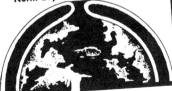
The advertisement for Raymond Bernard's *The Hollow Earth* (1963) which, seen by the author in the mid-sixties, started his quest after the true history of the Hollow-Earth Theory. Fieldcrest is no longer in business, but one small publisher or another has kept Bernard's book in print for more than twenty-five years.

Walter Kafton-Minkel

—

Subterranean Worlds:

100,000 years of dragons, dwarfs, the dead, lost races & UFOs from inside the earth

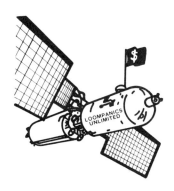

Loompanics Unlimited
Port Townsend, Washington

For Carol and Emily,
who put up with all this,

and with special thanks
to Frank Brownley,
without whose help
this work would be
nowhere near
as complete.

This work was written and typeset
with an Apple Macintosh SE/30 computer
and LaserWriter II NT printer
using Microsoft *Word*, and Adobe's
Century Old Style font for body text and
Stone Sans Bold font for titles and headers.
Some of the graphics were drawn with
Deneba's *Canvas* and Claris's *MacDraw II*.

SUBTERRANEAN WORLDS

© 1989 By Walter Kafton-Minkel
Printed in the USA

Published by:

Loompanics Unlimited
PO Box 1197
Port Townsend, WA 98368

ISBN 1-55950-015-8
Library of Congress Catalog Card Number 89-084325

Subterranean Worlds
Walter Kafton-Minkel

Table of Contents

Introduction:

Why I wrote about a "crazy idea"

In the spring of 1966 I was thirteen and surfacing from a fearful childhood. For longer than I could remember I had been terrified of a thousand monsters lurking on the fringes of my life, none of which I had ever actually seen. At the age of four they were formless beasts with huge mouths, waiting to gobble me wherever it was dark and I had to go alone—in my bedroom closet, the basement, or the garage. At five there was a skeleton lying among the dustballs under my bed, waiting to grasp my wrist in its cold white fingers if I thrashed in my sleep and thrust my hand out from under the covers. At eight there were the "Watchers," shrouded figures with phosphorescent eyes. The Watchers stepped silently into my room once my eyes were closed and stood at the foot of my bed and watched me—and all they did was *watch* me, as long as I kept my eyes closed. At ten there were a thousand shiny green devils, their bat-wings greasy like olive skins, passing to and from Hell through a secret door that lay beneath a thick patch of ivy beneath my bedroom window. I had seen the devils and the secret door in a particularly vivid nightmare, and even when we prepared to move away from the house two years later, I could not bring myself to walk into that patch of ivy to check whether that secret door was really there. At eleven I was still nervous in the bathroom at night; I knew that one evening, after washing my face, I would wipe my eyes, look into the mirror, and see a reflection that wasn't mine. Even the toilet held a demon, a long arm covered in scales that would reach out of the bowl and pull me down into the dark sewer if I lingered alone in the bathroom too long.

Yet if someone had asked me, even when I was small, whether any of the monsters were real, I would have answered, "No." As long as I wasn't alone and the lights were on, I knew they were only in my imagination.

Nonetheless it shouldn't be surprising that I grew suddenly obsessed with the Occult and the Unknown in the spring of 1966. I read every occult book and magazine I could find, from the most esoteric text—and I will admit that the metaphysical and linguistic intricacies of the Kabbalah were beyond my understanding, and are as much now, I fear, as they were then—to the glossiest "Witches in America Today!" sort of article, with color photos of naked witches dancing in a suburban living room. I suppose I was asking myself subconsciously "What have I been so afraid of?" But at the time I was only aware of an almost sexual excitement in the presence of Ancient Secrets, of instructions for raising and controlling the demons and spirits which had so terrified me.

It was in the spring of 1966 that I discovered *Fate* magazine in the rack at the supermarket, and I quickly became a regular reader. While the "true psychic experiences" and reports on hauntings and poltergeist phenomena intrigued me,

I was most attracted by the pages of advertisements, which were a strange department store of esoterica. There were free catalogs available from spiritualist supply houses that peddled black mirrors, spirit trumpets, and "Expelling Demons" Brand Incense (I bought and burned the last item, and the smell, something like cork soaked in perfume, permeated the house for nearly a week; my parents were not happy). There were ads for tarot readings by mail and amulets to increase wealth and attract romance. There were invitations to join the Rosicrucian Order, the Astara Foundation, the Lemurian Fellowship, and other organizations claiming to possess the Ancient Secrets.

But there was one full-page ad that intrigued me more than the others with its sheer strangeness. I saw it in most issues, and I always read it all the way through, and then read it aloud to friends. Beside the picture of what appeared to be a wise and hoary Old Testament prophet—but was actually supposed to be Admiral Richard E. Byrd—I read in bold and insistent type:

IS IT TRUE?
The Underground World of
Supermen Discovered by Admiral Byrd...
Under the North Pole...
and Kept Secret by U.S. Government

The advertisement continued that Dr. Raymond Bernard, A.B., M.A., Ph.D., had written a book, *The Hollow Earth,* revealing that "the true home of the flying saucers is a huge underground world whose entrance is at the North Polar opening." Admiral Byrd, it claimed, had led a group of Navy explorers through this mysterious opening to discover plants and animals long believed extinct on the earth's outer surface, as well as a race of technologically advanced superhumans. But "the news of this discovery was suppressed by the U.S. government in order to prevent other nations from exploring the inner world and claiming it."

The ad read like the plot of a Saturday-matinee science fiction movie to me, but my imagination hopped and twitched anyway. I had seen the movie version of Jules Verne's *Journey to the Center of the Earth*—the one with James Mason and Pat Boone—at a Saturday matinee when I was seven, and I had loved the descent into the icy volcano, the battle of the giant lizards, and the huge underground sea. Here was a book suggesting it might be true. Could the earth really be hollow? Did the UFOs come from inside? Did the President know about a big opening at the North Pole, and was he keeping it a secret? I wondered how there could be an opening if airliners flew over the Pole and submarines sailed beneath it, but the image in my mind of a hole in the top of the world with UFOs flying in and out was too much fun to abandon. I was always tempted to order the book, but it cost more than my allowance could bear at the time. I checked at the public library, but they didn't have it, and after a few years had gone by, *Fate* stopped running the ads, I stopped reading *Fate,* and I forgot about it. I forgot about it until the spring of 1976.

It was ten years later that, entirely by chance, I found a paperback copy of *The Hollow Earth* by Raymond Bernard in an unlikely place—a chain bookstore in a huge shopping mall. It was cheaper than I remembered it, but my income was also greater, so I bought it and finished it before I went to sleep that night. When I finished it I didn't believe the earth is hollow, and I still don't. But Bernard's book was so strange, and contained so many quotations from, and references to, the fellowship of believers in a hollow earth and in strange countries, creatures, and races within the earth, that my curiosity was immediately challenged. I had heard of none of these hollow-earth theorists before and wanted to learn more about them, so I set off upon the trail of scores of obscure books, from *The Phantom of the Poles* to *A Journey to the Earth's Interior* to *Agharta*, and they aroused again my adolescent lust after Mystery.

I discovered authors who seriously proposed that there is a small sun, a hundred—or a few hundred—miles in diameter, suspended at the center of our hollow planet. Others suggested that races of giants or eyeless beings with blue skins live in the inner world. Another believed the earth is concave, that we live inside, that the sun and moon are small globs of molten matter orbiting within the great hollow, and that there is nothing on the outside.

How did all the varieties of belief in "a world inside the world" come about? Most of the books I read gave no clue. Not even most of the believers in an inner world seemed to know, when I read between the lines, where the idea began. I found other works written by skeptics that sketched bits of the idea's history, but too often they were of the "Let's laugh at the crackpots!" variety, crazy-quilting the inner-world theorists with flat-earth proponents, prophets of the end of the world, and ark-builders awaiting the next Great Flood. Such collections are entertaining, but they do little to suggest the true significance of nonorthodox views of the cosmos—or as I shall refer to them here, "alternative realities."

Beliefs in alternative realities are in many ways like religious beliefs; they are often revealed through voices, visions, and flashes of intuition rather than experimentation or other orthodox scientific procedures. They are often dogmatic, and many of them meet deep emotional and psychological needs in those who hold them. The resemblance of many UFO sightings and contactee stories to religious experiences and near-death experiences is now well documented, and the religious aura which surrounds psychic healers, mediums, and channelers is well-known to any objective reader of alternative-reality literature. Due to the highly journalistic, rather than analytic, nature of most alternative-reality literature, there has been too little discussion of the religious and psychological dimensions of unorthodox beliefs and their survival value to those who hold them. To suggest such discussion might imply dismissal or ridicule of alternative realities, and publishers often say that so little is published analyzing them because nobody wants to read such things.

Calling most alternative-reality views basically emotional, however, is not to deny their worth or ridicule their proponents. But I do believe that both believers and skeptics have over the centuries wasted a great deal of time discussing these views as if they were supposed to be objective truth.

Proponents of alternative realities are not scientists and shouldn't try to be scientists—they are artists and mythmakers for a constantly changing culture, and should be respected for their abilities as poets, shamans, tricksters, and storytellers. Scientists tell us what the universe, unattached to human needs and desires, is like, and teach us about nature. Mythmakers tell us how we, with very definite needs and desires, react to the world, and thus teach us about ourselves. For example, a discovery that the brain's biochemistry might cause a certain mental illness satisfies no basic emotional need in the average person. But proposing that humans can psychically "see" people and places across long distances, or move objects only with the power of their minds appeals to almost all of us on the deepest level. Practically *all* alternative reality theories and beliefs—psychic powers, reincarnation, visitors from other worlds or dimensions, Masters who secretly control historical events—appeal to basic urges most of us have, frighten us deliciously, or move us deeply. Most have precedents in archaic myth and folk belief.

Very often, an analysis of alternative realities—which are contemporary myths—can be aided by placing them side by side with traditional myth and folklore. Myth, both traditional and contemporary, should not be understood as outmoded or false belief, but as the natural poetry of every human culture. Thanks to the works of scholars like Joseph Campbell and Mircea Eliade, we are slowly realizing that we hold today many beliefs about ourselves, our governments, and our cultures that are myths—that is, they are literally false, but symbolically and emotionally true for those of us who hold them. These myths give meaning to our lives whether or not we share a particular religious belief. As I write, for example, the 1988 American presidential campaign has just ended. Throughout the campaign, references were constantly made to "the values of the traditional American family," a family with mother, father, children, and grandparents living close together and honoring each other. Yet Americans probably have fewer *whole* families—families which include both father and mother, with an extended family of grandparents, aunts, uncles, and cousins living nearby—than any nation on earth, and many historians claim that it has been this way since the United States was founded. The American people, however, see what they want to see, and this myth helps them cope with a world in which families regularly break apart and reform, and family members often live in cities a thousand miles apart.

For a certain group of individuals, whose story I shall tell here, the hollow-earth theory has been literally and emotionally true for over two centuries, and that makes it one of the longest-lasting myths of the scientific era. For those unsympathetic to the idea of an inner world, this belief and its proponents seem easy to laugh at. But like all myths it is grounded in archetypal images of birth, life, struggle, accomplishment, and death which all human beings share. It gives its believers important secrets to confide. I have traced the history of the hollow-earth belief back to its beginnings in folklore and embryonic science, and here I would like to set this history down. It is the history of one not-very-important, but extraordinarily strange, belief.

A world within the world is one of the most archaic concepts in world mythology, part of the archetypal image of Gaia, the Earth Mother. Many of our distant ancestors told or heard stories of their distant ancestors germinating in the dark cavern-wombs of the Earth Mother, and being born into the bright, cold world of the surface. They knew they would return to the Earth Mother's arms again one day in death. The knowledge that we had struggled from the earth's womb, the home of the dead and the not-yet-alive, became also a fear of being reabsorbed too soon into those dark places, where all sorts of dim "things" crept. In my research I learned that my greasy childhood devils climbing out of their secret door in the ivy and my scaly demon down the toilet were the relatives of a swarm of other "things" which have risen from the earth to frighten other children, and adults, for thousands of years. Many of the archetypal images of myth—the Earth Mother and her aspects as provider and devourer, her good and evil children, and the secrets she hides within her wombs and bowels—became part of the revealed science of the hollow-earth theory.

The subterranean worlds we are about to explore are sometimes revealing, sometimes entertaining, and sometimes completely ludicrous, but if you are like me—a person who likes to be lifted from his chair by his imagination—they can show us how our desires to shape the universe and our own natures into a compact, comprehensible form can lead us to believe strange things, and hint at everything humanity still does not know about nature and about itself. The hollow-earth theory in all its glory describes great powers and conspiracies moving behind a false picture of a round, solid, neutral planet. In an era still searching for the "true story" of a President's assassination nearly thirty years old, and intrigued by stories of the Illuminati, the CIA, and the Trilateral Commission operating behind the scenes of modern history, why not a suppression of the truth about the North Pole? Could the President still be hiding the entrance to the inner world from the public? As long as the lights are on and someone else is around to assure us he isn't, we can be certain the whole thing is in our minds.

About the notes

This is not a scholarly work, although I have tried to verify all my statements whenever possible. The history of alternative-reality beliefs is perhaps the worst-documented area in the entire field of—what? History of religions? History of science? The very fact that it is a sort of stepchild of academia, that few "name" scholars have wanted to have much to do with it, and that many of its primary sources are self-published books and pamphlets printed in tiny amounts and not collected by libraries, means that many times I have only one source for a particular statement—often a not-exactly-reliable source. Some of the most fascinating figures in this story appear to have gone to some trouble to conceal their pasts, and a lot of biographical information has been hard to find. Many of the hollow-earth books I read gave no sources for much of their most interesting information, as if they were whispered secrets handed down from the Masters; it makes a researcher's work difficult.

Most of the sources I have used are long out of print or are found only in large academic or special libraries, and some are letters and other unpublished items. A few are available in large public libraries and used bookstores, however. Rather than construct a wall of footnotes, I have listed in Bibliography A the sources used for each chapter so the reader can attempt to hunt them down. In Bibliography B I have provided a list of additional books and periodicals involved in the hollow-earth mythos and related topics, both fiction and non-fiction. If you choose to pursue the subject further, good hunting!

Chapter 1

The Earth Our Mother

> Our great fathers talked together. Here they arose and moved on. They stooped over and came out from the fourth world, carrying their precious things clasped to their breasts.
>
> They stooped over and came out from moss world, carrying their precious things clasped to their breasts.
>
> They stooped over and came out from mud world, carrying their precious things clasped to their breasts.
>
> They stooped over and came out from wing world, carrying their precious things clasped to their breasts.
>
> They stooped over and came out and saw their Sun Father and inhaled the sacred breath of the light of day.
>
> *—Zuni Indian chant*

In the year 1884, the Wanapum or Columbia River Indians of eastern Washington state, a small tribe of about two hundred, were being pressured by the United States Government to abandon their traditional ways. For centuries the Wanapum had wandered up and down the banks of the Columbia to hunt and fish. But now Major J. W. MacMurray of the U.S. Army had been dispatched to the Wanapum village at Priest Rapids, where he used a checkerboard to demonstrate how the whites divided land into squares. He urged the Wanapum to apply for homesteads under the new Indian Homestead Law, and explained that it would now be necessary for them to settle in one spot to avoid conflicts with the white settlers pouring into the Columbia Basin.

But Smohalla, chief of the Wanapum, was a great shaman and prophet, a small hunchbacked man whose name meant Big Talk on Four Mountains. Smohalla was also the leader of a popular Indian religious cult, the Dreamers. He had told his followers to refuse to deal with the government, and promised them through his dream visions that all the land taken from them by the whites would be theirs again. Smohalla warned his people that if they wanted their land once more, they must not take up the ways of the whites. He told Major MacMurray that treating their mother, the earth, like a checkerboard was wrong:

> You ask me to plow the ground! Shall I take a knife and tear my mother's bosom? Then when I die she will not take me to her bosom to rest.
>
> You ask me to dig for stone! Shall I dig under her skin for her bones? Then when I die I cannot enter her body to be born again.
>
> You ask me to cut grass and make hay and sell it, and be rich like white men! But how dare I cut off my mother's hair?
>
> It is a bad law, and my people cannot obey it... We simply take the gifts that are freely offered. We no more harm the earth than would an infant harm its mother's breast. But the white man tears up large tracts of land, runs deep ditches, cuts down forests, and changes the whole face of the earth. You know very well this is not right.

For Smohalla and the Dreamers, the earth was literally their mother, a living and sentient being whom they would not think of harming. Smohalla was said to possess a special relationship with the Earth Mother. During one of his dream visions, it was said, he predicted the major earthquake that shook the Pacific Northwest on the night of December 14, 1872. The earthquake, said Smohalla, told Indian and white alike of the Earth Mother's anger, and it gained him many followers.

Like most Native Americans—and most archaic agricultural and pre-agricultural peoples—Smohalla and his followers had an agreement with their Earth Mother as specific and binding as any modern business contract. She provided them with many gifts. The nuts and fruits they gathered were her favors, and herbs, mushrooms and grains sprouted from her flesh. Streams and springs flowed from her breasts and vaginal openings, and game animals trotted and flew from her womb.

A North African rock engraving shows a Mother Goddess as Mistress of the Animals, helping a hunter. Note the umbilical cord.

In return, her human children agreed not to mistreat her or waste her gifts. In many hunting cultures, agreements were made between hunters and the Earth Mother, or between hunters and the game animals themselves, in trance visions. Among the Cree and Ojibway of Canada all hunting was done under a ceremonial contract between the hunters, the game, and the Earth Mother. The spirit being of the hunter, in the dream-songs before a hunt, negotiated a quota of rabbit or deer with the spirits of those animals. As long as the hunter did not exceed this quota, game would be plentiful. If the hunter killed more animals than agreed upon, or allowed any of the kill to go to waste, the animals would flee from him and return to the Earth Mother, and the people would go hungry.

Another Canadian tribe, the Thompson River Indians of British Columbia, believed that game animals had worlds of their own underground. The entrances to these countries of game were well-hidden from humans, but the animals wandered in and out of them as they pleased. When they chose to conceal themselves there, game was scarce in the upper world.

Sex and the Earth Mother

When a people developed agriculture and settled in one place to farm, the comparisons between the earth and the human woman became even more profound than they had been in a hunting/gathering culture. The sexuality and generative power of the earth was indispensable to the men and women of these early agricultural societies, and they saw everywhere the relationships between the macrocosm of the earth and the microcosms of their own lives and bodies. All that occurred in the earth and sky was echoed in the human being, and all that occurred within and between human beings was echoed in the earth and sky, for all parts of the universe, great and small, were essential and inseparable to them.

Since the woman gave birth to children, since she was the one who generated new life for her people just as the earth gave birth to all kinds of new life every spring, women had always enjoyed a special relationship with the earth. The earth, in its turn, took its mythic image from the human female and became the Primal Mother. The image was established long before the "invention" of agriculture (recent anthropological theory suggests that women were in many places responsible for this invention), and it was enriched when men came to be seen as the sowers of seed in women, just as the first farmers sowed seed in the earth. In many mythic traditions the Father God (often the sky) fertilized the Earth Mother at the beginning of time, and she brought forth her first crop of living things.

Thus in many traditions women became symbols of the soil to be sexually tilled. The Koran tells Muslim men, "Your women are as fields for you." In an ancient Egyptian poem, a young woman in love cries out, "I am the earth," as she calls for her lover. Plato, that old misogynist, believed that woman "in her conception and generation is but the imitation of the earth, and not the earth of the woman." He considered the earth of Greece "the mother of men" because it "brought forth wheat and barley for human food, which is the best and noblest sustenance for men."

The birth of the first humans from the Earth Mother is a widespread mythic image. One tradition of the Andaman Islanders tells that the first man, after he had been created, had intercourse with an anthill, from which were born many offspring. An anthill can certainly be considered a vagina symbol—a hole out of which swarm hundreds of the earth's "children." In other creation myths, the first humans were simply dug up. The Baiga of India said that "the first gods, being hungry, went... to dig for roots; they dug up some of them, and out of that hole came a little man and woman, naked, and they all laughed and said, 'These are Naga Baiga and Naga Baigin,'" the legendary ancestors of the Baiga. Other Baiga simply told anthropologists that the first of the Baiga had come "from the womb of Mother Earth."

We find this image even in the Bible. In the Book of Genesis 2, 5-8, God creates Adam much like a farmer plants and nurtures a crop. Adam is created, in fact, alongside the plants:

> ...no plant of the field was yet in the earth and no herb of the field had yet sprung up—for the Lord God had not caused it to rain upon the earth, and there was no man to till the ground; but a mist went up from the earth and watered the whole face of the ground, and breathed into his nostrils the breath of life; and man became a living being. And the Lord God planted a garden in Eden... out of the ground the Lord God made to grow every tree that is pleasant to the sight and good for food...

Cultures scattered from Finland to Japan specified in earlier times that a woman giving birth must be lying or kneeling upon the ground in imitation of, and in close contact with, the Earth Mother. Still more frequently seen was the custom of placing the newborn infant upon the earth. The child was laid "in the arms" of the Earth Mother to receive her beneficent energies and her blessing, for any child of a human mother was the child of the Earth Mother as well.

In many of the most ancient creation myths, the Earth Mother gives birth to the first humans without a partner, through a sort of parthenogenesis. In his *History of Religious Ideas* (1978), Mircea Eliade tells us that "the memory of this 'mystery' [of parthenogenetic birth] still survived in the Olympian mythology (Hera conceives alone and gives birth to Hephaestus and Ares) and can be read in numerous myths and popular beliefs concerning the birth of men from the earth..." Some of these myths shared Smohalla's belief that stones are the bones of the Earth Mother. In creation stories from Central America to Asia Minor, the first humans were formed from stones. In the Greek myth of the Flood, the hero Deucalion threw "the bones of his mother"—which were stones—behind his back after the flood had receded, and from them sprang a new human race.

For pre-technological men and women the mineral world was not the lifeless jumble of stones and strata we see. Stones and mountains contained their own life forces. Precious gems and minerals were literally the fruits of the earth. A ruby or gold nugget grew within the womb of the earth as an apple or an ear of corn ripened on the surface. The Sanskrit *Jawahernameh* (Book of Precious Stones), an ancient Indian mineralogical text, referred to a diamond as a "ripe" gem, like a fruit ready for harvest by the miner, while a mere crystal was considered "green" or unripe. In ancient and medieval Europe and Africa, the entrances to exhausted mines were often blocked up with stones for fifteen or twenty years, after which the stones were removed and the mines re-worked. The miners believed that if left alone, the earth would grow new gemstones or send new veins of precious metals up from below, as a tree or vine produces new branches. In this way, the mine would once again become profitable.

The notion of the earth "growing" gems and precious metals lasted well into the seventeenth century. A dissertation published in Germany in 1665 stated that "stones are generated as plants are," and that "each species" of mineral "produces and multiplies itself." Renaissance alchemists, as well as the miners from whom they had gotten their information, believed that in the center of the earth grew a "Golden Tree." All veins of gold in the earth, they said, were branches of a vast living tree of gold which grew toward the surface through fissures in the stone. The German alchemist Johann Gottlob Lehmann wrote of the Golden Tree in 1735:

> I hold that the mineral veins which are opened up in mining are nothing but offshoots from an immense trunk which presumably goes down into the very depths of the earth and which, on account of its great distance from the surface, cannot be reached in min-

ing operations. The great mineral veins are large boughs of this tree, the smaller ones
the slender branches and twigs of these great metal-bearing boughs.

The Golden Tree was also described in an account of a voyage to His-
paniola published in England in 1577. According to this account, the natives in
one region of the island (a region in today's Haiti) mined enormous amounts of
gold, and had "founde by experience that the vayne of gold is a lyving tree." In
some parts of the island they had "sometimes chaunced upon whole caves
susteigned and borne up as it were with golden pyllers," which were boughs of
this monstrous tree. Its roots, the natives said, through which molten or va-
porous gold rose like sap, "extendeth to the centre of the earth and there taketh
noorishment of increase."

Stooping over and coming out

With the belief in the fertility of the Earth Mother so widespread, it is
only natural that caverns and other subterranean places came to be seen as her
wombs. In ancient Egypt the word *bi* signified both "uterus" and "gallery of a
mine," and the early Hebrew term for "well" could also mean "woman" or
"spouse." Many mythical traditions held that in "the first days," the first
members of the human race had been generated far underground in one or
many subterranean womb-worlds. The emergence myths which form an important part of many Native American traditions give us the best examples of
such realms. In these myths, it is only after dwelling for a time far beneath the
surface in a larval state, slowly developing at least a rudimentary human form
and consciousness, that the first humans are brought up to the surface to live in
the light of the sun. This birth—this reaching the surface—represents the tran-
sition from childhood and dependence on one's mother to maturity and
independence.

An early missionary to the Lenni Lenape or Delaware Indians of Pennsylvania wrote that

> the Indians consider the earth as their universal mother. They believe that they were
> created within its bosom, where for a long time they had their abode, before they came to
> live on its surface. They say that the great, good, and all powerful Spirit, when he created
> them, undoubtedly meant at a proper time to put them in enjoyment of all the good
> things which he had prepared for them upon this earth, but he wisely ordained that
> their first stage of existence should be within it, as the infant is formed and takes its first
> growth in the womb of its natural mother... The Indian mythologists are not agreed as
> to the form under which they existed while in the bowels of the earth. Some assert that
> they lived there in human shape, while others, with greater consistency, contend that
> their existence was in the form of certain terrestrial animals, such as the ground-hog,
> the rabbit, and the tortoise.

The first humans in many emergence myths dwell in the Earth
Mother's womb in animal or semi-animal form, and do not become fully human until they ascend to the surface. In an Iroquois version of the myth, the
first subterranean-dwellers were of human form, but lived as children might.

In their dark ignorance they were unacquainted with tools or weapons for hunting, and they were unable to capture any game larger than mice. This myth (recounted here by another missionary) told us that

> they had dwelt in the earth where it was dark and no sun did shine. That though they followed hunting, they ate mice, which they caught with their hands. That Ganawa-gahha (one of them) having accidentally found a hole to get out of the earth at, he went out, and that in walking about on the earth he found a deer, which he took back with him, and that both on account of the meat tasting so very good, and the favourable description he had given them of the country above and on the earth, their mother concluded it best for them all to come out; that accordingly they did so, and immediately set about planting corn, etc. That, however, the Nocharauorsul, that is, the ground hog, would not come out, but had remained in the ground as before.

There is a penalty to be paid, this myth tells us, for not leaving our mother's womb when the proper moment has come, for choosing instead to remain in the dark security of her embrace. The one who would not come out, who had decided against maturity and independence, reverted to an animal form.

The best-known and most complete cycles of emergence myths are those of the Indians of the American Southwest, notably those of the Navajo, Hopi, Pueblo, and Zuni peoples. The Navajo word for the earth is *Naestan*, which means the horizontal or recumbent woman, and both the Navajo and Zuni hold that within the Earth Mother there are four subterranean womb-worlds. Some of the Southwestern emergence myths are explicitly gynecological in their symbolism, some are less so. But all share the image of the earliest humans germinating underground and slowly forcing their way, with the help of legendary heroes, up to the light of the sun. Here is a synopsis of one version of a Zuni creation myth that expresses the symbolism of the earth as mother very clearly:

In the beginning there existed Awonawilono the Creator, alone in an endless void. When the Creator decided to manifest himself, he became the Sun and the void was brightened. The Creator took from himself two seeds and with them impregnated the great waters, and upon the waters there appeared a green scum that grew and became Awitelin Tsita the "Fourfold Containing Mother-earth" and Apoyan Ta'chu, the "All-covering Father-sky." These two lay together and many children were conceived in the lowest of the Earth Mother's four wombs, the Womb of Sooty Depth. As she grew big with her children, she pushed herself away from the Sky Father and sank down into the great waters. As many human mothers worry over their first-born before birth, so did the Earth Mother worry. "How," she asked the Sky Father, "shall our children, when brought forth, know one place from another, even by the white light of the Sun Father?" So the earth and sky prepared clouds, rain, trees, and corn for their children's welfare when their children reached the surface. But still the Earth Mother worried that her children were not ready, and she held them deep in her nethermost womb.

The beings who were to become humans and other creatures were meanwhile dwelling in darkness as unfinished beasts, like grubs or tadpoles. Their existence was crowded and unhappy; they crawled and tumbled over one another, grumbling, swearing, spitting, and complaining. After a time, a few of these beings attempted to escape. One of them, a hero named Poshaiyank'ya, crawled up through all four of the Earth Mother's wombs and reached the surface, which in those days was a huge, soft island. Poshaiyank'ya begged the Sun Father to deliver his people, and the Sun heard his pleas and came to his aid. Once again he impregnated the great waters and again twins were born, but the new twins were Uanam Ehkona and Uanam Yaluna, the Brothers of Light and Lords of Humanity. The Twins took their great knives made of thunderbolts, cleaved the mountains, and rode their cloud-shields down into the darkness.

When the Twins reached the Womb of Sooty Depth, they found many herbs and vines growing there. They breathed upon the stems of the vines, and soon the plants shot up toward the opening the Twins had torn in the earth. They formed a great ladder of the vines and gathered together all the miserable womb-dwellers. Then the Twins led them up the ladder to the second womb-world, the Umbilical-womb or Place of Gestation, where it was only as dark as a stormy night. Not all the creatures succeeded in making the climb, however. Many of them lost their holds and fell back into the darkness of the lowest womb. They were not to be delivered of the Earth Mother until many years had passed and they had been rendered into evil, deformed monsters by the earth's rumblings and quakings.

After a short existence in the second world, the Twins led the rest of the creatures up to the third world, the Vaginal-womb or Place of Sex-Generation, lit like a valley in starlight. Here the various tribes of humans and animals began to multiply and diversify, and soon the third world was too crowded. Again the Twins led them up the ladder of vines to the fourth world, the Ultimate-uncoverable or Birth-Womb, where the light was like that of dawn. When the fourth world became too crowded in turn, the Twins took the people and animals on their final climb to the earth's surface, up to the World of Disseminated Light, Knowledge, and Sight.

Avan Yu, Pueblo serpent of the underworld.

Even when they reached the surface, the first humans looked like cave creatures. Their skins were dark, cold, and scaly; their ears were long and deep like those of bats, and their toes were webbed. Even the light of a star stung their owl-eyes, and they squatted froglike on the ground, as they had in their cave worlds. But they soon grew accustomed to the dazzling light of the sun and made themselves clothing and plaited sandals to help them walk upon the soft, unstable earth.

But in their first days on the surface, these first men and women lived in fear. The Earth Mother, angry that her children had escaped from her protection, seethed, shook, and split open, and from the torn wombs stalked the monsters which had been left behind and imprisoned there. They attacked and devoured the new men and women. But the Twins, who by now had gone to live in the sky, sent their thunderbolts down to the earth and sparked great fires which consumed the monsters. Finally the Earth Mother's surface became a fit place to dwell.

For some of the Native Americans of the Southwest, notably the Jicarilla Apache, the Emergence is not yet completed. Some time in the future, they say, this world will no longer be able to sustain life, and the people will have to ascend to another land above the sky. Here is how one of the Jicarilla described that time to folklorist Morris Opler:

> The sun and moon will go up as before. This place will be dark and people will follow the sun and moon. They say that some of the material out of which the earth was made is still left... There is material for two more earths and skies. This material is kept somewhere now, covered over by a mountain...
> They say that this earth is to be destroyed twice, once by water and this has already happened... Sometime in the future the earth is to be destroyed for the second time, by fire. It will occur some day when Killer-of-Enemies [the Jicarilla hero of the Emergence, equivalent to the Twins] comes back. He is going to take care of these Indians before it happens. He is going to send them up to a place above the present sky.

Thus for the Jicarilla, the present surface world we live in covers a dark, used-up world and sky beneath us. People must progress upward through the ages, leaving behind the old worlds, or be left behind themselves in the darkness and destruction.

Where monsters come from

The cycles of emergence myths we find in many Native American cultures present the journey from deep within the Earth Mother to the surface—and even beyond, to a new earth—as a process of growth, an image of the passage from childhood to maturity. For each member of the Zuni or Jicarilla people, the myths tell symbolically of the long journey each of them must make out of the womb, through the dim but deeply experienced countries of infancy and early childhood, and into a fully conscious adulthood. But these myths, and those of other cultures, also tell us that there are very real penalties to be paid for immaturity and dependence on Mother. We have already seen how one of the first humans in the Iroquois emergence story refused to leave the security of the earth and reverted to the form of a groundhog. Those in the Zuni myth who were unable to scale the ladder out of the safe but stifling darkness of the Womb of Sooty Depth were transformed into monsters. In the Jicarilla emergence story as well as the Zuni, the Earth Mother released the monsters onto the surface after her now-mature children had left her wombs. It was up to Killer-of-Enemies to save the Jicarilla from the monsters, which included a giant elk, a pair of galloping rocks, and a beast called the Kicking Monster.

Although the Kicking Monster ventured out to the surface to claim its victims, it lived underground, in a lair beneath a hot spring. It would kick passersby into the boiling water to feed itself and its four daughters. Killer-of-Enemies battled the Kicking Monster, and defeated it by kicking it into the boiling water himself; then he traveled below to deal with its daughters. The daughters were, at that time, the only women possessing vaginas. In fact,

> they were vagina girls. They had the form of women, but they were in reality vaginas. Other vaginas were hanging around on the walls, but these four were in the form of girls with legs and all body parts and were walking around. It was because of them that so many men had gone along that road [to the hot spring, where they had been boiled and devoured].

The "vagina girls" were, in their way, the most terrible monsters for any man, for their vaginas were toothed to bite off and consume his penis. Killer-of-Enemies defeated the vagina girls by feeding them a special medicine of sour berries that puckered their lips and destroyed their teeth (throughout the story, their mouths and vaginas are treated as the same thing). He was then able to steal the vaginas from the walls and bring them to the women of his own people.

To bring sexual maturity and reproduction to the Jicarilla, Killer-of-Enemies had to travel below the surface to defeat one of the most frightening monsters of all, yet also one of the most attractive, to the child becoming an adult— the monster of sexuality. This monster is one of the last that must be defeated in the process of maturation, and Killer-of-Enemies defeated it by bringing sexuality "up to the surface," away from the darkness underground. Similar legends of a hero conquering a woman-monster with a toothed vagina have been recorded among other Native American peoples, the Ainu of Japan, the Samoans, and the Naga of India.

When the monster, of whatever kind, ventures up to the surface world, it comes to scare us, to make us insecure, to drag us back down into the dependent state of early childhood, and to return us to the jealous arms of the Earth Mother. Monsters do their best work in darkness, rising from the dark waters or the grave or the deep shadows of the forest, leaping into the light only long enough to drag us back into the darkness with them. Almost all monsters are "put together wrong"; they are not only misshapen, but actively chaotic. They are bits of animal and human jumbled together, as if thumbing their noses at the order of nature. Cast out by the Earth Mother's mature children, they seek her breast all the more hungrily.

One of the monsters closest to the dark earth is the vampire. He is doomed to be always "incomplete"—half alive and half dead, he must leave his grave to drink the blood of the living if his half-existence is to continue. He comes to life only in the "womb" of night; while the sun shines he is bound helplessly in his womblike coffin.

An Irish vampire in his burial shroud, by John Batten from Joseph Jacobs's *More Celtic Fairy Tales*.

In European folk belief, it was people who had been unsuccessful at integrating themselves into the order of society—who had not become mature and responsible members of that culture—who were most likely to become vampires. In one old dictionary definition, "dead wizards, were- wolves, heretics, and other out- casts become vampires, as do the illegitimate offspring of parents themselves illegitimate, and anyone killed by a vampire." Until the last century, suicides were thought to become vampires as well. In his *History of Vampires* (1914) Dudley Wright mentions that it was common in England to drive ash stakes through the hearts of suicides before burial until 1823, when a law was passed forbidding it.

Monsters are also the offspring of socially unacceptable behavior—sins personified. The monster Grendel in *Beowulf*, who lived beneath the surface of a great marsh, had been "conceived by a pair of those monsters born of Cain, murderous creatures banished by God, punished forever for the crime of Abel's death. The almighty drove those demons out, and their exile was bitter, shut away from men; they split into a thousand forms of evil..." Rejected by humanity—for they represented all that humanity must reject to gain harmony and culture—the tribe of Cain haunted the wild, chaotic places: deserts, swamps, regions underwater and underground, the places closest to the Earth Mother.

How does the image of the Earth Mother as jealous and resentful of those children who have grown mature enough to live in the light of the sun, sending her monster-children to drag them back down into the depths, square with the image of the beneficent Earth Mother who gives freely of food, materials for shelter, and mineral wealth? The Earth Mother has two faces and two names—the Good Earth Goddess and the Devourer—throughout world mythology. In ancient Greece there were words for these faces: *ge* and *chthon*, roughly corresponding to the English words "underground" and "underworld." Ge, which is the root of words like geology and geography, signifies the earth which is our home, the place in which we make our homes and grow our food, the source of life and fertility. Chthon, however, is the name of that dark, cold place, far below the surface, to which we journey in dreams and must make our permanent home after death. It is the home of our fears, and the great void which always lies open beneath us.

The world of dreams

For almost every psychoanalyst since Freud, that part of the subterranean world named *chthon* has symbolized the depths of the subconscious. To descend into this region is to leave behind the sunlit surface world of consciousness, to abandon rational self-control, and to expose one's self to the apparent chaos of the world of dreams, where there is much to lose, but also much to be won. Folklore, mythology, and fantastic fiction are full of examples of such underground journeys.

A familiar example is that in *Alice's Adventures in Wonderland*. Charles Dodgson, who wrote the story under the pen name Lewis Carroll, entitled his original manuscript "Alice's Adventures Under Ground." It is easy to forget that Alice is deep beneath the earth throughout most of the story, however, because the story possesses such a dreamlike quality. The ending makes it clear it has been a dream, and the famous fall down the rabbit hole ("Down, down, down. Would the fall never come to an end?") reminds the reader of falling asleep and dreaming, doing the old schoolboys' trick of squatting, hyperventilating, standing up and passing out, or even of the dark spin into unconsciousness one felt breathing ether before surgery in the days before modern anesthetics.

The folktales collected by the Brothers Grimm contain several examples of underground regions that can symbolize the unconscious. In his book *The Uses of Enchantment* (1977), Bruno Bettelheim points out the symbolism of two such tales, "The Three Feathers" and "Mother Holle." In the first of these stories, Dumbkin, the youngest and most foolish of a king's three sons, competes with his brothers to determine which of them will succeed his father. Dumbkin follows a drifting feather to a trap door opening into the earth; descending, he is led to an underground kingdom of toads. The Toad King gives him rich and wondrous gifts enabling Dumbkin to succeed at the difficult task his father has set. He is able to best his brothers because they seek only the easiest of goals; they are unable to see past the surface of things. It isn't difficult to see that Dumbkin represents an immature, undeveloped person who nevertheless listens to his unconscious and learns the lessons it has to teach. The voice of the unconscious, of Dumbkin's "animal nature," is symbolized by the Toad King. With these lessons Dumbkin is able to act upon his inspirations and desires to lead a fully realized life.

"Mother Holle" has a similar theme. Here a young girl is forced by her stepmother to jump down a well in pursuit of a lost spindle. Falling, she loses consciousness and awakens in a beautiful land where she meets an old woman with large teeth named Mother Holle and becomes her housekeeper. After a time the girl is rewarded for her service when Mother Holle sends her through a doorway leading back to the surface world, where a shower of gold pours down upon her. When she returns with the gold, her envious lazy stepsister decides to descend and enter Mother Holle's service as well. But the stepsister refuses to perform the tasks Mother Holle sets her, and when it is time for her to leave, the doorway covers the stepsister with black pitch that can never be removed. It does not pay to trifle with the orders of one's subconscious.

The archetypal impression that a descent into the earth is a plunge into the world of dreams, and the discomfort and disorientation most of us feel in dark, enclosed places, have inspired dramatic uses of caverns and subterranean chambers for many thousands of years. When used in religious ceremonies and the meetings of secret societies, underground temples and lodges impress upon initiates the need for secrecy. They also carry a strong feeling of the closeness of birth and death.

In medieval Europe, reports of the activities of socially outcast groups often included rumors of subterranean gatherings in the dead of night. In his history of European witchcraft, Jeffrey Russell tells of several cases of subterranean rites described by chroniclers of that time. It was common knowledge in that period, he writes, that "demons cannot stand the light of day... and must be called up either at night or underground." "In 1340," it was reported, "heretics were found in Salzburg who rejected the Church, the sacraments and the Trinity. They argued that nothing done underground was sin, and they held orgies on Catholic feast days. They revered Lucifer [and] hoped for his restoration to heaven." The chronicler Caesarius reported "of heretics in Verona about 1175 that they congregated in a large hall underground, heard a blasphemous sermon, put out the lights, and held an orgy..."

The important feature of such stories, whether literally true or not, is the impression we get that medieval men and women felt it was natural to go underground to engage in a socially proscribed activity. Holding orgies and raising demons rejected God and satisfied the "lower urges." Underground, one was in closer contact with one's emotions and far from the guardians of "higher" morality. There it was easier to peel off the many prohibitions the medieval Church placed on one's behavior.

But the most dramatic ceremonial journeys into the archetypal world of birth and death, and away from the surface world of conscious logic, were conducted by the secret religious societies of many cultures in their rites of initiation, or "second birth." Such rites were impressive, frightening, and often violent—a "shock treatment," as Joseph Campbell tells us of the Paleolithic ceremonies of 30,000-10,000 B.C. These ceremonies converted "babes into men, dependable hunters, and courageous defenders of the tribe." The ceremonies were usually for pubescent boys at a time when women held that special bond with the earth that made their roles more sure (although initiation ceremonies for newly-menstruating girls were common in some cultures). They might involve cutting off the joint of a finger, ritual scarring, circumcision, or beatings. Whatever the trial, it was certain to be the most solemn and terrifying the culture could muster, for only after a boy passed the initiation rites could he become a man, trusted with the deepest secrets of his people.

To become an adult, the child had to be reborn, and in some societies which dwelled near caverns or grottoes, this rebirth was performed in these dark, womblike places. Joseph Campbell describes the Paleolithic ritual caves of southern France and northern Spain as truly dreadful and awe-inspiring:

> A terrific sense of claustrophobia, and simultaneously of release from every context of the world above, assails the mind impounded in these more than absolutely dark abysses, where darkness no longer is an absence of light but an experienced force... [During the rites] everything was done, even in the period of the paleolithic caves, to inspire in the youngsters being symbolically killed a reactivation of their childhood fear of the dark.

Campbell reminds us that the fear of the dark, which seems to be universal among children, had been said not only of inability to see potential dangers, but also "a function of the fear of returning to the womb." It is the fear that the child's "recently achieved daylight consciousness and not yet secure individuality should be reabsorbed." It is a longing for the light, for open space, and for freedom, for self-control rather than control by another. To be a mature human being is to seek the light and its freedom, which allows one to perform the tasks of an independent life.

The land of the dead

Yet even the earliest humans knew that when death came, the time had arrived to return to the great dim arms of the Earth Mother. It was time to enter the land of the dead, perhaps to be reborn someday in another form. Possibly as early as 200,000 B.C., the Neanderthals of Europe began returning the bodies of their dead to the earth in burial. Some Neanderthal skeletons have been unearthed which had been placed in a fetal or sleeping position, suggesting they were expected to awaken or be reborn into a new life. Many of them were buried on an east-west axis, which also implies rebirth as the sun is reborn in the east and travels west every day (the land of the dead was located in the west in many cultures, in the place where the sun sets). Many Neanderthals were buried with sacrificed animals and other food supplies, perhaps to provide the deceased with food in his or her new existence. The almost universal belief in an afterworld seems to have been with us since the beginning of human history.

"Crawl toward the earth, thy mother," wrote the Vedic poet to one about to die. Death, like birth, was bound up intimately with the Earth Mother. We come out of her womb (intuitively and symbolically, if not actually) and we return to her womb when our time on the surface is over (actually, in burial). Just as there arose the mythic cycles of emergence stories, in which the first humans germinated underground, there also arose a belief in an underworld into which the spirits of the dead must travel. In most cultures it was imperative that the dead be properly buried and well-supplied for the journey, lest they return as ghosts to trouble the living or even try to claim the bodies of relatives or fellow tribe members by stealing their souls.

Therefore the underworld had to be well secured. Both its entrances and exits needed to be well-guarded, so the dead could not escape nor the living enter. The Lipan Apache have a story of a woman who, knocked unconscious in an accident, began descending to the underworld. On her way down she passed a juniper tree, and "she saw that parts of bodies, lips, ears, eyes, teeth, were on that tree. This was the tree upon which hung the missing parts of people still living. When these people die and come to the underworld they pick up the part of the body they have lost and go on, whole again." She descended further until she met the spirit of her father. He told her to go back: "It's not time for you to come down here!" He forced her to return along a different trail (for the path to the underworld goes only in one direction) until she found her body, entered it, and regained consciousness. For the rest of her life, this woman was given the name "Going to Die."

There were other ways to insure that the dead reached the underworld and stayed there. Beneath the red earth of the western slope of the Sierras in Calaveras County, California is a small-time tourist attraction called Moaning Cave. The cave received its name in the nineteenth century, when wind blowing past its limestone cavities produced a loud, unearthly moan. The cave hasn't moaned since the 1920s, though, when an ambitious retired shipbuilder, anxious to create a monument to his talents, painstakingly carried down—through a tight, dripping, zigzag entranceway—and welded together a hundred-foot-tall iron staircase. The staircase spirals down from the stone balcony overhanging the cave's vertical main room to the room's floor. This main room is so deep and narrow that to look up from the bottom makes one dizzy and disoriented.

Some interesting discoveries were made in Moaning Cave in the 1850s. A group of Frenchmen, exploring the depths of the cave, claimed to have discovered three hundred petrified human bodies. Anthropologists a century later identified the few dozen skulls, bones, and artifacts that remained as those of the "Middle Horizon" people, who lived in that area about two thousand years ago, before they gave way to the Miwok Indians. At some point in their history, the Miwoks discovered the remains and ever afterward avoided the cave. They called Moaning Cave the lair of Chehalumche, a stone giant who dragged his human victims underground and there devoured them. But why were there so many remains of the Middle Horizon people at the bottom of the shaft in the first place? Anthropologists speculate that the Middle Horizon people had cast their dead into that howling pit because they believed it was the most direct route to the underworld.

The land of the dead is often separated from that of the living by terrible obstacles—oceans, mountains, or ferocious beasts. But there are those who make that journey often. The Altaic shamans of central Asia travel in trance states to the underworld to bargain for the return of the soul of one who is seriously ill or accompany the soul of one who has died to the afterlife. Mircea Eliade's *Shamanism* (1964) contains a vivid description of one of these trance-journeys, performed before a crowd of friends and relations:

The "black" shaman begins his journey from his own yurt. He takes the road to the south, crosses the nearby regions, climbs the Altai Mountains and, in passing, describes the Chinese desert of red sand. Then he rides over a yellow steppe that a magpie could not fly across. "By the power of songs we cross it!" the shaman cries to the audience, and then intones a song which the audience carry on in chorus. Finally he reaches the Mountain of Iron, *Temir taixa*, whose peaks touch the sky. It is a dangerous climb; the shaman mimes the difficult ascent, and breathes deeply, exhausted, when he reaches the top.The mountain is sown with the whitened bones of other shamans, whose strength did not suffice them to gain the summit, and of their horses. Once he is across the mountain, another ride takes the shaman to a hole that is the entrance to the other world, *yer mesi*, the "jaws of the earth," or *yer tunigi*, the "smoke hole of the earth."

An Altaic shaman's drawing of a trip to the land of the dead.

Entering it, the shaman first reaches a plain and finds a sea crossed by a bridge the breadth of a hair; he sets foot on it and, to give a striking image of crossing this dangerous bridge, he totters and almost falls. At the bottom of the sea he sees the bones of countless shamans who have fallen into it, for a sinner could not cross the bridge. He passes by the places where sinners are tormented; he has time to see a man who having listened at doors in his lifetime, is now nailed to a post by one ear; another, who has slandered, is hung up by the tongue; a glutton is surrounded by the choicest dishes without being able to reach them; and so on.

Even now the shaman risks his life. He must next evade the fierce dogs that guard Erlik Khan, the King of the Underworld, bribe the guard at the door of the king's yurt, and rush into the ferocious king's presence to request an audience. He gets the king drunk with strong wine brought along for just this purpose, and thus receives the blessing of Erlik Khan and permission to retain the soul of the patient. The shaman, his mission successful, returns to earth on the back of a goose. Rousing himself from his trance, he announces that the one who is ill will recover.

Few cultures have considered the land of the dead a pleasant place, and most people have feared the day they must make that journey. But in the region around the Mediterranean, the underworld grew more and more terrible until it became the Christian Hell, a vast flaming pit crawling with demons and tormented sinners. The development of this horrible underworld of punishment began in the cosmologies of ancient Egypt and Mesopotamia. The Egyptian *Book of the Dead*, placed in the coffin to help the deceased gain a happy afterlife, supplied passwords which allowed his or her spirit to reach the un-

derworld safely, as well as supplications to the judges he or she would meet
there in the "Hall of Double Justice."

Many a tomb mural and painted papyrus depicted the scene of judgement. Osiris, lord of the underworld, sat at one end of the hall. In the center
stood a great scale where Maat, goddess of truth and justice, weighed the deceased's heart. Nearby stood Amemait, the Devourer—a huge female monster,
part lion, part hippopotamus, part crocodile—waiting to consume the souls of the
wicked. Forty-two judges, some with human heads and others with the heads
of animals, all dressed in their winding-sheets, sat at Osiris's sides. Each asked
probing questions of the deceased, hoping to reveal past sins. For some incorrigi-
ble sinners special horrors waited. In a popular Egyptian tale written down in
the second century A.D., the hero, after wishing that his funeral would be as
grand as that of a wealthy man he witnesses, is led down in a vision into the
underworld. There he sees a virtuous poor man, whose body had been rolled up
in a mat and tossed into the ground; now he is an "exalted personage" clothed in
"garments of fine linen," and he sits near Osiris's side. But the wicked rich
man, who had been buried with such pomp, has been punished by having the
door of the underworld "planted in his right eye and rotating on this eye
whenever the door is opened or closed, while his mouth utters great cries."

The Mesopotamian underworld was even grimmer. *Kur-nu-gi-a*, "the
land of no return," was often described as a gloomy metropolis in the depths of
the earth, with seven walls and seven gates and covered with the dust of death.
Here the dead dwelled side by side with the monsters of the underworld, and
good or evil, rich or poor, high priest or lowly slave, all faced a wretched existence, "their sustenance earth, and clay their food." A proper burial was the
only virtue the deceased might carry into the afterlife, for the Mesopotamian
dead became hideous shadowy beings called *edim*, and if they had died far from
home or had not been buried with the proper rites, they were not even allowed
to enter Kur-nu-gi-a. These unfortunate edim were compelled to wander the
earth, digging for food in the piles of garbage that lined the streets of
Mesopotamian towns, growing more and more envious of the living. Such
edim usually took their vengeance against the living at last by becoming
vampires.

Hell

The ancient Hebrew tribes used the gloomy underworld of the
Mesopotamians as the basis of their own underworld, *She'ol*. In the Book of Job
10, 21-2, She'ol is described much like Kur-nu-gi-a:

> Let me alone, that I may find a little comfort
> before I go whence I shall not return,
> to the land of gloom and deep darkness,
> the land of gloom and chaos,
> where light is as darkness.

She'ol was either a deep pit or, once again, a dusty walled city. Yahweh, god of the Hebrews, did not seem to care what happened to those in She'ol; all there enjoyed an equally miserable and shadowy existence, far beneath the sunny world of the living.

In time, however, this image of She'ol was to change. In the apocryphal *Book of Enoch* we find descriptions of several journeys made by Enoch to the afterworld. He visits a flaming pit in which the fallen angels are forever punished; he also visits She'ol, depicted as a huge mountain with four great hollow places.

Idol of Moloch in the Valley of Gehinnom.

The angel Raphael tells Enoch that these hollow places were created "that all the souls of the children of men should assemble here... till the day of the great judgement." One of the hollow places holds the "spirits of the righteous" and the others are for "sinners when they die... their spirits shall be set apart in great pain till the day of judgement."

By the beginning of the Christian era the Hebrew underworld had evolved further. The place of the righteous became known as Paradise, and the place of punishment was called *Gehinnom* or *Gehenna*, which probably took its name from the valley of Hinnom south of Jerusalem. The valley of Hinnom had at one time been the scene of child sacrifices to the Canaanite god Moloch, and later it became the garbage dump for Jerusalem, where trash and animal carcasses were burned. Gehinnom was usually described as an enormous realm in the depths of the earth with three entrances—one in the sea, one in the desert, and one in Jerusalem itself. Here the souls of the wicked were punished in flames and gnawed by worms and serpents, and this conception of a subterranean realm of torment was assimilated rapidly into the new Christian religion.

Between about the third and seventeenth centuries, Hell was the ultimate fear of every Christian, and the terror of Hell shaped much of Christian society. Hell became a place where a soul might be punished eternally and brutally for a few momentary transgressions. Hell was hidden forever in the depths from the light of the sun or, for those in earlier times who pictured the earth as flat, it was the dark hemisphere beneath us and in the earth's shadow, mirroring and inverting the bright bowl of the heavens.

Throughout its many depictions in religious writing, Hell seems to be a macrocosm of the lower half of the human body, which in both its anatomy and its urges—to eat, to copulate, to excrete—reminded the medieval Christian of his or her own mortality and sinfulness. To those who think along such lines, the lower half of the body mocks the aspirations of the upper half—the faith and intelligence of the heart and brain and the creativity of the hands—as the underworld mocks the heavens and the sunlight. In some cultures, the dead in the underworld live "upside down." A popular belief of the ancient Egyptians held that the dead in the underworld walked upside down, with their feet on the ceiling. Their digestive systems were also upside down; the dead ate with their anuses and defecated from their mouths. In the underworld the low was exalted and the high brought low, and the exaltation of the body's mortality and urges filled the Christian Hell. Hell was in the "bowels of the earth," and like the human bowels, it was filled with stinking gases—the traditional brimstone—waste, and filth, plus the decay of the grave.

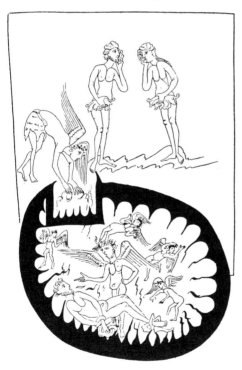

The Devil's emissary returns to a womblike Hell after bringing about the Fall of Adam and Eve. From the medieval *Archaeologia*.

Descriptions of Hell unintentionally stressed the fearsome, devouring aspect of the Earth Mother. The very concept of an Earth Mother would have been heretically pagan to those who depicted Hell and its terrors, yet many of the descriptions suggest that sinners damned to Hell were being drawn back into the womb to be restrained and consumed. James Joyce, in his *Portrait of the Artist as a Young Man*, rendered well the claustrophobia of the tormented in the Jesuit priest's terrifying sermon, based on sermons Joyce heard as a boy:

> In earthly prisons the poor captive has at least some liberty of movement, were it only within the four walls of his cell or the gloomy yard of his prison. Not so in Hell. There, by reason of the great number of the damned, the prisoners are heaped together in their awful prison, the walls of which are said to be four thousand miles thick: and the damned are so utterly bound and helpless that, as a blessed saint, Saint Anselm, writes in his book on similitudes, they are not even able to remove from the eye a worm that gnaws it.

When Joyce's Jesuit, delivering this sermon, says the walls of Hell are "said to be four thousand miles thick"—a perfect image of constriction—he may be referring to the Hell described by another Jesuit, Drexelius. Drexelius said Hell consisted of a mere cubic mile of space at the center of the earth, packed with 1,000,000,000,000 damned souls.

Other descriptions of Hell are equally claustrophobic. The monk Wettin, who was privileged to see a vision of the afterlife, said that lecherous churchmen and their lovers were doomed to be bound tightly to stakes for all eternity and flogged continuously on their genitals; another sinful monk in his vision was imprisoned forever in a casket of lead. In the *Inferno* of Dante, the damned are swallowed by mud, buried under rocks, and frozen into solid ice.

In the sixteenth century Saint Teresa of Avila suffered a mystical experience of Hell, which she called in her *Autobiography* "one of the greatest mercies that God ever bestowed on me," since it made the terrors awaiting the sinful all too real for her. She wrote that in her vision she was drawn into a narrow, muddy tunnel, "which smelt abominably and contained many wicked reptiles." At the tunnel's end was a small cavity into which she was squeezed, where she could neither sit nor lie down. To be damned to Hell was to be eternally smothered and consumed by the earth.

Hell was commonly pictured in the Middle Ages as a great dragon or monster with a gigantic mouth, devouring the wicked. In the medieval Vision of Tundale, reportedly the story of an Irish knight's vision while deep in a coma, a bright angel showed Tundale souls of misers eaten by a monstrous, flaming mouth. This mouth was so large that nine thousand people could fit easily within it, and the souls of the avaricious were continually prodded by demons down the vast throat, howling as they were roasted and digested.

The Hell-Mouth image has often been connected with openings in the earth. Numerous cave openings in Europe have been called entrances to the afterworld; one of the best known is "St. Patrick's Purgatory," a cave on an island in Ireland's Lough Derg. The cave was supposedly discovered by a hermit named Patrick who lost himself in the darkness, prayed to God to show him the way out, and while praying, he heard wailing and moaning deeper in the cave. After reaching the surface safely, he told others of his experience, and after Patrick's death, "pious people" built a chapel on the site. By the twelfth century the chapel had become a favorite destination for pilgrimages by both the devout and the curious. The monks in residence had long since covered the entrance to the cave with a stout door, but many knights and nobles making the pilgrimage persuaded the abbot, donations in hand, to open it.

Some of those who entered claimed to see horrible visions within the cave of demons, "wykked gostes," and the sinners they punished. Others said they saw nothing. But the abbey grew so excessively rich from the donations of curious pilgrims that in 1497 the Purgatory was walled up on orders from the Pope.

In England, there was a cave opening in the Hertfordshire area called Hell's Gate (although in Victorian times the name was changed to a more proper Cave Gate). A folktale connected with the cave runs that a blind fiddler bet a group of farm workers that Hell's Gate was no more than an ordinary cave. With only his fiddle and his dog, he entered the cave, and the farm workers followed the sound of his fiddle under the fields until they heard a horrible shriek and the fiddling stopped. The laborers ran back to the entrance, and soon they heard the faint sound of running. The fiddler's dog rushed out suddenly, minus its tail and with all its hair burned off. The dog howled, ran away, and was never seen again.

The fiddler was never seen again, either, and all presumed he had met his end at the hands of the Devil in the depths of the cave. No one had the courage to look for his body; the laborers covered the cave's mouth with stones and mortar instead. This wonderful story appears to be sheer folklore, however. Not only are there similar versions of the same tale connected with other British caves, but in 1965 the wall covering the mouth of Hell's Gate was torn down, an exploration party entered—and the cave went only a few yards before it ended in solid rock.

In other parts of the world, the Hell-Mouth image is clearly linked to the Earth Mother. In India, the tradition of the Terrible Devouring Mother is very old; we need think only of the goddess Kali, "dark, all-devouring time, the bone-wreathed lady of the place of skulls." Kali is also, as Erich Neumann tells us in his book *The Great Mother* (1963), "the hungry earth, which devours its own children and fattens on their corpses." Amemait, the Devourer of the Egyptian Hall of Double Justice, is a female monster with a huge mouth.

The Mouth of Hell, from the *Kalendrier des Bergiers.*

The Earth Mother is also monstrous in the mythology of ancient Mexico. In a Nahua creation myth, the earth began as a beast with numberless mouths, swimming in the waters of the great void and devouring all she encountered. She was defeated by the gods Quetzalcoatl and Tezcatlipoca, who tore her in two. Her lower half became the heavens, her upper half the earth, and her mouths became the caverns which descend into her belly. But she still wept if she was not fed; if she did not receive human blood, she would not bear fruit. The blood bowl in which the hearts of the Aztecs' sacrificial victims were offered to the sun had the symbol of the Earth Mother, a land tortoise, on the bottom. The Aztec death goddess was also a devourer; her mouth and vagina bristled with teeth and knives.

These great consuming mouths of the earth and the Hell-Mouth can probably best be seen as reactions to our own mortality. Most humans throughout history have feared death and the loss of freedom and life's pleasures that accompany it. Many cultures have myths of a "golden age" in the first days, in which people never got sick, never aged, and never died, until the gods or an evil or foolish human tricked them into losing their immortality. The rest of us have sickened, aged, and died ever since, and no matter how we try to rationalize our way out of our mortality, we're angry and fearful about it. Our fear of being swallowed by the underworld is part of our anguish at being mortal and having a fragile and perishable body, whose "lower" urges sometimes rule our lives.

The Christian Hell is an inverted celebration of our mortality. So it isn't surprising that Hell was placed by the Church fathers not only at the center of the earth, but at the center of the medieval universe as well. The earth was the center of the Ptolemaic/early Christian cosmos, but Hell was its real, concealed center. The spheres of the elements, the sun, the planets, and the stars circled Hell as certainly as they circled the earth. It is almost as if the philosophers and theologians anticipated Freud by two thousand years when they identified each man and woman as a microcosm of the universe. Our conscious minds are like the bright surface of the earth, and our ideals look heavenward. But the huge, dark subconscious lies beneath that surface, and it is the hidden center of each man's and each woman's urges and motivations.

The underworlds of myth are an uneasy combination of kindly womb and terrible gullet. Although we are all born from the earth, and it nourishes and shelters us, it waits hungrily to swallow us again. Out of these mixed emotions were born some of the Earth Mother's other children: fairies, gnomes, serpents, and giants. They are strange, wonderful, and fearsome children, and they draw us into their subterranean realms at our peril.

The torment of a sinner in Hell, from Father G.B. Manni's *The Eternal Prison of Hell for the Hard-Hearted Sinner,* 1692.

Chapter 2

The Earth's Other Children

> The kabouters are the dark elves, who live in the forests and mines... They are short, thick fellows, very strong and are strenuous in digging out coal and iron, copper and gold. When they were first made, they were so ugly, that they had to live where they could not be seen, that is, within the dark places.
> —William Griffis, *Dutch Fairy Tales for*
> *Young Folks* (1918)

The Welsh chronicler Giraldus Cambrensis wrote down a curious story in the twelfth century; he had heard it from his uncle David II, Bishop of St. David's. The bishop told his nephew about an old priest named Elidor who had once spoken wistfully about his childhood. As a boy Elidor had been sent to a highly regarded teacher to be educated for the priesthood, but the child was lazy and the teacher beat him frequently. Finally Elidor ran away one day when he was twelve and hid in the hollow bank of a stream for two days. Growing hungrier by the hour, he looked up and saw two small men watching him. One of them said, "If you would like to come with us, we will take you to a very pleasant country where you can play many games."

Elidor was perfectly willing to go to such a place, so he followed the two small men into a cave opening and traveled for hours through subterranean passages. At last the three came into a beautiful, green, but strangely dark land. The days there always seemed overcast, and the nights were totally black, without moon or stars. Elidor was brought before the king of that country and his court, and they examined him very carefully. The king approved of the boy and made him a playmate for his own son, who was about the same age.

Elidor was happy in that country and marveled at the ways of its people. They were slightly shorter than the people of the surface, and much more lightly built, with long, curling blond hair. The language they spoke, Elidor realized later in his life, was very similar to Greek. They ate no meat, living instead on milk, butter, and cheese mixed with saffron. The underground people held the surface folk in great contempt, and they often told the boy how greedy surface people were for trinkets and baubles while spurning the search for the real values of life.

The subterranean kingdom contained a great many precious gems and gold nuggets, and when Elidor was allowed to return to the surface to visit his mother, he told her of the wonders and riches of his new home. She listened closely to his tales and asked him if he could visit her again and bring her a little trifle of gold. One little trinket, she said, would surely never be missed by people who had so much. So one day after he returned to the underground kingdom, while playing with the prince and his friends, he grabbed their golden ball and ran through the passages to the surface. But as he crossed the threshold of his mother's house, he tripped and dropped the ball. It rolled back into the hands of the two small men, who had followed him unseen. Before they vanished they looked at the boy sorrowfully, as if they had realized there was no hope for the people of the surface.

Elidor never saw any of the underground race again, and the cave that had served as his entrance to their kingdom seemed to have vanished. He returned sadly to his old life, his teacher, and his lessons, and years later he became a priest. But even as an old man he never forgave himself for the ingratitude he had shown those kindly people.

An illustration of Elidor and the "small men" from the cavern world, by John Batten from Joseph Jacobs's *More Celtic Fairy Tales.*

Beings light and dark

In the Celtic and Germanic countries of Europe there are long traditions of races of small humanoids which dwelled inside hills, mountains, or ancient burial grounds. These beings ventured out onto the surface mostly at night, holding feasts and dances in woods and meadows, or roaming the earth about mysterious business of their own. They stole away babies and children, and sometimes lured adults into their subterranean homes. In England they were known as Fairies or Elves, in Ireland as Sidhe or Gentry, in Scotland as Sith or Good People, in France as Fees, and in Brittany as Korrigons. Fairy lore is a complex subject, for beliefs in Fairies often differed as much from village to village as they did from nation to nation. They did, however, share some basic traits throughout western Europe.

The Fairies were usually divided into two races—the "Fair Folk" or "Light Elves," who resembled the inhabitants of Elidor's underground kingdom, and the "Dark Elves"—swarthy, squat, and often hairy beings who seemed more truly creatures of the earth. The race of Dark Elves has included Brownies, Kobolds, Gnomes, Dwarfs, Trolls, and a host of cavern and mine spirits.

But the more human-seeming Fair Folk were usually associated with the insides of hills and barrows as well, and the European villager feared and respected their power far more than the modern image of the gauze-winged, Tinkerbell-style "fairy" would suggest. Even the smallest of the Fair Folk could cause more than mischief if angered or offended. A number of illnesses were commonly attributed to harmful Fairies before the last century. Strokes, for example, were believed to be caused by elf-shot; the term "stroke" is itself a shortening of "Fairy stroke." The Fairy stroke felled its human or animal victim, which the Fairies carried off invisibly, leaving a "stock" in its place. The stock was a Fairy or a log transformed into the victim's likeness, but corpselike or only minimally functioning. Victims of polio and other disabling illnesses were suspected of being stocks or changelings, and the recognized cure, as Fairy-lore expert Katharine Briggs tells us, was "incredibly harsh treatment" of the supposed Fairy child. In an effort to convince the Fairies to return their "true" child from their underground realm, many well-meaning parents beat or starved their disabled or retarded children to death. It is very likely that the dull, babbling, and listless changelings of many fairy stories were based on real-life autistic or Down's syndrome children.

Sometimes the appearance of the Fair Folk was a harbinger of death. In a typical tale of this type, a young Lancashire man saw a funeral cortege of Fairies bearing a coffin which held a tiny corpse looking exactly like himself. He died in an accident a month later. Such stories as these, when tied to the common association of the Fair Folk with ancient burial mounds, have led many folklorists to associate Fairies with the ghosts of the long-ago dead.

In popular tales, mortals often visited Fairyland, but usually at their peril. In Fairyland, time passed much more slowly than on the surface; a year on the surface went by in the space of a day, or even an hour, among the Fair Folk. This tradition of different rates of time, when seen in the light of modern relativity theory, has led several alternative-reality writers to question whether the Fair Folk might be visitors from a parallel universe or another dimension.

In another popular tale—this one from the twelfth century—there was a king of the ancient Britons, Herla, who was invited to attend the wedding of a great king of the Fair Folk. A small man led Herla and his retinue into a cave in the side of a cliff and they journeyed through darkness until they reached a luxurious palace lit by thousands of torches. Here the wedding was celebrated with great pomp and feasting. Herla and his men were loaded down with rich gifts of fine horses and hunting dogs, in particular a miniature bloodhound which was placed in the lap of one of his retainers. The Fairy who had led them into the cliff warned the Britons not to dismount until that dog had leapt from the saddle.

Back on the surface after what had seemed like three days, Herla asked the first man he encountered about his queen, and named her. The man appeared confused, and replied, "Lord, I scarcely understand your language, for I am a Saxon, and you a Briton. I have never heard the name of that queen, except in the case of one who they say was Herla's wife, queen of the earliest Britons. He is fabled to have disappeared with a dwarf at this cliff, and never to have been seen on earth again. The Saxons have now held this realm for two hundred years, having driven out the original inhabitants."

The Britons were dumbfounded, and in their astonishment, a few of them dismounted; they immediately crumbled into dust. Herla ordered that no one else should dismount until the bloodhound leapt down, but according to one version of the legend, the dog still has not touched the earth, and Herla and his men continue to ride aimlessly through Britain.

If a visit to the country of the Fair Folk could cause such disorientation and risk to mortals, the reverse was rarely true. Fairies were seen wandering and dancing through the European countryside fearlessly on numberless occasions. One of the few exceptions, however—and an important one for our story—was the tale of the "Green Children," found in the medieval English chronicles of both Ralph of Coggeshall and William of Newbridge. In his *Fairy Mythology*, Thomas Keightley gives the following translation of Coggeshall from the Latin:

> Another wonderful thing happened in Suffolk, at St. Mary's of the Wolf-pits. A boy and his sister were found by the inhabitants of that place near the mouth of the pit which is there, who had the form of all their limbs like to those of other men, but they differed in the colour of their skin from all the people of the habitable world; for the whole of their skin was tinged of a green colour. No one could understand their speech. When they were brought as curiosities to the house of a certain knight, Sir Richard de Calne, at Wikes, they wept bitterly. Bread and other victuals were set before them, but they would touch none of them, though they were tormented by great hunger, as the girl afterward acknowledged. At length, when some beans just cut, with their stalks, were brought into the house, they made signs, with great avidity, that they should be given to them. When they were brought, they opened the stalks instead of the pods, thinking the beans were in the hollow of them; but not finding them there, they began to weep anew. When those who were present saw this, they opened the pods, and showed them the naked beans. They fed on these with great delight, and for a long time tasted no other food. The boy, however, was always languid and depressed, and he died within a short time. The girl enjoyed continual good health; and becoming accustomed to various kinds of food, lost completely that green colour, and gradually recovered the sanguine habit of her entire body. She was afterward regenerated by the laver of holy baptism, and lived for many years afterward in the service of that knight (as I have frequently heard from him and his family), and was rather loose and wanton in her conduct. Being frequently asked about how she came into this country with the aforesaid boy, she replied, that as they were following their flocks, they came to a certain cavern, on entering which they heard a delightful sound of bells; ravished by whose sweetness, they went for a long time wandering on through the cavern, until they came to its mouth. When they came out of it, they were struck senseless by the excessive light of the sun, and the unusual temperature of the air; and they thus lay for a long time. Being terrified by the noise of those who came on them, they wished to fly, but they could not find the entrance of the cavern before they were caught.

In his account, William of Newbridge adds that the Green Children appeared during the reign of King Stephen (who died in 1154), that the girl called her country St. Martin's Land, and that the people of that land were Christians. William writes also that he did not believe the story until he had investigated it at some length, although he did not say what his investigations entailed.

The story of the Green Children is unusual in its attention to small, slice-of-life details, as well as its suggestion of great mysteries beneath the "Wolf-pits" of Suffolk, and it has attracted a good deal of attention from alternative-reality writers. In his book *Secret of the Ages*, Brinsley le Poer Trench concurs with fellow ufologist Harold Wilkins's theory that the Green Children may have been two young members of a technologically superior underground race who were trapped by humans when they ventured onto the surface. Jacques Bergier, in his *Extraterrestrial Visitations from Prehistoric Times to the Present* (1973), tells the story of the Green Children in almost exact detail, except that for some reason the locale is transferred to nineteenth-century Spain. Sir Richard de Calne, for example, becomes Ricardo da Calno, local justice of the peace. Bergier asserts several times that the story is true and that the Children were examined by "specialists from Barcelona." He is unclear as to exactly who the Green Children might have been, but he implies that they were part of an experiment set up by extraterrestrials or extradimensionals to test the reactions of humans.

Before considering such theories of the origin of the Green Children, we should examine the story in the light of folk belief. The subterranean home of the Children, and the "loose and wanton" behavior of the girl fit very well within local beliefs about the Fair Folk of that time. There exists an even more intriguing possibility to consider—that the tale began as a rumor of two children who had returned from the land of the dead, or had been buried alive and then rescued. Katharine Briggs reminds us that in Celtic countries green was the color of death and that beans were widely held to be the food of the dead.

Dark elves and mine spirits

"Dark elves" were rough, crude-looking, earthy beings. Goblins from George MacDonald's *The Princess and the Goblin*.

While the Fair Folk dwelled beneath the earth's surface in many folk traditions, their physiques were slim, light, and airy; they were not creatures truly *of* the earth. The Dark Elves, however, were quintessentially earthy beings. Those we know best today are the Dwarfs of Germanic folklore, those short, broad, brawny miners from the Grimm tale of Snow White and the fantasy novels of J.R.R. Tolkien. According to Germanic myth, in which they play an important role, the Dwarfs originated as maggots in the flesh of the cosmic giant Ymir, who had been slain by the god Odin and his brothers, and whose corpse became the earth. The gods formed the maggots into dwarfs, but as burrowers they began and burrowers they remained. The gods ordered them to dwell within the earth and allowed them to come to the surface only after nightfall. If a Dwarf remained on the surface after sunrise, he was turned to stone.

Dwarfs were stronger, craftier, and more skillful than humans with metals and precious stones, creating magical weapons, ornaments, and machines in their underground forges. Among the wonders of Dwarf manufacture that have entered literature and myth is the magic girdle of Spenser's *Faerie*

Queene which served as the ultimate chastity belt, for only a chaste and virtuous woman was able to wear it. Another is the magic sword Tyrfing, capable of splitting iron and stone; once Tyrfing was unsheathed, it could not be returned to its sheath until it had shed blood.

The Dwarfs lived in an underground kingdom often called *Svart-alfaheim* ("home of the Black Elves"). Their king, who reigned from a vast palace studded with gems, was commonly named Alberich or Oberon, both names probably deriving from the same root and both familiar to us today—the first from the *Niebelungenlied* and the second from Shakespeare's *Midsummer Night's Dream*. The Dwarfs were constantly occupied with mining and smithing, and their cavern homes were reputed to be piled with heaps of precious metals, gems, and the treasures they created from them. But the Dwarfs seemed to derive little pleasure from their wealth—only from accumulating more of it. While in some regions the Dwarfs were described as well-disposed to humans, even aiding hard-working humans in their chores during the night, in other places it was said that the Dwarfs were envious of the tall statures and fair complexions of the gods and humans, and hated them both equally. They considered themselves the guardians of the earth's treasures and would rarely part with their creations willingly. The Dwarf smiths would sometimes curse the swords and jewelry they made under duress for humans, and their owners found little joy in possessing Dwarf-craft.

According to Germanic myth, there were no Dwarf women, and thus no Dwarf children born in the usual way. Instead the gods supplied them with two princes who molded new Dwarfs out of the earth when members of their race died or disappeared.

Germany was the home of the Dwarfs, but beneath the mountains of Norway and Iceland there lived a similar race called the *Huldre Folk* or Hidden Folk. Among the Norwegians the most important of these beings was the Huldre or Hill-Lady, who appeared from the front as a beautiful woman dressed in a blue smock and white linen hood. From behind, however, she was hideously ugly, with her back hollowed out like a trough, and with a long tail she had difficulty concealing. She was a fine singer and dancer, and she would appear to mortal herdsmen or farmers and ask them to dance. If such a man had his wits about him and remained calm when her tail suddenly swished from beneath her skirts, the Huldre would reward him richly for his tact. The Huldre was often reported to have large teeth as well, and Mother Holle, from the Grimm tale mentioned in the previous chapter, is supposed to be derived from the Hill-Lady.

A race similar to the Dwarfs—and descended from them—but of occult philosophy rather than traditional lore was the race of Gnomes. Paracelsus, the Swiss doctor and occultist of the early sixteenth century, wrote that there were four races of beings called Elementals, one corresponding to each of the four classical elements of air, water, fire, and earth. Invisible to the common eye, Elementals nevertheless filled the natural world like sawdust filled a carpenter's shop. "Yet the Elementals are not spirits," wrote Paracelsus, "because they have flesh, blood, and bones; they live and propagate offspring; they eat and talk, act and sleep... They are beings occupying a place between men and spirits, resembling men and women in their organization and form, and resembling spirits in the rapidity of their locomotion."

The Sylphs were the Elementals of air; similar to the Fair Folk in appearance, they controlled the wind and weather. The Undines were the Elementals of water; Paracelsus based his description of them on classical mythology and the mermaids of popular folklore. The Elementals of fire were the Salamanders, who took the form of either knights in fiery armor or the amphibians which today bear their name. The Gnomes were the Elementals of earth.

The word "Gnome" probably derives from the Greek "genomus" or "earth dweller." Paracelsus seems to have coined the term himself and meant by it a particular class of being, but "Gnome" soon passed into popular speech as a synonym for "elf," "goblin," or "dwarf," and by the nineteenth century the four words had become almost interchangeable. The race of Gnomes seems to have found its resting places today in overly precious children's books and in numerous British and American suburban gardens as the plaster or plastic garden gnome.

Paracelsus's Gnomes, however, were intended as serious personifications of the powers of the earth. Physically they were like the Dwarfs—small, thick humanoid creatures. They could pass through the solid earth as easily as humans passed through air or fish through water. Paracelsus wrote that the Gnomes "are of the length of about two spans, but they may extend or elongate their forms until they appear like giants." Unlike the Dwarfs, the Gnomes were of two sexes; the females were sometimes called Gnomides. Both sexes were pictured wearing rough clothes of earthy colors. Their disposition toward humans was a matter of dispute. "The earth is filled well nigh to its center with Gnomes," wrote the Abbe de Villars, a seventeenth-century cabalist, "people of slight stature, who are the guardians of treasures, minerals and precious stones. They are ingenious, friends of man, and easy to govern." But other occultists considered Gnomes tricky and malicious beings who hampered the progress of those who worked in the earth or searched for buried treasure. One book of spells, the *Clavicule of Solomon*, calls Gnomes jealous guardians of the earth. They, "seeing the evil purposes to which treasure may be put, become intolerant to the seekers, and often kill them."

Since as a young man Paracelsus worked as a doctor among German miners, he probably based his ideas about Gnomes on those miners' folk beliefs. Any hazardous occupation is bound to gather about itself a large body of superstition, and mining, which is not only dangerous but carried out within the dark places of the earth, has traditionally been a superstitious trade.

In Germany and Britain particularly, the miners believed that a race of little men—wizened reflections of themselves a few feet high—worked the mines, rarely seen but often heard. The German miners called them *Kobolds* (the metal cobalt is named after these beings), and frequently heard them at work, tapping and picking in distant parts of the mine. The miners usually kept well away from the sounds the Kobolds made, for the Kobolds were malevolent creatures who did all in their power to frustrate the mortal miners' work, often causing cave-ins.

A nineteenth-century engraving of a Kobold.

Other German miners claimed there were two races of Kobolds, one malicious and one helpful. Georgius Agricola wrote in *De animantus subterranibus* (1651) of "goblins who labored in the mines," acting as if they were digging, blasting, and picking away furiously, hauling away great mounds of ore. Yet all their "work" was deceit, for when the miners approached to examine the digging, the rock had never been touched.

The "Knockers" of Cornwall's tin mines were better disposed toward humans. Robert Hunt, in his *Popular Romances of the West of England*, writes that "miners say they often see little imps or demons underground. Their presence is considered favorable; they indicate the presence of lodes, about which they work in the absence of miners." The Knockers, who were also known as Buccas, Nickers, and Spriggans, were generally believed by the Christian population to be the ghosts of Jews who had been responsible for the Crucifixion. Instead of sending them to Hell, God had sent them to labor in the tin mines. This belief, based on the fact that many Jews were involved in tin mining during the eleventh and twelfth centuries—it was one of the few trades they were allowed to pursue at that time—was magnified by the endemic anti-Semitism of the Middle Ages. One legend has it that these Jewish ghosts were tormented by having to sing carols deep in the mines on Christmas eve, but in a similar tale related by Hunt, the little miners seem to have been Christians and to have sung willingly:

> On Christmas Eve, in former days, the small people, or the Spriggans, would meet at the bottom of the deepest mines, and have a Midnight Mass. Those who were in the mine would hear voices, melodious beyond all earthly voices, singing "Now well [Noel]! Now well!" and the strains of some deep-toned organ would shake the rocks.

If the little miners were friendly, they would often warn their human colleagues of impending danger in the mines. Sometimes their tappings would ring out vigorously in a portion of the mine that would soon collapse or be the scene of an accident.

When many of the Cornish miners emigrated to California during and after the Gold Rush, they brought their belief in the Knockers with them. In the California quartz mines the little men became "Tommy Knockers," and the belief in them caught on among many of the Americans. The Tommy Knockers were, like the other small beings of the mines, extensions of the miners' anxieties.

A nineteenth-century illustration of gnomes terrorizing a miner.

Some miners said that any human hearing the raps of the Tommy Knockers' picks would be the next to be killed in a cave-in or to be poisoned by underground gas. Following the lead of the Cornishmen, the miners would set a clay figure of a Tommy Knocker with a pipe in its mouth and match-head eyes at the entrance to the mine for good luck. Often the Tommy Knockers were considered the ones responsible when equipment broke down—as in these lines from "Hardrock Hank," a California miner who dabbled in verse:

> I'm a hardrock miner an' I ain't afeard o' ghosts
> > But my neck-hair bristles like porcupine quills
> An' I knock my knuckles on the drift set posts
> > When the Tommyknockers hammer on the caps an' sills
> An' raise hallelujah with my picks an' drills!

There were mine spirits in other parts of the world as well. The Chinese miners told of the Celestial Stag, a seemingly helpful creature who would lead them to veins of gold or silver, then beg to be taken up to the surface. But if allowed to leave the mine, the Stag would change into a poisonous fluid that spread disease. In some ill-fated mines there were many Celestial Stags; if the miners resisted their entreaties, there would be a series of fatal "accidents." The only way to defeat the Stags was to take hold of them and bury them in clay within the mine. The Chinese, strong believers in *feng shui*, divination by the power of the earth, had tales of a great many earth spirits and were reluctant to dig very deeply into the earth for fear of angering them. Among them were several races of hill and mountain spirits who lived under rocks and in caves. The spirits of one such race ate earth, were sexless, and had no calves to their legs. After they died their hearts did not decay, but lay dormant like seeds for a hundred years and finally sprouted into human beings.

Giants and serpents

The huge body of the earth was not always considered female. Among the old Scandinavians the earth was formed by the gods from the corpse of the frost giant Ymir. Ymir was a personification of the wild, chaotic power of the cold, and he was slain by his grandsons Odin, Hoenir, and Lodur, the first three Aesir gods. The three gods shoved the enormous corpse into the pit of Ginungagap, and the torrent of brine that poured from Ymir's wounds overflowed the pit and became the oceans. The Aesir gods then fashioned Midgard, our world, from the floating body—Ymir's bones became the stony mountains, his flesh the soil, his skull the dome of the heavens, and we have already seen how the maggots burrowing through his flesh became the Dwarfs.

A Chinese "one-horned mountain spirit" who dwelt among the rocks and caves.

Ymir had also given birth to many monsters while he lived. From one of his armpits had sprouted the primeval pair of Jotuns, a malevolent race of giants. A six-headed Troll had burst forth from the flesh of his feet. The giants and trolls multiplied by scores, but when Ymir was slain, they all drowned in the ocean of brine save one male and one female Jotun, who swam to the northland on the far shore. That frozen land became Jotunheim, and there the giants and Trolls prospered once again. Because the Jotuns were destructive beings of the polar darkness and the cold, they hated both the Aesir gods and the humans the gods created.

In popular Nordic folklore, the Jotuns and Trolls also roamed the mountains and forests of Midgard. Like the Dwarfs, they dwelled underground in huge caves behind heavy stone doors which could not be distinguished from the sides of the mountains. These caves were filled with great hoards of gold and gems taken from their human victims or as tribute from the Dwarfs. The Trolls and Jotuns were engines of brute strength, tearing up trees, devouring livestock, and often dining on unwary humans. But they, like the Germanic Dwarfs, could venture from their caves only after dark, for if the sun should shine upon them, they turned to stone, and many unusual rock formations and piles of boulders were pointed out to travelers as the remains of giants who had stayed on the surface or been tricked by crafty humans.

Popular folklore told of many giants dwelling in the caves and among the rock formations of Cornwall as well. A typical Cornish giant was Trebiggan, described by Robert Hunt in his *Popular Romances of the West of England.* Trebiggan lived in a cave near Land's End, and his arms were so long that he could pull sailors from their ships when he desired. He was also said "to have dined every day on little children, who were generally fried on a large flat rock which stood at a little distance from his cave." The Iroquois of northeastern North America also had in their folklore a race of Stone Giants, huge, primitive, but very powerful magicians made of the stones of the earth, who did not know how to use the bow, but instead fought among themselves savagely during storms. They tore the greatest trees out of the ground for clubs, and threw boulders at one another.

The giant Finn M'Cool as a force of nature, building the Giant's Causeway in Northern Ireland.

It is said that the giants of folklore are based on our collective memories of being a small child in a world full of grown-ups. The "giant" adults could pick us up and put us down wherever they liked, paddle us when we did something they didn't approve of, and in general seem to be engines of mighty power. Giants also represent forces of nature; in folk traditions the world over, they move mountains and rivers, cause earthquakes and volcanic eruptions, and wipe out villages with a poorly placed foot. In "Koisha Kayn," a Celtic folktale from Scotland, the hero, seeking his kidnapped mother and sister, sails to an island ruled by a great giant who lives in a cave. The giant sucks ships onto the island with his breath; an old woman who lives there warns him:

> ...every one of the ships that you see he has taken in from the ocean with his breath, and he has killed and eaten the men. He is asleep at present, and when he wakens he shall have you in a similar manner. A large iron door and an oak door are on the cave. When the giant draws in his breath the doors open, and when he emits his breath the doors shut; and they are shut as fast as though seven small bars, and seven large bars, and seven locks were on them.

Here once again, we see an image of a cave mouth as the mouth of a devourer, but here it is a male devourer—a terrible Father. The only way the hero may defeat the giant, once he is sucked into the cave, is to take his "short spear," which isn't difficult to see as a phallic symbol, and remove the giant's head with one blow.

The giant dwelling in the earth has a reptilian colleague, the serpent. The ancient Egyptians regarded the snake as "the son of the earth," and the Greek author Aelian called the earth the mother of dragons. In the mythology of India, snakes were considered guardians of wealth. Each cobra supposedly guarded a treasure-crock which he had hidden beneath an anthill. There were also many tales of the Nagas, a race of semi-divine serpents, who were said to rule a subterranean kingdom, Patala, filled with incredible wealth. Patala was said to be the lowest of the seven regions of the Indian underworld, yet it was not a place of darkness and fear, but one of civilized wonders. The *Vishnu-purana* says, "What can be compared to Patala, where the Nagas are decorated with brilliant and beautiful and pleasure-shedding jewels? Who will not delight in Patala, where the lovely daughters of the Daityas and Danavas [other races of demigods] wander about, fascinating even the most austere... Splendid ornaments, fragrant perfumes, rich unguents, the blended music of the lute and pipe and tabor; these and many other enjoyments are the common portion of the Danavas, Daityas, and snake-gods, who inhabit the region of Patala." Few mortals were ever allowed to enter the lower world, yet there were said to be many hidden entrances in the mountains of India and Kashmir. In popular folklore, a passage in every anthill reached Patala eventually.

One of the few mortals to venture into this underground paradise of the Nagas was Utanka, a young Brahmin scholar, in a legend found in the *Mahabarata*. His queen gave Utanka a valuable pair of diamond earrings to deliver to the wife of his tutor. She warned him to be careful, for Takshaka, King of the Nagas, lusted after these gems and might try to steal them in a careless moment.

As he traveled, Utanka noticed that a poor beggar was following him, sometimes approaching to beg, but at other times vanishing. Utanka stopped to perform his ablutions, and when he set the earrings on the ground the beggar, who had been in hiding, stole up and carried them away. Utanka ran after the thief, but as soon as he grasped the beggar, the Brahmin found himself clutching a huge snake. The beggar was actually Takshaka, and he slipped from Utanka's grasp and into a cleft in the earth.

Upset by the theft, Utanka rammed his staff into the cleft, but Takshaka was already well on his way back down to Patala. The god Indra, watching the young Brahmin, took pity on him and sent his thunderbolt down to earth. It entered the cleft through the staff and tore the cleft into a great tunnel. Utanka followed the tunnel down to Patala, and when he arrived he was awestruck by the beauty of the Naga kingdom. When the serpents gathered about him, he chanted a long hymn in their praise. The Nagas drank up the flattery, but refused to return the earrings.

Unsure of what to do next, Utanka entered into meditation. Days and seasons passed in a vision before him, and suddenly Indra himself appeared, mounted on his horse. Utanka chanted praise to Indra, and the god asked the young man how he might help him. "Put the Nagas into my power," said Utanka, and Indra replied, "Breathe on the crupper of my horse." When Utanka did so, Indra's mount burst into sheets of flame and mountains of smoke that filled all of Patala. The Nagas were terror-stricken, and at last Takshaka shot from his palace and returned the earrings to Utanka. Indra then placed the young man upon his steed and delivered him to the tutor's door in the space of a second. He arrived there exactly at the moment appointed to turn over the jewels.

Far beneath Patala there dwelled another, and far greater, serpent. This was Shesha, the serpent who holds up the world—an immense cobra with a thousand heads. Shesha was the servant of the god Vishnu, and often the god was pictured sleeping among Shesha's coils, in the shade of his great hood. When Shesha shakes one of his heads the earth quakes, and at the end of each kalpa—every 3,420,000,000 years—he writhes convulsively and destroys the world in fire.

Northern Europe has a long tradition of evil dragons who preyed on humans and their flocks and guarded great treasures. In his *Religion of Ancient Scandinavia* (1906), William Craigie wrote of dragons:

> In various places all over the country there are still shown holes in the earth out of which they are seen to come flying like blazing fire when wars or other troubles are to be expected. When they return to their dwellings, where they brood over immense treasures (which they, as some say, have gathered by night in the depths of the sea), there can be heard the clang of the great iron doors that close behind them.

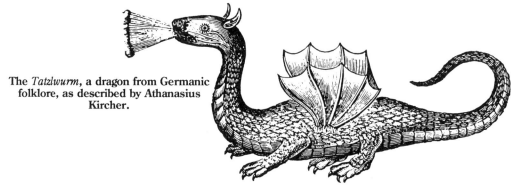

The *Tatzlwurm,* a dragon from Germanic folklore, as described by Athanasius Kircher.

The seventeenth-century Jesuit writer Athanasius Kircher (whom we shall meet in more detail in the next chapter) collected many dragon tales from throughout Europe and Asia and reached some interesting conclusions about the lives of dragons and serpents. Kircher believed that the earth was honeycombed with subterranean passages that were filled with a fantastic fauna and flora of their own, including many kinds of dragons and serpents.

One tale he related came from Switzerland, in which one Victor, a barrel-maker from Lucerne, fell into a deep crevasse while searching for wood for wine casks one autumn evening. He was unable to climb out, but discovered several caves, the biggest of which was the home of two winged dragons. The dragons were quite friendly toward Victor, and he lived there with them for six months, spending cold nights wrapped in their coils, and living on little else than the water dripping from the underground rocks. When spring finally came, the dragons grew restless. Suddenly, one of them spread its wings and flew up, out of the chasm. When the second prepared to follow, Victor seized its tail and was carried back up to the mountainside, eventually making his way back to Lucerne. His tale was met with great wonder, but his return to a regular diet caused his death.

In ancient Greece, a version of the myth of Apollo's battle with the serpent Python at Delphi dating from about 300 BC shows us again the relation between the serpent and the earth. The oracular shrine at Delphi, says the myth, was once ruled by the earth goddess Ge. Ge herself spoke the oracles, and her shrine was guarded by the great serpent Python. The god Apollo, when only a boy, came to the oracle and was attacked by Python; Apollo shot a hundred arrows at Python, finally killing him. After cleansing himself of the serpent's blood, Apollo took possession of the shrine, and the speakers of the oracles were ever afterward priestesses of Apollo. The myth is symbolic, once again, of the transfer of power from the Earth Mother (Ge) to the individual consciousness in the light of the sun (Apollo, who was also a solar god).

All of the "children" of the Earth Mother we have surveyed briefly in this chapter—the Fair Folk, the Dwarfs, Giants, and Serpents—we shall see again later in this story. All of them, in different ways, represent the not-quite-human powers that lie "beneath the surface" of both the earth and human consciousness. They are the child deep inside us that never grows up and the powers and urges that propel us through life, yet we fear might take control of us if we are not careful. They are the forces of a dangerous world, lying always beneath the sunny surface.

A "devourer" giant about to be slain at the mouth of his cave, by John Batten from Joseph Jacobs's *More English Fairy Tales.*

Chapter 3

The Inaccessible Center

> Presently she began again. "I wonder if I shall fall right *through* the earth! How funny it'll seem to come out among the people that walk with their heads downwards!"
>
> —Lewis Carroll, *Alice's Adventures in Wonderland*

Although *Homo Sapiens* has left its footprints in the dust of the moon and tossed space probes beyond the limits of the solar system, technology has not yet allowed humanity to pry more than a few miles beneath the surface of its home planet. After intensive study of the pressure waves in the earth's mantle using supercomputers, geologists have gone so far as to draw a detailed "map" of the planet's interior. But if scientists are correct, there may never be a way for us to actually visit the center of the earth.

In a 1976 interview, Julian Goldsmith, professor of geophysics at the University of Chicago, was doubtful we could travel any significant distance beneath the earth's crust:

> Going down is not possible. You reach a point where the pressure and temperature are so high you can't keep a hole open. At a pressure of about 10 kilobars (150,000 pounds a square inch)—that's something over 30 kilometers or over 18 miles deep in the earth—all the pores or cavities of solid rock close and the hole would squeeze shut. There's no way you can maintain a cavity or hole in the earth deeper than that. That's the absolute limit. I doubt you could ever send an instrument down even that far. We'll never reach the deep earth—that is, anything below 10 miles.

Geologists today tell us that the earth's interior is layered like the proverbial onion. They have placed a molten core about 1600 miles in diameter at the planet's center, made up of incredibly dense iron mixed with nickel, carbon, silicon, and sulfur at a temperature of over 10,000° F. This inner core is not a smooth ball, but a rough sphere flattened, like the planet itself, at the poles, and with its own "oceans" of molten rock and "rains" of iron particles. Surrounding this inner core is an outer core, another 60 to 200 miles thick and 7500°, of solid rock squeezed into ripples and depressions. Embracing the cores is the 1400-mile-thick mantle, a monstrous, many-layered mixture of heavy rock under the high pressures Professor Goldsmith described. These pressures are so intense that although the mantle is made of solid rock, it shifts and flows like a liquid (but is best defined as *plastic*). Resting uncomfortably on the mantle is the fragile crust of relatively lightweight rock, such as granite. The crust is fifteen to twenty-five miles thick under the continents, but only about five miles thick beneath the oceans.

The high temperatures of the earth's interior are generated by the tremendous mass of the planet—some 6,600,000,000,000,000,000,000,000 tons of matter—pressing in upon itself and breaking down the radioactive elements like thorium and uranium in the cores. It is well-documented that temperatures rise steeply even a short distance down into the crust. Parts of the Western Deep Levels diamond mine in South Africa, for example, reach a depth of almost two and a half miles; the temperature of the rocks at that depth average 130° F and the mine must be refrigerated to be worked. At six miles down, at the bottom of one of the world's deepest gas wells in Oklahoma, the temperature of the rock reaches 475° F. Geologists have long planned to drill all the way to the upper limits of the mantle; when they do, they estimate they will meet temperatures of at least 1600°.

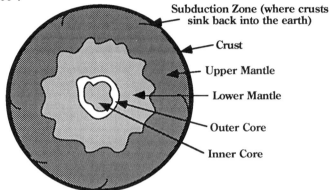

How geologists pictured the earth's interior in the late 1980s.
The cores, once pictured as perfect spheres, are now
believed to have "mountains," "valleys," and molten-iron "lakes.'

Thus we live our lives on the thin skin of a globe that is far from cold and dead; it is held together only by the gravitational power of its own mass. Anyone who has experienced an earthquake has felt the movement of the great stone plates of the crust shifting on the slow but unbelievably powerful convection currents of the mantle. Even when the ground seems calm, the plates of the crust move in different directions from one to six inches each year, slowly changing the shapes of the continents. Most people living along California's San Andreas Fault know that in a few million years Los Angeles and San Francisco will be in approximately the same location. So it isn't difficult, once we consider how small we are compared to our home planet, and the thinness of the crust that separates us from heat and pressure that could vaporize us in a few seconds, to put ourselves in the places of other humans in other times who imagined other great powers, kingdoms, and creatures beneath us.

The shape(s) of the earth

Geology sprouted from the soil of mythology, and the center of the earth began its slow separation from the land of the dead under the care of the early

Greek philosophers. Thales (640–572 BC) pictured the earth as a flat disk floating "like a piece of wood or something of that kind" on the waters that had given birth to all things. Anaximandros (611–545 BC) believed the earth, like everything else in the cosmos, had been formed "from the nature of the infinite," and was only one of a series of worlds constantly forming, changing, and dissolving. Anaximandros's earth was like a thick disk suspended in space with the air, the stars, the sun, and the moon circling above and beneath it. Humanity dwelled on the top surface of the disk; neither the sides nor the bottom were habitable. Leucippus (c. 450 BC) modified Anaximandros's great disk into a hemisphere, the lower half of a globe capped with an upside-down bowl of air. His earth was surrounded by a series of concentric crystal spheres, containing in turn the moon, planets, and sun, with the stars scattered about beyond them.

Tradition attributes the concept of a spherical earth to Pythagoras in the sixth century BC, but the idea in its written form appeared in *Phaedo*, one of Plato's dialogues. Here Plato has Socrates, in the last few hours before he consumes the fatal hemlock, give us a strange and detailed portrait of our planet. Socrates calls it "a round body in the center of the heavens" with "therefore... no need of air or any similar force to be a support." The earth is kept from falling or inclining "in any way by the equability of the surrounding heaven and by her own equipoise." Pythagoras had taught that the earth sat in space precisely at the center of the universe, and thus had no direction to incline towards. It had a spherical shape because a mass at the center of the universe would naturally take a spherical shape, and this globe would thus be habitable on all sides, not just its "top" surface.

Socrates continues by describing the features of the globe itself. The earth, he says, is like a ball of vast size and various colors, mottled with pits and hollows. We delude ourselves, he says, by believing we live on the earth's upper surface. Instead we dwell in one of the larger hollows, stretching from "the river Phasis to the Pillars of Hercules"—in other words, all the world Plato knew. We will never be able to see the true "upper" surface of the earth, Socrates tells his listeners, until we can climb to the top of the atmosphere and look out, like a fish might peer out of the water at the human world. This "upper" earth is far more beautiful than ours; the hills are covered with trees, flowers, and precious stones more colorful and perfect than anything we know here. The people and animals living "about the air as we live about the sea" have "no disease, and live much longer than we do, and have sight and hearing and smell, and all the other senses, in far greater perfection." Instead of air, these beings breathe ether, a highly refined "element" in comparison to which air and fire are gross and heavy, and earth and water unspeakably so (as late as the eighteenth century, ether was referred to in scientific writings as the stuff filling the space between the stars and planets).

But the hollow we live in is by no means the only one:

> ... there are divers regions in the hollows on the face of the globe everywhere, some of them deeper and more extended than that which we inhabit, others deeper but with a narrower opening than ours, and some shallower and also wider. All have numerous

perforations, and there are passages broad and narrow in the interior of the earth, connecting them with one another; and there flows out of and into them, as into basins, a vast tide of water, and huge subterranean streams of perennial rivers, and springs hot and cold, and a great fire, and great rivers of fire, and streams of liquid mud, thin or thick.

Finally Socrates tells us that there is "a chasm which is the vastest of them all, and pierces right through the whole earth." This chasm is Tartarus, through which all the waters and winds of the earth fall, only to rise again in an eternal cycle. There are four principal rivers in Tartarus; the greatest is Oceanus, "which flows round the earth in a circle." The next is Acheron, "which passes under the earth through desert places into the Acherusian lake; this is the lake on the shores of which the souls of the many go when they are dead, and after waiting an appointed time... they are sent back to be reborn as animals." The third river is the Pyriphlegeton which, passing between the two previous rivers, "pours into a vast region of fire, and forms a lake larger than the Mediterranean Sea, boiling with water and mud." The last is the Styx, which originates on the far side of the earth; flowing through a "wild and savage region, which is all of a dark blue color, like lapis lazuli... [it] falls into and forms the Lake Styx" in the underworld.

Unencumbered by the mythological speculations Plato added to it, Pythagoras's cosmology was closer to fact than those of his contemporaries—and closer than those of philosophers in general would be for a thousand years. But Pythagoras himself was not immune to imaginative speculation; he believed that earthquakes were caused by armies of the dead battling in Hades. Living in a region beset by frequent earthquakes and volcanic activity, the proto-geologists of classical times did, however, struggle to produce a truly scientific explanation for them. Aristotle attributed earthquakes to turbulent winds inside the earth. The poet Lucretius, in his *On the Nature of Things* (c. 58 BC), described the Sicilian volcano Mt. Etna as a hollow funnel of hot winds that struck sparks from the underground rocks and hurled hot stones and ashes onto the surrounding countryside. The pressure of these winds pushing against the earth's surface from below raised mountains, and their heat warmed geysers and hot springs.

In contrast, the underworld painted by the Roman writer Seneca (4 BC–AD 65) seems ominously peaceful:

Be assured that there exists below, everything that you see above. There are [caverns] vast, immense recesses and vacant spaces, with mountains overhanging on every hand. There are yawning gulfs stretching down into the abyss which have often swallowed up cities that have fallen into them. These retreats are filled with air, for nowhere is there a vacuum in nature; through their ample spaces stretch marshes over which darkness ever broods. Animals are also produced in them, but they are slow paced and shapeless; the air that conceived them is dark and clammy, the waters torpid through inaction.

Here, as in Plato, these early attempts at a "scientific" description of the earth's interior are tinged with the dimness of the land of the dead. For these writers, as for their ancestors and many of their descendants, what is up is more perfect and what is down is more imperfect; the interior world is a reflection of the surface world in muddy water—shadowy, chaotic, and second-rate.

Antipodes and Torrid Zones

The earliest concepts of the earth as a globe were fairly abstract. In the end it was a need for symmetry, the need to comprehend a perfect sphere of land and sea, that projected the speculations of the early geologists into what lay beyond the lands circling the Mediterranean. The skewed rotation of the stars around the North Pole implied a South Pole and other lands surrounding it, at least to most philosophers (Leucippus asserted his tympani-shaped earth had merely "sunk toward the south"). But these lands seemed incredibly foreign and distant to the Greeks, and many of them held that the earth was habitable only in two temperate zones, one in the Northern Hemisphere and one in the Southern. Between the two zones lay the impossibly hot and dry Torrid Zone, its description based on tales of the Sahara. The Phoenician sailors and traders, to whom the Greek philosophers owed many of their notions about other lands, and who may have penetrated down the African coast as far as the Cape of Good Hope, protected their profitable trade routes by telling the Greeks a few tall tales. The seas of the Torrid Zone were said to be boiling hot, impassible due to thick clouds of steam, and filled with monsters large of jaw and long of tooth.

This theory of two separate zones of human life became a major legacy of the Greek writers to the theo-geologists of the Middle Ages. When the Venerable Bede (673–735) compared the earth to a vast egg, he also brought in the notion of Torrid and Temperate Zones:

> The Earth is an element placed in the middle of the world, as the yolk in the middle of an egg; around it is the water, like the white surrounding the yolk; outside that is the air, like the membrane of the egg; and around all is the fire, which closes it in as the shell does... The ocean, which surrounds it by its waves as far as the horizon, divides it into two parts, the upper of which is inhabited by us, while the lower half is inhabited by our antipodes; although not one of them can come to us, nor one of us to them.

The idea of these two exclusive zones on our planet troubled the medieval theologians, for it implied there had been two separate creations. If we could never reach them, the Antipodeans could not be the children of Adam and Eve, and this possibility (combined with the whiff of sulfur accompanying the notion of beings living under our feet) made it difficult to accept. St. Augustine was said to have been particularly bothered by the idea of Antipodeans, and he suggested strongly that the entire Southern Hemisphere was covered with water. His followers carried the suggestion to such a degree that they proposed a sort of double earth with two spheres, one of earth floating in one of water, and each with a distinct center, like this:

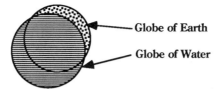

To those wondering how a globe of earth could float in a globe of water, since water is lighter than earth and no one had ever seen stones or clods of dirt floating in ponds, the Augustinians had only to point at Genesis 1:9 for their justification. There God, creating the world, had separated the land from the waters.

Another solution to whether Antipodeans existed was suggested by Dante at the end of the *Inferno*. There Virgil told him that when Satan fell, he was cast into the earth on the Antipodean side, and the land there, "for dread of him," rushed to the other side of the earth. Thus there was no land at all on the opposite side of the world, except for the Mount of Purgatory, rearing out of the sea at the point of the globe directly opposite Jerusalem (which is a spot in the South Pacific a little to the south of Tahiti).

Religious and superstitious belief continued to underlie both common and learned beliefs about the earth in medieval and Renaissance times. In 1374 Conrad von Megenburg wrote his *Book of Nature* and in it offered an explanation for earthquakes. First he dismissed the ideas held by many in his day:

> It often happens in one place or another that the earth shakes so violently that cities are thrown down and even that one mountain is hurled against another mountain. The common people do not understand why this happens and so a lot of old women who claim to be very wise, say that the earth rests on a great fish called Celebrant, which grasps its tail in its mouth. When this fish moves or turns the earth trembles. This is a ridiculous fable and of course not true but reminds us of the Jewish story of the Behemoth.

Yet when Megenburg gave his own hypothesis, it was basically astrological:

> Earthquakes arise from the fact that in subterranean caverns and especially those within hollow mountains, earthy vapors collect and these sometimes gather in such enormous volumes that the caverns can no longer hold them. They batter the walls of the cavern in which they are and force their way out into another and still another cavern until they fill every open space in the mountain. This unrest of the vapors is brought about by the mighty power of the Stars, especially by that of the God of War as Mars is called, or of Jupiter and also Saturn when they are in constellation. When these vapors have for a long time roared through the caverns, the pressure becomes so great that they break a passage through to the surface and throw the mountains against one another. If they cannot reach the surface they give rise to great earthquakes.

But even after reaching the surface the vapors were destructive, for they were highly poisonous. Megenburg believed the Black Death, which wiped out about a third of Europe's population during the fourteenth century, had been caused by underground vapors released during earthquakes.

The Great Fire

By the beginning of the sixteenth century, it had been established to the satisfaction of most academics that the earth was round, with land and sea on all sides. But what lay inside the globe was still a matter of debate. The concept of an eternal fire raging in the center of the earth, which dated back to Plato's time, grew increasingly popular among philosophers, and a lively discussion arose among the members of the "Plutonic" school, as it was known, over how the Great Fire was kept burning in the earth's bowels. The heat and force of volcanic activity required a great source of power, but how did the fire rage for thousands of years without consuming the whole earth?

Gabriel Frascatus, writing in 1575, proposed that since the center of the earth was also the center of the cosmos, it was the point at which the rays of the sun, stars, and other heavenly bodies converged, like spokes to the hub of a huge wheel. The center of the earth/cosmos was thus the hottest spot in the universe, and there the Great Fire would burn until God brought the material Creation to an end. The alchemist Johann Becher (1635–1682) agreed with Frascatus, adding that great torrents of salt water pour into the interior of the earth through cracks in the ocean floors, resulting in swirling clouds of steam among the central fires. Becher was thus able to confirm that Hell was indeed in the earth's center, since the violence he described corresponded fully with the horrors of the Pit to be found in the Scriptures.

Not everyone subscribed to the idea of a central fire, however. The Franciscan monk Marin Mersenne (1588–1648) believed the earth's crust was a hollow shell filled with water that supplied all the world's springs. This great tank of water had been formed when the waters of Noah's flood had drained away.

Athanasius Kircher (1602–1680), the Jesuit who was perhaps the most renowned scholar of his day, put the fire and water theories together in his mighty work *Mundus Subterraneus* or The Subterranean World (1665). In Kircher's eyes, everything in nature was "marvelous" and "wonderful," and he was notorious even in his own time for his ability to accept even the tallest of tales as evidence for his own theories (one critic called him "that universal scribbler and rhapsodist"). He lived in Rome, at the heart of the vast Jesuit missionary enterprise, and had ample opportunity to collect a thousand stories of the world's peoples. He told a tale of a Sicilian fisherman who spent so much time underwater that his fingers grew webs between them and his lungs so expanded that he could spend a full day below the surface. He wrote of an unfortunate Thuringian who once drank some stagnant water and later felt a great pain in his stomach as if something were alive inside him. He visited a doctor who, on a hunch, hung him upside down over a dish of warm milk—and a six-foot snake crawled from his mouth and was captured as it took a drink.

Kircher's unquestioning enthusiasm extended to his ideas about the earth; in *Mundus Subterraneus* he told of the dragon-haunted passages perforating the planet, of the discovery of mummified giants 200 cubits tall that crumbled to dust when they were touched, and the role of astrology in locating veins of gold and other precious metals. Like Megenburg three centuries earlier, Kircher believed the earth's interior was affected by the rays of various heavenly bodies, turning sulfur to gold and mercury to silver among the kettles of the Great Fire.

The earth Kircher described resembled nothing so much as a great round ball of Swiss cheese. Many thousands of passageways honeycombed the planet, he wrote; some were the home of giants and dragons, as well as subterranean spirits and demons who tended to gather in mines (he did not believe in dwarfs in mines, however, writing that they "are no longer found today"). Other passageways were the culverts and pipes of a worldwide plumbing system that connected vast reservoirs of hot and cold water. Still others were filled with fire and lava; he wrote that "What spiritous blood is in the human body, that subterranean fire is in the veins of the earth." Beside one of the huge, elaborate engravings in the work, a diagram of the "ideal system of subterranean fire cells from which volcanic mountains arise" (but which looks today more like a cross-section of an atomic bomb in the instant between its detonation and its explosion), Kircher wrote:

Diagram from Athanasius Kircher's *Mundus Subterraneus* showing the earth's oceans being sucked into an opening at the North Pole and spewed out at the South Pole.

> This drawing portrays the compartments of heat or of fire, or what is the same thing, the fire cells, throughout all the bowels of the Geocosm, the wonderful handiwork of GOD! These are variously distributed so that nothing be lacking which is in any way necessary for the preservation of the Geocosm. Also it is not believed that the fire is located exactly in the way the drawing shows, nor the channels placed exactly in this order. For who has examined this? Who among men ever penetrated down there? By this drawing we only wished to show that the bowels of the earth are full of channels and fire chambers, whether placed in this way or in another.

Kircher's underground water system was ingeniously designed. He told how the winds pushed the waters of the ocean through passages leading to huge lakes beneath the great mountain ranges. One of these reservoirs lay beneath the Alps, another beneath the Andes, and others under Asia and Africa. The heat of the Great Fire forced the water from these reservoirs to the surface, forming the springs that supplied the world's rivers. He also described subterranean rivers connecting the Black Sea, the Caspian Sea, and the Persian Gulf; were it not for the leveling influence of these channels, the Mediterranean would overflow.

Attempting to explain the mechanics of ocean currents, Kircher told his readers that there was a great passage through the earth from the North Pole to the South, and that all the earth's waters were sucked in through a great whirlpool in the Arctic and spewed out again in the Antarctic. He wrote that any explorer trying to approach the South Pole would never reach it because all currents flowed away from it, and any explorer attempting to reach the North Pole faced an inevitable death in the maelstrom.

Athanasius Kircher's Central Fire fed subsidiary centers of fire scattered through the earth's interior. Those reaching the surface formed volcanoes.

Donato Rossetti of Livorno, lecturer on logic at the University of Pisa, did Kircher one better in his *Antignome Fisico-Mathematiche* of 1667. Rossetti proposed that at the center of the earth there beat a colossal heart, like a human heart; its two ventricles "dilated and contracted with diastole and systole every twelve hours." The throb of the planetary heart could be felt in the change of the tides and the shifting of the winds. Johannes Herbinus, too, wrote in 1678 that the oceans swirled forever through "the earth's viscera" from the North Pole to the South.

In 1685, Edmond Halley, the scientist who first predicted the return of the comet that now bears his name, became the editor of the *Philosophical Transactions* of the Royal Society of London. In 1692, Halley published a paper there that planted the seed of the hollow-earth theory, and set the stage for the rest of this story.

The four concentric earths

Halley (1656–1743) was a man of wide-ranging interests. He was among the first to study trade winds, tides, and weather scientifically and begin to disprove Kircher's exotic theories. He attempted to calculate the age of the earth by the rate of salt accumulation in the oceans and angered a number of prominent bishops by concluding that the age of the planet to be computed from scriptural genealogies was far too short. He also anticipated Immanuel Velikovsky, author of *Worlds in Collision,* by nearly 300 years when he suggested that the Biblical Flood may have been caused by a comet passing too near the earth.

Halley was a master of statistics, of assembling data into a usable form. One of his most ambitious projects was a collection of readings of the magnetic needle that showed an appreciable degree of deviation, as if the North Magnetic Pole was wandering. Halley's paper of 1692 presented an intriguing hypothesis to account for these deviations of the compass. He proposed that the seemingly solid earth is actually a hollow shell about 500 miles thick containing three smaller concentric spheres, the diameters of the planets Venus, Mars, and Mercury. Each sphere was separated from the others by about 500 miles of atmosphere and prevented from colliding into its neighbors by the newly-discovered forces of Newtonian gravity. Halley believed each sphere had its own set of magnetic poles, but all four spheres turned "about the same common Axis... only with this difference, that the Outer Sphere still moves somewhat faster than the Inner." The difference in the rate of rotation among the spheres, however slight (Halley believed they amounted to no more than a few seconds per day), were the cause of the magnetic variations.

But Halley did not stop there. Once he had proposed the inner spheres, he felt the intrigue of what every hollow-earth proponent has felt since his time: the attraction of a new world to design, of millions of mysterious square miles to fill with hypothetical countries and creatures. To those readers "that shall enquire into the use these included Globes can be," he admitted they would not support human life as we know it. But "since we see all the parts of the Creation abound with Animate Beings," why should not the Creator, in His wisdom, have designed beings to inhabit the inner spheres? It only made sense that the Almighty would have created the earth to provide as large a living area as possible. "We ourselves," Halley wrote, "in Cities where we are pressed for Room, commonly build many stories one over the other, and thereby accommodate a much greater multitude of Inhabitants." To those who objected that "our Inward Globes" would be unfit for living things without light, he suggested "that there are many ways of producing Light which we are wholly ignorant of." The atmosphere between the spheres might itself be luminous, or the inner sides of the spheres might themselves shine. Perhaps, he speculated, there are small suns within the spheres—"peculiar Luminaries below, of which we have no sort of Idea."

Halley's article attracted a great deal of attention and was reprinted several times, not only in abridged editions of the *Philosophical Transactions,* but also in a special volume of the Royal Society's "most valuable" discourses. Nevertheless, few of its readers took the hypothesis seriously. The French scientific community, for example, welcomed Halley's tables of magnetic variations, but laughed at his explanation for them. Halley, however, continued defending his hypothesis as he gathered more data. He spent the years 1698–1700 sailing around the Atlantic taking magnetic readings (and putting down a mutiny attempt along the way). In 1716, he was offered an opportunity to develop his theory even further.

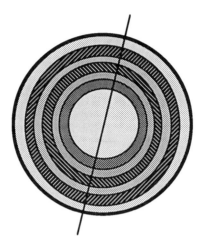

Diagram based on that in Edmond Halley's article in the *Philosophical Transactions*, 1692, showing the three concentric inner spheres of his proposed earth.

There was a magnificent display of the *aurora borealis* over much of Europe on March 6th of that year, and the Royal Society asked Halley to write a description of the phenomenon. He complied willingly, and the resulting article contained his theory of the aurora's origin as well. Isaac Newton had recently demonstrated that the earth's diameter was slightly less at the poles than at the equator, and Halley interpreted Newton's finding to mean that the outer sphere of his four-part earth was thinnest at the poles. It was thin enough, he argued, to allow the escape of some of the luminous material that provided light to the interior spheres, and once the luminous material had leaked into the outer atmosphere, it was set in motion by the earth's magnetic field.

Halley's hypothesis of several magnetic poles within the earth—one for each of four concentric spheres—and the possibility of (in Halley's words) "a more ample creation" those poles and spheres implied was soon consigned to the wastebasket of mainstream science as later researchers continued measuring the earth's magnetism. But his theory was of interest to several of the leading minds of the day, most notably the indefatigable churchman Cotton Mather. In his book *The Christian Philosopher* (1721), Mather included it in his discussion of "magnetical Vertue":

Isaac Newton has demonstrated the Moon to be more solid than our Earth, as nine to five; why may we not then suppose four Ninths of our Globe to be Cavity? Mr. Halley allows there may be Inhabitants of the lower Story, and many ways of producing Light for them... The Diameter of the Earth being about eight thousand English Miles, how easy 'tis to allow five hundred Miles for a Medium capable of a vast Atmosphere, for the Globe contained with it!

But it's time to stop, we are got beyond Human Penetration; we have dug as far as 'tis fit any Conjecture should carry us!

But conjecture was to continue for a while longer among a few orthodox speculators before the evidence piled up too strongly against a hollow planet. About seventy-five years after Halley's original paper appeared in the *Transactions*, Leonhard Euler (1707–1783), one of the most important mathematicians of the last three centuries (he invented the binary logarithms and produced a more sophisticated calculus) and a somewhat lesser physicist (he believed firmly in the critical role of Plato's ether in conducting light rays), again proposed a hollow earth. Unlike Halley's complex set of nested spheres rotating at different speeds, Euler's globe was simply a great hollow bubble. But it was not empty, for in its center he placed a small molten core that served, for this inner world's hypothetical inhabitants, like a miniature sun, eternally at the zenith of the interior "sky."

Sir John Leslie (1766–1832), a Scottish physicist and mathematician best known for his studies of heat radiation, proposed a similar theory at about the same time. Where Halley had only suggested the possibility of "peculiar Luminaries" within the earth, however, and Euler proposed a glowing core as an interior sun, Leslie went a step further. Taking his cue from the recent discovery of binary stars by the astronomer Sir William Herschel, Leslie imagined a binary molten core for his hollow earth. He even gave his two "little suns" names: he called them Pluto and Proserpina.

The publication, and rejection, of Leslie's and Euler's theories marked the last gasp of the hollow-earth idea among orthodox scientists, but the idea itself was just beginning to blossom. Leslie was still alive in 1818 when the world first heard from a retired U.S. Army officer from the Missouri Territory, John Cleves Symmes, and his "Theory of Concentric Spheres." Symmes claimed that the road into the inner world lay open, waiting only for those courageous enough to travel it.

Chapter 4

Symmes's Hole

Has not Columbia *one* aspiring son,
By whom the unfading laurel may be won?
Yes! history's pen may yet inscribe the name
Of SYMMES to grace her future roll of fame.
—Moses Brooks, for a Symmes fund-raiser, 1824

In the center of Ludlow Park, in the middle of the middle-sized city of Hamilton, Ohio, stands a monument to the central character of the story of the hollow-earth idea. It is the gravestone of a man stubbornly obsessed with the idea of a new world inside the world. When I visited it in 1977, the monument squatted sadly in a nest of weeds, behind an iron-and-concrete fence placed there to frustrate vandals, although at the time it shared its little plot with an abandoned tire. I had to press my face against the fence to read the nearly illegible inscription on the north side of its weatherbeaten sandstone pillar:

> Captain John Cleves Symmes was a philosopher, and the originator of "Symmes' Theory of Concentric Spheres and Polar Voids." He contended that the earth is hollow and habitable within.

Atop the five-foot pillar sits a pitted, sorry-looking model of the earth, turned almost on its side to reveal a large cylindrical hole from the North Pole to the South.

There is little about the gravestone of John Cleves Symmes to inspire most people. But the man and the idea the monument commemorates were very much on the minds and tongues of Americans in the decade between 1820 and 1830. On at least nine occasions, petitions signed by hundreds of the Captain's supporters were presented and debated before Congress, with the goal of financing an expedition to discover the lands within that vast opening in the North Pole. John Cleves Symmes was determined to be the leader of the first journey from the outer to the inner world, and to conquer the inner world for the United States.

"Not considered a gentleman"

Symmes was born November 5, 1779 in Sussex County, New Jersey. He was the namesake of an uncle, Judge John Cleves Symmes, who had been a New Jersey delegate to the Continental Congress during the American Revolution and who later moved west to help found the city of Cincinnati. Not much is recorded of Symmes's early life, other than that he received a "good common English education" and from the beginning showed a strong interest in mathematics, the natural sciences, and stories of exploration. "I remember at the age of eleven, in Jersey," Symmes wrote a few years before his death, "while reading a large edition of 'Cook's Voyages,' my father, though himself a lover of learning, reproved me for spending so much of my time from work, and said I was a book-worm. About the same age I used to harangue my play-mates in the street, and describe how the earth turned round; but then, as now, however correct my opinions, I got few or no advocates."

Nevertheless, the occupation Symmes chose was not that of a scientist, but a soldier. In 1802, at the age of 22, he enlisted in the U.S. Army as an ensign. He served at several forts in what was at that time the distant Southwest of the new nation—Mississippi and Louisiana—and while stationed at Fort Adams, Mississippi, Symmes fought a duel with a fellow officer, one Lieutenant Marshall.

The incident was described by Symmes in a long letter to his brother that nearly burst with prissy self-righteousness. It seems that Symmes's air of overconfidence irritated some of his peers, and a rumor spread that he had extorted money from a subordinate he had granted a leave. When Symmes one day demanded to see some records of Lieutenant Marshall's company in a tactless fashion, Marshall handed them over with the remark that Symmes was "not generally considered a gentleman." Symmes was outraged and immediately challenged Marshall to a duel, but the Lieutenant declined to fight one of Symmes's reputation. Symmes fumed off, but soon after challenged Marshall again; again the Lieutenant refused. Finally Symmes stormed over to Marshall in a frenzy of temper after parade, swearing to "fall in with Mr. Marshall when he had his sword on, and wring his nose." Symmes drew his own sword and challenged Marshall to fight him on the spot. The weary Lieutenant finally agreed to the duel, to be fought the next morning.

John Cleves Symmes, father of the Hollow Earth Theory, a few years before his death.

Symmes was ecstatic. "I... glided to my quarters (if possible) like a man intoxicated with pleasurable passion. One of my messmates said I had been drinking wine." When the duel was fought, Symmes aimed for Marshall's hip, but instead shattered Marshall's thighbone, leaving the Lieutenant with a lifelong limp. Marshall's bullet nicked Symmes in the wrist after passing through the seat of his pants. Symmes coolly ignored the wound; it became infected and he spent the next six weeks in bed with a fever, satisfied that his honor had been defended. One of Symmes's biographers tells us that Marshall "was afterward befriended by Captain Symmes, who always spoke of this duel with regret."

At the beginning of the War of 1812, Symmes was senior Captain of the First Regiment of U.S. Infantry, stationed at the mouth of the Missouri River. In 1814 the regiment was ordered to the Canadian border, and almost as soon as they arrived they were sent into a battle known afterward as the Battle of Lundy's Lane. The commanding general praised Symmes's courage in leading his troops, and soon after the battle Symmes and his men made a successful raid against the British. Symmes became a minor hero in this raid when he "spiked the first cannon with his own hand."

Symmes retired from the Army in 1816, a year after the war's end. He had long since chosen the life of a frontiersman; he obtained from the Governor of the Missouri Territory a special license to trade with the Indians and supply the troops, and he set up a trading post in St. Louis. In 1808 he had married Mary Anne Lockwood, the widow of a fellow officer, and to her six children he added four more. One of them was a son with the auspicious name Americus Vespucius Symmes; another was a daughter named Louisiana.

In St. Louis Symmes returned to his beloved science books, and he bought a telescope to study the planets. We can be fairly certain that one of the books he read was Cotton Mather's *Christian Philosopher*, with its description of Halley's concentric-earths idea. Coming as he did from an educated family with a Puritan background—Mather had mentioned one of Symmes's ancestors in another of his books—the *Philosopher* could not have been unknown to him. From it and other books Symmes gradually conceived the idea that was to become known as "Symmes's Theory of Concentric Spheres, Polar Voids, and Open Poles." As he described it, his theory was simply

> that the earth as well as all the celestial orbicular bodies existing in the universe, visible and invisible, which partake in any degree of a planetary nature, from the greatest to the smallest, from the sun down to the most minute blazing meteor or falling star, all are constituted, in a greater or less degree, of a collection of spheres, more or less solid, concentric with each other and more or less open at the poles; each sphere being separated from its adjoining compeers by space replete with aerial fluids; that every portion of infinite space, except what is occupied by spheres, is filled with an aerial elastic fluid, more subtile than common atmospheric air, and constituted of innumerable small concentric spheres, too minute to be visible to the organ of sight assisted by the most perfect microscope, and so elastic that they continually press on each other and change their relative situations as often as any piece of matter in space may change its position, thus causing a universal pressure, which is weakened by the intervention of other bodies in proportion

to the subtended angle of distance and dimension, necessarily causing the body to move toward the points of decreased pressure.[1]

In other words, Newton was wrong; gravity, such as it is, is produced by the pressure of countless tiny particles of "aerial fluid" pushing against all solid matter in the universe. These particles take the form of hollow concentric spheres, and the matter they act upon tends to coalesce into sets of hollow concentric spheres, open at the poles, as well.

Thus all heavenly bodies in the universe, including the earth, are actually a series of concentric spherical bodies open at the poles. The huge circular opening Symmes proposed at each end of the planet set Symmes's theory apart from Halley's, which included no such entrances to the inner spheres. Symmes studied all the reports of explorers of the polar regions he could find, and he became convinced that the difficulties exploring parties faced reaching the poles lay not in the terrible cold and bleakness of the Arctic and Antarctic—in fact, Symmes believed there was no more ice beyond a certain point as one traveled closer to one of the poles—but in the true nature of the polar regions. He grew more certain after reading *The Botanic Garden* by Erasmus Darwin (Charles Darwin's grandfather), a very long and—to modern tastes—unreadable poem describing the earth's wonders. According to Symmes, Darwin implied "there was a great secret, yet to be explained, at the poles."

Captain Symmes did nothing by halves; the openings he proposed at the poles were so enormous that they transformed the figure of the earth from a sphere to something vaguely resembling a donut. The north polar opening, he said, was about four thousand miles in diameter, with the *verge*—the ringlike point at which the earth and sea began descending into the inner world—sweeping through northern Alaska, Siberia, and Greenland. The south polar opening was even larger, encompassing not only the entire Antarctic continent (which was only hypothesized in Symmes's day), but also Tierra del Fuego, Tasmania, and the South Island of New Zealand within its six-thousand mile span. Symmes wrote that although explorers had sailed well within both polar openings on many occasions, they would not be likely to realize it, since it wasn't evident one had crossed over one of the verges until a ship was hundreds of miles beyond it. The verges, in addition, did not circle the poles perfectly; both were slightly askew, reaching further north on one side of the globe than the other.

Symmes estimated that the outer sphere of the earth was a thousand miles thick, and that the circumference of the lip of each polar opening—that is, from the outer verge to the inner verge—was about 1500 miles. His concept of the earth's shape led him to some interesting proposals regarding earthly and celestial phenomena. Due to the great distance between the North Geographic Pole and the North Magnetic Pole (about 1100 miles), for example, the magnetic compass is unreliable in the Arctic. Symmes believed the entire northern verge

---

[1] Symmes was no writer. This statement is all the more remarkable when you realize that it is all one sentence.

was magnetic, confusing explorers who subscribed to the orthodox picture of the earth. These explorers merely wandered about on the verge instead of actually entering the opening. Until an explorer reached the Arctic with a true idea of the earth's shape, the reality of the polar regions would never be known to orthodox science.

An even stranger hypothesis was Symmes's theory of the true nature of the Magellanic Clouds, those two nebulae visible only from the southern hemisphere. Perhaps the sightings of the Clouds available to Symmes had been made only from the South Atlantic; in any case, he proposed they were not celestial phenomena at all, but the reflections of Tasmania and the South Island of New Zealand, seen across the rim of the southern opening!

The concept of holes at the poles was not, however, original to Symmes. We can find it in *The Messiah*, a massive religious poem written by Friedrich Klopstock (1724–1803), an early German Romantic, and first published in 1748. In the first canto of *The Messiah*, the angel Gabriel descends from heaven into the hollow center of the earth through a great opening at the North Pole concealed by a cloud. Klopstock's inner world is like the one proposed by Leonhard

The earth as conceived by John Cleves Symmes, showing the North Polar Opening and the inner spheres. Adapted from an illustration in Americus Symmes's book.

Euler, with the addition of the polar opening and various theological trappings. Here the hollow is the home of angels responsible for outer-world affairs, as well as the location of Limbo:

> Where, far from us, the earth turns on its center, is a vast concave filled with a pure ether, in the midst of which is a sun which swims in a luminous fluid. From this source, life and warmth ascend into the veins of the earth...
> On this sun Gabriel alighted. Around him assembled the guardians of monarchies, the angels of war and death... Round the seraph also flocked the souls of those tender infants who had just entered into life; but fled weeping with the piteous cries of childhood.

The Messiah, however, has never been well-known in English-speaking countries, although Klopstock was one of the premier poets of his time in his native Germany, and *The Messiah* was his *magnum opus.* It is possible that Symmes was familiar with it, but we cannot know for sure. In any case the Captain, once he had decided the earth was hollow, needed a way to enter the inner world, and since the poles were the only large areas of the earth still unexplored in his day, they were the logical locations for openings.

Although Symmes, as we shall see, did his best to fabricate physical laws allowing for the formation of a toroidal earth, it was his notion of polar openings that earned him the greatest ridicule. As Ohio historian Henry Howe put it in 1900: "'Symmes' Hole' was a phrase more or less... on everybody's tongue; the papers in the decade between 1820 and 1830 were more or less full of Symmes' Hole. If one suddenly disappeared, the reply often was, and with a grin: 'Oh, he's gone, I expect, down into Symmes' Hole.'"

"Hollow, and habitable within"

After two years of zealous study, contemplation, and—we can be sure— heated discussions over the counter of his trading post, Symmes composed and printed a circular for the world to consider. He sent copies of his *Circular No. 1* to every city and town of any size in the United States, every college and scientific association in America and Europe, and all the members of Congress:

> LIGHT GIVES LIGHT, TO LIGHT DISCOVER—"AD INFINITUM."
>
> > ST. LOUIS, (Missouri Territory,)
> > North America, April 10, A.D. 1818.
>
> TO ALL THE WORLD!
>
> I declare the earth is hollow, and habitable within; containing a number of solid concentrick spheres, one within the other, and that it is open at the poles 12 or 16 degrees; I pledge my life in support of this truth, and am ready to explore the hollow, if the world will support and aid me in the undertaking.
>
> > *Jno. Cleves Symmes*
> > Of Ohio, late Captain of Infantry

N.B.—I have ready for the press, a Treatise on the principles of matter, wherein I show proofs of the above positions, account for various phenomena, and disclose *Doctor Darwin's Golden Secret.*[2]

My terms, are the patronage of this and the new worlds.

I dedicate to my Wife and her ten Children.

I select Doctor S.L. Mitchell, Sir H. Davy, and Baron Alex. de Humboldt, as my protectors.

I ask one hundred brave companions, well equipped, to start from Siberia in the fall season, with Reindeer and slays, on the ice of the frozen sea; I engage we find warm and rich land, stocked with thrlfty vegetables and animals if not men, on reaching one degree northward of latitude 82; we will return in the succeeding spring.

J.C.S.

Symmes appended to his circular a certificate testifying to his sanity, so he must have realized the boldness of his proposal; he felt, no doubt, like Martin Luther nailing a new set of theses to the door of Science. But the *History of Butler County* (Ohio) tells us that the circular was "overwhelmed with ridicule as the production of a distempered imagination, or the result of partial insanity. It was for many years a fruitful source of jest with the newspapers." Most of the scientists and academics who received the circular ignored it. The Paris Academy of Sciences looked at it and dismissed it as "not worthy of consideration."

But Symmes, proud and stubborn, simply stepped up his pamphleteering. In 1819 he sold his trading post—he had spent so much time on his researches and writing countless letters to newspapers that he had almost totally neglected his business—and settled his family on a farm near Newport, Kentucky. In 1820 he launched the first in a series of lecture tours to promote his theory, speaking in large and small halls all over Kentucky and Ohio (he sometimes lectured on other subjects as well, such as the superiority of rain water over well water for drinking).

Unfortunately, the Captain was not much of a speaker. One of his biographers, John Wells Peck, wrote frankly, "The arrangement of his subject was illogical, confused, and dry, and his delivery was poor." Symmes had neither a sense of humor nor the ability to understand why so many people could not accept his "overwhelming" proofs that the earth was a set of hollow, concentric spheres. His lectures were nonetheless well-attended, no doubt out of sheer novelty. His reputation for heroism in the late war helped him, and his faith and enthusiasm lent him a certain charisma. He converted a sizable number of his listeners to his views; many Ohioans and Kentuckians, even those with little faith in the idea of a hollow earth, took pride in the Westerner challenging the Eastern scientists, and they felt Symmes should be given the benefit of the

---

[2] Symmes refers here to *The Botanic Garden*, Canto IV, Line 320:

O Sylphs! disclose in this inquiring age
One golden secret to some favour'd sage.

In Symmes's opinion, the secret was the true nature of the polar regions, and the "favour'd sage" was, of course, Symmes himself.

doubt until a polar expedition proved him wrong. They also enjoyed Symmes's suggestion that the inner world could, like America's west, be subdued, and even one day join the Union.

At each lecture Symmes took a collection to promote his proposed expedition, but he never collected much more money than he needed to feed his large family. The wealthy benefactor he sought so earnestly did not step up to back him. But like many of today's alternative-reality proponents, the Captain's lectures and ideas proved irresistible to the press. A writer for the *Western Courier* of November 27, 1822 speculated on what might be the news 328 years in the future *if* Symmes was right:

THE YEAR 2150 ANTICIPATED.

Cincinnati, December 7, 2150.—The marble monument at Newport, which, in 1838, was erected by our ancestors to the memory of that great philanthropist and philosopher, John Cleves Symmes, fell to the ground on the 5th...

Thus the records of fame, which committed solely to such perishable materials, live but a few transitory ages, and ultimately fall in with the general decay; but the memory of Symmes shall be as unfading and lasting as time itself. We need no frail stones to remind us of his name, who first separated truth from error, and banished ignorance from the world.

Washington, December 11.—Two members of Congress from the State of *California* arrived yesterday in this city by the inland route. They inform us that the other (twenty-one) members from that State had proceeded through the canal at the Isthmus of Darien, to Mexico, where it was their intention to join the Mexican members, and charter a vessel for their conveyance to this city.

The members from *Chu-san*, in the interior regions, via the North Polar opening, arrived on the 9th inst.; those from *Pestchee-le*, via the South Pole, reached the United States on the 30th ult.

Symmes also asked his listeners to petition the government in favor of his polar expedition, and many of them did. One of the first such petitions was presented to the House of Representatives by Rep. J.T. Johnson of Kentucky in January of 1823; it requested Congress to outfit an expedition to the North Pole, to be led by Captain John Cleves Symmes, not only for the purpose of making "new discoveries in geography, natural history, geology, and astronomy, but of opening new sources of trade and commerce."

Representative Johnson moved to refer the petition to the Committee on Foreign Relations, but Rep. Farelly of Pennsylvania, who felt Congress had little time to waste on such foolishness, moved to table it. Another representative suggested the petition be referred to the Commerce Committee, "the object of the memorialists being probably to establish a commerce with the interior inhabitants." But the motion to refer lost, and the petition—although filled with "many respectable signatures"—expired on the table. More petitions followed rapidly; one was from South Carolina, another was from Pennsylvania, and five came from Ohio, but all met the same fate. Senator Benjamin Ruggles of Ohio brought a pro-Symmes petition before the Senate with an equal lack of success.

"A great saving of stuff"

This lack of faith on the part of the government he had served so devotedly was disheartening to Symmes, but it only strengthened his resolve to keep striving for vindication. Among his converts he found two valuable allies in that struggle. The first was James McBride, one of southern Ohio's most important social and intellectual figures of the first half of the nineteenth century. McBride wrote a respectable history of the founding of the state, served on the board of trustees of Ohio's Miami University, and performed the feat of gathering a six-thousand-volume library in the rough frontier town of Hamilton.

McBride was probably instrumental in convincing the Captain to move in 1824 to a farm his uncle had left him near Hamilton, and with Symmes's guidance he set himself the task of organizing the Captain's letters, circulars, and other chaotic scraps of theory into a cogent whole. The result was a small book published in Cincinnati in 1826, entitled *Symmes' Theory of Concentric Spheres, Demonstrating that the Earth is Hollow, Habitable Within and Widely Open About the Poles—by a Citizen of the United States.* Why McBride used a pseudonym is uncertain. Perhaps he sensed that having his name connected with a theory that was widely considered a joke was risky business, but he may simply have wanted the full credit for the theory to go to Symmes himself.

McBride's book was torn apart with both relish and distaste in the *American Quarterly Review*, one of the prominent intellectual journals of the day. In the light of claims that have since been made about the feasibility of a hollow earth—claims we shall be following in the next few chapters—it is revealing to set several of McBride's statements alongside rebuttals by the anonymous reviewer:

McBride first described Symmes's basic idea—that the set of concentric hollow spheres is the most widespread form in nature. This form, he argued, was the perfect expression of the balance between the pulling of centrifugal force on a rotating mass of matter (such as a planet) and the pushing of all the little spheroids of aerial fluid, otherwise known as gravity. As McBride put it:

> Were the matter of this globe thrown into a confused, disorganized state, and then put into a quick rotary motion, such as it is known to have, it would throw off from the centre towards the surface, first the heaviest, and next the lighter substances, which is the very order in which they are found to be arranged, in the composition of the earth.
>   This principle, for it is simply the principle of projectile force, will account for mountains, hills, valleys, plains; and for nearly all the inequalities on the face of the earth. These circumstances depend on the density of substances composing the earth... Hence we find that mountains are composed of heavy masses of rock... hills, or the next highest eminences, of earth of the next specific gravity; and plains, or level lands, of lighter substances.

Unfortunately for McBride and Symmes, this notion not only contradicts a very conspicuous fundamental of geology—erosion—but some plain laws of physics as well, and the reviewer was quick to point them out:

Nothing can be more completely at variance both with reason and with facts, than the principle which is here asserted. The centrifugal force to which a body is subjected is proportional, not to its absolute velocity, as our author always seems to suppose, but to the deflection from the tangent, produced by the rotation, in a given time... It has been found that, at the equator, where the centrifugal force is the greatest, and that of gravity is the least, the former is but one 289th part of the latter... It is therefore absurd to suppose that this could have raised the Alps and the Andes, or have produced the many other wonderful effects ascribed to it in the new theory.

The reviewer also pointed out that one of Symmes's greatest embarrassments was the lack of a clear process by which the inner spheres of the earth, if they existed, could have been formed. If the earth had been formed the way McBride described, it would look like a single hollow bubble, not a set of concentric bubbles. McBride, for his part, pleaded that he "has long had strong doubts whether the laws of gravity are well understood," and chose instead to "take the broad principles of nature for his guide"—in other words, to reason by analogy. He suggested that the earth must be a series of concentric spheres because water on the side of a cutler's grindstone arranged itself into "something resembling concentric spheres, one within another, and the surface of the earth revolves with much greater velocity than any grindstone."

He said also that hollowness was more "natural" than solidity. "Inquire of the botanist," McBride contended, "and he will tell you, that the plants which grow up spontaneously, agreeably to the established laws of nature, are hollow cylinders.... Inquire of the anatomist, and he will tell you, that the large bones of all animals are hollow." To this the reviewer merely asked his readers why stones are not hollow, nor the trees in the forest.

But McBride's most pressing argument was primarily emotional. He could not "perceive any thing more derogatory from the power, wisdom, or divine economy of the Almighty, in the formation of a hollow world, than in that of solid ones." He felt that if "all the orbs in creation" were formed as Symmes said they were, it "would display the highest possible degree of perfection, wisdom, and goodness; the most perfect system of creative economy; and... *a great saving of stuff.*"

Here the truth comes out. Here we find again the "economy" argument Halley used in his *Philosophical Transactions* article—an argument that has appeared wherever the hollow-earth idea has. It is illogical but attractive—the earth is not hollow because the evidence points irrevocably to the fact that it is. The earth is hollow because it is more satisfying to have it so, because it feels right, because it would be wasteful to have all that matter stuffed uselessly into the center of the planet.

But Symmes found his proofs not only in plants and bones. His observations of other planets were also important, and it was, curiously, the rings of Saturn that he considered conclusive proof of his theory. McBride wrote:

The appearance of Saturn, I conceive, establishes the fact, that the principle of concentric spheres, or hollow planets, does exist, at least in one instance, in the solar system. And if the fact be established that it exists in one case, is it not fair, nay, is it not almost a certain and necessary consequence, that the same laws of matter which formed one planet into concentric spheres, must form all the others on a plan more or less the same? ...If we form any opinion in relation to our own planet in particular, whose poles have never been explored, would not reasoning from analogy bring us to the conclusion, that all bodies of matter are formed similar to that of Saturn, unless we have positive evidence to the contrary?

That Symmes managed to mistake the rings of Saturn for one in a set of concentric spheres is testimony to his obsessive desire to see the earth proven hollow. He didn't stop with Saturn, however. He also said that what astronomers called the Martian polar cap was actually a polar opening allowing us a look into a concentric Mars. Symmes and McBride also asserted that the cloud belts of Jupiter were in reality a remarkable set of concentric spheres; the outermost sphere was ringlike and each succeeding interior sphere was more narrowly cylindrical. Thus the Jupiter they proposed looked something like this:

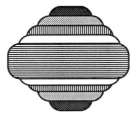

Both Symmes and McBride made much of the reports of Arctic explorers who, it appeared, had witnessed many animals and fish migrating north for the winter instead of south, and returning well-fed. "Whales, mackerel, and herring come down from the north in spring at their best and fattest," ran the proof. "The frozen zone could not produce nor sustain them. Obviously they came over the rim from the fair country within the earth!" The problem with this argument, stated the *Quarterly* reviewer, was that it was simply not true, as it was based on fragmentary and undocumented reports—and observations made by biologists in the nearly two centuries since have proven the reviewer correct. "The deer, musk ox, and other quadrupeds, mentioned by our author, are not properly migratory animals, and their occasional changes of situation are irregular, and seem to be governed only by the search for food." In Symmes's day it was not known that the Arctic Ocean included the North Pole, and it was not known that a permanent ice cap covered much of the Arctic Ocean. The migrations of fish and marine animals in high latitudes have been well documented today, and they do not migrate further north in the winter. Yet reports of animals migrating north for the winter—and by implication into the warmth of the inner world—were used by hollow-earth proponents, as we shall see, until the 1960s.

The *American Quarterly* reviewer saved the greatest scorn, however, for the idea of inner-world inhabitants. He pointed out meticulously that once inside the great hollow earth-shell Symmes proposed, a person standing in any spot would be attracted by the gravitational pull of the hemisphere above him (or spheres above him, in the case of concentric spheres) almost as much as the hemisphere he was standing on. Inside the earth, the centrifugal force of the earth's rotation would reinforce gravity rather than oppose it, but the earth's centrifugal force is so weak it would have little effect on the inner-world gravity. Thus if we imagine a single hollow shell 150 miles thick, a 150-pound man standing on the inner equator—where the centrifugal force would be greatest—would weigh eight ounces. The same man at 60° inner latitude would weigh only four ounces, and "might fly through the air, with great ease, by the aid of a lady's fan."

The only problem with the pleasant concept of feather-light inner-world folk is that, ironically, they would be more likely swimming than flying. The power of gravity on the oceans of the outer world would be so strong that all our oceans would be sucked into the polar openings like bathwater down the drain. To be fair, Symmes had provided for the gravity of the inner world. His inner-world people—and oceans—were pressed against the sides of the inner spheres by the force of the aerial fluid filling the spaces between the spheres. But those who questioned the existence of the inner spheres were equally unconvinced of the existence of the aerial fluid.

Expeditions that might have been

Such arguments were only hostile quibbling to the Captain. He was convinced that all the evidence supported his theory. "I challenge any opposers of my doctrine," he wrote in 1825, "to show as sound reasons why my theory is not correct as I can show it is." He was more determined than ever to win the world to his side, and he applied to join a Russian expedition being formed to explore Siberia. The American minister to Russia presented Symmes's request to the Chancellor, Count Romanosov, in St. Petersburg. The Count, eager to exploit his nation's vast Siberian territories and interested in all possibilities, granted the Captain's request. But Symmes was forced to withdraw at the last moment—he was unable to scrape together the money to pay his passage to the Russian capital. It must have been a great disappointment to Symmes, for of all the governments he had proselytized, the Russians had expressed the greatest interest in his ideas.

Undaunted, he struck out once more upon the lecture circuit with new vigor, accompanied by the second of his two important converts, a young lawyer and newspaper editor named Jeremiah Reynolds. Reynolds arranged an Ohio-to-East-Coast lecture tour for Symmes in 1825, and when Symmes collapsed after exhausting himself on the Ohio leg of the tour, Reynolds began lecturing frequently in his place with better results than Symmes had ever achieved. Reynolds was a pleasant and guileless-looking young man who had two things Symmes did not—a sense of humor and a sense of perspective—and he used them to advantage on the lecture platform. When Reynolds lectured to a skeptical audience in Chambersburg, Pennsylvania in January of 1826, he easily persuaded them (according to the local newspaper) to support a polar expedition, for "the cost of the experiment would be trifling, and discoveries of importance would probably be made, tho' Symmes' theory should be found erroneous." He addressed the Pennsylvania State Legislature at Harrisburg, inspiring fifty of the legislators to send the President a letter asking for approval of the expedition. Symmes's theory, they stated, was "quite as reasonable as that of the great Columbus" and "better supported by facts."

When Symmes and Reynolds reached Philadelphia, however, the two men began to argue. Reynolds felt that since he was now doing most of the lecturing, he should be able to interpret the theory his own way—not as a certain truth, but as a possibility. Reynolds's interest in the theory itself had begun to wane as his passion for promoting an American polar expedition had grown. Symmes's sheer mulishness, however, had not declined with his health; he refused to let Reynolds speak of his theory as if it were only a possibility, and the two men parted.

Reynolds did not, however, abandon Symmes's theory entirely; he continued lecturing on his own interpretation of the Captain's ideas in Philadelphia, Baltimore, and other eastern cities, and in 1827 he even published a little book, *Remarks on a Review of Symmes' Theory*, defending the Captain's ideas against the attacks in the *American Quarterly Review*. But even there his doubts showed through. He admitted that the round shadow cast upon the moon by the earth in partial eclipse did not indicate a toroidal earth; he said he could not prove the existence of a hollow earth, only that "it might be so." But he asserted that evidence indicated that there was an icy circle around each polar region "which once being passed, the ocean becomes less encumbered with ice, 'and the nearer the pole the less ice.'"

After a time, however, Reynolds left Symmes's theory behind to become America's leading proponent of Antarctic exploration. He made friends with Samuel Southard, John Quincy Adams's Secretary of the Navy, and pushed hard for a "United States Exploring Expedition" to the South Pole, with himself as leader. All Reynolds was able to get in the end, however, was an 1829 expedition with three small and poorly-prepared ships that was notable only for its complete lack of success. The crew, suffering from scurvy, mutinied off the coast of Chile and the ships had to turn back before they could even leave South America behind. Reynolds remained in Chile to explore and returned two years later to publish an account of his travels. Among the articles that came out of his experiences was a tale he had heard from an old salt. Retold as "Mocha Dick or the White Whale of the Pacific," it was published in *The Knickerbocker* and read with interest by Herman Melville, who was later to expand it into his classic novel.

Whether or not Reynolds still wanted to prove Symmes correct with his abortive voyage is unknown. But there was another expedition that had already been successful at reaching Symmes's inner world: a fictional one. *Symzonia: a Voyage of Discovery* was published in New York in 1820, two years after the Captain issued his first circular. *Symzonia* is partly a satire of Symmes's theory, partly a parody of the memoirs-of-a-sea-voyage genre of literature so popular in the early nineteenth century, and partly a utopian fantasy. The title page gives the author as "Captain Adam Seaborn", obviously a pseudonym. Some scholars—and the Library of Congress—attribute the work to Symmes himself, but this is very unlikely. The Captain was a simple man, a poor writer—not that *Symzonia* is very well written, but Symmes's own prose was far worse—and so humorlessly devoted to his theory that he never would have parodied his beliefs. The author of *Symzonia* was more likely a sophisticated Easterner, someone like the Jared Sparks who wrote a ruthless tongue-in-cheek review of the book for the *North American Review,* a Boston journal, in 1821. Sparks spent the entire review lampooning Symmes and paid little attention to *Symzonia* itself.

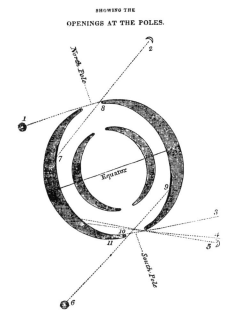

SECTIONAL VIEW OF THE EARTH.

SHOWING THE

OPENINGS AT THE POLES.

EXPLANATION OF THE PLATE.

Fig. 1.—Rays of the sun when in the equator, refracted 3 degrees.
2.—Moon's rays in 28° north declination.
3.—Sun's rays in 9° south declination.
4.—Sun's rays in 23°   do
5.—Moon's rays in 28°   do
6.—Sun's rays in 23° 27' south declination, refracted 3°.
7.—Supposed place of Belzubia.
8.—Place of exile.
9.—Symzonia.
10.—Token Island.
11.—Seaborn's Land.

Frontispiece diagram of the hollow
earth from *Symzonia* (1820).

Symzonia satirized the "manifest destiny" attitude of Americans of that day—the belief that the world belongs to America to explore and exploit. "Captain Seaborn" tells us how he sailed southward on a sealing voyage, planning to sail into the South Polar Opening, but not telling his crew of his plans until the last minute. He exults at all the new lands he discovers as he passes over the "icy hoop" of the southern verge, and he takes possession of all of them for the United States, naming the new islands and seas after himself and members of his crew. Dollar signs roll in his eyes when his first mate, Mr. Boneto (i.e. Bonito—most of the crew are named after fish) announces a take of a hundred thousand sealskins. When the ship has passed completely within the opening and reaches Symzonia, the large inhabited country beneath the Southern Hemisphere, Seaborn is prepared to treat the Symzonians as ignorant savages. He is shocked to find them more civilized and intelligent than the Americans.

An intriguing aspect of the meeting of the Americans and the Symzonians is the manner in which they view each other's skin color. Since no direct sunlight reaches Symzonia—only refracted light—the Symzonians' skins are almost pure white. Seaborn writes:

> I am considered fair for an American, and my skin was always in my own country thought to be one of the finest and whitest. But when one of the internals placed his arm, always exposed to the weather, by the side of mine, the difference was truly mortifying. I was not a white man, compared with him.

Symzonia is a utopia ruled by a council of the wisest men of the country (in true nineteenth-century fashion, the women of Symzonia demonstrate their wisdom by their devotion to Motherhood), and the most grievous sins of their culture are war and materialism. Any "internals" found guilty of either crime are banished to a country on the northern verge that is exposed to sunlight, and over generations, these transgressors and their descendants grow darker, weaker, and more sinful. On first encountering Seaborn, the Symzonians thought he was one of these banished folk, and their mistake led Seaborn to speculate

> that we externals were indeed descendants of this exiled race; some of whom, penetrating the "icy hoop" near the continent of Asia or America, might have peopled the external world. The gross sensuality, intemperate passions, and beastly habits of the externals, all testified against us.

Although the criticism here is aimed at the proud, materialistic white American, it also implies that the darker one's skin, the more degenerate one's soul. The racist notion that the inner-world inhabitants are a superlatively *white* race, and we are their darker and—depending on our skin color—more or less degenerate offspring inspired (as we shall see) Edgar Allan Poe, and has popped up with disturbing regularity in inner-world lore of the twentieth century, culminating in a number of hollow-earth proponents today who believe the true home of the Aryan race is "inside."

But Seaborn meets a fate suitable for a would-be exploiter. When the internals realize how violent and materialistic the visiting Americans are, Seaborn and his crew are banished from Symzonia and warned never to return. On the voyage back to the United States, all evidence Seaborn has collected of his visit to the inner world is lost in a storm, and when he reaches home, he loses his fortune by selling his cargo of sealskins to a crooked middle-man. At the end of the book, writing in a tiny attic, he offers his memoirs to the public in the hope of gaining financial backing for another trip "inside." Seaborn clings to the very last to his dream of making a fortune establishing trade with the Symzonians.

In his review of *Symzonia,* Jared Sparks was even less gentle with the dream, often propounded by Symmes, of an American empire inside the earth:

The addition to our jurisdiction [would be] almost immense. It is well known that in the vocabulary of political science, all nations, for the first time discovered, are heathen, savage, and barbarous; of course wholly without right or claim to the land on which they live, of which the property immediately vests in fee simple and unqualified sovereignty in the discoverer;—who becomes authorized, to use an expressive phrase, to "extinguish the Indian title," in which process it commonly happens that the Indian is extinguished with it.

Sparks also considered the fortunes to be made from trade with the inhabitants of the inner world:

...we shall probably gain a great market for our produce. There is no reason to believe that the Internals will not be glad to eat flour, and wear Waltham shirtings, and smoke tobacco; and it was ever a feature of the benignant colonial policy, that the colony should feed and clothe itself from the mother country.... Should the Internals refuse to eat, drink, and smoke, as we direct, there then will doubtless be found ways to compel them. As to the latter article, there can be no difficulty. No one takes tobacco at first without nausea, and if we actually put it down their throats by main force, a struggle, more or less, is of no consequence. Or we shall have but to draw a large curtain over the opening at the poles, and we can have them upon their knees, for their very sunshine.

"A benefactor of his race"

But let us return to Symmes, who when we left him had just parted ways with Jeremiah Reynolds. The Captain, accompanied by Anthony Lockwood, one of his stepsons, lectured in Philadelphia, New York, Boston, and eastern Canada. He carried with him a model of the hollow globe, and he demonstrated to the students at Harvard with a magnet, iron filings, and a bowl of sand how matter tends toward hollow, concentric spheres. But wherever he went in the Northeast, Symmes lectured to the accompaniment of hoots and ridicule. He pushed himself so long and so hard that he collapsed in 1827 as he had two years earlier in Ohio. He stayed in New Jersey for a time with a friend of his father's, advertising in the newspapers for financial help, until he was well enough to return to Cincinnati. But Symmes never regained his health. In February 1829 he was carried to his home in Hamilton on a bed set in the back of a spring-wagon. He grew weaker and weaker, and he finally died on May 29, 1829, "aged," his monument tells us, "forty-nine years and six months."

The Captain was buried with full military honors in the Hamilton cemetery, and in the 1840s his son Americus replaced his simple headstone with the sandstone monument that stands there today, long after the old Hamilton burying-ground has been converted to a park. But even the monument wasn't taken seriously; soon after it was erected, the hollow globe was broken off to grace a neighboring porch for a time. And William Dean Howells, writing of his boyhood in Hamilton, described how he used to tremble at the sight of a gravestone, especially the monument "set at the grave of a philosopher who imagined the world as hollow as much of the life is on it."

**Symmes's wooden model of the hollow earth that accompanied him on lecture
tours; now in the Academy of Natural Sciences in Philadelphia**

It is interesting to speculate what Symmes might have done had he lived
longer. The world would have seen more lectures, more circulars, more proposed expeditions, to be sure. But in 1841, his fellow Ohioan William Henry
Harrison became President, and Harrison's wife, Anna Symmes Harrison, was
the Captain's cousin. The Captain named one of his sons after Harrison, and it
isn't difficult to imagine Symmes at 61 on the doorstep of the White House, offering to lead an expedition over the north polar verge.

Americus Symmes remained a strong believer in his father's theory, and
he collected a group of the Captain's lectures and circulars, with a few speculations of his own, into a book. It was published in Louisville, Americus's home,
in 1878, with the familiar title *The Symmes Theory of Concentric Spheres,
Demonstrating that the Earth is Hollow, Habitable Within, and Widely Open About
the Poles.* Americus's additions to the theory included his misinterpretations of
reports from Arctic expeditions since his father's death, plus Americus's
conviction that the inhabitants of the inner spheres were none other than the
Ten Lost Tribes of Israel. Since their migration from the surface world, the Ten
Tribes had built a magnificent civilization in the inner world. It appears he
used the civilzation described in Symzonia as his model—and it also appears he
believed Symzonia was a true story. The son's prose style differed little from
the father's: "Reason, common sense, and all the analogies in the world,"
Americus wrote, "conspire to support and establish the theory."

A few years later, in 1884, the Louisville correspondent for the New York
Times interviewed Americus Symmes. He described the Captain's son as "an
honest, kindly, rare old man" in his seventies, but he was unsympathetic to
Americus's beliefs:

> There is no question now that Mr. Symmes is insane on the subject of his father's theory,
> but in many quarters his occasional lectures are listened to with a profound interest that
> could only proceed from an ignorance of the subject fed by the most minute and
> astonishing details of a country and people as fabulous as the lost Atlantis. Every few

weeks Mr. Symmes invades the columns of some obscure paper with a wonderful account of the latest intelligence from "Symzonia," as the interior of the earth is called in his tracts. At other times he invades the local newspaper offices with voluminous manuscripts, or he delivers a lecture for the benefit of some struggling church or charity, and the burden of all his thought is "Symzonia."

"I am in constant communication," says he, "with all those engaged in perfecting inventions looking to the discovery of means for reaching the north pole. I have lately received a letter from a gentleman in Boston who has invented a ship with an iron hull. The hull will be heated to a white heat as she streams into the ice regions, and the ice-floes will be melted as she moves to allow her to pass. It is a very ingenious idea, and may yet solve the problem."

Another invention upon which he looks with equal gravity, but less confidence, is a ship which will be constructed of steel, with a razor-like keel. When the ship approaches a floe she will be propelled with immense force, jump out of the sea and fall upon the floe with such force as to crush through it. Still another is a cigar-shaped balloon, propelled by an electric engine...

Outside of Louisville, Americus's book attracted little attention; the interviewer noted that many copies "were left on his hands, some of which he sells occasionally." But the Symmes theory had also been given national exposure again in an article in the *Atlantic Monthly* for April 1873 by an author identified only as P. Clark. Clark had been a senior at Union College in Kentucky during the winter of 1826-27, when the Captain gave a series of lectures on his theory to the students and faculty. Clark was taken with the Captain's ideas and took detailed notes; presenting the theory nearly fifty years later, Clark—like Americus—felt that subsequent explorations of the Arctic had only confirmed Symmes. He regretted that the Captain seemed to have been forgotten:

> ...if his theory had been made fully public long ago, much hardship, suffering, and expense would or might have been avoided in the futile attempts to find a passage through the bleak and desolate regions around Baffin's Bay. That Behring's Straits offer the best route into the Arctic regions admits of little or no doubt, and an expedition for the purpose from the Pacific coast is well worth the consideration of the government.

Clark concluded with one last pitch for recognition of the Captain's genius:

> Time, the great revealer of secrets, will soon determine whether this startling theory is true, in whole or part, and whether its author was a visionary enthusiast, or a profound philosopher whose name will be honored among men, like that of Franklin or Newton, as a benefactor of his race, and an honor to the country which gave him birth.

Now both poles have been reached, and Symmes has long been almost completely forgotten; for most of those who do hear his name, he is at best either a footnote to the early history of Ohio or one of a collection of "classic eccentrics" who will always have a home in the literature of trivia. But the Captain was something else as well—the prophet without honor in his home who nonetheless set in motion a small movement, one of believers in a hollow earth, that has been around for nearly two centuries. What follows is this movement's story.

Chapter 5

Inward the Course of Empire Takes Its Way

> Who knows what oceans, what continents, what nations, it may be
> of men like ourselves, may not exist in a subterranean world?
> Who knows what gold, what silver, what precious stones are there
> piled perhaps mountains high?... I call for volunteers for the inte-
> rior world!
>
> —William Bradshaw, *The Goddess of*
> *Atvatabar*

Chicago's Religio-Philosophical Publishing House brought out in 1871 a thick, curious volume with a title to match: *The Hollow Globe; or the World's Agitator and Reconciler—A Treatise on the Physical Conformation of the Earth. Presented through the Organism of M.L. Sherman, M.D. and Written by Prof. Wm. F. Lyon.* "This book is addressed," Professor Lyon began, "to the reasoning intelligence of Humanity,—to all inquiring and reflective minds, everywhere upon the earth." He felt that perusal of its pages "may save multitudes from many superstitious beliefs and shadowy dogmas, respecting natural phenomena, as well as theological teachings, which have hitherto overclouded their minds."

The Hollow Globe was conceived in Lyon's office on J Street in Sacramento in September 1868. As he told the tale, he was busy at his desk (doing what, or what Lyon was a professor of, I have never discovered) when a strange-looking man entered and introduced himself as Dr. M.L. Sherman. Lyon asked him to sit down, and Sherman did, murmuring, "You are the man that I have been searching after; the very man I was to find, and we have a large amount of business that we must transact together, but I am not fully prepared to state the nature of that business, for I do not seem to understand it myself."

Lyon was neither surprised nor impressed by Sherman's pronouncement. "In my experience," he wrote, "I had heard things of a similar nature previously." Nevertheless, in time the two men formed a partnership, and Lyon came to believe Sherman was indeed "a very remarkable and peculiar personage, whose day and hour to be known to the world, has probably not yet fully come."

Dr. Sherman was a medium. He began his career, probably not long after the first burst of interest in spiritualism in America in the 1840s, as a public speaker in New York State. During his talks, he would go into trances and provide descriptions of the afterlife and the world of spirits, and communicate with dead friends and relations of audience members. After a few years, however, his trance statements grew disconnected and confusing, so he left public performance. He continued exploring the world of spirits at home, and there lapsed into longer and longer trances. His longest, in 1861, lasted twelve days. "For four days of this time," Lyon wrote, "he was to all appearance dead, so much so that a prominent physican of the town pronounced him dead to all intents, with the remark that they might use his head for a football if he ever breathed again upon the earth."

But at the end of the twelve days, Sherman woke and wrote a thirty-eight page booklet titled *My Experiences in Spiritual Phenomena.* Unfortunately, it "was not well received," and the spirits told Sherman to seek a certain man with whom he would perform a truly great work. His search took him to Lyon, and while in a trance Sherman's spirit voices told the Professor to take pens and paper and write down the teachings they were about to reveal. The result, heavily larded with Lyon's comments, was *The Hollow Globe.*

An emotionally satisfying cosmos

Humanity is unaware of the true nature of the earth and the universe, wrote Lyon, because it clings to either the old belief in a single Creator who formed the cosmos by speaking a word—which defied natural laws—or the materialistic doctrines of modern science, which were unable to conceive a grand destiny for the earth and its people. The universe was actually created by the spirits themselves through the use of natural laws, and it is the spirits who keep the earth in orbit around the sun, the tides turning, and the winds blowing. The spirits are life entities, and all living organisms contain spirits in some stage of development. They transmigrate from amoeba to insect to pig to human until, fully developed, they are ready to join the beings who run the universe. The "natural laws" of Lyon and Sherman's cosmos were based on the interaction of opposing forces—life and death, male and female, light and darkness—and the goal of the spirits was to expand the positive force of life into the dark negativity of space.

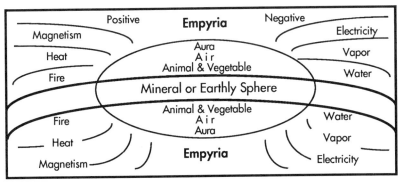

Lyon and Sherman's diagram of how "positive and negative forces," interacting with one another, can produce the form of a hollow sphere.

This process of expansion went on continuously. The spirits controlling stars with planetary systems, like our sun, began their work by condensing nearby clouds of interstellar debris into small, hollow, planets. All planets were hollow because it was the simplest and most economical shape for them to take. Lyon used the soap bubble as an analogy to describe the earth's true form. Soap bubbles represented "precisely the principles upon which worlds may be commenced and established; they represent in miniature just the kind of superstructure we require to insure the greatest amount of strength compatible with the smallest amount of material." The orthodox geologists of his day held that the earth was a molten sphere with a crust forty miles thick; Lyon thought this idea ridiculous and a waste of good material. Such an earth was "horrifying to the finer sensibilities that exist in the minds of civilized humanity." The spirit-architects would never assemble such a seething, unstable globe. The forty-mile crust, Lyon insisted, *was* the earth.

After the spirits had coalesced the interstellar material into a hollow globe, they placed it in an extremely fine spiral orbit around its mother star. When it had reached a point sufficiently distant from the star—in about the location of Venus, for example—the spirits began forming another planet in about the location of Mercury. In this way, all the many planetary systems in the cosmos had been shaped. As each planet spiraled farther from its star, it grew larger—Lyon admitted he had no idea how this was done, but he knew the spirits could do it—and as it grew it began imitating its star, building moons of its own under the control of its planetary spirits. Lyon had only to point at the configuration of the solar system to make his point, for the smallest planets were closest to the sun and had few or no moons (Pluto was not to be discovered for another sixty years), while the outer planets were considerably larger and possessed many moons. When a planet reached its full size and generated a complete family of satellites, its spirits transformed it into a star. The new star, with the beginnings of its own planetary system, left its parent to continue filling the universe's dark vastness.

One cannot help but smile appreciatively at the beauty of Lyon and Sherman's well-run, growing, emotionally satisfying cosmos. Although Lyon described the process as "mechanistic," it is really organic. The planetary systems they depict reproduce themselves in great, slow spirals like the shoots of a colossal plant growing in the garden of infinitely wise spiritual beings.

As the guiding spirits of the cosmos desired to constantly expand into the empty, wild places of space, so did the spirits within us compel us to explore and conquer the wild places of earth. Lyon believed this desire was most actively developed in the "American or Anglo-Saxon race." The spirits had in the past compelled the Anglo-Americans to travel to the New World, wage and win the Revolution, conquer the Indians, settle the West, and span the continent with a railroad. But soon, Lyon warned, the West would be filled with farms, banks, homes, and schools. "What is to be done," he asked, "with that restless, uneasy mass that have always been going ahead, seeking out new territory, and preparing the way for the more quiet, stay-at-home class who only follow in the wake of the Pioneers? The required territory must be found of necessity."

Where was this new territory? Inside the earth, of course, and the time was ripe for the entryway to be found. The spirits told Lyon that a ship could find its way into the interior "by following the warm Oceanic current through Behring's Straits; an accessible gateway will be discovered that will lead the navigator to all the territory we can occupy for many thousand years." The interior world, Lyon wrote, was "accessible by a circuitous and spirally formed aperture that may be found in the unexplored open Polar Sea." Thinking perhaps of the upcoming 1876 centennial of the United States, Lyon predicted the passage would be found by that year, and he felt certain its opening would set in motion the greatest age of American expansion. "Let every reader do his utmost," he urged, "to aid in this enterprise... for when all that lies within the polar circle is revealed to mankind, then humanity will take another stride in advance."

But *The Hollow Globe* disappoints the reader in the end, for although they called the interior world "beautiful" and "in a more highly developed condition than the exterior," Lyon and Sherman revealed nothing of significance about their inner world. After four hundred pages of abstruse mystical physics, Lyon mentions that neither he nor the spirits had any intention of giving "a more graphic description of that interior world which we claim has an existence." He feels that any such description "would be found of little profit to the reader."

Were Lyon and Sherman hedging their bets, afraid of being proven wrong when the inner world was actually discovered? Did the spirits refuse to reveal more to them? Before vanishing into obscurity, Lyon and Sherman produced a second edition of *The Hollow Globe* in 1876, and another book, *The Gospel of Nature*, in 1877, but their work seems to have been ignored even by the Spiritualist community. Their work might have had more influence had they spent less time with abstractions of the cosmos and more with their new American empire inside the earth.

A "new" theory

Another would-be prophet of a hollow earth was Frederick Culmer, Sr., of Salt Lake City, Utah, who published a little booklet, *The Inner World: A New Theory*, in 1886. Culmer believed he had arrived at an important *new* idea— that the earth is hollow and habitable within, and open at the poles—perhaps because he lived in a place far from most newspapers and magazines. Culmer had heard of Symmes's theory. But his knowledge of Symmes's ideas came from a poorly-written article translated from a French magazine, which gave a confusing description of "the great basin of Symmes." This "great basin" was "a vast plain at the interior of our globe, lighted and warmed by the refraction of the sun's rays." Culmer was misled into thinking Symmes had proposed not a hollow earth, but a hole—with a bottom—at each pole, like this:

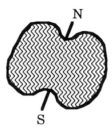

Culmer felt an apple-shaped earth made little sense, and asserted that the earth was instead hollow all the way through. "This idea," he claimed, "has never before been suggested."

Like Symmes, Culmer created an ingenious set of physical laws to explain how a hollow globe might be formed. They weren't too different from the physics Symmes had invented, but they were better articulated. All molecules, Culmer said, possess both "forces of attraction," which draw their matter toward a common center, and "forces of repulsion," which push their matter away in all directions. He claimed that these forces strike a balance in the formation of each atom and molecule, depending on its density. Thus if an atom of platinum were greatly magnified, it would look like a small, dense

hollow sphere like this: ●, while an atom of hydrogen would be a larger,

thin-shelled sphere, something like this: ◯

Just as all atoms take the forms of hollow spheres, so does the earth—which is, after all, simply a collection of atoms of different densities. All celestial bodies, in fact, were hollow, and Culmer used astronomical observations to make his point much as the Captain had. "Sun spots," Culmer wrote, "seem to reveal that our luminary itself is a hollow globe whose gaseous circumference is sometimes rent to show the space that is within; and so far as daring astronomers have been able to demonstrate, the universe is a hollow globe of which the Milky Way is the circumference."

Culmer neglected to mention how the earth, if formed according to his theory, could have a thousand-mile hole at each pole, but he was certain the openings existed. He was also convinced that gravity was centered within the shell itself, and thus "a man's weight would be about the same on a concave as a convex surface." Although this statement sounds reasonable, and it is true that gravity could not be most intense at the empty center, we have already seen that a person standing inside a hollow earth would weigh less than a pound because both hemispheres of the shell would exert an almost equal gravitational force. Culmer didn't realize this fact, however, and confidently continued to propose that with a strong gravitational pull from the hemisphere of the shell beneath it, the inner atmosphere "would seek the surface of the land, exactly as on the exterior, increasing in density as it approaches the earth and becoming attenuated towards the centre." The center of the hollow would be a vacuum "as absolute as that of interplanetary space." Unfortunately for Culmer, if the earth was hollow with holes at the poles, the interior would exert a stronger pull on the oceans and atmosphere than the exterior. Unless the hollow was completely filled with either water or air, the surface of the outer world would resemble the surface of the moon.

Culmer had little faith he would live to see the earth declared hollow by the scientists. But that day would come: "My belief," he concluded, "is that no man will be able to plant the standard of his country on any land [in the polar or interior regions] worth one dime to himself or anyone else at present, because, as I proceed, I am more than ever convinced that the time is not yet come when the great secrets of the ice-bound regions of the North or South shall be unlocked."

"No one can get to the poles"

William Reed, author of *Phantom of the Poles* (1906).

In 1906, just three years before Robert Peary finally reached the North Pole and proved to most of the world that the Pole was on the earth's surface and not an imaginary point within it, another dedicated layman tried to prove the earth was hollow. A new book, *The Phantom of the Poles*, was written by William Reed, who in his frontispiece portrait looks like a pleasant, grandfatherly fellow, more like a stereotypical turn-of-the-century druggist or grocer than a geological theorist. But Reed was a man obsessed with the mysteries of the polar regions—an armchair explorer puzzled over why so many expeditions had come within a few hundred miles of the North Pole, but had never reached it. Reed had obviously read Symmes, because many of his proofs were those used by the Captain and his disciples, yet he never mentioned Symmes in his book. His conclusion and the Captain's were also the same: the poles had never been reached because they were unreachable.

Reed had scoured many scores of books and newspaper and magazine articles reporting every polar expedition of the previous century. *The Phantom of
the Poles* presented dozens of reports of unusual polar phenomena taken from
these books and articles; Reed wrote of polar meteor showers, snowfalls colored
by pollen, the strange behavior and stranger contents of icebergs, and unusual
fluctuations of temperature, and he interpreted them all as originating within
the earth. Near the beginning of the book he asked his readers twelve questions
about polar phenomena, questions that appeared in hollow earth literature published into the 1960s:

1. Why is the earth flattened at the poles?
2. Why have the poles never been reached?
3. Why is the sun invisible so long in winter near the farthest points north or south?
4. What is the Aurora Borealis?
5. Where are icebergs formed, and how?
6. What produces a tidal wave?
7. Why do meteors fall more frequently near the poles, and whence do they come?
8. What causes the ice-pressure in the Arctic Ocean during still tide and calm weather?
9. Why is there colored snow in the Arctic region?
10. Why is it warmer near the poles than six hundred to one thousand miles away from
    them?
11. Why is ice in the Arctic Ocean frequently filled with rock, gravel, sand, etc.?
12. Does the compass refuse to work near the poles?

Reed's faith in the existence of a hollow earth led him into some very
creative theorizing as to why the poles hadn't yet been reached. He answered
his questions with the sort of baroque ingenuity that leaves the objective modern reader squinting at the page. When most people hear that the earth is
"flattened at the poles," for example, they realize it means that the diameter of
the earth at the equator, due to centrifugal force over billions of years, is slightly
greater than its diameter at the poles. But Reed did not, or chose not to, understand this meaning; he believed instead that if one looked at the earth from a
point several thousand miles over the equator, the polar regions would appear
literally *flat*. Thus he wrote, "Why is the earth flattened at the poles? As the
earth is hollow, it could not be round, is the answer to that. Again, the opening
to the interior would detract from its roundness just in proportion to the size of
the opening."

His answers to the other questions were similarly reasoned. The aurora,
as well as the polar meteor showers and the dust and stones found in Arctic ice,
are the light and debris of volcanic eruptions and forest fires in the interior
world. The sun is not visible at the poles during the winter because the observer
is within the opening. Reed proposed that most icebergs are formed from fresh
water within the verges and float out into the external seas, and as they drift
southwards they cause tidal waves. The poles, of course, had never been
reached because they didn't exist. "The poles are but phantoms," Reed wrote.
"The earth is hollow, or all principle of reasoning must fail."

When he was asked what the interior of the earth was like, Reed admitted he was hesitant to commit himself. He did, however, offer a few possibilities:

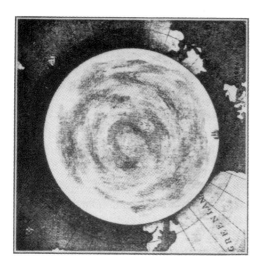

"A bird's-eye view of the opening to the interior of the earth," from William Reed's *Phantom of the Poles* (1906).

From what I am able to gather, and from analysis, game of all kinds—tropical and arctic—will be found there; for both warm and cold climates must be in the interior—warm inland and cold near the poles. Sea monsters, and possibly the much-talked-of sea serpent, may also be found, and vast territories of arable land for farming pupuses. This theory is based on the great quantity of pollen that finds its way to the exterior of the earth, and falls with the snow in such great quantities that it colors it, and thus produces the colored snow of the Arctic Circle. This would require millions of acres of land to grow. Minerals may be found in great quantities, and game of all kinds. The earth contains minerals and gems, and they are as likely to be in the interior of the earth as on the exterior. We may succeed, too, in finding large quantities of radium, which could be used to relieve the darkness if it should be unusually dark.

But Reed did not believe it would be dark inside the earth. He wrote that for each year we experience on the surface, the inner world would experience "two summers of four months' duration" during the spring and fall equinoxes of the outer world. This speedy change of seasons would make each year in the inner world only six months long. Reed, like Symmes, believed the southern opening was a bit larger than its northern counterpart; thus it would allow in more sunlight for a longer time, and every other inner summer would be a few days or weeks longer. The result of this halving of the seasons, according to Reed, would be an even, balmy interior climate, "about such a climate as San Francisco, I should judge, where one has to stop and think whether it is June or January." Reed unfortunately placed far too much faith in the ability of the inner atmosphere to refract the rays of the sun into the interior. Although he proposed herds of game and forests of plant life, he didn't—or again, chose not to—realize that the direct rays of the sun, which are necessary for most plant and animal life as we know it, would reach at most only a few thousand miles into the interior, and then for only two or three months out of the year in any one spot. So little sunlight would hardly create a paradise for humans. Yet a paradise what just what William Reed longed for between the lines of *The Phantom of the Poles*.

He ignored a great many facts, such as that salt water will freeze (making it unnecessary to propose that there were not enough outer-world glaciers to supply all the icebergs in the Arctic), that might appear to constrain his theorizing. His appeal was again emotional; like his predecessors, Reed stressed the symmetry and economy of a hollow planet and the wastefulness of a solid one. He suggested, for example, that objects in the inner world would weigh less than on the surface, but not because of the pull of an opposite hemisphere. They would weigh less "for the reason that the laws of the universe are so perfect that nothing is wasted, and a substance requires less force to hold it to the inside of a hollow ball in motion than to hold it to the outside." Anyone who has taken an elementary physics course would have a little difficulty explaining *that* statement.

America's greatest opportunity

But the most entertaining, and in its ardor the most persuasive, of the early hollow-earth tracts was written by Marshall Blutcher Gardner, the inventor of a number of ferocious-looking sewing machines used to assemble corsets and eventually the owner of the Gardner Sewing Machine Co., in which they were made. Dwelling prosperously in the coincidentally-named town of Aurora, Illinois, Gardner labored over his own version of the hollow-earth theory for twenty years, poring over what must have been hundreds of books of polar exploration, astronomy, geology, and geography. In 1913, at the age of 59, Gardner withdrew his savings to publish *A Journey to the Earth's Interior; or, Have the Poles Really Been Discovered.* It was an impressive volume with a large frontispiece portrait of its author, a burly, mustachioed fellow looking rather uncomfortable in a stiff collar and tie. Like Symmes, Gardner was convinced he was the "favour'd sage" who had discovered what the scientists, in their stubborn conservatism, had missed. Like Symmes, he would listen to none of their trivial objections. Like Symmes, Gardner was an evangelist; he mailed scores of copies of his book to professors, legislators, presidents, and kings. Like Symmes, his ideas were featured, often with tongue in cheek, by the newspapers.

But Gardner scorned Symmes as a visionary fool, and he took great pains to demonstrate that his theory bore no more resemblance to the Captain's than the sun did to a flashlight. "Some very unintelligent readers," Gardner wrote in the expanded second edition of his book, "have accused us of putting forward a theory that is not new but merely a rehash of Symmes' Theory of Concentric Spheres." On the defensive, probably because Symmes's ideas had inspired him in the first place, but unwilling to share any of the credit for his theory of a great new world inside the earth, Gardner heaped scorn upon the Captain with a shovel. He called Symmes's theory "a cranky idea," and he accused the Captain of weaving dreams upon guesses:

> [Symmes's theory] was based on a supposition, and the author argued from his supposition down to what the facts ought to be. He said in effect, "According to my principle

there ought to be within the earth a series of spheres each one inside the other." But he did not know and he never went down to see. We take the opposite course. We begin with the facts.

Gardner, like most of the hollow-earth proponents since Symmes, abandoned the unwieldy idea of concentric spheres, but he also resurrected an idea just as awkward, but far more useful— Leonhard Euler's central sun. Gardner was probably unfamiliar with Euler's proposal, but he had obviously read both Symmes's writings and Reed's *Phantom of the Poles* and realized that the greatest single stumbling block to an inner world which the human race could settle was the lack of light and warmth only the sun could provide. He estimated that an inner sun, floating in the middle of the hollow sphere, would need to be about six hundred miles in diameter to produce a pleasant, subtropical warmth inside the planet, and so it became. Once he had decided that the inner sun existed, proofs of its existence came to him quickly.

Marshall B. Gardner in 1913.

Where Symmes, for example, had claimed the *aurora borealis* was caused by the outer sun's rays reflecting upon the internal oceans, and Reed had proposed that it was caused by fires or volcanoes inside the northern opening, Gardner was able to offer a much neater explanation for the Northern Lights. They were the rays of the inner sun shining through the opening.

The central sun played a critical role in Gardner's novel theory of planetary formation. He proposed that the earth had begun its career as a spiral nebula, and gave the Andromeda Nebula as an example. The nebula's swirling arms formed into a ring around a small central star, and over millions of years this gaseous ring contracted into a solid toroidal planet, with its openings at each pole and the central sun still shining within. Gardner tried to demonstrate this process with illustrations of several well-known nebulae, such as the Ring Nebula in the constellation Lyra, that indeed look like shells of gas surrounding a star. Nebulae like this one were even called "planetary nebulae" in the astronomy texts of that day because they look much like planets in low-powered telescopes. But Gardner read the astronomers selectively, ignoring the vast differences in size between these nebulae and the earth. The findings of astronomers since his time make his theorizing seem far off base; the Andromeda "Nebula," for example, is not a nebula at all, but a galaxy larger than the Milky Way. The central star of the Ring Nebula is much larger than any known planet, and the shell of gas surrounding it, millions of miles across, is expanding, not contracting. The Ring Nebula is the remnant of a nova or exploding star, and its central star is far more likely to contract into a white dwarf or even a black hole than a sun which could coexist with a planet the size of the earth.

But much of this information was unknown in Gardner's day; the astronomers of that time seemed overly cautious and conservative to him, and he felt free to speculate. He realized that the inner world he proposed, even with a sun of its own, could never be like the outer world, for its sun could never set. But Gardner turned this difference into an asset. Imagine, he wrote, an inner world in which the sun is always shining:

> Owing to the heat and moisture... vegetable growth is not only rank and luxuriant, but it grows four times as rapidly as the vegetable matter on the earth's outer surface. They do not stop growing as our outer plants do, because there is no setting of the sun, and they do not pause in their growth in the winter because there is no winter.... We should be amazed at the abundance of insect life. On the water would be water flies of various kinds and sizes. Newt-like forms would be scrambling from water to land or sunning themselves in the pools. Occasionally under the dense undergrowth we should espy a serpent or serpent-like creature wending its way...

Gardner also believed that animals that had become extinct on the surface survived in the inner world, and he devoted a long chapter in his book to presenting evidence that the mammoth had not died out. He recounted many stories he had read in newspapers and magazines announcing discoveries of whole frozen mammoths in Alaska and Siberia. Most people with even a vague interest in paleontology have read of these finds, which still turn up from time to time; the mammoth's carcass, although thousands of years old, is found almost as well-preserved as if some giant had put it in the freezer a month before, with undigested food still in the creature's stomach and the meat—it is reported—fresh enough to eat. Gardner quoted with relish stories of explorers dining on mammoth steak, like the American author/explorer James O. Curwood, who was present at the discovery of one of these beasts in Alaska. Curwood claimed to have tried mammoth steak and wrote that "the flesh was of a deep red or mahogany color.... The flavor of the meat was old—not unpleasant—but simply old and dry. That it had lost none of its life-sustaining qualities was shown by the fact that the dogs throve upon it." This report was later revealed as a hoax, as were several other I-ate-mammoth-steak stories, but Gardner pointed to the tale and asked whether it was possible for a mammoth to remain edible after fifteen or twenty thousand years. It was much more likely, he said, that mammoths survived in the inner world. While in search of tidbits which grew near the interior glaciers, they occasionally lost their footing, fell into the ice, and were quick-frozen and delivered over the verge by the Arctic currents.

Gardner's "sensible" explanation of the frozen-mammoth discoveries, when compared to the scientists', only emphasized the blind conservatism of orthodox science in his eyes. The scientists, he believed, were so convinced that mammoths were extinct that they were unable to comprehend proof of living mammoths when it was placed in front of them. "It never occurs to... any explorer," wrote Gardner, "to think anything else than what he has always thought." The scientists and explorers tried to explain away the freshness of the mammoth carcasses by claiming the ice had preserved them, but Gardner knew better. Unfortunately, it is clear that Gardner once again chose his evidence carefully to arrive at a conclusion determined in advance. While many frozen mammoth carcasses have indeed been found near the shore of the Arctic Ocean, many more have been found far inland, frozen into the tundra hundreds of miles from the ocean. How these mammoths have remained so well-preserved over thousands of years remains a mystery—speculations have ranged from individual mammoths falling into glaciers by accident to catastrophe on the order of an earthquake or polar shift that simultaneously killed an entire mammoth population. But of all theories, Gardner's appears probably the least plausible.

Gardner believed the inner world was the home of human inhabitants as well. In fact, he believed it was the original home of both the Eskimos and all the East Asian peoples. "From where comes the up and outward position of the eye that we associate with the Chinese?" he asked his readers. "May it not be a modification of the ordinary eye position induced by the fact that in the interior the sun is always in the zenith?" But because Gardner was interested in an inner world that the United States would be able to explore and conquer, he was careful to stress that any race dwelling within the earth would be primitive and highly exploitable. "The tribes would certainly be numerous and prosperous owing to the easy living conditions," he wrote, "although we might expect to find them very lazy, being so well provided for."

But Gardner hurried on in his second edition to the real message of his book and the reason for all his proposals. It was a pitch to a United States which had found itself, at the end of the First World War, the strongest nation in the world. The time had come, he crowed, for America to reach its zenith by establishing an empire in the inner world:

A new territory almost as vast as that which the [outer] world occupies now would be opened to mankind. How much of it America could claim is problematical but she could certainly claim a tremendous area. The minute we began to take the riches of this area from the interior to our own country our national wealth would increase tremendously. In fact the whole burden of poverty would be lifted. There would be new careers for all who wished them. A new world would mean the disappearance of most of the woes of the present half-world on which we dwell, ignorantly taking it to be the whole world.

Such is the opportunity that confronts us as a nation. Every patriot who is also intelligent must see that to help realize this opportunity is in itself to be a patriot just as much as if he were helping on a field of battle—the battle for subsistence, for plenty, for progress, for supremacy, for all that makes life worth living. For this discovery would add the most glorious page yet written to the annals of the United States. Once we have made this discovery in actual physical fact—as it is already made in reason and thought—feeding Europe would be a mere bagatelle. We could feed the world and have an unlimited plenty left over. We could not only feed the world but we could transform the world. A new and glorious chapter in the history of the human race would have opened.

Between these lines it is easy to feel Gardner's passion to prove himself a new Columbus, another Newton, and a savior of humanity. His desire to find the most spectacular of new earthly frontiers re-created the earth in a new form, a form in which wonderful but accessible discoveries still awaited the explorers and scientists. Marshall B. Gardner constructed a mystery out of carefully selected phenomena and then solved it, making himself—in his own mind at least—one of the great geniuses of-the century. But his greatest challenge lay before him, and continued to do so until the end of his life—to convince the rest of the world of his genius.

"Don't laugh too loud"

Gardner never stopped trying to place his ideas before people of influence. In his enlarged second edition of *A Journey to the Earth's Interior,* published in 1920—again at his own expense—he recounted his struggles to impress the stubborn academics and heads of state with his theories. He included, as one example, Arthur Conan Doyle's polite reply:

> Dear Sir:
>   I read your little book (and big theory) with great interest. It is so very original and actually explains so many facts, that if it were not that both poles had actually been attained, I should be a convert. But I must thank you none the less for a most interesting exposition.
>
>   Yours Sincerely,
>   Conan Doyle.

But Marshall Gardner did not believe either pole had been attained, and he devoted a lengthy chapter in his second edition to disproving the discovery of the North (and by implication the South) Pole. He sneered at the cynical reader who "has read the newspapers and 'knows' that Peary—or Cook—discovered the Pole."

Although it has been almost forgotten today, a great controversy raged in the years 1909 and 1910 over just who had reached the North Pole first. Dr. Frederick Cook, a New York physician who joined Robert Peary's first Arctic expedition in 1891, was so impressed by the cult of heroism growing around the headstrong, egocentric Peary that Cook decided to grab a little glory for himself. In 1907 he put together his own Arctic expedition and disappeared into the North for two years. In September 1909 he reappeared in Copenhagen, announcing that he had reached the North Pole on April 21, 1908. Two days after Cook's announcement, Peary wired his wife from Greenland that he had arrived at "the old pole" on April 6, 1909. Peary was furious when he learned of Cook's claim; he roared that Cook was an upstart trying to hoax him out of his greatest achievement. Although a case can be made for Cook's attainment of the Pole, and there is no guarantee, since the North Pole is always covered by a moving mass of ice, that either man ever reached it, the data on landmarks and astronomical sightings brought back by Peary have always been considered more complete and accurate than Cook's. In December 1909 the University of Copenhagen ruled that Cook's data were insufficient to substantiate his claim. The debate raged on in the newspapers until 1911, when Congress voted to recognize Peary officially as the discoverer of the North Pole, and other nations quickly followed their lead. In 1988 the controversy was revived by the announcement that Peary's notes—supposedly made at the Pole itself—had been discovered; Peary wrote he had seen the sun rise, which would have been impossible unless he had been at least a hundred miles to the south.

Gardner must have followed the controversy with interest. Since he recognized neither man's claim to have reached the Pole, he exulted in the charges and countercharges the Cook defenders and Peary defenders hurled at each other, and he utilized some of them to show that the Pole had not been reached at all. Both sides claimed the sextant readings of the other were incorrect, as well as insufficient proof of arrival at the Pole, since in April the sun was, at its highest, only a few degrees above the horizon. Gardner latched onto this contention and worked it for all it was worth. Obviously, he wrote, both Cook and Peary had spent months wandering lost on the northern verge, deluded by the angle of the sun into thinking they were approaching the Pole. "Owing to the notorious difficulty of finding one's way around in a neighborhood where observations of the sun are not possible in winter—and the sun was barely above the horizon when both explorers were there—where distances are deceptive, where the compass is useless... we must not be astonished," said Gardner, "at the failure of these two men to find out where they really were."

Gardner tried other tactics as well to awaken the public to the facts about the polar regions. He had an enormous globe constructed of laminated wood that split in half to show the lands of the inner world illuminated by an electric bulb that represented the central sun. The globe was first displayed in the window of Sawyer's millinery and book store in Aurora in 1913, and the exhibit was favorably reviewed in the Aurora *Daily Beacon-News*:

> On the start [Gardner's theory] sounds rather "fishy," we admit. So did Columbus' theory that the earth was round instead of flat, but in the face of bitter opposition and biting ridicule he set out and proved his theory to be correct. So if you laugh at Gardner don't laugh too loud, for some day the laugh might be on you. Those who have read his book are not nearly so ready to laugh as they were before, and those who have seen a demonstration of the interesting working models which Mr. Gardner has prepared to illustrate his theories feel pretty sure that he is right.

But Gardner placed his greatest faith in the hundreds of copies of *A Journey to the Earth's Interior* he sowed through the mails. Most of them struck barren soil. The Smithsonian Institution, acknowledging receipt of the book, noted curtly that "the Institution is unable to approve its contents." The copy he sent to King George V of Great Britain was returned, "as it is contrary to rule for His Majesty to accept books from those who are not his own subjects." The well-known astronomer F.R. Moulton of the University of Chicago was blunt in his opinion of the theory. "Mr. Gardner," he wrote, "seems to have no conception whatever of the thoroughness with which scientific men work, or of the requirements of the proof of a theory before it may find acceptance.... His book is well written, but his conclusions are, in my judgement, entirely unfounded." When W.W. Campbell, Director of the University of California's Lick Observatory, replied to Gardner, he concluded, "It may be a disappointment to you to learn that we are placing your book in the class which contains pamphlets we perennially receive on such subjects as 'The Earth is Flat,' etc. It is surprising how many of these contributions there are which ignore, with apparent deliberation, the great body of modern scientific knowledge."

Not all reactions to Gardner's book were hostile. Several periodicals praised his work, although more for his imagination and style than the plausibility of his ideas. The *Scientific American* said, "The sheer ingenuity of his arguments makes the little book worthy of the Jules Vernean reader." The *Buffalo Medical Journal*'s reviewer was realistic but wistful: "Mr. Gardner's hypothesis is so alluring in many ways, practical as well as theoretic, that we are inclined to express the hope that the discoveries of the poles will prove incorrect."

Those who placed the greatest faith in Gardner and his ideas were, as one might suspect, those least likely to be found in the company of scientists or heads of state. In 1932 he received a letter from "The School of Wisdom—The Teachings of the Masters of Wisdom, taught by The Brothers" in Los Angeles. One of "The Brothers" told him:

> ...the main reason of this message is the desire to tell you the points you have brought out in your book which agree with the Wisdom Teachings, and can be confirmed by one who is a student of the Path. We have used your book as a reference in lectures on the poles as entrances to the inner earth.... It has been very interesting to us to see how you have approached the subject from the reasoning or semi-scientific angle, whereas our teacher has brought out practically the same thing from the esoteric or inner view...
>
> P.S. Many of our students also own your book; in fact we have picked up about all of the available copies in the city.

And we shall see, in the chapters to come, what use the students of "the Path" made of Gardner's ideas.

He received another supportive letter from one J.K.P. McCallum, who signed himself "Civil War Veteran and Octogenarian," and wrote, "Since the people do not know what the conditions are inside of the earth, your opinion seems plausible." He urged Gardner to continue working to interest a corporation or government in sending an expedition to the inner world, and concluded by saying, "I found a copy of your book in a second-hand store in San Diego... and I infer the fellow who had bought it, had thrown it away..."

And a writer for the Chicago *Sunday Tribune* of August 13, 1913, allowed himself to get carried away in a feature article:

> Can it be possible that down in the middle of the earth there is another earth? That a few hundred miles or so away, separated from us by ground and rock and vapor and such things, there is a great country inhabited by a great race?
>
> Scientists innumerable have discovered life, vegetable and animal, upon other planets. Long ago seers and wise men peopled the heavens. Exploration has stretched out

toward the truth in all directions save this one. It remains for an Illinoisan to lead us—in theory—down, down into the earth's uttermost recesses and the wonders thereof.

But like the other inner-world philosophers, Gardner led no one into the earth's recesses who didn't already nurture the desire to be led there. Gardner lived until 1937, dying in a prosperous retirement at the age of 83, laboring until the end to convince the outer world of the inner world's existence. He predicted in his book that the interior would be explored first by airplane or dirigible, so one wonders what he must have thought in 1926 when Richard E. Byrd flew over the North Pole, followed in the same year by Roald Amundsen and Lincoln Ellsworth in a dirigible. No doubt he felt that Byrd, Amundsen, and Ellsworth, like Peary and Cook, never realized where they *really* were.

"The earth bisected laterally through the polar openings," from Marshall Gardner's *A Journey to the Earth's Interior* (1920 ed.).

Chapter 6

The Man Who Lived Inside the Earth

> Who shall call his dreams fallacious?
> Who has searched or sought
> All the unexplored and spacious
> Universe of thought?
> Who, in his own skill confiding,
> Shall with rule and line
> Mark the border-land dividing
> Human and divine?
> —Henry Wadsworth Longfellow
> *Hermes Trismegistus*

In his book *Dark Trees to the Wind* (1949), New York historian Carl Carmer recorded his conversation with one of the followers of Dr. Cyrus Read Teed, the man who called himself Koresh, who believed that he was the second incarnation of Jesus Christ, and who taught that we live on the inside of a concave earth:

> "Now if you've got time I'd like to tell you the first scientific principles of Koreshanity."
>
> "First," I said, "I'd like to know how you were converted."
>
> "I was barbering at the Sheraton Hotel in Chicago. Left my room for a walk down State Street. The nineteen-hundred elections were going on. Speakers were hollering about that on one corner and on another the Salvation Army was holding a meeting, but I wasn't paying anybody mind. I was out for a walk. Then I saw a fellow speaking beside a post that had a sign on it—same sign you see there on the wall—WE LIVE INSIDE. What he said made sense and I stopped to listen. I bought a copy of the *Flaming Sword* from a man standing beside the speaker. It was three cents but I gave him a nickel and said 'Keep the change.' I read it in bed that night. Before I went to sleep I was inside."

And it was easy, he continued, to prove that Koresh was right. If you stand on the south shore of Long Island Sound on a clear day, you can see Connecticut ten miles away:

> "Have you ever seen Connecticut from there?"
>
> "Yes, on clear days."
>
> "All right, and you know the curve of the earth's surface runs about eight inches to the mile. If we're living on the outside of the round world you couldn't possibly see it. There'd be a bulge in between taller than you are. How come you can see it?"
>
> "I don't know," I said weakly.
>
> "It's because we live inside," he said triumphantly. "The curve of the earth is eight inches to the mile but it curves up instead of down. We live on a concave surface—not a convex."

Blessed by the August Motherhood

Cyrus Teed was born on a farm in Delaware County, New York, on October 18, 1839, and grew up in Utica, in the center of New York State. His father, Jesse Teed, was quick with his hands and brain. Jesse invented a good number of farming devices, but he won real fame as a healer; he cured many local people of a strange plague called "Black tongue." There must have been some spiritual bent in the family, for a distant cousin of the Teeds was one of the most successful prophets of modern times—Joseph Smith, founder of the Mormon Church.

Cyrus had little interest in conventional schooling; he quit at eleven to take a job on the Erie Canal. When he was twenty he began studying medicine with his uncle, Dr. Samuel Teed, who had an office in Utica. In 1860 he married Delia Row, and soon afterward they had a son, Douglas, who later became well-known in the South as a landscape painter.

Teed discovered he had a real talent for medicine. A year after the Civil War broke out, he interrupted his apprenticeship with his uncle to enlist in the Union Army Medical Corps, where he served as a private for a little over a year. At the war's end he entered the Eclectical Medical College of New York. Eclecticism was a medical sect that flourished in the mid-nineteenth century, but faded away a decade or so before the century ended. It relied on herbal remedies used with treatments taken both from orthodox medicine and Homeopathy, its major rival. Eclectic doctors were a mixed lot; some were quacks, others skilled herbalists, depending on their education and inclinations; almost all of them practiced in small towns. Teed graduated in 1868, and returned to Utica with his wife and son to set up a practice of his own.

But strange ideas were brewing in the mind of Cyrus Teed as he reached his thirtieth year. A devout Baptist in his youth, Teed was confused and saddened by the expanding forces of rationalism, capitalism, and general godlessness he saw around him. The universe that the scientists were busy unfolding seemed terrifyingly infinite to him, enveloping a tiny earth in a vast darkness. What Teed desired intensely was a cosmos on a human scale—one that could be measured in thousands, not billions, of miles, and one like that of Biblical times, in which the earth loomed large and important.

In search of answers, Teed set up a laboratory a short distance from his home where he could, in solitude, pursue his studies of "electro-alchemy," a discipline of his own devising. One midnight late in October of 1869, Teed was sitting in his laboratory lost in meditation when he felt in his head first a buzzing sensation, and then a great vibration, that spread throughout his body and flowed outward into the air around him. Carmer, quoting from Teed's own writing, gave a wonderful description of what happened next:

> Impelled to recline upon "this gently oscillating ocean of magnetic and spiritual ecstasy," he was conscious of the fading of his senses and to test his hearing spoke aloud.
>
> Lying upon the vibratory sea of his delight, he heard from his own lips a voice he had never heard before:

"Fear not, my son," it said, "thou satisfactory offspring of my profoundest yearnings! I have nurtured thee through countless embodiments... in superlative attitudes of earthly glory and thence descending to the lowest depths of degradation into which the human animal can decline."

Then, as the young doctor, eyes closed in awe, knelt on the floor of his laboratory, the voice told him that through his many past incarnations the speaker had witnessed his triumphs and his defeats. She had seen him destroy his body by loathsome disease, had seen him fall before enemies whom his own ambitions and grasping ego had made. "Then," she said, "I have clothed thee in another body and watched thee therein."

Bidden to open his eyes, Cyrus Teed saw emerging from a sphere of purple and golden light the exquisite face of a woman, and the neck, shoulders, and arms "equally exquisite... to the very finger extremes adorned with the most delicate, matchless finger nails so framed as to challenge admiration." Her hair falling over her shoulders was long, luxuriant and golden, and she wore a robe of purple and gold whose folds fell in a long train behind her.

"I have brought thee to this birth," said the vision, "to sacrifice thee upon the altar of all human hopes, that through thy quickening of me, thy Mother and Bride, the Sons of God shall spring into visible creation.... Thou shalt possess me henceforth.... My son, receive now the blessing flowing from my august Motherhood..."

Teed's experience was plainly erotic as well as mystical, reminiscent of the mingled pain and pleasure of Saint Teresa's visions, but Teed the former Baptist took pains to stress that while in his ecstasy, his "Mother and Bride" had revealed some remarkable truths about the cosmos. The time had come, she said, to announce them to the world. Whatever we may think about Teed's ideas, he did take one step few religious leaders are willing to take even today— he championed the femininity in God. He taught that God has both a male and female aspect, as any true Creator must. The Lady of his vision was no less than the female face of God, and she told Teed that he was to "reform the race." He accepted this revelation with due modesty.

"I shall achieve the victory over death," he told himself, "not for myself, but for those to whom I come as a sacrificial offering."

Does this sound familiar? It should; at the same age at which Jesus Christ began his mission as the Savior of Men, Cyrus Teed realized that he was Christ in his Second Coming. Instead of Christ, Teed took the title of Koresh, which means Cyrus in Hebrew. Instead of Christians, he called his followers Koreshans. Instead of Christianity, he announced his teachings to the world as Koreshanity.

A cosmic egg in a golden shell

Among the secrets revealed to Teed by the Lady was the fact that the Copernican cosmos is inside out. The earth, she disclosed, is not a tiny ball floating in endless space, but a great concave hollow shell containing the oceans, the sky, the sun, the moon—in fact, everything that has ever existed. "The Koreshan System," Teed wrote, "maintains and demonstrates that the universe is a unit; it is an alchemico-organic structure, limited to the dimensions of 8,000 miles diameter. According to the great law of analogy, we hold that its form is cellular; that all life is generated in a cell—*omne vivum ex ovo!* [all live within an egg!]" But it was not within an egg or cell that Cyrus Teed had placed his universe, although both those images indicate the direction of his desire for a closed cosmos. In a mythological sense, Teed placed his universe within the womb of the great Lady herself. By enveloping him in a secure, all-enclosing, and sexual aura "of magnetic and spiritual ecstasy," and based upon the cosmos she showed him, she revealed herself to us as an aspect of the Earth Mother. Once Teed had experienced the ecstasy flowing from the Lady and her womb-world, he reveled in it and burned with the desire to spread the security he found to the rest of humanity.

Just as the Twins led the Zunis out of the deepest womb of the Earth Mother, Teed set it as his task to lead us all back in again. He spoke and wrote endlessly about the virtues of a closed cosmos—one that had been closed for all eternity and would forever remain so. Only a closed universe, he taught, was knowable and secure. On that October night, Teed shut himself into that womb for the rest of his life, away from his fear of infinite space, as a bullied child might shut himself away with paper and pencils to draw maps of a fantasy kingdom that he alone rules, where he can lord it over the bullies—the scientists—with his magical powers. "Why do we care to know whether the earth moves or is stationary?" Teed wrote. "If the universe be illimitable, it is equally incomprehensible. Why then should humanity waste its energies in the investigation of that which it has already pronounced incomprehensible, unknown, and unthink-

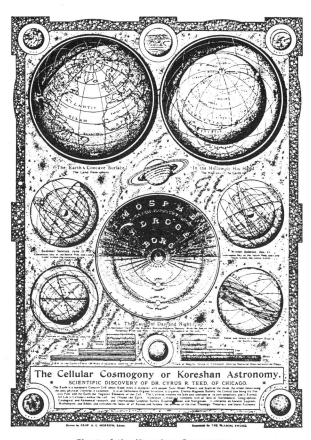

Chart of the Koreshan Cosmogony.
Showing the Principal Astronomical Features, in Explanation of the Phenomena of the Heavens.
Etching No. 8.

Diagram of Cyrus Teed's "Koreshan Cosmogony."

able,—because illimitable? We sought to know the exact form of the universe...
that through conscious knowledge we might enter into and become its power."

The Koreshan Cosmogony was the blueprint for a huge and intricate
clockwork universe that ran by laws existing only in Teed's electro-alchemy.
The concave shell of the earth has seventeen layers, according to Teed. We live
on the outermost of five geologic strata; beneath these lie five layers of minerals,
and deeper still lie seven layers of metal. The innermost of these layers is pure
lead; beneath it run layers of—in descending order—tin, iron, zinc, copper, and
silver. The outermost layer, which is also the outer shell of the cosmos, is pure
gold. Between the metal shells are spaces filled with mercury. The whole
earth-husk acts as the negative pole of the "great voltaic pile," a gigantic battery
powering the sun, which is also its positive pole. Teed's sun is quite small, a
"heart-shaped disc" a few hundred miles across that rotates at the center of his
cosmos; it is bright on one side and dark on the other. We never see the *real* sun,
however; it is hidden from our view in the furthest layer of the atmosphere, the
aboron layer. We see only the reflection—or as Teed put it, the "refocalization"—
of the sun upon the upper surface of the lowest layer of the atmosphere, the ni-
trogen/oxygen layer we breathe and live in. There is also a hydrogen layer between the two; it has its own refocalization of the sun, but we can't see it.

Due to the action of many extremely intricate and obscure optical laws
discovered by Teed, the pseudo-sun that we see only appears to rise and set on
the horizon. Actually there is no horizon, and the rays of the sun simply sweep
around the inside of the globe like those of a rotating light on a police car. Koresh's more skeptical listeners constantly asked him why, if his teachings were
true, we cannot see the real sun, and especially why we cannot point a telescope
straight up and see the people of New Zealand hanging upside down. He would
reply, a little impatiently, that a three-story atmosphere eight thousand miles
across is simply too dense to see through; it thus gives us the illusion of infinite
space.

The moon, stars, and planets are "not worlds or systems of worlds; they
are not wanderers or erratic orbs, but points of generation of energy.... The real
planets are discs of mercury in the earth, between the metallic shells; they are
concave to the center. They focalize the sun's energies in the atmosphere above
us. They are what their names indicate—plan-ets, little planes."

But the question Teed was asked most often was, "If the entire universe
exists within the shell of the earth, what is on the outside?" His answer was
simple—nothing:

> The shell of the earth is the circumference—the limit of the universe. It environs all that
> exists. Outside the environ or limit of existence, there is nothing. There is no infinite
> space. Space is measure and dimension of things that are; it is definite. Limitation is a
> factor of form; form is a factor of existence. Hence if the universe exists it is limited, be-
> yond which there is no existence.... No matter how absurd this may be to the average
> person, sufficient thought on the problem will reveal the fact that our conclusions as to
> what is not on the outside are reasonable, loyal, and absolute.

Koreshanity attempted to demolish science in the quickest way possible—it revealed all the "givens" of science as illusions. The convexity of the earth was an illusion, the rising and setting of the sun were illusions, and the infinite expanses of space and the vast sizes of the stars and galaxies were illusions. The atheistic Copernican cosmos and the godless laws of physics were turned inside out like pairs of socks. The only truth was the truth revealed to Koresh. "To know of the earth's concavity and its relation to universal form, is to know God; while to believe in the earth's convexity is to deny him and all his works," he wrote. "All that is opposed to Koreshanity is Antichrist."

The fortunes of the Second Christ

Not long after his vision, Teed began telling his patients that he was the new redeemer—the "Cyrus" spoken of in Isaiah 45:1, "whose right hand I have holden, to subdue nations before him, and to loose the loins of kings." He told them he was the Second Christ, and that we live inside the earth. The results were predictable; his patients began looking for another physician. Tales began circulating among the conservative Uticans about the "crazy doctor." Some people were outraged by his blasphemy; others merely thought him insane. But whatever people thought, Teed soon found himself unable to make a living in Utica. So he packed up his family and his practice and moved from small town to small town in central New York state. Everywhere Teed preached Koreshanity to prospective patients, and everywhere he was subsequently avoided. Under the continuing stress of being a target of ridicule wherever she went through no fault of her own, Delia Teed suffered a nervous breakdown. Soon after, she took her son and walked out on Cyrus, never to return.

But his wife's desertion and the ridicule of the state of New York didn't stop Teed. By 1880 he had attracted five followers, all women—one was his sister Emma; another was a cousin. Teed's parents offered him their Moravia mop-making business, and he gratefully accepted. In Moravia he established the first small Koreshan community, which made mops and published a largely-ignored newsletter, *Herald of the Messenger of the New Covenant of the New Jerusalem.* But both mop and messenger businesses proved unprofitable, and two years later Teed took his flock to Syracuse, where he set up another practice with his younger brother Oliver, also an Eclectic. For a time the brothers' practice prospered; by 1884 they had their office on one of the wealthiest streets in Syracuse. But in that same year the practice dissolved in the midst of a widely publicized scandal. Cyrus was sued by Mrs. Charles Cobb, who charged that he had persuaded her and her mother to give him a good deal of money "under the plea that he is the 'Second Christ.'" The *New York Times* account of the incident continued that:

> He also claims that when he was 30 years of age he received divine manifestations, and that when he is 46 he will be translated to heaven whence he will return in 50 days to found a kingdom where all will be love. By love he means only mind love of great purity and elevation. Those who follow him... will live forever in this world.

The lawsuit generated such unfavorable publicity that Teed decided to carry his teachings to the world at large instead of small towns. So he moved his tiny band of Koreshans, now numbering *four* women, to a flat in Manhattan. Until 1886, the world at large paid little attention to Koreshanity. But in September of that year, the Fates changed their minds about Cyrus Teed.

He was invited to address the convention of the National Association of Mental Science in Chicago, and the speech he delivered was so powerful, and his presence so charismatic, that he was elected president of the association. Before the entire convention, Teed healed a woman who until then had only been able to walk a few steps; she walked all the way home, praising the powers of Koresh. Teed had suddenly found a receptive—in fact adulatory—audience, and his fame spread quickly to both coasts. By the end of the 1880s, in addition to the nucleus of 126 followers Teed had won in Chicago, groups of disciples had gathered in Lynn and Springfield, Massachusetts, Baltimore, Denver, San Francisco, and Portland. With money donated to Teed, the Assembly of the Covenant (as he now styled his church) purchased a huge, ornate mansion in Washington Heights that Koresh christened Beth-Ophra. It served as a cooperative dormitory for the Koreshans, and from its bowels Teed began churning out another newsletter, *The Guiding Star*, which was soon succeeded by a more ambitious publication, *The Flaming Sword*. He also set up a "College for Life" at Beth-Ophra that held courses in electro-alchemy, metaphysics, and mental science.

Cyrus Read Teed or Koresh, the "Second Christ."

Never a humble man, Teed let the adulation he was receiving go completely to his head. As a young man, friends and relatives had recognized his potential and had urged him to go into the ministry, but he had chosen medicine instead. Now he began preaching with a vengeance and played the role of prophet to the hilt. The *Chicago Tribune* described Teed in 1894 as "an undersized, smooth-shaven man of 54 whose brown, restless eyes glow and burn like live coals.... He exerts a strange, mesmerizing influence over his converts, particularly the other sex." He appeared in public in stark black and white, favoring Prince Albert coats, white silk ties, and broad-brimmed felt hats. His confidence in himself must have made him truly magnetic; by the mid-1890s he claimed four thousand followers. He told his followers about the power of his own thoughts, "If I would throw everything I write or ever have written right here into the waste basket, or if it would be burned or otherwise destroyed, so that no human eye would get to see it, its spiritual substance, nevertheless, would go out, carried by waves, electric waves that fill the air we breathe."

With his church prospering, Teed began turning his mind toward political goals. In 1891 he established the Bureau of Equitable Commerce, a Koreshan subsidiary devoted to the conversion of the working classes. The Bureau promoted the idea of a cooperative sharing of goods and a fight against the monopolies. Teed envisioned a grand goal—a communist (with a small "c") country of Koreshans all under his rule. In an interview with a reporter from the *Pittsburgh Leader* in 1891 he said that

> as soon as his system of government prevails, which he says will be within ten years, he will build a six track railroad between the Atlantic and Pacific coasts, in one year employing a million men in its work. He will also construct a pneumatic passenger way across the continent which will carry one to San Francisco in 12 hours; the cars will run without wheels. More wonderful than all, Dr. Teed says one of his members in the Chicago office has a device whereby he can, from his desk in that office in Chicago, set the type for every newspaper in the country by wire and that an application for a patent is now on file in Washington.

Teed was a supporter of black-white racial equality, and in one 1893 issue of *The Flaming Sword* defended racial intermarriage, a topic of extreme controversy at that time, although he believed the highest virtue was to be found in celibacy. "It is impossible," he wrote, "to conceive of any kind of civil equality, in which there is a recognition of a social compatibility between the whites and the blacks, without the recognition of a marital equation; and until the moral right for the marital union of the black and white races is recognized social equality is out of the question." In carefully convoluted language, he then proposed that "the circumcision of the females of the black race" would make possible, through "conservation of that energy which made the Hebrew race the greatest nation in the earth," the interbreeding of a newer, stronger American race. Teed believed that America was soon to be threatened by "the Mongolians," invaders from East Asia, and the nation needed to be ready.

Alongside Teed's political ideas came a strange set of sexual beliefs that seem like those of the late twentieth century blended with those of the early fourth. He believed strongly in the equality of the sexes (which may have been one of the reasons so many of his disciples were women), but for women to attain an equal estate with men, sexual energies had to be channeled into other ends. For those who desired to gain immortality in this world, celibacy was all-important. "The wild, lustful, and dissipating pleasures of sexuality," Teed wrote, "have blinded the human mind to the sanctity of the potencies of proliferation and the higher uses to which the hidden energies of being should be devoted." Men and women were rigidly segregated in the Koreshan dormitories. But Teed himself didn't seem to follow his own beliefs; from about 1890 to the end of his life, he lived with Annie Ordway, a church member to whom he gave the name Victoria Gratia and the title "Pre-eminent." There were also many rumors that the love he had for his many female disciples was not entirely spiritual.

The Holy City and the Rectilineator

Burning with the desire to govern his little womb-world, Teed realized that he would have to accomplish two goals to win people over to Koreshanity—he would need to establish a model city that could demonstrate the truth of his political ideas, and construct an experiment that would be undeniable proof of his scientific ones. To reach his first goal, he had long dreamed of a star-shaped city in the wilderness that would be first the center of Koreshanity, next the capital of the United States, and finally the center of a new world government. Like most utopians and cult leaders, Teed began searching for an unspoiled location in which he could both give his noble experiment some isolation in which to develop, and exert unquestioned control over his followers.

Soon the bit of paradise Teed desired was laid at his feet. In 1883 Gustav Damkohler, a German of mystical inclinations, had come to the wild southwest coast of Florida in search of solitude. Standing on the banks of the Estero River a dozen miles south of Fort Myers, Damkohler heard a bodiless voice. It said, "Take and dress until the Lord comes." So he bought 320 swampy acres of palmettoes and mosquitoes near Estero Bay, built a house, sent for his wife and six children, and waited for the Lord to come.

He had a long, hard wait. Over the next seven years his wife and five of his children expired in the unfamiliar climate. But one day in 1890 he was in the nearby village of Punta Gorda picking up his mail, and he happened upon a pamphlet announcing the appearance of Koresh, the new Messiah, and describing his teachings. Damkohler trembled with excitement, for he knew he had been meant to find that pamphlet. He wrote a letter to Chicago and invited the new Messiah to Estero Bay. It took Teed, who was busy establishing himself in the North, nearly four years to get to Florida, but on New Year's Day of 1894, Teed arrived at Damkohler's house, accompanied by three of the highest-ranking Koreshan women. Damkohler was swept away by Teed's very presence; he knelt at his feet and called Teed "Master." Teed, for his part, was not unimpressed with his new disciple's lush landholdings. Soon Damkohler, in exchange for lifetime care[1], had signed over his 320 acres to Koresh, and Teed began preparing the foundations of his holy city. He told his followers back in Chicago that he had found the "vitellus of the Great Cosmogonic Egg," which is only a euphemism for the center, or navel, of the earth. It was an ideal location, he said, for the future capital of the world. Within a year a hundred Koreshans had moved from Chicago and erected a village on Estero Bay—a house for Teed and Victoria Gratia, a communal dining hall and women's dormitory, and a scattering of other buildings, all built of logs cut on the property. Teed was pleased with the village; he called it the Koreshan Co-operative and Communistic Colony.

Now Teed turned to his second goal—an experiment that would provide absolute proof of his revealed science, proof that even the "deluded followers" of Copernicus could not deny. And just as Symmes found James McBride to serve as his apologist, Teed found Ulysses Grant Morrow. Professor Morrow, of Teed's College for Life, was a young man from Corning, Iowa, whose field was not exactly cosmology. His *magnum opus* before his conversion to Koreshanity had been a little pamphlet titled *Phonography; or Phonetic Shorthand: What it is and How to Learn it.* But Morrow took the need for a real proof of the Koreshan System to heart, and in 1896 he completed work on a device that would do the job—the Rectilineator. His invention was essentially ten T-squares set horizontally, alternately head-to-head and tail-to-tail, mounted on ten carefully adjusted legs. Morrow took great pride in his creation. "The material of which the sections of the Rectilineator are constructed," he boasted, "is inch mahogany, seasoned for *twelve years* in the shops of the Pullman Palace Car Co."

Morrow's idea was a simple one. If the surface of the earth curves upwards, as Koresh taught, then an absolutely straight line, parallel to the starting surface and set at a certain height would, if extended far enough, strike the earth at both ends. Morrow set the height of the Rectilineator at 128 inches—the idea being that if the curve of the earth is eight inches upwards to the mile, the line set by the device would touch the earth at a distance of four miles.

On January 2, 1897, the Koreshan Geodetic Survey, as Morrow styled himself and his little band of assistants, arrived at the long, level beach of Naples, Florida, a winter resort south of Estero Bay. They had made the journey from Chicago "with apparatus, and all appurtenances and instruments, and plans of operations, which required five months' careful observations and accurate work to execute." They erected the Rectilineator and began their measurements. The device was precisely calibrated to be parallel with the beach, and four weeks were spent merely checking the microscopic adjustment of the right angles.

It took the Koreshan Geodetic Survey five months to move the Rectilineator, section by section, the distance of four miles. But on May 5, 1897, the

---

[1]Damkohler was given the job of tending the gardens and apiary at Estero, but grew increasingly disenchanted with Teed's control over, and failure to educate, his remaining son. Damkohler eventually instituted legal action against the Koreshans for the return of his land, and agreed to accept the return of a small portion of it (80 wild acres out of the original 320) and the release of his son from the colony's influence.

line struck the water and a great cheer of thanksgiving arose from Morrow and his men. Their work was not in vain; Koresh was right. The earth was concave.

Two views of the Rectilineator on the
beach near Naples, Florida.

Teed was delighted, and he and Morrow collaborated on a book, *The Cellular Cosmogony, or the Earth a Concave Sphere,* published by Estero's Guiding Star Publishing House in 1898. It is an impressive little volume filled with intricate charts and diagrams, and every word of the text shines with the absolute confidence of its authors. Teed announced in the introduction that "the mechanical Geodetic demonstration has been carried forward to a successful geometrical and mathematical conclusion and climax,—irrefutable and overwhelming." Morrow chimed, "That the earth is convex, there has never been any direct and positive evidence offered; the most eminent astronomers are unable to place the matter within the range of certainty," a statement that would no doubt raise the eyebrows of many eminent astronomers. "The Koreshan System alone has been able to reduce the question of the earth's shape to a specific and pivotal demonstration. It rejects no truth; endeavors to set aside no well-established and demonstrated fact, and does not fear the most crucial test of its premise." Although *The Cellular Cosmogony* went through three editions, and despite its "irrefutable" proof, the science of Koresh had little effect on the astronomy and geology textbooks. In fact, it had no effect on them at all.

By the turn of the century, the Estero colony had a population of a little over two hundred, and in 1903, the home office of the Koreshan Unity (Teed had changed its name again) packed up and moved south to Florida. Teed, who had been dividing his time between Chicago and Estero Bay, settled in Florida permanently. The colony was definitely prospering. More log buildings went up, and the Guiding Star presses turned out thousands of copies of the *Flaming Sword* every month for an ever-widening circle of subscribers. Teed told the Koreshans that in ten years, ten million people would live in Estero. Accordingly, the Unity purchased nearly six thousand acres of surrounding land and cut roads deep into the pine woods; a great city was surveyed and plotted out, with business and residential districts extending—on paper—far from the colony center like rays from a star. A huge sign was erected over the entrance to the colony that read "WE LIVE ON THE INSIDE," and Koreshans wore badges bearing the same message when they rode into Fort Myers or greeted visitors to Estero. The Cellular Cosmogony was celebrated by the colonists in a regular cycle of solar and lunar festivals, and the Koreshan Art Hall featured a prominent display of charts of the concave earth devised by Professor Morrow, and a globe that came apart to show the nations of the world on the inside.

Teed stressed the study of the arts in his new and improved College for Life, which he had given the grander title "Pioneer University of Koreshan Universology." The University's brass band went to the Florida State Fair in Tampa one year and returned with the first prize in its competition. Self-sufficiency in food production was also important to Koresh. By 1903 two thousand acres of Koreshan land were under cultivation; huge citrus orchards were planted and soon the colony's produce was considered among the finest in the state.

Any outsider who desired to join the good life at Estero was handed a prospectus, written by Teed, which read in part, "There is no differnce between one who has placed one penny in the common treasury and one who has contributed a hundred thousand." Colony members received no wages for their work; the colony secretary issued requisitions for supplies and food that were redeemed at the Estero general store. The prospectus was clear about Teed's control of his followers. "When a family comes into the Koreshan Unity it comes with the understanding that there is a separation; that the children no longer belong to the parents, but to the institution and that the Unity claims the right to direct the education, industry, and care of the children exclusively.... the male children belong until they are twenty-one, and the female children until they are eighteen... and all children should be taught that they belong to the Unity and not their parents."

Teed did not believe that everyone should swear themselves to celibacy, and thus immortality; only the "higher ranks" of the population need do so. Colony members were required to join the "ecclesia," the group of celibates who would gain eternal life and set an example for others; the ecclesia gave all their personal possessions to the Unity with the understanding that if they chose to quit the order at a later date, their money and other possessions would *not* be returned. The lower stratum of Koreshanity was the marital order, to which many of Teed's disciples scattered around the country belonged. Members of the lower order were allowed to marry, keep their children and their property, yet support the Koreshan movement with their labors and frequent donations.

The Progressive Liberty Party and the Great Red Dragon

The Estero colonists lived in peace and happiness until the summer of 1904, when all hell broke loose in Lee County, Florida. The Democratic political machine in Fort Myers, which had controlled county politics for many years, had been a little uneasy about having a large body of voters living in their midst who preached—and lived by—such radically socialist ideals. But until 1904 the Koreshans had always voted Democratic—every one of them—under Teed's orders. But as the presidential election drew near, Teed decided he was not happy with Alton Parker, the Democratic candidate who was opposing the Republican, Theodore Roosevelt. The word reached Fort Myers that the Koreshans were *not* going to vote Democratic in November. The Lee County officials began quietly arguing that the Koreshans should be disenfranchised before the election because Teed was telling them all how to vote. When Koresh heard what was happening, he called his flock together and told them to gird their loins for battle. He established a new party, the Progressive Liberty Party, and began printing a party newsletter, the *American Eagle*, on the Guiding Star presses. He toured the county with hand-picked candidates, the Koreshan brass band, and a full platform: public ownership of utilities, equal division of wealth, free schools, and protection of natural resources. By October, an impressive number of Lee County residents, pleased about the Koreshans' fight against the county machine, were actively supporting the Progressive Liberty Party.

The county politicians began displaying real anxiety, and tempers grew short on both sides. On October 13, the hulking marshal of Fort Myers strode up to Teed on the streets of that city. The two began to argue, and soon the marshal began punching Teed violently on the side of the head until he knocked him down. A moment later the marshal was knocked down himself and nearly torn to pieces by a crowd of angry Koreshans before he was able to draw his gun and arrest them all. Teed was helped back home to Estero after a lengthy shouting match at the police station.

The Progressive Liberty Party lost the November election, but the results were very close; in its first time on the ballot, the party of Koresh had shown surprising strength. Teed himself, however, began to grow weaker. He was now approaching seventy, and the marshal had injured him more seriously than the Koreshans had at first realized. The blows left him plagued with spells of great pain that grew more severe over the next four years.

Teed probably realized that his life, at least in his present body, was drawing to an end. In 1908, his last year, he wrote his final and most ambitious work, *The Great Red Dragon; or, The Flaming Devil of the Orient*, a "prophetic novel" that was also a supreme example of "yellow peril" hate literature. It is Teed's scenario for the future, a prediction of the great battles to come between nations, religions, and social classes, and of the final flowering of his mighty city of Koreshans. The story, which is told in the past tense, details the consolidation of "the money power of all Christendom" with the governments of the Western nations into a great totalitarian power. But while these forces merged, the working classes also united into a huge socialist army of opposition, and the two were soon locked in battle. "All the principal cities were in consternation," wrote Teed of this class struggle; "the contending armies now numbered nearly two million and hundreds of thousands were added every week. Tens of thousands were being sent daily to their last resting place in that gory carnage."

While this war devastated the West, the East was arming itself for conquest:

> Military and naval activity was everywhere apparent in Japan and China. Both peoples had been excluded from American soil, as well as from England and the other Western countries. Much of the work in both the army and navy of the "yellow" nations was secretly conducted...
> The result of the first battle between the corporate powers and the masses was flashed around the world; and with the same lightning-like velocity, the Oriental peoples were aroused. War began with England in her Imperial possessions in India; China and Japan were quick to measure the extent of the disaster, and England's power abroad began to wane.

Of course, it wasn't long before the East attacked Europe and America themselves:

> A great fleet of foreign vessels stood off the Pacific coast, and another was approaching the harbor of New York, on the Atlantic coast. The character of this display was not yet understood. Following this report it was ascertained that Japan and China were moving with an army of ten to fifteen millions, making their way into Europe, conquering all before them.... The movement of the military force of China, Japan and India was accompanied by a corresponding and social progress. Men, women and children marched with the army, taking possession of the territory conquered by the invading forces of the Oriental world.... Christianity was driven from every quarter of the world toward America, which up to the present time, had not been overridden...

But soon after:

> The entire Pacific coast had been occupied by Japanese and Chinese, for Japan had sent a vast navy and transportation fleet, with hundreds of thousands of fighting men to occupy the territory of the United States.... The attempt to portray the carnage of the effort to defend the coast of the United States from the host of Asiatics swarming to our shores, would be an unwarrantable prolixity; and I leave this part of the subject to the imagination.

Yet as these battles raged, an even greater trial was in store for the peoples of the earth. For some time, Teed had been predicting in his writings and speeches that the ecliptic was due to shift thirty degrees to the south, with massive changes in the apparent movement of the sun and the celestial bodies. When the ecliptic shifts, he wrote, "the limit of movement of the sun, north and south, will then be fourteen degrees. The north and south polar axis will be proportionally shortened, and the habitable portion of the earth will be reduced to this space." He also said that the sun would begin to rotate faster; not only would the days become shorter, but the refocalization of the sun would be stretched into a long ellipse. And so it happened in *The Great Red Dragon*:

There had been issued statements of a calamity that was to overtake the world in which millions would be destroyed in the universal cataclysm... [But] God had never brought disaster upon the human race `without first sending His prophets to invite the world to the haven of safety that He had provided for His people. The human race was called upon to gather toward the tropical regions of the earth...

There was to be no delay in this gathering of the people of God.... Thousands began to heed the warning and prepare for the transmigration; but many scoffed, not heeding the voice of God as declared through His Messenger.

As people sought the place of safety, wonderful changes were observed in the geological foundations, which underwent processes of transformation. There was a shortening of the axis of the earth; the stars of the northern and southern constellations began to fall, and there disappeared one-third of the stellar universe. A marvelous change commenced to affect the sun, which elongated from east to west. There were upheavals in various waters of the earth, and the land began to sink in other places.

People from every nation under the sun had gathered either in proximity to the Central City, or within the limitations of the area of the contracting sphere.... From northern climes the people had migrated south; and from northern climes they had migrated north.

Teed described this cataclysm as the dawn of his dream, but it would be the coming of a claustrophobic nightmare for most of the rest of us. His "wonderful changes" are actually the tightening of his womb-world; but the womb of the Earth Mother is not contracting in preparation for birth. It is just contracting, squeezing its inhabitants into a smaller and smaller area. Many are squeezed into Teed's Central City, a thinly-veiled Estero, and into a tightly-controlled existence:

During all of the militant activity operative among the nations, there had been planted a colony on the Gulf of Mexico, which was in process of rapid growth. The world at large was ignorant of the significance of the energy displayed, and of the character of the forces at work in the various phases of the mechanical and other enterprises. The vast machine shops, with every conceivable kind of intricate and mystical combinations, were operated by thousands of men. There was no talking except upon the business of the shops during the hours of employment.

The place was characterized by a spirit of religious enthusiasm which pervaded it.... Neither whiskey nor tobacco was used; there was neither profanity, nor vulgarity, nor obscenity.

Peculiar looking machines were being multiplied in thousands of disassembled parts. The work went forward day and night...

The industry of the world was to be regulated and organized. There were to be no idlers; the energies of children even were to be directed in such a manner as to contribute to their pleasure, while the juvenile mind and body were trained on lines of moral, physiological and mental development. It had been contended that there could be no greater evil than that of maintaining children in idleness.

Many people gathered into the mystic city, and became parts of its congregations. The wealth of nations flowed into its treasury, and was devoted to the progress of the work and to the prosperity of the gigantic operations of the municipality.

Here is the description of a state that any reader of Orwell might find familiar, down to the mumbo-jumbo of its language.

The Theocrasis of Cyrus Teed

But Teed was never to see Estero become the center of the world; he died, quickly and quietly, on Estero Island on December 22, 1908, at the age of sixty-nine. He had predicted his death back in 1892 in *The Flaming Sword*: "Dr. Teed will die; the termination of his natural career will be tragic. He will reach his death at the instigation of a people who profess the religion of Jesus the Christ of God." His prophecy—although with a four-year delay—turned true enough, but many of the Koreshans refused to believe that he was really dead. Some of them were sure that he would slough his worn body like a snake sheds its skin and be reborn before their eyes. Others remembered his teachings concerning *theocrasis*—"incorruptible dissolution, without decay of the flesh, of a physical body by 'electro-magnetic combustion'"—and they waited for his body to vanish in a burst of holy light. In either case, they agreed, his body should not be buried. So it lay in state for nearly a week in the midst of a midwinter hot spell, and as it decayed, some of the Koreshans, who had halted work to keep a vigil over Koresh, claimed to see the "remarkable physical changes" that preceded rebirth. But when the remains of Cyrus Teed had reached a definite state of decomposition without incident, health authorities from Fort Myers paid a visit and ordered a speedy burial. So the Koreshans, confused and shaken, quickly constructed a concrete tomb on Estero Island that bore these words:

CYRUS
SHEPHERD STONE OF ISRAEL

and what was left of Cyrus Teed was laid to rest.

But over the next decade, a group of Koreshans who believed that Teed's body had "dematerialized" in the tomb tried to break it open several times. The rest of the Unity assigned a guard to the tomb, however, and the "theocrasites" were always unsuccessful. Finally, one November evening in 1921, a hurricane hit Estero Island with all its force and carried away the tomb, the inscription, and the remains of Koresh. Nothing of Teed was found and the Koreshans were awestruck; their founder had, after twelve years of waiting, experienced theocrasis.

There is another version of Teed's "translation" that was told in Florida in the 1930s that is definitely apocryphal, but it's worth relating anyway. After his death, the story runs, Koresh's body was laid out on a cypress plank on the bank of the Estero River, and his followers held a vigil over it for several weeks, waiting for him to rise again. He didn't rise again, and the Koreshans were eventually forced to place the remains in a bathtub, which was set back on the plank. Soon after, a hurricane roared through Estero and the Koreshans had to leave the corpse and flee for cover. When they returned, the bathtub and the body had disappeared, and although the river and the surrounding woods were searched for weeks, not a trace of either was ever found. But the plank was still exactly where they had placed it; it had not budged an inch, and the faith of the Koreshans in their leader's divinity was restored.

Unfortunately, the Koreshans' faith in themselves was not so easily restored after the death of Koresh. In the first months of 1909, the group split into fragments. Gustav Faber, the man who had nursed Teed in his final days, and had even built a special "electrotherapeutic machine" to cure him, claimed that Koresh had designated him the new Supreme Counselor of Koreshanity with his dying breath. Victoria Gratia contended that she was Teed's rightful heir, but when she left Estero, only a few followed her. Another group of Koreshans established an "Order of Theocracy" in Fort Myers, but it faded into obscurity along with Faber and Annie Ordway.

Those who remained in Estero continued to live much as they had before Teed's passing, and they continued to welcome new converts since, being sworn to celibacy, Koreshanity could not otherwise continue. The Guiding Star presses continued running as if Teed had never died, and in fact his death was never mentioned in the *Flaming Sword*—and the *Flaming Sword* was published regularly until 1949, when the printing plant burned down. In 1909 *The Great Red Dragon* was posthumously published, but under the unlikely pseudonym of "Lord Chester." The remaining Koreshans had little success in convincing a new generation of young people to join them in celibacy within a concave earth; by 1950, only a dozen or so were left, most of them over seventy. As it became obvious to them that the Estero colony was dying, they began to quarrel among themselves over the title to the vast colony properties. But in the end, the board of the Unity met and decided that it would be best, and most honorable to Koresh's memory, to give the land to the state of Florida. They offered the colony property to the state in 1952, and after nearly ten years' worth of red tape, the Koreshan State Park was established in 1961. The fields and orchards of the colony have been converted to a tropical arboretum, and the few remaining Koreshans in the area publish a revived *American Eagle*, now a monthly newsletter along the lines of a local *Christian Science Monitor* (although a recent issue in my possession announces an upcoming Lunar Festival), and give tours of the old colony grounds.

The remaining Koreshans, including those who moved elsewhere, did not give up their beliefs. In 1969, Elizabeth Bartosch of Miami, one of their number, privately published *The Last Days and the New Age*, which had been written in 1940 by Dr. Willis G. Sheeman. Bartosch revised the book, and in her introduction told us that Dr. Sheeman—who died in 1956—believed he was "destined to bring forth, in these last days, the teachings of Dr. Cyrus R. Teed." Sheeman's goal was to demonstrate that not only does the Bible definitely indicate that Teed was the second Messiah, but the stones of the Grand Gallery of the Great Pyramid do as well. Sheeman shared Cyrus Teed's belief in Anglo-Israelitism—both believed the Great Pyramid revealed that the Ten Lost Tribes of Israel were the ancestors of the Teutonic and Anglo-Saxon peoples. "The Pyramid of Gizeh," Sheeman wrote, "contains within its enormous structure of stone the complete history of the Anglo-Germanic race, past, present and future." He claimed that the "Anglo-Germanic race," and not the Jews, are God's "chosen people," and the "promised land" of the Bible is not Palestine, but the United States.

Since he was writing on the eve of America's entrance into World War II, Sheeman also pointed out that the prophecies of *The Great Red Dragon* were a warning of Japan's ambitions in the Pacific and the need for American vigilance; the harbingers of war were the first indications that the last days were upon us. Composing her revised ending nearly thirty years later, Bartosch ignored the fact that the sun did not lengthen soon after the war, nor did continents rise and sink. She concluded, "Let me urge you to take seriously the prophetic warnings given in this book, for we are indeed living in the last days. The Great Battle of the Ages is being fought to the finish in order that those who are of the Elect may find their way back to the pathway of right living, and take part in the glorious work of the New Age."

Some things will never change, and one is the wish for Paradise for oneself and confutation for one's opponents. The New Age, whether within the earth or without, will always be coming next year or in another decade. Words like Bartosch's—and Teed's—were shouted and written a thousand years ago, a century ago, last year, and yesterday. Barring unforseen events, they will be shouted and written tomorrow and a century from now.

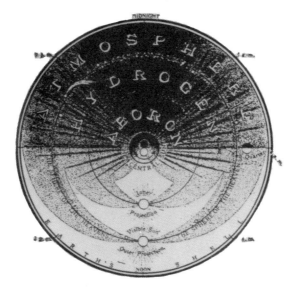

THE CAUSE OF DAY AND NIGHT.
Cross-Sectional View of the Gigantic, Electro-Magnetic Battery with the sun as the Perpetual Pivot and Pole. The Southern Hemisphere of the Cell.

**Cross-section through Koresh's
concave earth.**

Chapter 7

The Hidden Masters' Hiding Places

> "Then bring me the Father of the Father of Nadd!" ordered the
> King. "He knows about everything in all my kingdom, in all
> the world beyond, and in all other worlds that may happen to
> be."
>
> —Dr. Seuss, *The 500 Hats of*
> *Bartholomew Cubbins*

The basis of the alternative-reality tradition in the West
may well be the notion that there is a body of "Ancient Wisdom," a secret collection of knowledge about the cosmos given to humanity by a Higher Power before recorded history began. The idea of hidden wisdom is probably as old as religious belief—as old as the secrets held by the shamans, priestesses and priests of every archaic culture. The initiatory cults, such as those of Isis, Mithra, Dionysus, and other gods, claimed during the early Christian era special knowledge for their members. Perhaps today the best-known "secret doctrine" of that time is the *gnosis*, the secret way to salvation, taught by the Egyptian Gnostics in the first three centuries AD. It was in about the third century that the *Book of Hermes Trismegistus* was assembled in Alexandria; this was a collection of magical ritual, alchemical knowledge, Gnostic and Neoplatonic teachings, and astrology texts. The *Book of Hermes Trismegistus* was considered in medieval and Renaissance Europe to be the oldest book in the world, dating back to the time just after the Deluge, and to be the ultimate source of the Ancient Wisdom.

It was also in the early years of the Christian era that the figure of the Magus became popular among those who sought the Ancient Wisdom. The Magus is a man—or very rarely a woman—who serves a civilized culture as shaman and magician. A Magus is one in possession of secrets, one in contact with invisible powers, one able to break society's rules, one who is forcefully charismatic and able to appear and disappear from the earthly scene without warning. The great figures in the history of the alternative-reality tradition, from Pythagoras to Paracelsus to Aleister Crowley, have all been considered Magi. The religious scholar Robert S. Ellwood, Jr., calls the Magus a person "who appears like one who has been through the ultimate transformation, yet is visible here"—in other words one who, like the shaman, serves as a bridge between the sacred and the profane, between the seen and the unseen worlds.

The cults and brotherhoods that gathered around the Magi came to shine in their founders' reflected light, and indeed sometimes became—as a group—Magi themselves. They collected about themselves a body of myths transforming them into "hidden brotherhoods." These brotherhoods, the myths ran, were secret societies charged with preserving the Ancient Wisdom in its purest form, and concealing it from the eyes of those not ready to receive it. Tales of hidden brotherhoods surfaced from time to time in medieval and Renaissance Europe, and flourished between the seventeenth and nineteenth centuries—a period when several European secret societies, real and mythical, political and mystical, like the Freemasons, the Rosicrucian Order, and the Illuminati occupied an awesome and sinister place in popular mythology. The Masons in particular have been accused for centuries of everything from devil-worship to human sacrifice at their secret meetings; in America in the 1820s, they were popularly accused of plotting to take over the government, and in France fifty years later, they were considered to practice the vilest forms of black magic behind closed doors.

The Rosicrucian Order shared the Masons' sinister aura, even though there is no proof of the existence of a real Order by that name before the mid-nineteenth century. Two of the seminal documents of the original "Rosicrucian Order," the *Fama Fraternatis* (1614) and the *Chemical Wedding of Christian Rosencreutz* (1617), which actually may have been political rather than mystical in nature, invoked great clouds of symbolic mystery. They described prophecies, arcane rituals and grand ceremonies, as well as the discoveries of secret vaults into which "the sun never shined," lit by magical lamps or glowing carbuncles and containing hidden wisdom, strange inscriptions, and unheard-of wonders. Nineteenth-century occultists embroidered upon the Rosicrucian documents to produce further gothic tales of the mysterious Order, and in these tales the hidden sanctuaries of the Order were frequently located underground.

Masons engaged in devil-worship, from a nineteenth-century anti-Masonic book.

Hargrave Jennings, one of the more fanciful occultists and folklorists of the last century, told one such tale in his romanticized "history" of the Rosicrucians (*The Rosicrucians: Their Rites and Mysteries*) published in 1870, a tale he claimed came from a seventeenth-century *History of Staffordshire* that never actually existed. In the tale a Staffordshire farm laborer, digging a trench in a remote field, uncovered a great stone buried in the earth. He levered the stone aside and found beneath it a stairway, and collecting his courage, he descended hundreds of steps into the darkness until he reached a faintly-lit passageway, leading into a vast underground temple or crypt. He turned a corner and was nearly blinded by light streaming from a huge and ancient lamp. Beneath the lamp sat a hooded figure, bent as if in concentration.

Frightened, but compelled to approach the figure, the laborer drew closer until he could no longer contain his fear. He cried out, and the hooded man turned to face him; the figure's wise and aged eyes flashed in anger as he took up a great metal rod. He brought the rod down upon the lamp with enormous strength. For a second the chamber was lit more brightly than ten suns; then all went black and a great rumbling was heard, as if something huge and powerful was moving through miles of passageways under the earth.

The rustic was never seen again, Jennings wrote, and when the opening in the earth was discovered it was supposed that he had stumbled upon a Rosicrucian sanctuary and paid dearly for his curiosity. Such tales of well-hidden and well-guarded vaults of the hidden brotherhoods, where wonders sat heaped upon wonders far underground or deep within a mountain, became a standard feature of alternative-reality lore in the latter part of the nineteenth and the early part of the twentieth centuries. Some of the stories grew ineffably bizarre. Arthur L. Bell, the founder of "Mankind United," a cult that flourished in California in the 1930s and 40s, told one prospective member that several miles under the earth's surface there lived a "race of men with metallic heads, very large to indicate their mental development," who controlled the planet's earthquakes and floods. Bell also told his followers he was the spokesman for the "International Institute of Universal Research and Administration," headquartered in subterranean laboratory-cities where super-scientists labored over mysterious devices that would stop all wars by rendering cannons, guns, and bombs useless, or placing all the world's armies into simultaneous suspended animation.

The members of these hidden brotherhoods came to be seen as the Masters—beings who are physically impressive, yet unencumbered by their physical bodies when they desire to leave them. They lack no material thing, yet need or desire no wealth. They are supremely confident and forcefully charismatic because they know—not guess about, or believe they know, or theorize about, but *know*—the secrets of the universe.

Three assumptions were implicit in the concept of a hidden group of ruling Masters: first, that the universe exists for a purpose, to fulfill a pre-determined plan in which human spiritual development is the key; second, that culture, religion, and civilization did not evolve, as secular historians would have it, within the last few thousand years, but were rather the degenerate and half-remembered scraps of a wisdom given the human race by a higher power before recorded history began, and third, that only a minority of mortals were prepared to accept the Masters' teachings, or even that the Masters exist; thus the

Masters must work for the advancement of humanity in extreme secrecy. We could not find them, but they were constantly watching us from their hidden sanctuaries.

Although these sanctuaries of the hidden brotherhoods were usually remote and well-guarded, there have always been those like Arthur L. Bell who know about the Masters' secrets, have often been invited to share in them, and have returned to tell the rest of us about them. There was one woman in particular whose knowledge was critical to the rest of this story. She revealed much to the world about the keepers of the Ancient Wisdom and their sanctuaries, and before we can investigate any further we must make a brief survey of her career.

Madame Blavatsky and the Masters

Probably no individual has had more effect on the modern alternative-reality tradition in the West than Helena Petrovna Blavatsky. Anyone with a more-than-casual interest in the occult has no doubt encountered this extraordinary woman's name many times. Few, however, have probably read more than a chapter or two of her monstrous but important works *Isis Unveiled* (1877) and *The Secret Doctrine* (1888). In these books Madame Blavatsky, or "H.P.B.," as her friends and disciples called her, first popularized many of the ideas widely held by alternative-reality enthusiasts today. She proposed that the earliest humans advanced under the guidance of extraterrestrial "wise ones," that the statuary heads of Easter Island were the remnants of a once-mighty civilization centered in the Pacific, and that there is no such thing as "coincidence." H.P.B. molded the scattered fragments of nineteenth-century occultism into a vigorous, if not quite coherent, body of dogma, and with it she loudly challenged the scientists and clergy of her day. She hated both orthodox science and orthodox religion for their cool Victorian faith in materialism and reasoned progress, and for their denial of a hidden destiny for humanity and superconscious powers in the human soul.

She was born Helena Petrovna von Hahn in 1831, the daughter of an officer in the Czar's army and a mother who was one of Russia's most popular novelists, and who died when Helena was only eleven. From the beginning Helena was a wild, headstrong child fascinated by legends and secrets. Largely ignored by her busy mother, she would disappear into the cellar or the attic to read ghost stories and fairy tales, and she frightened her brother and sister by telling them she saw forest-spirits in the trees around their home. She would leap on a horse, ride off, and visit the local "wise woman," whom everyone else in Helena's social class avoided. When Helena was sixteen, she announced that she was repulsed by the prospect of becoming a wife. "When I was young," she later wrote, "if a young man had dared to speak to me of love, I would have shot him like a dog who bit me." She thrust her leg into a kettle of boiling water to avoid attending a fancy ball.

Yet when a group of girls at a party made fun of her strangeness and laughed that not even "old General Blavatsky" (who was thirty-nine) would marry her, she walked over to him, charmed him, and a year later married him (although others believe she was forced to marry General Blavatsky against her will). She left Nikifor Blavatsky a few months later out of boredom, however, and escaped with the help of a British steamer captain to Constantinople, where she rode bareback in equestrian shows and served as a companion to elderly noblewomen. Then she met Agardi Metrovich, an aging Hungarian opera star, and became his mistress, traveling with him all over Europe. She left Metrovich in Paris and became an assistant to Daniel Dunglas Home, the famous medium, and held a few seances of her own.

She returned to her parents' home in Russia in 1858, returned for a while to General Blavatsky, and then left him again almost immediately when Metrovich came to Russia to sing. One of her cousins, Count Witte, met Helena about this time, when she was twenty-nine, and left us a description of her. Her once-handsome face, he wrote, "bore all the traces of a tempestuous and passionate life," and she had become fat and slovenly; "but her eyes were extraordinary.... When she spoke with animation, they sparkled in a fashion which is altogether indescribable. Never in my life have I seen anything like that pair of eyes."

In 1861, Helena found herself pregnant, perhaps by Metrovich and perhaps by another man. Her son, Yuri, was born near the end of the year, but he was born severely disabled and was not expected to live long. She and Yuri went with Metrovich to Italy, but after Yuri's death at the age of five, Helena and Metrovich went to Kiev. All went well until Helena began ridiculing the Governor-General of Kiev in public, and she and Metrovich were forced to leave the city in disgrace. They lived in poverty for a while until Metrovich was offered the chance to sing in Cairo. He accepted eagerly and booked passage for both of them on a steamer, the SS *Eumonia*. But on the way, in July of 1871, the boiler burst, the *Eumonia* sank, and Metrovich saved Helena's life at the expense of his own. She was picked up by a freighter and taken the rest of the way to Egypt, where she set up a spiritualist society and made a living, although not much of one, giving seances.

Helena P. Blavatsky

After she was caught manipulating a cloth "spirit arm" during a seance, she left Egypt for Europe, and made her way at last to America. In July of 1873 she landed in New York, forty-two years old and with only a few cents to her name. Like many other European immigrants in that time and place, she lived in miserable poverty for a time, using the same coffee grounds over and over, making artificial flowers, and saving what little money she was able to scrape together to buy tobacco for the cigarettes she smoked in incredible volume. But she quickly involved herself in the widespread spiritualist movement (spiritualist groups were as common in America in the 1870s as yoga and meditation groups were to be a hundred years later), and she soon latched on to Colonel Henry Olcott, a lawyer-journalist who chronicled the spiritualists for several New York dailies. Olcott was searching for something to believe in, and H.P.B. was searching for a publicist; the two soon became almost inseparable.

They spent much time discussing and investigating occult phenomena, and H.P.B. hinted that she was the key to a higher wisdom, and to the "Masters" who preserved it. One day in May of 1875, Olcott received a mysterious letter, postmarked Philadelphia (where H.P.B. was then living). Written in gold ink on thick green paper, it contained a message Henry found strange and exciting:

> FROM THE BROTHERHOOD OF LUXOR, Section the Vth to Henry S. Olcott.
>
> Brother Neophyte, we greet thee.
>
> He who seeks us finds *us*. Rest thy mind—banish all foul doubt. Sister Helen is a valiant, trustworthy servant.... She will lead thee to the Golden Gate of truth.... Brother John hath brought three of our *Masters* to look after thee.... Thy noble exertions on behalf of our cause now give us the right of letting thee know who they were: Serapis Bey; Polydorus Isurenus; and Robert More.
>
> > TUITIT BEY
> > Observatory of Luxor
> > Tuesday Morning
> > Day of Mars.

This letter, which everyone but H.P.B.'s disciples is convinced she wrote herself, marks the first appearance in print of the Masters, who were soon to become the hidden sources of all her teachings. The "Brother John" of the letter was "John King," Helena's spirit guide during her American seances. She told Olcott that John King had been visiting her while she was in trances and bringing her guidance from a distant body of "adepts." Olcott had heard, of course, of such brotherhoods before, but largely in legendary or fictional form, such as the ageless Rosicrucians of Edward Bulwer-Lytton's occult novel *Zanoni*. Now he was awestruck with the prospect of communicating with real Masters, and he begged H.P.B. to help him continue the correspondence. In the long exchange of letters that followed, Olcott grew convinced that the Master Serapis Bey was his personal guardian. He wrote of Serapis Bey often in his diary and even referred to him as "Dad" or "Daddy."

Not long after Olcott received the letter, H.P.B. described the Masters to the readers of a spiritualist newspaper, *The Banner of Light*, but only in vague and mysterious terms. She could only say "that such a body exists, and that the location of their Brotherhoods will never be revealed... until the day when Humanity shall awake." H.P.B. and Olcott soon gathered around them a small but sincere group of seekers after the Ancient Wisdom, and out of their meetings and discussions, the Theosophical Society—from the Greek "theosophy" or "God-knowledge"—was formed in September 1875 in Manhattan.

A painting of the "Master Morya" of the Theosophists.

The Society was not much of a success at first, although its members applied themselves diligently to unconventional ceremonies and experiments. When one of the Society's first sponsors died asking to be cremated, they held the United States' first cremation service. To the publicity-loving H.P.B.'s joy (and Olcott's keen embarrassment), the service was attended by a huge crowd of curiosity-seekers and was written up in the newspapers as an outrageous pagan rite. On another occasion the Theosophists attempted to determine whether levitation was caused by electrical energy by applying a pair of live wires to H.P.B.'s cat. The reluctant feline, as might be imagined, instantly rose several inches into the air, to the experimenters' delight; but the trial, as described by Olcott, came to an unhappy end. The animal "was then, in spite of my warning, electrified more powerfully; and of course, the poor cat suddenly expired." Such investigations as these were conducted to, as H.P.B. put it, "make an experimental comparison between spiritualism and the magic of the ancients."

But Madame Blavatsky saw a more important task before her—to place before the public proof that "the magic of the ancients" had indeed been fact, and that the scientists and clergy had strayed far from the path of truth. Around the time the Theosophical Society had been formed, she told Olcott that John King had instructed her to write a book to be called "Skeleton Key to Mysterious Gates." With Olcott's help (and, according to Olcott, the Masters' astral assistance), the book appeared two years later with the title *Isis Unveiled*. It was thirteen hundred pages long, and the first edition—all one thousand copies of it—sold out in ten days. The reactions of reviewers varied; some were bowled over by the sheer bulk of Ancient Wisdom it revealed, but many agreed with the reviewer of the Springfield *Republican*, who called *Isis* "a large dish of hash." After H.P.B.'s death, a dedicated anti-Theosophist scholar told the press that *Isis Unveiled* contained almost two thousand passages lifted without credit from other works, as well as seven hundred incorrect names, figures, and quotes, and six hundred easily verifiable errors of fact.

Whatever its failures, *Isis* offered something very important to the mystically-minded of the last century. In a time when many felt their place in the universe had been diminished by materialistic science in general and Darwinism in particular, when it seemed as if humanity had no destiny greater than inventing ever-more-ingenious machines, H.P.B. championed the idea of a hidden but sacred Plan for the human race. She likened the scientific community to a "squirrel upon its revolving wheel... doomed to turn their 'matter' over and over again," and she contrasted the vanity and sterility of modern materialism with the glories of past civilizations which had lived by spiritual and occult truths. "Many are those," she wrote, "who infected by the mortal epidemic of our century—hopeless materialism—will remain in doubt and mortal agony as to whether, when man dies, he will live again, although the question has been solved by long-ago generations of sages." The ancient truths were soon to be revealed again. "The whole of antiquity [will] be vindicated," she wrote; "much that is now considered fiction may yet be proved fact, and the 'facts and laws' of modern science found to belong to the limbo of exploded myths."

Desiring to be closer to the Ancient Wisdom, H.P.B. and Olcott left for India soon after *Isis* was published. They had found that the teachings of Theosophy were held in greater respect by Hindus and Buddhists than Christians (which is not surprising, since the scrappy H.P.B. spared no insult when she spoke and wrote of Christianity), and Madame Blavatsky's ideas began taking a strongly Asian point of view. Reincarnation and the doctrine of karma assumed important roles in the new Indian version of Theosophy, and the Egyptian Brotherhood of Luxor faded into the mists as the Masters headquartered themselves in the most remote reaches of Tibet. From the time she first landed in America, H.P.B. had been telling everyone in her circle that during the early 1860s (the time in which she had actually been living with Yuri and Metrovich in Italy) she had made her way secretly to Tibet to sit at the feet of the Tibetan adepts. Now the Masters of the Himalayas took center stage in Theosophical teachings.

For her followers in India—both Indians and British colonists—she "precipitated" (that is, pulled out of nowhere) numberless letters from these Tibetan Masters, particularly two named Koot Hoomi and Morya. Constantly barraged with questions about the home of these all-wise spiritual fathers, she once produced a picture of their headquarters in a hidden Himalayan valley. Nestled in a steep, tree-lined gorge, it took the form of a beautiful complex of vaguely oriental temples and towers, where the Masters lived communally in the midst of many apprentices preparing for initiation. But H.P.B. stressed that much more lay beneath the valley than within it. The earth under the buildings was honeycombed with miles of tunnels, secret chambers of all sizes, and a vast occult library containing, in astral prototype, every great artistic or literary work humanity had ever created or would ever create—which implied that every great work was inspired by the Masters in a human ready to undertake it. All the lost wisdom of the ancients was preserved in the subterranean library as well.

No one, however, could find or enter this valley if the Masters did not allow it—and they allowed it only rarely. H.P.B. hinted that in her past she had encountered "more than one Russian mystic" who had "traveled to Tibet via the Ural mountains in search of knowledge and initiation in the unknown crypts of Central Asia. And more than one returned years later, with a rich store of such information as could never have been given him anywhere in Europe." She implied that there were sanctuaries of the Ancient Wisdom beneath the sands of the Gobi Desert as well, filled with the remains of a once-mighty civilization that had been guided by the Masters. "Built deep in the bowels of the earth," she wrote, "the subterranean stores are secure; and as their entrances are concealed... there is little fear that anyone should discover them." She added that according to legend, "Bahti—hideous, but faithful gnomes—guard the hidden treasures of this prehistoric people, awaiting the day when the revolution of cyclic periods shall again cause their story to be known for the instruction of mankind."

She also wrote in *Isis Unveiled* of similar sanctuaries hidden beneath South America. Within the mountains of Peru and Bolivia, she said, ran thousands of miles of "mysterious catacombs" built under the directions of Atlantean magicians. At a later date the tunnels had been used by the Incas as concealed storehouses for their treasures. When Pizarro and his men conquered the Incas, enormous mounds of gold were sealed in the passages to prevent their seizure by the Spaniards, and there the treasure has remained to this day. H.P.B. claimed that when she was in Peru (no evidence indicates she was ever anywhere near South America), she heard about these tunnels first from a Peruvian and later from an Italian who had heard the story from a dying priest. The Italian supposedly gave her a detailed description of the passages. The entrance to one branch of the system

> was in the neighborhood of Cusco, now marked beyond discovery. This leads directly into an immense tunnel which runs from Cusco to Lima, and then, turning southward, extends into Bolivia. At a certain point it is intersected by a royal tomb. Inside this sepulchral chamber are cunningly arranged two doors; or, rather, two enormous slabs which turn upon pivots, and close so tightly as to be only distinguishable from the other portions of the sculptured walls by the secret signs, whose key is in the possession of the faithful custodians. One of these turning slabs covers the southern mouth of the Liman tunnel—the other, the northern one, of the Bolivian corridor.

If this treasure-filled Andean tunnel system sounds familiar to some readers, it should be no surprise. Erich von Däniken resurrected it successfully in 1973 for his book *The Gold of the Gods*. Although many caves have been discovered in the Andes through the years—some of which have been over-anxiously identified as entrances to this pre-Incan tunnel system—no proof has ever been uncovered for the existence of these thousand-mile tunnels.

The Stanzas of Dzyan

A few years before her death in 1891, H.P.B. wrote her greatest work, *The Secret Doctrine*, an outline of the True History of the cosmos. She claimed to have read this history in the "Stanzas of Dzyan," the oldest of all books, written in the incredibly ancient and symbolic Senzar language. The Stanzas were one of the works preserved by the Masters in their subterranean library, and only she and a few other well-chosen mortals had ever set eyes upon them. She described them in *The Secret Doctrine*'s opening lines:

> An Archaic Manuscript—a collection of palm leaves made impermeable to water, fire, and air, by some specific unknown process—is before the writer's eye. On the first page is an immaculate white disk within a dull black ground. On the following page, the same disk, but with a central point...

Out of these symbols, H.P.B. divined that both the creation of the material world and the progression of human civilizations are parts of an immensely long, complex chain of evolutionary steps out of the astral, into the material, and back into the astral again. All life, she wrote, evolved in cycles of seven—that most mystical of mystical numbers—under the direction of the *Dhyan Chohans*, seven powerful entities or "rays" that shaped and developed the universe. Humanity had to progress through seven Root Races, each with seven sub-races, before it reached perfection. In her rejection of Darwinism, H.P.B. was careful to stress that her version of evolution was both physical and spiritual. The earth and the human race had slowly jelled out of the astral together millions of years ago.

The First Root Race was almost totally astral, and first appeared in an equally astral continent, the "Imperishable Sacred Land." This land was designed by the Dhyan Chohans to "last from the beginning of humanity to the end.... It is the cradle of the first man and the dwelling of the last divine mortal." Thus the Imperishable Sacred Land still exists; H.P.B. was vague about its location, but implied it might exist at or around the North Pole. In another part of the book, she suggested that when mortals finally reached the North Pole, they would find something there that would change the course of history.

The home of the Second Root Race was near the North Pole as well; it was called Hyperborea, a huge, misty, partially-solid continent of which only pieces like Greenland and Spitzbergen remain. The Third Root Race lived in Lemuria, another huge continent filling what is now the Indian and Pacific oceans. While the first two Root Races had been amorphous since their bodies were primarily astral, the Third Root Race was primarily material and grew ever-more-human in form as its sub-races developed. By the fourth sub-race or so, the Lemurians resembled giant apes—they stood sixteen feet tall, with long arms, short legs, and eyes almost on the sides of their heads. They also lacked true sentience, for they had no souls or consciousness.

At this point, about eighteen million years ago, spiritual beings called *Kumaras*, or "princes," began entering the bodies of the Lemurians, and they brought the developing race both conscious minds and sexual reproduction (previous races and sub-races had divided in a protoplasmic fashion). Unfortunately, some of them received sex before consciousness; a group of the yet-soulless Lemurian males, carried away by their new urges, copulated with "huge she-animals.... They begat upon these dumb races... a race of crooked monsters going on all fours." As punishment, the transgressors and their offspring were denied souls by the Kumaras, and these crooked ones eventually evolved into both the apes—in H.P.B.'s neat reversal of Darwinism—and what were called in her day "the inferior races.... The world knows them as Tasmanians..., Australians, Andaman Islanders, etc." She stated that these peoples had no souls, and that there were other races, among them the Africans and Polynesians, which had only recently reached a level of development at which the Kumaras would enter their bodies.

The "monsters" fathered by the soulless Lemurians brought more misfortune to the world, for the monsters attacked and devoured the newly sentient Lemurians, and murder and sin came into the world. Although the sentient Lemurians appealed to the Chohans for help, and beings from the planet Venus, known as "the wise Serpents and Dragons of Light," came to their aid, Lemuria was doomed. Volcanoes and earthquakes broke the continent to bits, and Australia, Madagascar, and the Pacific Islands are all that remain of it today. The Serpents and Dragons of Light did help the remnants of humanity through the crisis, however, by teaching them agriculture, weaving, and other skills necessary to life in a sinful world. They also taught the most virtuous of the remaining humans the secret teachings, and these recipients of the teachings became the first Masters—the "elect custodians of the Mysteries revealed to mankind by the Divine Teachers." The Masters continued to dwell alongside their less advanced brethren, guiding them but remaining hidden from all but a few apprentices.

With the fall of Lemuria, Atlantis rose from the sea and the Fourth Root Race took the stage. Their first sub-race was the Rmoahals, a nation of black-skinned giants; the second was the Tlavatlis, a red-skinned, wandering people. The third sub-race, the Toltecs, was guided by the Masters for a time, and the Toltec empire, using occult knowledge wisely, lasted a hundred thousand years, until they abandoned the Masters' teachings. As soon as they did, they began degenerating; a secret society of evil magicians took power in Atlantis and lured the people into worshipping elemental spirits with bloody rituals. In the end the Toltecs were conquered by the barbarous Turanians (the fourth sub-race), the ancestors of the Aztecs. They were replaced in succession by the Semites, ancestors of the modern Jews, the Akkadians, who settled the lands around the Mediterranean, and the Mongolians, ancestors of the modern East Asians.

A small group of Semites traveled to Central Asia and under the direction of the Masters evolved into the Aryans, the Fifth Root Race. H.P.B. felt the Aryans were the pinnacle of creation at the time she was writing, but they were soon to be replaced as the dominant race by the Sixth Root Race, which was evolving in America. Annie Besant, H.P.B.'s successor as head of the Theosophical Society, believed the new race was developing from the most spiritual Anglo-Saxons living in Southern California. The home of the Sixth Root Race was to be a new Lemuria, due to rise out of the Pacific just west of San Diego. In another few thousand years, the Seventh Root Race was to evolve from the Sixth in the vicinity of South America and humanity would return to its starting point in the Imperishable Sacred Land, once again an astral race in an astral country. Once the earth and the human race had faded again into the non-material, the curtain would fall on the earth cycle and a new, more perfect cycle of seven would begin on the planet Mercury.

This evolutionary "hierarchy" of races was a key element of Theosophy in its early days, but even more important to the history of alternative-reality ideas in general was the notion of an endless, but hidden, succession of Masters. The Theosophical Masters were the first incarnations of those wise ones who watch over humanity, stepping in to affect history when necessary, but always guarding their privacy carefully and revealing themselves only to those mortals they considered ready to receive their teachings. The Masters in various forms have become central figures in Anglo-American occultism; today they are often extradimensional or extraterrestrial, but for most of this century they were very much of this earth, and most often hidden *within* it. Let us pay a visit to the best-known underground sanctuary of the American Masters, and a magnet for thousands of those who would be their initiates.

The mountain of the Masters

On the high plain of northernmost California stands one of the world's most beautiful peaks, Mount Shasta. In the late spring, clear of clouds and covered with snow, Shasta appears even more enormous than it is—14,162 feet high—and stands like a white beacon. Its magnificence draws thousands of hikers to its slopes every summer and thousands of skiers every winter. But it has also been a sacred mountain in the eyes of many occultists for over a century. Many believe the last descendants of the wisest Lemurians dwell within the mountain, and they call the mountain a "point of power," a place at which rays of cosmic force and earth energy converge. Groups of believers visit the mountain throughout the year, hiking, meditating, and holding ceremonies on its sides. Forest rangers in the area have cleaned up innumerable crosses of branches, symbols carved on trees and painted on rocks, ceremonial altars, and other occult paraphernalia left behind by the seekers. Many occultists have settled in Weed, Dunsmuir, and Mt. Shasta City, the three towns near the foot of the mountain.

Many stories have gathered around this sleeping volcano, some of which seem more like tall tales than legends that inspire serious belief. They are kept alive and circulating by the Mount Shasta Chamber of Commerce, which knows a good thing when it sees one. In one of the Chamber's newsletters can be found the story of two cities, Ilethelme and Yaktayvia, supposedly flourishing inside the mountain. The Yaktayvians are said to be the world's greatest bell-makers. Using the precise vibrations of their huge bells and chimes, the Yaktayvians in ancient times hollowed out the interior of the mountain, allowing the cities' construction. Both cities—which are referred to together as "The Secret Commonwealth"—are lit by the continuous ringing of bells, which vibrate "the atoms of ether in such a way as to produce light." On Shasta's northwest slope, there is also reputed to be an invisible Yaktayvian bell "made of a transparent substance that reflects no light." The wind, passing under the mouth of the bell, produces an ultra-high-frequency vibration that drives away any climber approaching the outer entrance to the Secret Commonwealth. Other bells can be heard on the wind miles from the mountain, and it is said that often people driving within the sound of the bells will suffer a stalled motor, which refuses to start again until half an hour after the bells stop ringing. "People are sometimes lost on Mt. Shasta," the story continues, "but after awhile they begin to hear the bells, and by following them, and by going in the direction from which they come, they finally arrive safely home." This whimsical tale dates back to the 1930s, at least.

Mount Shasta in midsummer.

Mount Shasta's magical reputation is very old; it existed long before any white settlers came to California. The Modoc, Shastika, and Wintun people living near the mountain considered Shasta the home of the gods, the pivot of the earth, and the pillar reaching up into the heavens and rooting down into the underworld. In those days Mount Shasta was still an active volcano; it appears to have last erupted between 1810 and 1825, just before the first white explorers arrived in 1827. One myth about Shasta—or Ieka, its original name—was collected by California writer Joaquin Miller in the last century. It communicates well the religious aura of the mountain:

The Indians say the Great Spirit made the mountain first of all. He first pushed down snow and ice from the skies through a hole which he made in the blue heavens by turning a stone round and round till he made this great mountain; then he stepped down out of the clouds on to the mountain top and descended and planted the trees all around by putting his finger on the ground. The sun melted the snow and the water ran down and nurtured the trees and made the rivers. After that he made the fish for the rivers out of the small end of his staff. He made the birds by blowing some leaves which he took from the ground among the trees. After he made the beasts out of the remainder of his stick, he made the grizzly bear out of the end, and made him master out of all the others. He made the grizzly so strong that he feared him himself and would go up to the top of the mountain out of sight of the forest to sleep at night.... Afterwards, the Great Spirit, wishing to remain on earth, and make the sea and some more land, converted Mt. Shasta by a great deal of labor into a wigwam, and built a fire in it and made a pleasant home. After that his family came down, and they all have lived in the mountain ever since; they say that before the white man came they could see the fire ascending from the mountain at night and the smoke by day, every time they chose to look at the mountain.

Shasta was the focus of other tribal beliefs as well. In the 1870s, during one of California's last Indian wars, the Modocs were inspired to battle by shamans who prophesied that their ancestors would be resurrected and come to their aid, while the earth would open and swallow the white soldiers. At the same time, one of the Shastikas announced that a crow had brought him the news that the spirits of slain Shastika warriors were hovering about the peak of Shasta, ready to swoop down and join the battle.

Many of the Indian peoples also had tales of mysterious beings living inside the mountain. Grant Towendolly, son of a chief of the Wintuns, told a Dunsmuir folklorist in 1953 that he had heard stories as a boy of a race of giants living in the mountain before the coming of the whites. The giants were called the Shupchers, and they would "waylay the Indian people, kill them and take them to their caves. The giants carried no weapons but squeezed people to death. A young Indian and his brother became local heroes when they killed one of these mighty giants and threw his body into the river, where they weighted his body down with a huge rock." Towendolly also said that the same two brothers slew another giant who lived in a cave in the shadow of the great mountain. "This cave had a subterranean passage to the top of Mt. Shasta," he said. "The boys built a fire to flush out the giant; the smoke from the fire could be seen belching forth from the the summit of Mt. Shasta." The Wintuns also believed that a race of small, invisible people lived on the mountain. Sometimes these beings could be seen for a moment before they vanished, but most often only their laughter, like the laughter of small children, was heard.

Stories like these, passing from the Indians to the white settlers, helped continue the mountain's magical reputation in the last century. But the first piece of actual alternative-reality literature dealing with the mountain was the curious occult novel *A Dweller on Two Planets; or, the Dividing of the Way*, by "Phylos the Thibetan." Its author, Frederick S. Oliver, who set down the text between 1884 and 1886—when he was still in his teens—claimed it was only being channeled through him and that it was the story of an actual Master. In his introduction, Oliver wrote that while "in sight of the inspiring peak of Mount Shasta," his mind and writing arm were seized by "Phylos... one of those mysterious persons—an adept of the arcane and occult in the universe." Oliver called Phylos's tale "absolute revelation," but it was similar in many ways to *Isis Unveiled* and Ignatius Donnelly's *Atlantis, the Antedeluvian World*, both of which had been recently published.

"Phylos" had, according to Oliver, been incarnated twice upon the earth before he became a Master. His first incarnation had been as an Atlantean miner named Zailm, who worked his way up to become a prince of the lost continent. But he ultimately fell into dishonor—and wronged the law of karma—by loving two women at once. To atone for his sin he was reincarnated in the nineteenth century as Walter Pierson, a gold miner who made a fortune on his claim near Shasta. While working his claim, Pierson met Quong, a Chinese of great charisma and personal power. Pierson felt nothing but contempt for the Chinese laborers in the mines, so he treated Quong warily until one evening when Quong tamed an attacking grizzly bear with a word and revealed himself to Pierson as one of a hidden brotherhood of mystics dwelling inside the mountain. Quong told Pierson that he had only assumed the form of a Chinese laborer but was actually a superior being; he then invited Pierson to join the order. In the middle of the night, the two men met near the mountain and entered Shasta through a concealed door in the end of a canyon. They passed into the home of the brotherhood, a *sanctum sanctorum* of great beauty:

> ... the walls, polished as by jewelers, though excavated as by giants; floors carpeted with long, fleecy fabric that looked like fur, but was a mineral product; ledges intersected by the builders, and in their wonderful polish exhibited veinings of gold, of silver, of green copper ores, and maculations of precious stones. Verily, a mystic temple...

Pierson then met the other Masters, who initiated him into the order in a turgidly mystical ceremony. Quong then placed Pierson in the care of another Master who flew Pierson to Venus in his astral body. Here Pierson learned of his previous incarnation as Zailm, and many of the secrets of the universe as well. After many chapters of characters addressing each other as "thee" and "thou," and interminable lectures on improbable revealed science, Zailm/Pierson at last became Phylos, one of the guardians of the cosmos; the "Thibetan" portion of his title seems to have been added for Mystery's sake.

A Dweller on Two Planets was not very good fiction, but it did establish all the main elements of the modern Mt. Shasta mythos. In it, a secret order of Masters lives simply in a luxurious temple inside the mountain; the story of the sinking of the lost continent from which they came is told, and the technological glories of past ages—for example Zailm takes a vacation from Atlantis in a cigar-shaped flying machine called a *vailx* that is remarkably similar to many reported UFOs—are described in wondrous detail. These are the secrets the Masters must guard until the mass of humanity is ready to receive them.

The Lemurians of Mt. Shasta

When *A Dweller on Two Planets* was published at the turn of the century, it became immediately popular with the alternative-reality community. The book made a strong impression on H. Spencer Lewis, the former publisher and advertising man who founded AMORC (Ancient Mystical Order Rosae Crucis), the group better known as The Rosicrucians who advertise in popular magazines. Under the pseudonym of Wishar Spenle Cervé—an anagram of Harve[y]

Spencer Lewis—he published *Lemuria: the Lost Continent of the Pacific* in 1931, transplanting Phylos's Atlantis to the opposite ocean.

According to Lewis, the story of the Lemurians began about 150,000 years ago. At that time, the area now occupied by the Pacific was almost filled by the enormous Lemurian continent. Since all the displaced ocean had to go somewhere, most of the rest of the earth's surface was a vast marsh. Thus Lemuria had the role of *"Cradle of the Human Race* and the original *Garden of Eden."* Lewis had read Blavatsky well; he assured us in an aside that "the earliest records indicate that man was created coincident with the creation of other living creatures, and that he was *not* a descendant from any lower species of the animal kingdom, but always of human form and expression and with dominant control over the other creatures around him." This passage is an example of why Lewis's "Rosicrucian" teachings have continued as a part of America's alternative-reality culture while those of similar groups have burst into the limelight and then died out. Lewis always wrote in a simple advertiser's prose with a clear view of his audience—people who had been brought up as traditional Christians and were dissatisfied with mainstream churches, but still held basically traditional beliefs. He skilfully blended Theosophy with enough fundamentalist Christian ideas to make concepts like reincarnation and karma palatable to a broad spectrum of Westerners.

Although humanity did not evolve in Lewis's story, he wrote that the earth began "passing through a regular and continuous program of evolutionary changes" about 100,000 years ago. "Magnetic waves" caused the western half of Lemuria to break up and sink, and the other continents began rising. Twenty-five thousand years ago Lemuria and the newly-formed North America, which had been drifting toward one another, collided at the spot where California is today. He also revealed that most of today's California had not been formed as part of North America, but was the remnant of the mountainous eastern coast of Lemuria—the only part of the lost continent that didn't sink when the two continents met. Before the collision, a party of the wisest Lemurians, seeking refuge from the impending cataclysm, journeyed eastward from their sinking cities to settle within the caverns of the mightiest peak of Lemuria—which was, of course, Mt. Shasta. There they have remained, secretly, to this day.

The Lemurians Lewis described would not have been difficult to spot in a crowd. They averaged seven feet in height, with larger heads, longer arms, higher foreheads, and shorter legs; they were not too different from H.P.B.'s sentient Lemurians of the Third Root Race. Their hair was short and thin on top of their heads, but long and thick in back and on the sides, and it "was often arranged in very fancy forms across the shoulders or down the back." But their most interesting anatomical feature was a growth in the center of their foreheads, about an inch and a half above the bridge of the nose and looking something like a flesh-covered walnut. This growth was their "third eye," an organ alluded to in *The Secret Doctrine*; it was used to receive sensory impressions at a great distance and for mental telepathy. The third eye was the result of centuries of "sustained development" on the part of the Lemurians. At the height of their civilization, they used the third eye to learn all that could be known about the astral and material universes, all of human history—past, present, and future—and all about the life to come (they knew they were to be reincarnated). After Lemuria vanished into the depths of the Pacific, most of its people scattered and succeeding generations lost the third eye and the knowledge it had given them. The only members of the race retaining its powers at the highest pitch were those few groups hiding in a handful of remote retreats, and Shasta was one of the most important of them.

The existence of the Lemurian colony within Shasta became an important part of AMORC's teachings in the 1930s. While doing research in the Shasta area, I was told by two long-time residents that during the decade, the Rosicrucians sent several exploring parties from their San Jose headquarters to the slopes of Shasta to search for the secret entrance to the colony. One of the first of these parties spent most of the fall of 1930 combing the mountainsides for some clue to its location, but without success. Such setbacks didn't dampen the searchers' enthusiasm; in fact, the Shasta myth boomed after publication of Lewis's book, fed by the stories he told:

> Many years ago it was quite common to hear stories whispered in Northern California about the occasional strange looking persons seen to emerge from the forests and the dense growth of trees in that region, and who would run back into hiding when discovered or seen by anyone. Occasionally one of these oddly dressed individuals would come to one of the smaller towns and trade nuggets or gold dust for some modern commodities. These odd-looking persons were not only peculiar in their dress and different in attire from any costume ever seen on the American Indian, and especially the California Indian, but distinctive in features and complexion; tall, graceful, and agile, having the appearance of being what one would term *foreigners*, but with larger heads, much larger foreheads, headdresses that had a special decoration that came down over the center of the forehead to the bridge of the nose, and thus hid or covered a part of the forehead that many have attempted to see and study.

Lewis also told of mysterious lights seen on the sides of Shasta, silhouetting strange figures performing ritual dances, and sounds of chanting and weird, beautiful music carried down the mountain by the wind. Curious folk who tried approaching the source of the lights and music were invariably turned away by "a strange and peculiar set of vibrations or invisible energy" that "would seem to emanate toward the investigator and force him to remain fixed in his position." Once struck by the vibrations, the luckless explorer had no choice but to head back down the mountain. One Frater Selvius, writing in the May 1931 issue of *Rosicrucian Digest*, noted that "many testify to having seen the strange boat, or boats, which sail the Pacific Ocean, and then rise at its shores and sail through the air to drop again in the vicinity of Shasta." He added that the boat "has neither sails nor smoke-stacks."

Stories like these circulated primarily among the occultists themselves, and then among the citizens of Weed, Dunsmuir, and Mt. Shasta City, who suddenly found themselves selling groceries and renting rooms to seekers after the mysterious colony. The general public read of the myth in a sensational article that appeared in the *Los Angeles Times*'s Sunday magazine for May 22, 1932. Edward Lanser, its author, wrote that while bound from Los Angeles to

Portland on the *Shasta Limited*, he woke before dawn and went up to the train's observation platform to watch the sunrise. As he looked out at Mt. Shasta in the distance, Lanser suddenly saw the whole southern slope of the mountain "ablaze with a strange, reddish-green light." He thought at first it was a forest fire, but there was no smoke. After breakfast he asked the conductor about the weird light. "His answer," Lanser wrote, "was short but enticing.

"'Lemurians,' he said. 'They hold ceremonials up there.'"

On his return from Portland, Lanser stopped for a while in Siskiyou County to discover what he could about the Lemurians. In Weed, he found the existence of the hidden colony was accepted by just about everyone. "Business men, amateur explorers, officials and ranchers in the country surrounding Shasta speak freely of the Lemurian community, and all attested to the weird rituals that are performed on the mountain side at sunset, midnight and sunrise." When Lanser proposed a climb up to the Lemurian village, "they freely ridiculed my avowed trek into the sacred precincts, assuring me that an entrance was as difficult and forbidden as is an entrance into Tibet."

Lanser, like Lewis, said that he heard that the Lemurians were often seen in the area; sometimes they were fleetingly glimpsed in the forests, but never for long. "They possess the uncanny secret knowledge of the Tibetan masters and, if they desire, can blend themselves into their surroundings and vanish," he wrote. But again as in Lewis's book, they did venture into the towns, bearing large gold nuggets to purchase specific supplies. The Lemurians reportedly bought sulfur and salt in huge quantities, and carried off large gobs of lard in transparent bladders they brought with them. The local merchants were always glad to see them, for the gold nuggets they traded were always worth much more than the value of the merchandise. Some of Lanser's informants, it appeared, believed the Lemurians were concealing an enormous vein of gold within the mountain.

He also claimed that one man had successfully penetrated the Lemurians' wall of secrecy—"no less an authority than the eminent scientist, Prof. Edgar Lucien Larkin, for many years director of the Mt. Lowe Observatory in Southern California." Lanser wrote that Larkin, armed with a powerful telescope, had stationed himself on a promontory overlooking a Lemurian village, and had watched them as long as he dared. His telescope revealed "a great temple in the heart of the mystic village—a marvelous work of carved marble and onyx, rivaling in beauty and architectural splendor the magnificence of the temples of Yucatan." Larkin counted nearly a thousand Lemurians living there, hidden in a lush glen tucked into the slopes of Shasta. Larkin somehow also learned that the weird lights and the chanting were parts of a ceremony celebrating the escape of the ancient Lemurians from their sinking continent and their safe settlement in "Guatama," which he said was the Lemurian name for America.

Lanser seems to have written the article with his tongue in his cheek; by the 1930s all parts of Shasta (the outer parts, at least) had been thoroughly explored, by airplane as well as by foot; he also concluded that the "really incredible thing" about the Shasta Lemurians was their ability to resist the neon signs and hot dogs of modern civilization. Anyone who did a little research would also quickly discover that Professor Edgar Lucien Larkin, Lanser's major source on the ways of the Lemurians, was hardly an "eminent scientist." Larkin was in fact a rather woolly-brained occultist who had died in 1924, eight years before Lanser's article appeared. Larkin's "Mt. Lowe Observatory" was not in any sense a scientific institution, but a tourist attraction operated by the Pacific Electric Railway in the mountains just northeast of Los Angeles, near the well-known Mount Wilson Observatory. The railway paid Larkin to point his not-very-impressive telescope at the moon, Mars, or the rings of Saturn and show them to tourists.

Edgar Lucien Larkin

Larkin authored several alternative-reality works with titles like *Radiant Energy* and *Within the Mind Maze,* as well as a newspaper column on mystical subjects for the Hearst papers. In one of his 1913 columns he described how he had read *A Dweller on Two Planets* with the absolute certainty that it was the truth, and in another he told of his discovery of the Lemurian village by telescope, although from an observatory.

Larkin's story was one of those that Lewis used to corroborate his thesis in *Lemuria: the Lost Continent of the Pacific,* and the perceptive reader who first peruses Lewis's 1931 book and then Lanser's 1932 article would probably be correct to assume that the latter—except for Lanser's "own role" in the story— had been lifted almost entirely from the former. Yet Lanser's story was seized upon eagerly by lost-continent enthusiasts as further evidence of the Lemurians' existence. Lewis included Lanser's "experiences" in the 1935 second edition of *Lemuria.* Even a fairly level-headed lost continent scholar like folklorist Lewis Spence, in his *The Problem of Lemuria* (1932), thought Lanser's tale worthy of consideration. The legend of the Shasta Lemurians continued growing and changing, built largely over one layer of wishful thinking over another, and more was to come.

The violet-blue eyes of Saint Germain

In 1934 Guy Warren Ballard, using the pseudonym Godfré Ray King, added to the mythos with the publication of his first book, *Unveiled Mysteries.* Born in Kansas in 1878, Ballard worked until 1930 or so as a mining engineer and promoter with a dubious reputation; science-fiction writer L. Sprague de Camp has written that Ballard "graduated from selling stock in imaginary gold mines to old ladies, into occultism." Ballard pored over the Theosophical and Rosicrucian writings in public libraries, joined a group of spiritualists, and married a medium, but his "enlightenment" did not come until 1930, when he was

52. *Unveiled Mysteries* is the story of this enlightenment, and his meeting with the greatest of the Masters of Shasta.

Guy W. Ballard at the height of his influence in the 1930s.

In the summer of 1930, Ballard wrote, he was working with a mining company near the mountain. He had long been aware of the mountain's reputation, so on his day off, he decided to climb the peak, asking God to direct his path. When he stopped at a spring for lunch, he felt an electrical charge pass through his body, and he turned to see a young man "who, at first glance, seemed someone on a hike like myself." But the young man asked Ballard for his cup, filled it with a strange creamy liquid, and handed it back to Ballard, who drank it. "While the taste," Ballard continued, "was delicious, the electrical vivifying effect in my mind and body made me gasp with surprise." The young man told him he had filled the cup with "Life—Omnipresent Life," and he asked Ballard to sit down:

> I did as he requested and in perhaps a few minutes, I saw his face, body, and clothing become the living breathing tangible "Presence" of the Master, Saint Germain, smiling at my astonishment and enjoying my surprise.
> He stood there before me—a Magnificent God-like figure—in a white jeweled robe, a Light and Love sparkling in his eyes that revealed and proved the Dominion and Majesty that are his.

This encounter was the first of many Ballard was to have with Saint Germain (the Comte de Saint-Germain was a notorious eighteenth century occultist who, it was rumored, had discovered the secret of eternal life; H.P.B. identified him as one of the Tibetan Masters). After Ballard proved his faith and courage when he tamed a hungry panther by looking into the animal's eyes with Love—in a scene very similar to Quong's taming of the grizzly in *A Dweller on Two Planets*—Saint Germain whisked him off astrally to one of the Masters' sanctuaries, two thousand feet beneath the Grand Tetons of Wyoming. Here, in a magnificent maze of gold-and-onyx-lined corridors and chambers, again like those in Oliver's book, Ballard was led to a vast subterranean library filled with containers of strange spindles. These spindles were wound with golden ribbons that behaved not unlike videotape, containing the complete history of the universe and the "Cosmic Divine Plan" for humanity that the Masters were to carry out. The sub-Teton chambers also held great mounds of gold brought from the sinking of Atlantis and ready to be released into the outer world when the right cosmic moment arrived. "No one in the world," Saint Germain told Ballard, "ever accumulated a great amount of wealth, without the assistance and radiation of some Ascended Master.... It is we who really govern the wealth of the world, and use it as a test of the soul strength of the individual."

In other out-of-body trips, Ballard was taken to see scenes from his past incarnations. Whether as a priest of ancient Egypt, a prince of the Incas, or even as George Washington, Ballard was always a model of enlightened spirituality and correct behavior, and in all of them, he worked closely with previous incarnations of his wife and son, as well as with Saint Germain himself. The Master also showed him the hidden, and carefully preserved, remains of a mighty civilization buried under the mud of the Amazon River, one in which the virtuous citizens were tall and golden-haired, with eyes of "violet-blue." He showed Ballard the underground treasure-houses of the Incas and carried him back in time to the days when the Incas were ruled by a caste of righteous, blond, "violet-blue"-eyed kings (the Inca people themselves were new souls on the material plane and spiritually undeveloped; they were dark-skinned and dark-haired).

The concluding scene of *Unveiled Mysteries* was a great convention of the Masters in the sanctuary beneath the Tetons. Saint Germain gave a short concert on the organ, after which twelve beautiful Masters (both male and female) from the planet Venus—all with "violet-blue" eyes—were hailed by the group. All at the gathering looked forward to the coming of the "Golden Crystal Age" upon the earth. In the next century, Saint Germain said, "the sinister force attempting to create chaos and destruction throughout the world, will be completely destroyed. When that is accomplished the mass of humanity will turn to the 'Great God Presence' within each heart and also governing the universe." The United States would lead the world in every way imaginable.

Unveiled Mysteries was followed quickly by a sequel, *The Magic Presence*. This more ambitious work followed Ballard and a group of virtuous souls on a spiritual odyssey through a series of caverns in Colorado, Arabia, Egypt, and India to receive instructions from Saint Germain and other Ascended Masters, while battling a group of Communist Sinister Forces in Washington and Paris. The outcome of the battles was never in doubt, for as soon as Saint Germain appeared and glared at them, the Sinister Forces threw their hands up in defeat and were led away meekly in handcuffs. In *The Magic Presence* Saint Germain also revealed much about the realms inside the earth. Deep within the Colorado cavern, he showed Ballard and friends a marvelous radio that received broadcasts not only from the surface world, but from other planets and the cities far beneath the earth's crust as well. When the radio operator tuned into the special "low" frequencies, he was able to speak with a Master with an appropriately deep voice dwelling hundreds of miles below them:

> This is Pelleur. It is interesting and encouraging to know, there are those on the earth's surface who have some idea... that God-Beings can and do exist within the interior of the earth. We think we have less to contend with than you, for we do not have extremes of temperature, nor seasons of heat and cold.... Our climate is very delightful, like that of the semi-tropics on earth.... We have what might be called the "Eternal Sun of Even Pressure." This produces an atmosphere that is always of equal pressure and harmonious to all who live within it.

Saint Germain added that those who think the center of the earth was "a mass of fire" were completely wrong: "Self-conscious individual beings" who had spent "many cycles of work" had learned to master the "fire element" within the planet to render the interior habitable and "accomplish the fulfillment of the Divine Plan for that part of the earth."

In *Unveiled Mysteries*, Ballard called the Masters "wholly Pure, Perfect, All-powerful beings who never make a mistake," and the powers he attributed to them in *The Magic Presence* were miraculous. In one scene Saint Germain cured a hopelessly disabled girl in about a minute; in another, one Master drew a cloak of invisibility around the car he and Ballard were riding in to deceive the Sinister Forces. Even small things were marvels; the food Saint Germain pulled out of the air for his students was always delicious and completely unlike anything in the outer world. When the meal ended, the plates vanished and reappeared clean for dessert, scrubbed spotless by special vibrations. Saint Germain never tired of saying that all these wonders would be humanity's one day very soon, after our race abandoned vicious thoughts and learned to become one with the great power of the cosmos, the "Mighty 'I AM' Presence."

It is difficult to imagine books more pretentious or disagreeably pious than Ballard's; yet they are not without their attraction. The idea of a body of all-wise and omnipotent Masters who watch and guide us is alluring in an age when the screws holding the world together seem dangerously loose. Even as I chuckled over the excesses of Ballard's prose, I felt myself wishing the Masters were real. Who couldn't stand a little loving care and guidance from a Perfect Being one could sit down and talk to?

This desire for the guidance of the Masters on the part of many ordinary people made Guy Ballard and his wife Edna astoundingly successful in attracting followers during the years between 1934 and Ballard's death in 1939. Bearing the title of "Accredited Messengers" of the Masters, the Ballards and their son Donald traveled the United States preaching the coming of the "Golden Crystal Age" to thousands of Americans. In a short time the Ballards' cult—"The 'I AM' Activity"—surrounded itself in a controversial mystique like that surrounding the Scientologists and the Unification Church today; the Ballards might be seen, in fact, as the spiritual parents of L. Ron Hubbard and Sun Myung Moon. The Ballards used a multi-sensory approach to indoctrinating their followers. They toured the country in a cream-colored Cadillac towing Edna's concert harp. Ballard was obsessed with the mystical values of colors, particularly pinks, blues, and violets. At each public appearance, he wore a pastel suit and shoes, and Edna, who came to dominate the meetings as time went on, wore striking jewels and evening dresses. *Time* magazine described the "I AM" Activity in 1938:

> Like many other psychological religionists, devotees of the Mighty I AM Presence believe in self-improvement. Like Mormons, they abstain from alcohol, narcotics, tobacco. They also abjure onions and garlic, feeling that their odors are repugnant to the Ascended Masters to whom they pray. Furthermore, they do not keep pets in their houses. People who follow these precepts and live an "I AM Presence-like life" are called "Hundred Percenters." Meeting in I AM reading rooms and auditoriums—of which there are five in California, two in Florida, others in Seattle, Chicago, Philadelphia—these Hundred Percenters pray together, believe their group prayers are more powerful than single ones.
>
> Mr. & Mrs. Ballard and Son Donald sell their followers pins, I AM rings ($12), phonograph records of the discourses of the Accredited Messengers (also harp solos by Mrs. Ballard), and pictures in all sizes of St. Germain, of Jesus Christ. Pictures of the Mighty I AM Presence, showing two figures, the upper one of which emits rays of light, loom large in the cult's meditative meetings. Such pictures, garishly colored, may cost the faithful as much as $15. Originally Mr. & Mrs. Ballard and Son Donald declined to accept money from people who attended. After they hit their stride holding I AM meetings, however, the meetings have burgeoned with ushers in white, microphones, colored charts and pictures to illustrate the theology of the I AM Presence.... They now hand out envelopes labeled I AM, Love Gift, and explain that they no longer deny to their followers the right to make contributions.

At the meetings, a master of ceremonies would lead the audience in song, after which the Ballards would call upon the "Great God Presence" in each of them to fill them with love and power. They told them that the coming age would bring the Masters out of their subterranean retreats to walk among the faithful. Mount Shasta, one of the retreats, hummed in preparation; many I AM devotees saw "flying boats" like those of the Rosicrucians entering and leaving the mountain on mysterious errands.

But for teachers urging love and virtue, the Ballards had powerfully intolerant streaks when it came to those they saw as tools of the Sinister Forces. Surrounded by the faithful in a room filled with colored light, they led them in ceremonies of "blasting" or "decrees," directed at unbelievers, labor agitators, Communists, and anyone else who didn't stand totally behind America and the I AM Activity. Waving his arms, Ballard would shout:

"Everyone who opposes the Light, silence them forever!"

The devotees responded, "Annihilate!"

"Anyone who stands against me, I shall blast his carcass to pieces!"

"Annihilate!"

The I AM Activity collected many hundreds of thousands of dollars in Love Gifts during meetings, and by 1939, the Ballards claimed a world membership of 400,000 and set up an impressive headquarters in Chicago. But Guy Ballard's death, on December 29 of that year, nearly shattered the movement. Like the Koreshans had with Cyrus Teed, many of Ballard's devotees had long expected that he would, instead of dying, ascend into heaven with a flash of light to join the Masters; Ballard himself claimed in 1938 he would not die before his Ascension. Unable to accept Edna Ballard's assurances that her husband had indeed ascended—she told her followers that "Our Blessed Daddy Ballard made his Ascension last night at twelve o'clock from the Royal Teton Retreat, and is now an Ascended Master," but his death notice, listing his death of heart disease in Los Angeles, appeared in the newspapers that afternoon—many believers left the fold. In 1940, Edna and Donald Ballard, with several of the other I AM leaders, were indicted for obtaining money under false pretenses, and during the rather messy trial, the membership shrank even more. But the Supreme Court acquitted the leaders, and the remnants of the cult, primarily the "Hundred Percenters," withdrew into their remaining temples.

Edna Ballard also established the I AM Youth Foundation near Mt. Shasta City in the forties on a large piece of land her husband had bought for that purpose. The citizens of Mt. Shasta City were not particularly happy about the influx of I AM devotees, and for more than a decade the two groups regarded each other coldly. The I AM folk erected "No Trespassing" signs all over their property, and the townspeople circulated rumors about the secret rituals that went on in those buildings so far from the road, as well as on the slopes of the mountain. There were tales of invocations of violet spirits and pagan gods—shocking behavior in that time and place.

Early in the history of the I AM Activity, the Ballards had discovered that their teachings had been much easier to accept once Jesus Christ had been included in the doctrine as an Ascended Master, so in 1955 Edna Ballard decided that the best way the I AM devotees could end the conflict with the local people would be to present a pageant of the life of Christ. She intended to demonstrate that the I AM followers had nothing but respect for God and Country, and she appears to have succeeded. Relations improved markedly afterwards, and the pageant is still performed every August, attracting hundreds of visitors to Mt. Shasta City's hotels and restaurants.

I attended the 1979 I AM pageant, presented in an outdoor amphitheater with an imposing view of the mountain. Edna Ballard, who wrote and directed the original pageant, had died in 1971, but the movement appeared to be going strong. Although the amphitheater was almost full, I overheard several of the devotees, who favored spotless white clothing, remark that attendance was down due to that year's gasoline shortage. The audience sat attentively in the hot sun for four hours to see Jesus revealed as the greatest of the Ascended Masters. Attended by a throng of blonde angels in violet robes, he traveled from scene to scene, instantly converting everyone he met to the power of the Love of the Great God Self. The entire presentation was so focused upon demonstrating the power of Love that the most potent episodes of Christ's life were left out—there was no King Herod, no Judas, and no Crucifixion. But the conclusion of the pageant was truly impressive. Christ climbed a hill at the rear of the stage, said goodbye to the crowd below, and began slowly ascending the side of a pine tree (actually, I was told, a concealed elevator) and vanished near its top in a flash of light. We were given to understand that thus did Jesus join the other Ascended Masters, and he was now waiting for us to live by his teachings and join him on a higher plane. After the Ascension, two clean-cut devotees marched out to the elevator carrying American flags, and as the cast and audience sang *America*, the flags rose to the top of the tree to symbolize the ultimate triumph of America in the divine plan.

I found it interesting that the actor portraying Christ was tall and particularly Nordic-looking, with long reddish-gold hair. I was, alas, too far away to determine whether he had "violet-blue" eyes.

Chapter 8

The Shaver Mystery

> And as they grew mis-shapen in body, they had grown in knowledge
> and cleverness, and were now able to do things no mortal could see the
> possibility of. But as they grew in cunning, they grew in mischief, and
> their great delight was in every way they could think of to annoy the
> people who lived in the open-air-story above them.
> —George MacDonald, *The Princess
> and the Goblin*

The attainment of the North and South Poles ended forever,
in most people's minds, the possibility that Symmes's "Golden Secret" might
still be uncovered. The completeness of the globe—which until then had been a
fairly certain educated guess—was now proven, and it allowed no room for
holes a few thousand miles across into which a ship might accidentally sail or
the sun could shine.

The completed sphere also changed the image of what the inhabitants of
the inner world might be like. During the "classical" phase of the hollow-earth
theory—which began with Edmond Halley's article in the *Philosophical
Transactions* and ended with Marshall B. Gardner's *Journey to the Earth's Interior*—the "Internals" had usually been imagined, if they were described at all,
as a race of happy, exploitable natives. Symmes, Lyon, Reed, and Gardner each
imagined himself as a new Columbus, opening a vast new territory to explore,
colonize, and capitalize upon. All four were Americans living in a time in
which the British, French, and Germans sat on great colonial empires in India,
Africa, and Southeast Asia, and they were anxious to see the United States obtain an empire of its own and win the envy and respect of the Europeans.
Given the cultural superiority complex of the West at that time, it was "sensible"
to view the inner-world people as simple savages. If the Americans could but
set foot in the inner world, they suggested, the Internals would have no choice
but to submit to the sovereignty of the United States.

But the discovery of the poles changed all that. So did the blossoming of
science fiction into the wildest form of popular literature. The time between the
World Wars was the time of the "pulp," the cheap newsprint story magazine,
and the science fiction pulps—*Astounding Stories, Science Wonder Stories, Captain
Future, Amazing Stories*, and many others—sold hundreds of thousands of
copies a month. They had great appeal, particularly to adolescent and pre-adolescent boys and young men, with their lurid full-color covers of bullet-shaped
spaceships and giant doodlebugs from Mars drooling at semi-clad spacewomen.
Along with the need that exists in every era for fast-action, escapist fiction, the
pulp science fiction story reflected the anticipation most Americans felt at the
promises held out by a booming technology. Science fiction is the genre of liter-

ature most concerned with technology's potential to help and to harm, and with new discoveries—television, helicopters, miracle drugs—announced in each new issue of *Life* or *Popular Science*, the pulp story served as a telescope looking into the future. But this telescope had a fun-house mirror for a lens, examining all the crazy possibilities of technology. Pulp fans loved the idea of a technology that could produce anything—travel by teleportation, mind-reading machines, robot lovers for the lonely, or a quadrupled lifespan. Yet there was always an uneasiness to confronting the new and strange, whether it be a Martian or a personal helicopter. What would happen if a master computer or robot or super-weapon fell into the wrong hands, or what if we became too dependent on machines and the machines revolted or failed us? If we met a superior race of aliens, what would keep them from conquering us and keeping us as a race of domestic animals or slaves? These ideas are cliches today, but in the 1920s and 1930s they were largely unexplored territory.

The wonderful new questions raised by a flourishing technology and the pulp science fiction story, as well as the notion of subterranean Masters transplanted from alternative-reality literature, transformed the Internals into something quite different from a race of simple savages. Where the inner world had been painted as a virginal Eden awaiting the inward march of "the Anglo-Saxon race," it soon became an empire of ineffably wise and technologically superior beings who, for humanity's own good, made certain that any surface explorer who stumbled into their realm never left alive. The Internals became UFO pilots who flew regular patrols over the surface world to keep an eye on us. This transformation was grasped eagerly and embroidered upon by a new generation of alternative-reality writers, but it was largely the work of one man: Raymond A. Palmer, who became the editor of *Amazing Stories* in 1938.

The trickster of the pulps

One day I hope someone will write a full-length biography of Ray Palmer, the editor of a colorful menagerie of science-fiction and alternative-reality magazines over a forty-year career—*Amazing Stories, Fate, Other Worlds, Flying Saucers*, and maybe a dozen more. He almost singlehandedly created the myth of UFOs as extraterrestrial visitors; he promoted many of the earliest "flying saucer" sightings, and he started the stories of a government "cover-up" of UFO reports. Palmer was the P.T. Barnum of alternative-reality promoters; he enjoyed playing verbal sleight-of-hand with an uneasy public waiting to have its uneasiness about the universe manifested, and they purchased millions of his magazines when he did. P.W. Fairman, one of his colleagues in the science-fiction business, wrote of him in 1952: "In these times of drab and unconvincing falsehood, there is still something to be thankful for. A Palmer promotion has the touch of genius. It has zing, sparkle, and true showmanship. It can be spotted a mile away by the bright lights. The thing to do is sit back and enjoy it."

Like most tricksters, Palmer was a bit of an egomaniac and loved to write about himself. In numberless articles of the "From the Editor's Desk" variety, he described in loving detail his struggles to bring before the public the *facts* about whatever mystery he was then promoting. Along the way he told his readers quite a lot about his life.

He was born in Milwaukie on the first of August, 1910. He once wrote that he had a vivid memory of being held at the window to see Halley's comet when he was one month old (when an indignant reader wrote him that the comet was not visible after July, Palmer replied in effect: Who knows? Perhaps I saw it psychically from my mother's womb). He also claimed that he read the entire newspaper daily at the age of four and sixteen library books a day when he was a teenager. But Palmer's early life was tragic. When he was seven, a butcher's truck ran him over and cracked one of his vertebrae. Over the next two years, pressure on his spine increased until he could neither stand up straight nor walk. The doctors performed a spinal graft operation on him, and it appeared successful, Palmer wrote, until that night:

> ...infection set in, and by morning the damage was irreparable. The graft had loosened, I had slumped down in bed until my spine was bent, and any attempt to straighten it would mean my death. I was given twenty-four hours to live, the infected and now open wound exposing my spine was painted with iodine (what agony!) and I was strapped down immovably.

Palmer lived, but he was permanently disabled. He grew up a hunchback, and was never completely free of pain. As an adult he stood four feet eight inches tall. He was hospitalized several more times in his teens and early twenties, and while bedridden he developed an obsessive appetite for science fiction. He read all the novels of Wells and Verne, and every pulp he was able to find; it wasn't long before he began writing science fiction himself. In 1926, when he was sixteen, one of his stories was accepted and published in *Science Wonder Stories*. He was determined to see his name in print again.

Ray Palmer in the mid-fifties.

He submitted his second story a hundred times—and had it rejected ninety-nine times. The next year he swore that he would one day become the editor of *Amazing Stories*, his favorite pulp. Over the next eleven years he wrote hundreds of stories at night—mostly stirring tales of virility for pulps like *Scarlet Adventures* and *True Gang Life*, with a little science fiction thrown in— while he worked days as a bookkeeper for a Milwaukie sheet-metal firm. He also wrote countless fan letters to *Amazing*, and in 1938, just after his twenty-eighth birthday, Ziff-Davis, *Amazing*'s publisher, offered him the editor's chair.

Palmer achieved almost instant success at the magazine by stressing straight, fast-action science fiction, and by keeping his writers very busy; he was known as "the little Napoleon" around the Ziff-Davis offices. While commissioning authors to turn out ten or twenty thousand words a month, he invited them over for frequent poker games (at which he was suspected, but never accused, of cheating), and he even organized an *Amazing Stories* bowling league. He negotiated a contract with Ziff-Davis which gave him a percentage of the magazine's profits as salary—at a time when most pulp editors earned twenty or thirty dollars a week—and he proceeded to raise *Amazing*'s circulation so much that he took home more money than the publisher's vice-president.

One day in September of 1943, *Amazing Stories* received a letter that changed both Palmer's career and the magazine's. Palmer wrote that

> a letter came in giving the details of an "ancient alphabet" that "should not be lost to the world;" it was opened by my managing editor, Howard Browne, who read it with typical orthodox attitude, and tossed it into the wastebasket with the comment: "The world sure is full of crackpots!"
>
> Even through the intervening wall I heard his remark, and the word "crackpot" drew me like a magnet.... I retrieved the letter from the wastebasket, examined the alphabet, made a few casual experiments with a dictionary, then a few more casual experiments. I went about the office to those who were familiar with other languages than English, and came up with a few more interesting results. That was enough. I published that letter in *Amazing Stories*.
>
> The results made publishing history...

The letter was indeed strange and unlikely to inspire confidence in an "orthodox" soul. It began, "Sirs: Am sending you this in the hopes you will insert in an issue to keep it from dying with me. It would arouse a lot of discussion. Am sending you the language so that some time you can have it looked at by some one in the college or a friend who is a student of antique time. This language seems to me to be definite proof of the Atlantean legend."

It hardly seemed proof of anything, but it was an odd code-alphabet. "A," for example, meant Animal, "B" existence ("To be"), "C" meant "Con. To see. (Con: to understand.)" Good and evil were symbolized by the letters "T" (which stood for integration and was "the true origin of the cross symbol") and "D" ("Detrimental, disintegrant energy"), respectively. The letter was signed by one S. Shaver of Barto, Pennsylvania, who felt the alphabet "should be saved and placed in wise hands. I can't, will you? It really has immense significance and will perhaps put me right in your thoughts again if you will really understand this. I need a little encouragement."

By itself, the letter as published might have appeared the product of a deluded and barely literate mind, but Palmer appended to it a sober invitation to the readers to try it for themselves:

> We present this interesting letter concerning an ancient language with no comment, except to say that we applied the letter-meaning to the individual letters of many old root words and proper names and got an amazing "sense" out of them. Perhaps if readers interested were to apply his formula to more of these root words, we will be able to discover if

the formula applies.... Is this really a case of racial memory, and is this formula the basis of one of the most ancient languages on Earth? The mystery intrigues us very much. — ED.

Palmer undoubtedly meant the whole thing as an experiment in attracting reader response, and the response was astounding. Hundreds of readers wrote in to tell him they had tried the alphabet, and it had worked! Palmer was certain now he was on to something hot, so he sent a letter to the mysterious S. Shaver asking for more information. Shaver replied with a ten-thousand-word letter, "typed," as Palmer described it later, "with what was certainly the ultimate non-ability at the typewriter," and emblazoned with the title "A Warning to Future Man." He revealed his full name, Richard S. Shaver, and told Palmer he was anxious to see his "Warning" published in *Amazing* as soon as possible. He didn't know how much longer he was to live and he wanted to warn humanity of the terrible dangers it faced.

Palmer read the entire manuscript—which was just as jumbled as the first letter had been, if not worse—and he decided he had a gold mine on his hands. "I put a clean piece of paper into my typewriter," Palmer wrote later, "and using Mr. Shaver's strange letter-manuscript as a basis, I wrote a 31,000-word story which I entitled 'I Remember Lemuria!' (complete with exclamation mark)." The story was published in the March 1945 issue, and all copies promptly sold out. Palmer introduced it as a true story, taken from Shaver's "racial memory," and gave the author's credit to Shaver alone. Soon letters began pouring into the Ziff-Davis offices again; readers wanted to know more about Shaver and his memories of Lemuria. Some of them claimed to have memories of Lemuria themselves.

"I Remember Lemuria!" is a strange story, as were almost all the Shaver stories, rewritten by Palmer or not. It is full of quirky obsessions and bizarre sexuality, which will be best understood after a synopsis of Shaver's personal mythology:

Over twelve thousand years ago, according to Shaver, the earth was populated by a race of mighty beings who had traveled from a distant planet to settle here. They were known as both "Titans" and "Atlans," the latter name taken from Atlantis, their first earthly home. The Titans had lifespans of thousands of years, remaining youthful and constantly growing; a mature Titan might stand three hundred feet tall. They were far more intelligent and technologically sophisticated that modern humans. They communicated by thought transference, and their scientists had discovered energies that could power spaceships at the speed of light. The Titans were also genetic engineers; they bred new races of beings to perform manual labor for them. One of the races they bred became our ancestors, but others had six arms to operate complex machinery, or sported horns and hoofs, or were half-human and half-serpent. Shaver claimed these races survived in our racial memories as the many-armed gods of Hinduism and the satyrs of Greek mythology. He called all these artificial races "robot races," not because they were machines but because they were under the mental control of the Titans, who used a device called a *telaug*—short for *tele-pathic aug*mentor—to enforce their wills.

The scientists of this super-race discovered one day that the sun had begun to change; it had started hurling radioactive rays into space that were poisoning the earth's atmosphere. The sun's radiation, absorbed into the air and drinking water, was causing the Titans to age prematurely. Their race appeared doomed if it remained on the surface, so the Titans went underground, constructing huge cave-cities, using natural caverns as the entrances. Over millenia, the cavern network grew enormous, and eventually its area totaled more than twice the land area of the surface. "More than *fifty billion* people inhabited the caves," Shaver wrote, "their civilization of such mechanical and scientific perfection that it was almost impossible to comprehend. Everything was done by machines built of metals almost imperishably built to last for tens of thousands of years.... Marvelous energies performed almost every miracle conceivable."

But even moving underground proved unsuccessful. The entire planet had become contaminated, and many of the Titans aged and died after only a few hundred years. Finally the Titan elders reached a decision—they must leave the earth as soon as possible, travel to a planet near an uncontaminated sun, and resettle there.

Unfortunately, there weren't enough spacecraft to transport all the Titans, plus all the robot races, to a new planet; nor, due to the great distance between the earth and the planet they had chosen as their new home, would they be able to return for all of them. So many of the robots were left behind to fend for themselves; those who became our ancestors returned to the surface, adjusted to the sun's radiation, and after many generations forgot about the caves beneath them. But many other robots remained in the cavern cities. They were shielded from some of the detrimental rays of the sun, but neither did they receive its beneficial rays; although they survived and reproduced, most of them degenerated into a race of psychotic dwarfs Shaver called the *dero*, short for *detrimental ro*bots. There were others in the caves who managed to stave off the the mental and physical deterioration of the dero, and did all they could to defeat them; they were the *tero* (in*tegrative ro*bots). But the dero, according to Palmer, were much more numerous than the few groups of tero, and the dero, unfortunately for us, had incredible powers at their command:

> These dero have access to the wonderful machines of the ancients, still in working order... and with these machines they are able to bedevil both the tero and the surface people. Among these machines are marvelous vision rays that can penetrate miles of solid rock, picking up scenes all over the earth without the need of a broadcast unit; transportation by teleportation instantaneously from one point to another...; mental machines which cause seemingly solid illusions, dreams, hypnotic compulsions (which account for the strange "urges to kill" of surface folk, such as the young girl who said, "God told me to stab mother with a knife.")
>
> They have death rays, space ships, giant rockets that traverse the upper air...; machines for the revitalizing of sex known as "stim" machines (in which these degenerates sometimes spend their whole lives in a sexual debauch that actually deforms their bodies in horrible ways almost beyond mentioning), ben rays which heal and restore

the body but are also capable of restoring lost energy after a debauch, and many other marvelous things which Mr. Shaver claims would revolutionize our surface science if we could but obtain them.

The dero live on in the caverns, using their wonderful machines in diabolical ways—starting wars, causing airline and traffic accidents, even tripping us as we walk down the stairs. No one felt the tortures of the dero more than their creator, Richard Sharpe Shaver.

The welder, the flesh, and the devils

Shaver steeped himself in an exotic brew of pulp science fiction and occultism, and he mythologized an entire pantheon of gods and demons, past and present, dwelling miles under our feet. But the demons took control of his mind and his writings, lurking in their caverns and turning their "ray mech" of unbelievable destructive power on him and the rest of the world. In his obsessive, rambling, disconnected writings, published in bulk by Palmer in the early 1960s under the title *The Hidden World*, Shaver placed the blame for almost every evil, great or small, in human history at the feet of the dero. One of their rays sliced the blood vessels in Franklin Roosevelt's brain and killed him just as World War II neared its end. The dero used the telaug to convince Lee Harvey Oswald to assassinate John Kennedy—perhaps the ultimate conspiracy theory. Hitler and the Nazi leaders were puppets of the dero, who designed the death camps and ran the Third Reich. Even Jesus Christ was crucified under orders from the caves.

Many of the details of Shaver's life are a little hazy; when he was asked, his biography seemed to change with his mood. He was born in either 1908 or 1910 in rural Pennsylvania. His father bought, sold, ran, and lost restaurants around the state, so the family was constantly moving during his childhood. Shaver's mother wrote poetry fillers and "true confessions" magazine stories under a variety of pseudonyms. His older brother, who died when Shaver was a teenager—Shaver later claimed his brother was murdered under telaug influence—wrote fiction for *Boys' Life* and similar periodicals. Shaver himself showed little interest in writing as a young man. He seems to have been a restless, unstable man through most of his life—never keeping a job very long and working when he felt like it. After high school he hauled trees for a landscaper for a while, and later he became—among other things—a meat cutter in a slaughterhouse, a crane operator for Bethlehem Steel, and a welder for Ford Motor Co. He was also married three times. His first two marriages seem to have lasted less than a year each, but his third wife, Dorothy, married him in 1947 and they lived together, happily by all accounts, until his death. She was, however, a fundamentalist Christian and never regarded his tales of dero and tero with more than a bemused tolerance.

One thing we definitely know about Shaver is his long-standing love of science fiction. He bought a copy of the first *Amazing Stories* in 1926 and remained a pulp fan the rest of his life. He was also fascinated by Charles Fort's collections of unexplained phenomena and by many occultist writings, from the Rosicrucians to Madame Blavatsky, and their influences can be seen throughout the Shaver Mystery stories. But the true how and why of the dero and tero lay in Shaver himself.

Richard Shaver in the 1930s.

He told several versions of how he first became aware of the invisible empire of the dero. The best-known version begins in 1932, when Shaver was a welder in one of the Ford Motor plants in Highland Park, Michigan, and by his own admission a confirmed skeptic in all matters supernatural. One day, clutching his welding gun on the assembly line, Shaver made an unusual discovery. Whenever he held the gun, he "heard voices, faroff voices of endless complexity." He found he could read the minds of his co-workers:

I knew what was in Bill's lunch box; which girl Bunny was going to take out that night, what Hank's mother was planning on for his wife. It was a dress, and quite a dress, too. More, I knew what the men upstairs were griping about; I heard everything I didn't want to hear all over the factory. That welding gun was, by some freak of its coils' field attunements *not* a radio, but a *tele*radio; a thought augmentor of some power.

After awhile I could read the thought of nearly everyone in the building.... But at last it began to get on my nerves.... I'll tell you why: I began to hear "thought!" I couldn't figure it out. I would hear a mean kind of voice say:

"Put her on the target!"

Then I heard a woman's screams, louder and louder and more and more agony in the screams—and at last a gurgle, a death rattle. Then later I could hear some person thinking about a spaceship, not a *new* spaceship, but an *old* one—*one he had been out in space with!*

I would hear a woman cursing and the lash of a whip—and feel a pleasure in the scream of the person getting the lash. It was all so mad, but I kept hearing such things, over and over. It got on my nerves, so I quit. I quit and went on the bum, for I didn't feel like working any more, because I believed—I *knew*—I heard the voices and if that is what telepathy gave a man to hear in America, I wasn't going to work for America. I was a *smart* guy—and pretty soon I was running a liquor truck between Detroit and Toledo. Easy money, I had the satisfaction of knowing I wasn't a sucker for any hidden bunch of devils like I figured out was running America, from what I heard.

Now we enter the foggiest part of Shaver's biography. He quit driving the bootleg truck after a while and bummed around until he reached Montreal, where he stowed away on a ship he thought was bound for England. Instead it landed in Newfoundland, where he was arrested and sent to jail for either twenty days, two years, or not at all, depending on which version of Shaver's life one believes. He was then deported to Boston, where he broke a leg and spent the winter in a charity hospital; another version of his life runs that he went into a mental hospital for the next eight years. Somewhere along the line, he also either was or wasn't arrested and sent to prison for running liquor over a state line.

Whatever occurred, it was during one of these prison or hospital stays that Shaver discovered the truth about the dero. He was visited in his cell—or ward—by a blind tero girl named Nydia, who told him the story of the Titans and revealed the existence of the underground world. After she had visited him several times, Nydia helped Shaver to escape and led him to a concealed cave entrance not far from the prison—or hospital. Here Shaver was able to join a group of tero and live among them for several years. He learned that the "voices" he had heard on the assembly line were those of the dero and their prisoners. Using the tero's televiewers—for the tero had some of the Titans' devices too—Shaver witnessed many of the horrible dero torture sessions, in which young women abducted from the surface were flogged, torn to pieces, roasted, or devoured by the evil dwarfs.

More than anything else, the dero are sexual perverts. Although they must reproduce somehow, they do not seem to engage in conventional sex; they either loll about in the stim rays or find their arousal in torture and dismemberment. Sadomasochistic sex was one of the dero's major pleasures. One of the weirder stories in *The Hidden World* was illustrated with a crude drawing by Shaver of a dero pitching dagger-tipped darts into an unfortunate young woman who had been stripped naked and chained to the wall of a cave.

Scenes of sexual torture were common in Shaver's writings, as well as in many of the Shaver/Palmer stories, but more to the point of our story—and far more pleasant to read about—was the depiction of the Titan women to be found in many of the early stories, particularly "I Remember Lemuria!" and its sequels. These women of the Titan race are an adolescent boy's fertility goddesses—huge, powerful, scantily clothed, and sexually vibrant. Princess Vanue of the Titans of Nor is easily recognizable as an aspect of the Earth Mother as Provider. As one of the Titan elders, she dwells deep in a chamber filled with "ionized and nutrient-saturated air." The reader is given a strong impression of a great power of fertility germinating in an earthly cavern. When Mutan Mion, the young protagonist of the story, is brought into Vanue's presence, he is consumed by the desire to grovel joyously at her feet:

> All of eighty feet tall she must have been. She towered over our heads as she rose to greet us, a vast cloud of the glittering hair of the Nor women floating about her head, the sex aura a visible irridescence flashing about her form.
>
> I yearned toward that vast beauty which was not hidden, for in Nor it is considered impolite to conceal the body greatly, being an offense against art and friendship to take beauty out of life. I was impelled madly toward her until I fell on my knees before her, my hands outstretched to touch the gleaming, ultra-living flesh of her feet.... As we touched her flesh, a terrific charge of body electric flowed into us. We fell face forward in unbearable pleasure on the floor.

Here we have the fertility goddess of a technological age. Whether created by Shaver himself or by Palmer using Shaver's writing as a guide, Vanue is a manifestation of the powerful, positive, fertile aspect of the Earth Mother. She is both a source of sexuality and a source of security—the story tells us that "all evil is restrained from entering" Vanue's chambers. Such a female figure is appealing to a man who feels persecuted or sexually insecure, and such figures appear in the Shaver stories frequently. Later in "I Remember Lemuria!" Mutan Mion fights alongside Vanue's legion of female warriors, and each of them is great and powerful:

> ...this was not the first time these warrior maids had seen action. They worked too smoothly. With the hand weapons and war harness they wore, they were formidable-looking Amazons. Their strength was unbelievable, and I knew it came from the inner growth of the incubator which increased the solidity of [their] flesh.

Not all of Shaver's superwomen worked for the power of good, however; some were dero, or allies of the dero in the persecution of surface people. Another story, "Cult of the Witch Queen" by Shaver and Bob McKenna, shows the other face of the Earth Mother—the Devourer—in the character of the Hag, who lives on Venus but controls an army of huge vampire-women lurking under the earth. These seductive and powerful creatures steal children from the surface and spirit them to Venus, where the Hag lives eternally by drinking their blood. The hero of the story sees the Hag in the vampire-women's interplanetary TV globe:

> The figure in the globe was big, standing twice the height of the figures around her. Her body was well-covered with flesh, still, she seemed bony. Barbaric ornaments were hung and fastened all over that huge harridan. Her face was a fierce Medusa mask from antiquity, covered with a network of fine wrinkles. She seemed to scorn clothes and her immense dugs hung down to her waist—the living incarnation of the foully evil Hindu goddess KALI! in the flesh.

And of course Shaver implied that Kali—and perhaps Medusa as well—were in fact racial memories of the Hag of Venus, absorbed into the legends of the Hindus and the ancient Greeks.

Have you heard voices?

With the phenomenal success of "I Remember Lemuria!" Palmer began including Shaver material in almost every issue of *Amazing Stories*. The magazine's circulation, previously 135,000, increased to 185,000; where it had once received fifty letters a month from fans, it was deluged now with 2500. Readers wrote Palmer to tell him they had heard voices, dreamed inexplicable dreams, seen strange phenomena while exploring caves, or remembered their previous incarnations as citizens of the Titan empire. Palmer was delighted with the torrent of mail; he increased the size of the letters column and added a new department, "Report from the Forgotten Past," to handle the meatiest new developments in what he dubbed "The Shaver Mystery."

Cover of the June 1947 *Amazing Stories*, devoted entirely to the Shaver Mystery.

With each batch of new letters, Palmer noted an increasing interest in the idea of visitations of the earth by alien spaceships on the part of his readers; he also noted that many readers seemed to believe that there was some truth about the earth's past that was being "concealed," that attempting to reveal such knowledge was dangerous, and that it was all connected somehow with Shaver's "racial memories." Palmer encouraged these feelings in his sensational introduction to the first installment of "Report from the Forgotten Past." *Amazing Stories,* he wrote, had been inundated with

> a tremendous flood of letters which are alike in one respect: namely, the writers emphatically insist that their letter NOT be used for publication and their name not be disclosed.... They have had experiences similar to Mr. Shaver's with cave people, or with strange humans who could not have been ordinary people. MANY OF THESE WARNED US TO DROP OUR CAMPAIGN OR WE WOULD RUN INTO REAL TROUBLE WITH THE CAVE PEOPLE! AND MANY OF THEM BELIEVED THEY WERE RISKING OUR LIVES BY WRITING TO US...
>
> There are certain people who believe that something is about to happen on this old earth which is so stupendous that it is almost beyond imagination. They are very few in number, but they have two things in common. First, they do not know whether or not they are reincarnated from a previous existence, members of an ancient race such as the Titans and sent here in human form, or what. But they do know that they are here for a definite purpose which has to do with whatever is going to happen. Second, they have spent their lives in perfecting certain trades and professions which do not overlap.... And indications are that when all these people are united they will make an organization which not only will have an expert on every subject... but their pooled knowledge will be FAR IN ADVANCE OF ANYTHING THAT HAS BEEN DEVELOPED ON EARTH TO THE PRESENT DAY!
>
> Thus, we urge every reader who has such convictions... to write to your editor, WHO IS ONE OF THOSE PEOPLE!

Palmer followed this wowser of an introduction with a few of the letters he received from readers who were, evidently, courageous enough to speak out against the dero. A man from Arizona, who appears to have been a follower of Doreal (see the next chapter), was concerned Shaver might be toying with forbidden knowledge:

> I sincerely hope that Mr. Shaver's intentions are good because it is clear that he has come into certain powerful knowledge from the past.... The Atlanteans and Lemurians were two different places and races. Both were wiped out by the great Masters because of failure to obey cosmic laws. The last remnants of the Lemurians are locked in a great cavern in the earth along with other der or negative creatures and can not be reached by any ordinary mortal, for which I give thanks to the Cosmos...
>
> There were other races besides the Lemurians and the Atlanteans. One of these was the Xians, who came from a dark planet. As to travel in space, it can be done if one travels through curves but not angles.

Palmer replied earnestly, "Your editor is sincere—and he'd like to know everything you know.... For instance, please explain this space-travel business—about curves and not angles."

The Lemurian Masters of Shasta put in an appearance as well. A woman from San Bernardino, California wrote in to profess her firm belief that "a strange tribe of people" lived within Mount Shasta. "Numerous searching parties," she continued, "have covered the slopes and crags of Mt. Shasta and found nothing. There are instances, however, of small groups [of searchers] disappearing there and not being found again. Perhaps they have found the entrances and the inhabitants have not seen fit to let them return with their story." But several of the Shasta inhabitants had also appeared, she said, in San Francisco in 1923 after a severe earthquake hit Japan. "They descended... and turned over to the Japanese consul there a large amount of gold to be used for the relief of the stricken people." Another woman wrote Palmer to tell about the time a "gorilla type creature" entered a polling place near Shasta and stared for a long time at one of the young women working there until the editor of the local newspaper threw him, or it, out. She also saw a UFO—although this was 1946, so she called it a "rocket"—appear to come from the direction of Venus and disappear on the east side of the mountain. "I believe," she wrote, "that it kept going and landed right in the Mountain, much as a plane might fly into a hangar." Later she heard a woman screaming for help, and the cry seemed to come from Shasta. "Of course I'm in favor of an armed expedition to clean out dero," she concluded, "but I don't think any but righteously advanced people can contact the good forces." Were the Masters at war with the dero?

Palmer printed an article written by one Ralph B. Fields describing the purportedly true adventure of Fields and a friend exploring a cave in California's Mount Lassen. Deep in a tunnel in the cave, the two men were kidnapped by three evil-looking "horloks," and placed on a toboggan-like vehicle which carried them miles deeper until they encountered another such vehicle carrying men with strange weapons, like "a fountain pen flashlight with a large, round, bulb-like affair on the back end and a grip something like a German luger" which emitted "a fine blue light" and killed the three abductors. Fields and his friend Joe asked what was happening and one of their rescuers replied, "I could not tell you too much as you could not understand.... The people on the surface are not ready to have the things that the ancients have left." After receiving their promise that they would not return to the cave, their rescuers took Fields and Joe back to the surface and released them. Fields concluded, "What is the answer to the whole thing?... We had been told just enough for me to believe down there somewhere there were or are things that might baffle the greatest minds of this earth." Palmer called Fields's story "amazing!"

Another group of readers from West Los Angeles warned Palmer that there "will be, in distant years to come, a contest. A contest between Mars and Jupiter to see who shall control the universe.... Earth must enter that mad 'contest' for superiority, win it, and show Mars and Jupiter that all men are created equal. THAT THERE SHALL BE NO MASTER PLANET." And there was another letter from a soldier just returned from the Pacific Theater, warning Shaver to be careful; he had received ray gun burns on his arm "the size of a quarter" when he tried to hide from the Japanese in a cave in Burma.

Read in retrospect, these letters—printed in 1945 and 1946—are shadows of the 1947 flying saucer craze cast before. Taking care to remain vague, Palmer stressed the connection between the Shaver Mystery and interplanetary visitations when he introduced "Cult of the Witch Queen." "If you don't think space ships visit the earth regularly, as in this story," he wrote, "then the files of Charles Fort and your editor's own files are something you should see.... And if you think responsible parties in world governments are ignorant of the fact of space ships visiting earth, you just don't think the way we do." He wrote these lines early in 1946, a year before Kenneth Arnold's sighting placed the term "flying saucer" in our language—a sighting Palmer would do a great deal to publicize. But even before Arnold entered the news, Palmer had already introduced the idea of a government cover-up of UFOs to a group of readers which included many people who would soon be big names in the UFO movement.

From 1945 to 1948 *Amazing Stories* was filled with Shaver, and Shaver fan clubs sprouted up all over the country. In one issue Chester Geier, one of *Amazing*'s writers, announced the formation of the "Shaver Mystery Club," begun with a thousand-dollar donation from Shaver himself. It was "organized to try and solve the mystery, and further, to advance the many wonderful ideas Mr. Shaver's stories present, which no one can deny would vastly improve our civilization—and God knows it needs improvement today!" But not all *Amazing*'s readers were happy with the situation; fans of good old science *fiction*, many of them scientists, protested the magazine's new fixation. *Fantasy Commentator*, a New York fan magazine, ran an article by Thomas Gardner that was not gentle at all when describing *Amazing*'s new readership:

> The crackpots, as they are called, number at least a million in the United States. They are, in the main, adults, and have educational levels ranging from near zero to those of Ph.D.'s engaged in technical occupations. A great many harbor seriously delusions of ancient civilizations superior to ours...
>
> [T]hese crackpots constitute a large potential buying power for magazines.... To capture these readers it is only necessary to publish issues of *Amazing Stories* containing stories which propitiate these crackpots' views in fictional guise.... Palmer has instituted this very trend.

And this wasn't all. The Queens Science Fiction League of New York passed a resolution that the Shaver stories endangered the sanity of their readers, and brought their resolution before the Society for the Suppression of Vice. A fan conference in Philadelphia was rocked by threats to draw up a petition to the Post Office Department, asking that *Amazing Stories* be banned from the mails.

Palmer, of course, loved the attention these protests brought him, and he used the threats and hostile letters he received as an excuse to shrug his shoulders, pick up a rallying banner—Suppression of the Truth—and wave it around:

> There have been some odd reactions [to the Shaver Mystery series], one of them being a promise by a fan group to "expose" our "hoax" (which was a compliment, by the way, because it was termed "the biggest ever attempted in modern science fiction history"). We are waiting for this expose, with interest—because we are curious to know how a hoax

which is not a hoax can be exposed as a hoax. We realize that a lot of our readers find it difficult to believe that we ourselves believe one single word of what Mr. Shaver tells us in his stories, but we'll keep on presenting the evidence as it comes in, and you can judge for yourself.

One can almost see Palmer winking between the lines.

The acme of the series appeared with the June 1947 issue, which was devoted entirely to "The Shaver Mystery, the Most Sensational True Story Ever Told." In his introduction to the issue, Palmer dropped some dark hints that the dero had done all they could to prevent its publication. Manuscripts and galleys vanished into the air, one page was printed with ninety-two errors not caught by the proofreader, and delay after delay hampered the staff. "Man does *not* rule this earth," Palmer concluded, "and it is based on *fact* that he does not. Roll on, Shaver Mystery!"

But the Shaver Mystery hadn't much longer to roll in the pages of *Amazing Stories*. Late in 1948, the series was stopped. The magazine ran a very few more Shaver stories it had already purchased at wide intervals into the early fifties, but the pages of letters, alternative-reality articles, and editorial tirades Palmer had provided disappeared. Palmer, as always, gave several versions of why the Shaver Mystery was cancelled: 1) William Ziff, the publisher, had received so many complaints and so many old fans had stopped buying the magazine that he ordered the series stopped; 2) Palmer himself decided the Mystery didn't belong in a *fiction* magazine; 3) Palmer hinted he had to stop running the series because the dero were tampering with the presses; 4) in 1961 he suggested, a little implausibly, that Ziff cancelled the series "because it contradicted Einstein." The first of these reasons seems closest to the truth—Ziff probably decided that enough was enough and called Palmer onto the carpet. Palmer knew now what he wanted to do.

In 1948, Palmer began a magazine of his own—*Fate, true stories of the strange, the unusual, the unknown*—and from the start it did well. The first issue of Fate featured "I *Did* See the Flying Disks," by Kenneth Arnold; it had been so heavily and sensationally rewritten by Palmer that the story, and the description of what Arnold had seen, bore little resemblance to Arnold's official report of a year earlier. Palmer's readers didn't seem to mind. Palmer left Ziff-Davis in 1949 to devote his time to his own publishing business; he was replaced at *Amazing Stories* by Howard Browne, the man who had thrown Shaver's original letter in the wastebasket and who later described the Shaver stories as "the sickest crap I'd ever run into."

Palmer sold *Fate* to another publisher a few years later and started other magazines. He began with *Other Worlds*, a science-fiction magazine which subsequently became *Other Worlds Science Stories, Flying Saucers from Other Worlds*, and finally just *Flying Saucers* as it became more UFO-oriented. He published a changing group of other, similar magazines as well, including *Imagination, Mystic*, and *Search*, and there were few of them that didn't run a Shaver article sooner or later. The Shaver articles were no longer disguised as fiction, but presented as solemn warnings. In the January 1956 *Mystic*, Shaver passed along more details on the cavern world:

> Today, the centers of population of the dero are located under great cities, for obvious reasons. There ARE ways to contact the surface, and much of the needs of the underground people, such as food, clothing, etc., can be gotten only from the surface. Down there, they call us "meat people." Literally. Because many of those who disappear every year never to be heard from again become meat in the markets of the dero. Many times I have been shown over telaug ray, hideous deformed deros gnawing on a bone, a bone that cannot be anything but human, as there are no animals in the caves. Some of these bones are those of fellow deros, some of unfortunate teros, captured in battle, but some of them are surface people—as many as 120,000 yearly in this country alone! Ask the F.B.I. about the number missing yearly, and never found.

But there were no longer many people reading Shaver's warnings. Palmer's magazines circulated among a dedicated group of Mystery fans that numbered perhaps a few thousand. By the mid-fifties the series that had torn the science-fiction world apart had been forgotten by everyone else.

Stones and secrets

Between 1961 and 1964, one of Palmer's biggest projects was publication of *The Hidden World*—"The whole truth at last" about the Shaver Mystery, "and nothing but the truth." By this time Palmer, his wife Marjorie, and their children were living on a farm near Amherst, Wisconsin. Richard and Dorothy Shaver bought a farm next to theirs which they tried unsuccessfully to make into a going dairy farm. The two men were, however, able to work closely on the series. The sixteen book-length issues, a total of nearly three thousand pages, were a rummage sale of the original stories, reprinted from *Amazing*, reams of Shaver's jumbled pontificating about how nobody believes him but they'd better wise up soon, a pompous turn-of-the-century hollow-earth novel called *Beyond the Verge*, and lots of letters and articles from Shaver fans.

The letters are the most fascinating part of the series. Most give evidence of "dero activity;" others offer theories about the influence of dero and tero on human history. Some of the letters are amusing, some are tedious, some are vague and mysterious. One reader offered an inner-world theory of his own:

> There are three underground cities beneath the Earth. Each one of them is built beneath a desert with the only entrance to these cities in the mountains near the deserts. It should not have been difficult for a thinking man to understand why these cities have been built beneath deserts. None of these cities are peopled by what Mr. Shaver calls deros, teros, or even zeros. More than likely you have met, and may even have talked to persons from at least one of these cities during your lifetime, but you wouldn't have known this except by the lack of color in their irises. The pigmentation of their complexion will darken about as quickly as it takes you to get a suntan. They are neither evil nor saintly but they do have more keenly developed sensitivities than the average human on the human on the surface of the Earth because they do not have to live under the destructive disintegrating energies of the sun.... To these people you are just another species of ani-

mal on the surface of the Earth and they regard you in the same way you regard the simian species...

He ended his letter with the comment that he would not have written at all if he had not been "protected in several ways."

During this time—in fact, for the last twenty years of his life—Shaver was deeply involved with a new manifestation of his beliefs. In the early sixties, he began advertising "Pre-Deluge Art Stones" in several UFO magazines. These were slices of agate, cut by Shaver with a diamond saw; he claimed the slices held actual pictures of the Titans and their world. The photo-stones had been printed by the "forgotten... masters who first discovered a way of making agate, and of mixing photo-sensitive chemicals with liquid stone and impressing upon the stone their very thoughts, their art and their history."

One of Richard Shaver's dero-infested paintings. The face in the upper left-hand corner has "Bad" painted on its cheek.

Many children see funny and monstrous faces in the linoleum swirls of the bathroom floor or the grain pattern of a door, and it appears Shaver found his pictures of the Titans in the same way. Even Palmer was impatient with the idea at first. "How would you feel," he asked the readers of *The Hidden World*, if you were shown a whole bushel basket full of stones and invited to look at the pictures on and in them—only to find that you saw nothing, except some vague resemblances that were quite obviously accidental?" Shaver nonetheless insisted the pictures were there, providing physical proof of the Titan civilization.

He developed a technique for bringing out the pictures in the stones. He projected the stone slices onto large pieces of cardboard with an opaque projector. He treated the cardboard with dye and laundry detergent, and painted over them with oils so everyone could see what he saw. In a *Hidden World* article titled "How to Make a Portrait of Dero Activity," Shaver detailed his process, and warned that the dero would show up in the picture as well:

> Enraged that you too can see pre-deluge art from record stone, fearing you may learn something of the ancient wisdom they're too stupid and too lazy to learn themselves, they tamper the picture with the ancient machines setting under your feet, to spoil your picture.... They change the face right before your eyes into new patterns, often a horrible portrait of a degenerate and ugly dwarf, possibly themselves, peering into the machines they have never bothered to understand. Anyway, you will see the distorting images they make print photographically before your eyes, and you will have a bona-fide proof of dero activity.

Shaver turned out hundreds of paintings and pastels of the pictures he saw in the stones, and they are a remarkable body of work. His technique was poor—he had little sense of design, and his paint-over-detergent method gave many of his pictures the texture of those velvet paintings one sees at flea markets. But the power of his vision was so strong it overshadowed his failings as an artist. Almost all the pictures are of human or humanoid figures; he did many of the beautiful Titan women, mermaid races, and Amazons locked in battle with wicked-looking monsters. Some are little masterpieces of *Art Brut*, and can hold their own beside the works of many recent professional artists for crude power and energetic use of line. The spaces between the swirling and jagged lines are filled with a confusion of little faces—the dero, of course, "tampering the picture." They peer from the pictures with hostile eyes and open mouths. In some pictures, we see nothing but whole masses of faces pressed together, overlapping each other and even appearing in cross section, like diagrams from an extraterrestrial *Gray's Anatomy*.

Shaver believed the keys to the Titans' technology were locked in the stones, and he worked at "reading" them for the rest of his life. He called them "rock books," and wrote they "will eventually point the way to build the saucer drives and space ships the elders used... toughest part is *not* translation or photography but to get *any* science interested, as they can't get it through them there actually *was* a previous civilization and all this work seems nonsense to them."

In the mid-sixties the Shavers moved to Summit, Arkansas, where he set up The Rock House Studio and stepped up advertising for his Pre-Deluge Art Stones (five dollars a slice; $25 to $100 for mounted wall plaques). Despite his continuing obsession with the story of the Titans, dero, and tero, many of those who knew Shaver in his later years desribe him as warm and intelligent. I wrote to UFO archivist Lucius Farish, who knew Shaver in Arkansas, and asked him his opinion of the man. He replied, "I definitely would not consider Shaver a 'madman' of any sort, which is not to say that I necessarily agreed with all his ideas. He was a kind man, a truly gentle man, extremely well-read and one of the most interesting conversationalists I've ever met." After I described several qualities in Shaver's works that might indicate fairly severe paranoia, Farish answered, "I am not at all convinced that such analyses are valid. Or, perhaps I should say, that if a person *is* paranoid, perhaps he has good reasons for his fears. *If* the basic elements of the Shaver Mystery are correct (and I realize that is a big 'if'), would you or I not also be considered paranoid if we *knew* such things to be factual and tried to tell others about them?"

Materialism and magic

Richard Shaver died of lung cancer in November 1975, with most of the world unconvinced of the existence—let alone the terrible deeds—of the dero. What are we to make of the Shaver Mystery? In many histories of science fiction, it's called the "Shaver Hoax," and it may in fact be better known by that name. Was it a hoax? From Ray Palmer's point of view, almost certainly. Palmer had an excellent feel for the anxieties of the Mystery-minded public, and in his last four years at Amazing Stories, he did a beautiful job of articulating Shaver's fears and beliefs into a more universal fear of having one's mind invaded by an evil power and of an omnipotent but uncontrollable technology—of machines that could work amoral magic. Despite his many protests that he was dedicated to uncovering the truth behind the Shaver Mystery, Palmer actually did all he could to scatter and camouflage the lack of physical evidence for Shaver's claims. By encouraging readers to write in their experiences and "feelings," he prolonged the Mystery, kept the readers entertained, gave them a sense of participation in an adventure, *and* sold a lot of magazines. It was a method he continued throughout his career, and it kept him going through good times and bad. Until his death in August of 1977, Palmer unearthed, sensationalized, and defended one mystery after another without ever saying directly he believed any of them were true. In one of his last works, *The Secret World*, a short autobiographical fragment bound together with a large collection of "rock book" paintings, he wrote of the Shaver Mystery: "It is [Shaver's] work, yet it is mine too—for none of it might have happened had not our minds met and our work meshed in that incredibly mysterious network of the Plan, as it is being developed by the Manipulator." Palmer himself was certainly a manipulator, and at times he could hardly keep himself from admitting it was all a gag.

Shaver is more of an enigma. He obviously believed that the world was under attack by a race of diabolical underground beings armed with a magical technology. Was Shaver insane? Most uninvolved writers who have looked at the Mystery have concluded that Shaver and his supporters were a group of like-minded paranoiacs who banded together to swap stories of their persecutions from the caves. But Shaver was no mere paranoiac—he was, in his way, a mystic, and something of a shaman.

He was a member of that ancient fellowship of receivers of revealed knowledge—like Moses and Joseph Smith and Cyrus Teed, Shaver heard voices and saw visions that disclosed hidden information about the cosmos. His predecessors were religious men, however; Shaver was not. He insisted the dero were real in a materialistic time, and here he made his mistake.

Shaver failed as a prophet because his materialism could not support his mythology. Over and over he asserted the reality of the caves, but when asked where the entrances were, Shaver hedged the question, claiming the dero camouflaged them with machine-generated illusions. He found himself in the uncomfortable position of a materialist who could offer no material proof for his beliefs. He hoped the rock books would provide this proof, but even the existence of the rock pictures became a revealed truth, one that could only be accepted by those long on imagination and faith, and short on geological knowledge.

But he did do an amazing job of building a mythology for a technological age. It was an earthy, dynamic mythology containing nearly all the elements discussed in the first two chapters. The time of the Titans was the Golden Age, the sacred time of creation, of Eden, of no death or disease. In the stories we see the two faces of the Earth Mother, the Provider and the Devourer. As in the classic beliefs surrounding the Fairies, Shaver described two races of underground folk eternally at odds, yet dwelling amidst vast piles of riches—in this case technological riches, magical machines. Here also was the underground Hell of punishment run by merciless demons, and here mortals were abducted from the surface to slave for those demons in a technological Fairyland. The dero were the demons, the monsters, the obscene whisperings in one's ear; they attacked us out of the dark earth, unseen.

The Shaver Mystery succeeded initially because it responded to the fears of many postwar Americans—particularly the fear of technology gone mad that grew in the wake of the bombings of Hiroshima and Nagasaki, and of the War itself. It offered myth based on science, myth that allowed magic *if* it was performed by a machine. The idea of the dero assembled the shards of twentieth-century chaos—wars, assassinations, disappearances, and all the other disasters that pepper the newspapers—into a comprehensible shape. But the Shaver Mystery ultimately failed to become a living myth—where popular ufology and parapsychology have done well—because it was overwhelmingly negative. Shaver simply kept repeating that the dero were slowly destroying us. "These secretive, reactionary, sadistic minds among them are today holding us back from ALL true development," he wrote. "They are striving with might and main to place all human life under a rule of malignance unimaginable, that is so horrible in its aims, in its degenerate cruelties, so destructive in its details of government that the race of man will perish if they succeed!"

Shaver was never able to offer his readers any *yang* to offset his pages of *yin*; he was never able to give them a plan of action, a way to defeat the evil creatures under the earth who denied us the hidden knowledge and magical machines of the past. Perhaps Shaver gave it all away in one tiny article at the end of one issue of *The Hidden World*, comparing us with the Titans:

> If only... we had love today instead of hate.
> If only... we possessed the knowledge of our predecessors.
> If only... our short lives were happy.
> If only... they had all died, and we had never been; would it not have been better?

So in the end, he felt it didn't matter what we did. We were doomed whether we realized it or not.

Chapter 9

The Secret War with the Snake People

> "That's it, Blug!" he shouted. "That's the idea, General! I'm
> King of the Under World, and my subjects are all miners. I'll
> make a tunnel under the desert to the Land of Oz—yes! right up
> to the Emerald City—and you will march your armies there
> and capture the whole country!"
>
> —The Nome King, in L. Frank Baum's
> *The Emerald City of Oz*

Among the many warnings *Amazing Stories* received in the early days of the Shaver Mystery about the dangers of probing too deeply into the secrets of the cosmos was a letter from one Dr. M. Doreal of the Brotherhood of the White Temple in Denver. Doreal claimed intimate knowledge of the subterranean realms, and he cautioned against trying to find and explore the caves of the dero:

> Like Mr. Shaver, I have had personal contact with the Dero and even visited their underground caverns. In the outer world they are represented by an organization known loosely as the "Black Brotherhood," whose purpose is the destruction of the good principle in man.... The underground cities are, in the most part, protected by space-warps, a science known to the ancients, but only touched on by modern science.... I note that many are wanting to enter these caves. For one who has not developed a protective screen this would be suicide and one who revealed their location would be a murderer.

From Shasta to Tibet

Maurice Doreal was born Claude Doggins in Sulfur Springs, Oklahoma in 1898 (or so have I heard). He looked more like a feed-store owner or small-town banker than the guru he became to his thousand or so followers. He founded his "Brotherhood of the White Temple" in 1929, naming it after a group of Masters of the same name often invoked by H.P.B.'s successor Annie Besant. He claimed that after serving in the First World War, he traveled to Tibet and spent eight years studying there with the Dalai Lama. Doreal amassed one of the world's largest and finest occult and science-fiction libraries—over thirty thousand volumes—but all he seemed to distill out of his studies was a long series of repetitive and poorly-written, but highly imaginative, booklets on occult subjects, written between about 1940 and his death in 1963. It is still possible at this writing, though, to send away for "Mysteries of Mt. Shasta," "Mysteries of the Gobi," "Polar Paradise," and similar booklets for a few dollars each from the Brotherhood of the White Temple, Inc. in Sedalia, Colorado.

In the late 1940s Doreal became convinced that an atomic war was to strike in May 1953 and gathered his followers to build "Shamballa Ashrama," an "atom-proof" city in a mountainous valley thirty-five miles southwest of Denver. With spiritual help, reported the newspapers, and because the surrounding mountains contained deposits of lead, Doreal and the other members of the Brotherhood of the White Temple believed they would "ride out the atomic attack in safety." In February 1953 the Denver *Post* reported that

> Doreal, who presides in heavy gold robes from his throne over meetings of the cult and is known to his followers as "The Voice," has issued orders that "no outsiders are permitted to enter the valley except necessary workmen."
> ...Doreal calls the retreat "Western Shamballa, or Shangri-La-in-the-Rockies." He said in a speech last week that the atomic refuge is now completely stocked and ready for "the end."

In a 1946 interview with a reporter from the *Rocky Mountain News,* Doreal said, "I had predicted atomic war years before it came. I saw atomic energy at work several years ago when the Dalai Lama of Tibet ushered me into the Great White Lodge 75 miles under the Himalayas."

In his writings, Doreal claimed to have visited many of the retreats of the Masters. In "Mysteries of Mt. Shasta," Doreal revealed that he was privileged to pay a visit "in the flesh" to the Atlantean—not Lemurian, he wrote, as is commonly believed—colony inside Mount Shasta. As he told it, while he was in Los Angeles delivering a series of occult lectures, two of the Shasta Masters walked up to him after one lecture and introduced themselves. They had been attending his talks for a week, they said, and were impressed with Doreal's knowledge. Would he like to visit their home inside Shasta that evening? Doreal demurred at first, since he had another lecture in just a few hours, but the Masters insisted; they could easily reach Shasta and return in time.

Doreal, leader of the Brotherhood of the White Temple, in a 1946 portrait.

They drove up to Topanga Canyon (a favorite locale for paranormal activities in Los Angeles), parked the car, climbed a hill, and the Masters took strange belts and cellophane masks from their pockets, giving Doreal one of each. He put on the mask and was instructed to push certain buttons on the belt. When he did, all three rose into the air, and fifteen minutes or so later they landed on the side of Shasta. They entered a small concealed stone building which carried them like a trolley to the top of the mountain, where they stepped out onto a great flat rock. The rock was a hidden elevator, and it began descending rapidly until it reached a point five miles within the mountain and far below sea level. They left the elevator, passed through two great pillars made of orichalcum, the shining white metal known only to the Atlanteans, entered another elevator, and descended two more miles. At last Doreal found himself in an enormous cavern "about twenty miles long and fifteen miles wide and it was as light as a bright summer day, because suspended, almost in the center of that great cavern of space was a giant glowing mass of light.... They told me later that it was condensed from a blending of the rays of the sun and moon and that it had all of the harmful rays in it extracted and only the life-giving and beneficial energies left." This light was collected by three power houses hidden on the mountain which purified the light and expelled the waste matter as colored rays. So when Larkin and Lanser saw those mysterious lights emanating from the mountain just before sunrise, they were seeing the Shasta Masters ridding themselves of the harmful solar and lunar rays.

Doreal described the Atlantean city inside Shasta as one of beautiful homes of white marble surrounded by gardens of flowers, vegetables, and fruits—the forebears of many had been saved from the sinking Atlantis and existed nowhere else. The Atlanteans knew how to turn sand into gold, and how to make clothing by simply drawing a picture of the garment they desired; the drawing was placed in a "projecto-scope" which displayed the actual garment on the screen. When it fell to the floor, it was ready to wear.

He concluded his description of the subterranean city by reminding his readers that one could enter Shasta only when invited. The seeker who was not "ready," but who tried to find the city anyway, might step into a space warp and find himself five miles away from where he wanted to be. But the Masters knew instantly of anyone approaching who is in the "right state of consciousness, and... they can pass into the inner temples."

The Atlanteans, like the other groups of Masters, served the cosmic plan by protecting us from forces we were not yet ready to use. Near the end of his letter to Palmer, Doreal emphasized, "I do know that the race Mr. Shaver calls 'Dero' exists, although I know them under another name." Perhaps he was referring to a group of Lemurian priest-kings and nobles whom he later wrote were kept prisoners in huge cities they had built beneath what is now the Caroline Islands. These evil Lemurians were held underground by a special team of 353 Atlanteans—who traveled back and forth from their Shasta headquarters by space ship—because the Lemurians had discovered a destructive force far worse than the atomic bomb, one that could mean the end of the human race if it was revealed to us. Doreal said this subterranean Lemurian city was mentioned in the Bible in Second Peter: "And Jesus spoke to the souls of those who were bound in prison during the three days his body lay in the tomb." Most people mistakenly thought this passage referred to the souls in Hell. Doreal didn't believe in Hell: "I have no superstition," he wrote to *Amazing Stories,* "am not a spiritualist or believer in the supernatural. I know that everything exists because of definite law."

Doreal did believe that although the ultimate headquarters of the Great

White Brotherhood "is on the star 'Antares' of the Pleiades[1]," there are seven subterranean "places of retreat" for the Masters in this world. Six of them are located 1) in the Gobi Desert, 2) in the Atlas Mountains of North Africa, 3) in the Northwest Territories of Canada, 4) beneath the ruins of a Mayan city in Yucatan, 5) in the Hartz Mountains of Germany, and 6) within Shasta. The seventh and most important of these retreats is Shamballa, located beneath Lhasa, the capital of Tibet. Some seventy-five miles beneath the Himalayas, Shamballa is protected from curious or malicious outsiders by a space warp "of ninth dimensional vibration." It became, in fact, a subterranean city because of this warp; it had been built on the surface long before the Himalayas existed, and when the mountains began rising, they simply lifted themselves over Shamballa as if it wasn't there. No human power could hope to harm Shamballa. "I was asked once," Doreal wrote, "what would happen if a bomb were dropped on it. Nothing. The person who tried to drop a bomb would find himself in another place so fast he would not have time to turn around.... You could stand outside of Shamballa and have all the big guns, tanks, and armies lined up and send them one by one into that shimmering wave of light around it, and they would vanish. They might find themselves on another planet of the universe." In the 1946 *Rocky Mountain News* interview, Doreal called Shamballa "center of all the occult lore of this planet" and said that in the cavern housing Shamballa, as in the cavern that housed the Shasta colony, "suspended, without apparent support, above the temple is a mighty globe of radio-active material. Around it shimmers a mist of opalescent light allowing only the life-saving and life-bearing rays to emanate." Seeing the might of these rays was Doreal's introduction to atomic power.

Doreal's Shamballa, like Blavatsky and Ballard's underground retreats, contained a library of "everything mankind ever did" or ever would do. Like the spools of golden ribbon St. Germain showed Ballard, the "books" in Shamballa's library consisted of spools of fine wire—each spool "no larger than my little finger"—and each was supplied with a tiny motor the size of a fingernail. By pushing certain buttons, the wire would flow past a crystal very slowly, and when the user looked into the crystal, pictures of the past would appear, like a videotape in miniature. When another button was pushed, the sound or narration came on, and if the spool was turned sideways, a three-dimensional image appeared in space about ten feet away.

Doreal wrote that this library was the most fascinating feature of a visit he made to Shamballa in his astral body. He was curious about events which hadn't occurred during any of his past incarnations, and described one of the recordings made many hundreds of thousands of years ago:

At that time, the present North and South poles were located at the equator and the earth's axis passed through two points on the present-day equator. The area which is today's North Pole was inhabited by "a giant God-like race

---

[1] Whatever the Masters taught Doreal, they neglected astronomy. Antares is a star in the constellation Scorpio, not the Pleiades.

that later became known as the Sons of God," of whom we are the sorry descendants. But what is now Antarctica was the home of the Serpent People, a vaguely humanoid race with heads "like a great snake and their bodies faintly scaled as [with] the scales of a serpent." Since the two races were utterly different in mind as well as in form, they did not understand each other at all. War broke out between them. The Serpent People possessed hypnotic powers which allowed them to appear human to the Sons of God and their other human allies, and they frequently passed among them as spies. But the humans developed a trick that could identify a serpent person immediately; the guards in the human cities and fortifications required all those entering to pronounce the word *Kininigin*. Doreal didn't say what Kininigin meant, but it was a serpent person's undoing, for that word "could only be pronounced by human vocal cords."

In a lush kingdom that is now the Gobi Desert, however, there lived at that time a blond, blue-eyed race of humans who had developed a super-weapon to use against the Serpent People, a weapon so powerful they did not know its full potential. But they pointed it at the land of the Serpent People and set it off, unleashing a catastrophe that almost destroyed the world. "The earth toppled to one side," Doreal wrote, "came out of balance, began to wobble and as it did so, great volcanoes broke, mountains were pushed up, [and] other land masses sank beneath the waters." The Serpent People were wiped out. Those at home in Antarctica quickly froze to death, for they suddenly found themselves at the South Pole; the few remaining in other parts of the world were slaughtered by the more numerous remnants of the human race.

The blond, blue-eyed Gobians were the only group of humans to survive in large numbers, and Doreal's story of their subsequent career gives us suspicions about what the name Great *White* Brotherhood really meant. He wrote that the wisest of the Gobians journeyed first to Atlantis, where they grew great in knowledge and power. They later fled the sinking of the continent to establish the "mystery schools" of ancient Egypt. They also became, he wrote, the priests of the Jews. "To the ancients," he continued, the Gobians "were known as Hebrews, not Jews.... The Hebrews were fair-skinned, blue-eyed and red-haired. Of such was the line of David; of such was Solomon; of such was Moses and of such was Jesus who became the Christ. Jesus was not of the Jewish race." There will, unfortunately, be more of this sort of anti-Semitic occultism in the chapters to come.

The other white Gobians remained in their homeland until "there came an influx of barbarous races from the Mongolian countries," causing them to abandon the Gobi and migrate to Scandinavia, where they have remained to this day. Doreal noted that while "most of the other races of the world today are admixtures of many races," the Scandinavians are "one of the few remaining pure races."

But he also revealed the existence of more races, of undreamed-of colors, dwelling inside the earth. One of them was the Blue Race, which had once lived in Atlantis, but moved underground when that continent began sinking. For thousands of years, said Doreal, they have inhabited an enormous maze of caverns honeycombing the entire planet at a depth of about two hundred miles. Although the caverns are filled with a luminous atmosphere, the members of the Blue Race don't need its light, for like many cave creatures, they long ago lost their physical eyes. After moving underground they attained a spiritual level high enough to "see," far better than we can, without eyes. But the luminous atmosphere is still useful to the Blue Race, for it is also edible—it "supplies all the needs of the body... if one merely breathes it."[2]

The members of the Blue Race did not move underground to live an easy life, however; they had two critical jobs to perform in the cosmic plan. One is guarding an imprisoned race of evil giants, the Xians (mentioned in one of the Shaver Mystery letters quoted in the last chapter), kept in a vast metal sphere suspended in a hollow at the center of the earth. These giants were, several million years ago, very similar to the people of earth, but they had the misfortune to inhabit a planet beyond the orbit of Pluto which Doreal called "Planet X." In that day the solar system passed near a point where "negation, disorder or inharmony, poured in suddenly upon the universe," and Planet X was completely saturated with these negative forces. They warped the minds and bodies of the peaceful people of Planet X; the Xians grew until they were a mile tall and immensely intelligent, cunning, and destructive. They built a fleet of spaceships, invaded the earth, and enslaved the human race.

Luckily for our ancestors, however, the earth had its own race of giants—the "Sons of God" who were later to battle the Serpent People. The Sons struggled with the Xians for decades and saw little hope of defeating them, since they could not be killed—they had absorbed so much negative force that death, the ultimate negativity, could not affect them. They were already "dead" a thousand times over. In a final desperate attempt, the Sons of God constructed an enormous globe a hundred miles in diameter at the earth's center "of grayish black matter, harder than anything we know of on the outer surface of earth, because it is composed of neutrons alone, matter subjected to such intense pressure that the electrons and ions are broken away from it." The Sons then tricked the Xians into the sphere and imprisoned them there.

The evil Xians are still there today, Doreal wrote, and every initiate of the Ancient Wisdom must travel down to that sphere at some time during his or her training. For millennia the Masters and their pupils have been working these with the evil giants, trying to remove the negativity from their bodies. But all attempts so far had proven unsuccessful, and the sphere has had to be guarded by a succession of inner-earth races. The Blue Race are the current guardians, but when another people of the surface have advanced enough spiritually to take on the job, the new race will take the Blue Race's place in the cavern world.

In an aside, Doreal noted that on two evenings of the year, Halloween and the last night in April—known in European folklore as Walpurgis Night—

---

[2] It is fairly obvious that Doreal's description of the "Blue Race" originated in the description of the "Guide" in John Uri Lloyd's occult novel *Etidorhpa*; see Chapter 13.

the Xians are "able to project their disorder and their inharmonious thoughts and desires, and it is for that reason that ancient man and even modern man have set aside those two times." The thoughts of the imprisoned giants can, on those two nights, "affect the sensitive among mankind and cause him to have nightmares of devils." But he reassured his readers that the giants' prison "is shut off from this world. They cannot come out and get you."

The other task of the Blue Race is watching over the earth's balance. There is a great circular passage, according to Doreal, circumscribing the interior of the earth, located approximately beneath the equator. Within this passage travels an enormous pyramid of energy "2500 feet in length, 200 feet in width and 500 feet high." Operating something like the needle of a slowly rotating compass, the pyramid is always located directly beneath that part of the earth's surface facing the sun, and its apex is constantly pointing in the sun's direction. In its daily perambulation through the great passage, the pyramid focuses the "infinite or cosmic energy" it receives from the sun to all parts of the globe, and it keeps the earth in its proper orbit. But the great passage is also connected to the maze of smaller caverns and passages that perforate the inner earth, and if the pyramid should by accident move into one of these smaller channels, the earth might lose its balance and wobble into the sun, or the North and South poles might change places. One of these unscheduled side trips sank Atlantis and Lemuria, so the Blue Race keep a close watch on the pyramid today.

The Blue Race, Doreal warned, are deadly serious about their work and are not to be trifled with. He cited the case of Floyd Collins, the doomed spelunker who died after being trapped for weeks in a limestone cavern in Kentucky in 1925. A rescue party kept Collins alive by handing food to him through a hole in the collapsed cavern, but they were never able to free him. Doreal reported that Collins's first words when they reached the spot where he was trapped were, "I have seen the most wonderful things that man has ever dreamed of. I have seen something that the world would not dream of unless they saw it themselves." (These were not Collins's actual first words when found; according to the most reliable sources, they were "Help Me!" or something very similar.) The rescuers asked Collins what he saw, Doreal continued, but he refused to tell them until he was released. What did Collins see? That cavern, said Doreal, was one of the entrances to the cave world inhabited by the Blue Race. The Blue folk "had no desire to harm him, but knowledge of their secret was inviolate." Collins promised not to reveal what he had seen, but "when he got almost to the surface he changed his mind and when he changed his mind the rock closed in on him. Why? Because that race has the mastery of the rock and of metals and of the earth."

Rainbow City and the Hefferlin Manuscript

The Masters took another guise in a new alternative-reality scenario which was first revealed to the public by Ray Palmer during the Shaver Mystery craze. The September 1946 issue of *Amazing Stories* contained four short articles written by a W. C. Hefferlin. Each described a wonderful new invention which had come to the author, in Palmer's words, "from Tibet by mental telepathy." One of them was a "circle-winged airplane" which sounded like a cross between a conventional airplane, a donut, and a dinner plate. Another was the GHYT—for Gas HYdraulic Turbine—motor, which Hefferlin implied was decades ahead of the internal combustion engine without being too specific about how it worked; he fetchingly introduced it with the phrase "Speed, *speed,* and more SPEED!" Still another was a method for burning water for fuel by releasing its hydrogen and oxygen through electrolysis (unfortunately the electrolysis required the burning of some other fuel; Hefferlin neglected to mention this). The final invention was a spiral power beam which today sounds vaguely like a laser, but just as vaguely like a science-fiction-story ray gun. It was described as if anyone with good mechanical sense could build it from Hefferlin's ambiguous instructions, yet it was clear that he had never built the beam device itself. The article ended in a gaseous climax: "POWER! Blasting material destruction! Or 'building blocks' for the expansion of all mankind!... It is yours, now. What are you going to do with it? Build or destroy? God help you!" In the October 1946 *Amazing Stories*, Hefferlin claimed that he had invented a wonderful method to eliminate static from the radio, although he made some major factual errors—stating, for example, that lightning is "of direct current nature," when it in fact oscillates.

Palmer was suspicious of Hefferlin's claims. He hinted that although "there are many people who 'say' they are the recipients of unusual information from Tibet," they might be unfortunates misled by the telaug whisperings of the dero. But whatever their origin, Hefferlin's articles could not inspire much confidence in the reader who studied them carefully, and it appears that Palmer enjoyed having readers take potshots at Hefferlin. One reader wrote that after reading Hefferlin's article on static, he could only "heartily suggest that Mr. Hefferlin buy a good book on radio and electricity and learn a little about the subject before he writes any more articles.... I honestly cannot see how anyone with a high school education could read Mr. Hefferlin's article without laughing." Hefferlin had given a few specific directions for building the circle-winged plane or the GHYT motor or the POWER! beam, but in each of the articles he left out several essential details, and without them the instructions were useless. When a doctor wrote Palmer and pointed out it would be impossible to build the POWER! beam device with the information Hefferlin had supplied ("Never in my life have I seen or heard of such a poor set of instructions"), Hefferlin replied in the next issue that "full construction information" could not be placed in the hands "of the *general* public," and that "we must consider the seriousness of the International Situation." He also made the ambiguous statement that the articles were "but a brief schematic of the entertainment field pertaining to the Rainbow City, its contents, etc." What was "the Rainbow City"? Palmer tacked on the titillating line that Rainbow City "is the headquarters, a deserted city of the Gods (or the Elder Race) under the ice of the [South] Pole, where all the gadgets mentioned and thousands more are perfectly preserved for thousands of years." Palmer also suggested that Rainbow City be given a seat in the then-new United Nations, but with those teasers, Rainbow City and

William C. Hefferlin disappeared from the pages of *Amazing.*

SPACE SHIPS IN ANTARCTICA

Admiral Byrd visited the South Pole in 1947, one of his exploration flights discovered a warm area on the continent. This area seemed to be artificial. Are those "mystery" aircraft based there?

The February 1948 *Amazing Stories* featured this painting of "Space Ships in Antarctica."

In 1947 and 1948, however, the Borderland Sciences Research Foundation, an alternative-reality group based in Vista, California, began issuing bits and pieces of a document called "The Hefferlin Manuscript," written by W.C. and his wife Gladys at their home in Livingston, Montana. In her introduction to the Manuscript, Gladys Hefferlin denied that their story had anything to do with the Shaver Mystery. "In our correspondence with Mr. Raymond A. Palmer," she began, "we requested him to keep our material separate from the Shaver Mystery.... Mr. Palmer ignored our request and has deliberately distorted our statements for his own purpose." Here in the Hefferlin Manuscript, she wrote, those distortions would be corrected and the real story would be told:

In 1927, according to Gladys, the Hefferlins were a young, mystically-minded couple living in San Francisco, and there they met and became friendly with a man named Emery[3] who shared their interest. They soon moved and lost track of Emery until 1935; but while in Elwood, Indiana, the Hefferlins

---

[3] The identity of "Emery" was long a controversy in Borderland Sciences and Shaver Mystery circles. Many thought he was Emery Deutsch, a once-well-known radio violinist; Deutsch denied it.

learned that Emery was in New York "in radio circles." They wrote to him and it wasn't long before the three of them had begun working on a sort of psychic telephone they called "Controlled Mental Communication." Gladys Hefferlin acted as the "mental link"—a conscious medium—on the Elwood end, while Emery, who was a powerful psychic, sent and received messages in New York. "Our communication," Gladys wrote, "is as fast as ordinary, open conversation." She would receive Emery's messages telepathically and speak them aloud to W.C., and if W.C. wanted to say anything to Emery, he merely had to speak it *at* his wife. Emery "hears all that is said if one speaks loudly enough. It is not necessary to shout—only to speak clearly. Street noises from here go through to him. There is no mystery about this channel, only a definite use of vibrational focus."

Soon after the three of them had established to their satisfaction that the telepathic messages were being accurately received on both ends, Emery began disappearing on mysterious errands around the United States and the rest of the world. Every so often he would send a psychic message to the Hefferlins to let them know where he was, but the reasons for his travels remained a mystery.

At about the beginning of the Second World War, however, Emery revealed to them he had been "working under orders" from a community of Masters beneath Tibet. It had begun back in the early thirties, when W.C. had been experimenting with a few ideas that had "come to him"—the circle-winged plane, the POWER! beam, and so forth—on a small scale, but he had been unable to find a backer with the capital to allow construction of full-scale working models. After being turned down by the U.S. Government, W.C. had sent a complete set of his plans to Emery to show to any potential backer he might encounter. While on vacation in the Far East, Emery somehow met and became friendly with "the Grand Lama, head of the temple in the Valley of Harmonious Peace... which we call Shangri-La." Emery showed W.C.'s plans to the Grand Lama, who was so impressed he ushered Emery into the secret underground lodge of the mysterious Masters of Human Destiny, "the Ancient Three, 'Who were, Who are, Who will be, Always.'"

The Ancient Three were wise enough to realize that W.C. was a reincarnated engineer of the ancients who had reinvented devices used in the forgotten past. They immediately ordered construction of a fleet of 350 circle-winged planes, powered by GHYT motors burning water for fuel, and using POWER! beams as weapons. Under the direction of the Three, work progressed rapidly, and when the fleet stood ready at last, an expedition was ordered to search the wastes of Antarctica for signs of Rainbow City. This deserted metropolis had been the home of the Three during their first incarnation on the planet Earth, and it was critical that the city be repopulated and brought to life if the cosmic plan was to be fulfilled. Emery was assigned to the search, and he spent painstaking months flying over the Antarctic, looking for clues that none but the initiated could detect. But on Thanksgiving of 1942, Emery sent a joyful message to the Hefferlins. Rainbow City had been found.

The Hefferlins were understandably anxious to learn more about the Ancient Three, and little by little, in their psychic conversations with Emery, they heard the story of the Three and the concealed history of the human race. Countless millions of years ago, Emery told them, humanity ruled an empire of planets stretching over a hundred galaxies. But at some point in their conquests, the ancient humans encountered the race which was to become their deadly enemy, the Snake People. The Snake People and the ancients battled for a thousand years, with the advantage passing first to one side, then to the other. But at last it became clear that the Snake People had won. They chased the human race from planet to planet, scattering the remnants of the Human Empire to a few lonely, inconsequential worlds. One of them was Mars, and the Red Planet was for hundreds of generations of the ancients a hospitable home. But as time passed the ancients realized Mars was dying—its oxygen and water were slowly evaporating into space.

The Great Ruler of Mars sent a fleet of spaceships to earth to investigate its potential as a new home. The scouting party returned full of praise for our planet, especially the subtropical Antarctic continent. So the Great Ruler told several thousand of his subjects they were to leave and prepare the way on the new world. They settled in Antarctica and built seven great cities there, modeled after the cities on Mars; each had a distinctive color and was called the Green City or the Blue City or the Red City. But the greatest of all was Rainbow City, so named because it was constructed entirely of plastic of all colors of the rainbow. From Rainbow City, the earth colony was ruled by the first earthly incarnations of the Ancient Three—the son and daughter of the Great Ruler, and the daughter's fiance, who was the son of one of the Great Ruler's ministers (as in most occultist scenarios, there was no such thing as democracy among the all-wise ancients). Under their guidance, the colony flourished mightily.

It was humanity's golden age, but it was not to last forever. A great catastrophe, probably a surprise attack by the Snake People, struck the earth and tipped it over on its axis. As in Doreal's history—but with the parties reversed—the people of Antarctica quickly found their paradise icy and uninhabitable. The survivors of the disaster abandoned the great cities to settle in the wilds to the north, and after thousands of years of adversity they lost their technological knowledge. Memories of the glorious days of the ancients became myths and legends. But even after all that time the great cities of the Antarctic still existed, buried now under thousands of feet of ice.[4]

Rainbow City sat deserted for a million years. It alone of the seven cities was free of ice, for hot springs beneath the city kept it and the surrounding valley at room temperature. Encircled by walls of ice ten thousand feet high,

---

[4] The circumstances surrounding the discovery of Rainbow City in the Hefferlins' story are reminiscent of H.P. Lovecraft's horror story *At the Mountains of Madness* (1936). In the tale, a scientific expedition bores a hole into the Antarctic ice crust and discovers a tunnel filled with the well-preserved corpses of alien life forms. Nearer the South Pole, the expedition discovers a great deserted city hidden behind mountains higher than the Himalayas and finds carvings telling the story of a race of "Elder Things" which settled at the Pole nearly a thousand million years ago and created the earth's life forms. When the "great cold" came, the Old Ones settled first in the oceans, and then traveled down to a sea in the interior of the earth.

Rainbow City has remained hidden from Antarctic explorers to this day—except for Emery and his band. They occupied the city and found it consisted of six levels, one on the surface and five beneath it. Since the technology of the ancients was infinitely superior to our own, the city was found with all its incredible machinery running as well as it had when the city was built two and a half million years ago.

Almost everything in Rainbow City was built of plastic. W.C. wrote that the roads leading into the city "are paved with plastic." The clothing Emery and his colleagues found hanging in the ancient closets "is woven of a plastic thread softer than the finest modern silks, lighter in weight, and... fire proof." All of their jewelry was of a plastic so hard "the surface of a diamond is cut and powdered as if it were ordinary glass." W.C. also wrote that Rainbow City is filled with gardens of "great shade trees and flowering plants, luxurious beyond belief, whose individual blooms often measure three feet in diameter." They are visited by enormous butterflies with wingspreads of seven or eight feet; their bodies would "fill a large sized turkey platter.... They are as large as full sized eagles and are beautiful beyond words." W.C. didn't mention anything about the four- or five-foot caterpillars such butterflies imply, but perhaps the people of Rainbow City didn't mind encountering huge, hungry larvae in their gardens because they were larger themselves. Emery estimated, after looking at the clothes and furniture the ancients left behind, that they averaged about eight feet tall.

While preparing Rainbow City for resettlement by the Ancient Three and their specially-selected followers, Emery and the others discovered many incredible devices abandoned by the ancients. Like Saint Germain's magical dishwasher, "vibratory flames" kept the plastic clothes, carpets, and dishes of the city eternally spotless. Other vibrations supplied the artificial sunlight for the underground gardens. Ancient books read themselves aloud when a button was pushed.

The ancients surpassed themselves, however, as transportation engineers. One of their most remarkable inventions was the "portal," a closet-like room with two doors that would warp space and deliver people or cargo to any point on the globe when the user merely concentrated on the destination. According to W.C., one of Emery's comrades was Kilroy, "a red headed Irishman with a puckish sense of humor." Kilroy was overjoyed when he learned to work the portal, and in his spare moments he would trip from place to place all over the world, appearing just long enough to scrawl "Kilroy was here" on a convenient wall.

The explorers also found and tested the ancients' enormous subway system. It was the *ne plus ultra* of subways, with hundreds of thousands of miles of tunnels from the Central Terminal beneath Rainbow City and snaking under all the continents and oceans. Enormous trains a hundred feet in diameter had flown through the centers of the tubes, held in place by vibrational power; the cruising speed of the trains was a touch over two thousand miles an hour. Emery's group explored a few of the nearby tunnels, and took one of the ancient trains on a short run beneath Antarctica, but the majority of the worldwide tube system was sitting unexplored and empty, as it had since the great disaster struck a million years ago.

There is something in W.C.'s description of the tunnels to tickle the scalp of any science fiction lover—an incredibly old network of huge tunnels under our feet, silent and sealed off into thousand-mile sections behind impervious steel doors, their entrances long buried by earthquakes and landslides. Emery located a few of the great sub-terminals of the system under Asia, Africa, and the Americas using the portals, and he found them filled with caches of unused atomic weapons—mostly personal "blaster types." The Hefferlins themselves discovered the end of one of the subterranean branch lines near their home, "some two hundred feet or more up the side of a mountain" west of Sheridan, Wyoming. "This tunnel seems to have been twisted and sheared off." Was this the work of the Snake People? "When we have time," W.C. wrote, "we shall use the portals to find the answer."

But in 1948 the servants of the Ancient Three had more critical tasks to perform. The Three had reincarnated in our era to begin a new golden age on earth, and they were already "guiding the destinies of three-quarters of the world." All the non-white races of the world, Gladys Hefferlin wrote, "already accepted their leadership and guidance." There were seven temples scattered across Asia, Africa, and South America, all provided with special vibratory jewels, or "thought machines;" from these temples the Ancient Three had for several decades broadcast their wishes to the minds of the non-Western world. Their message was that "each people, country, nation must earn its independence from the European Empire Nations." In the future, "no nation will exploit another nation, put burdensome taxes upon them, nor enslave them in any way. And war will be abolished." All races would be equal.

Under the guidance of the Ancient Three, all nations would merge into a world government on the model of the United States. "The Occident, the White Race, are hearing about this for the first time" because the Three had begun acting on their behalf as well. Who had stopped the Japanese from conquering Australia during the War? Gladys asked. Who had kept Rommel from taking the Suez Canal? The Ancient Three had worked diligently behind the scenes to assure the Allied victory. Now with the War over and Rainbow City in operation again, the time was ripe for the new golden age. The Three were sending squadrons of circle-winged planes into the skies of every continent to search for more traces of ancient cities that might be revived; when people saw the strange craft, they mistook them for alien spaceships and called them "flying saucers."

When the Hefferlins first announced the existence of Rainbow City, they were deluged with questions from the alternative-reality community: Where, exactly, *was* Rainbow City? How can I contact the Ancient Three? Can I go to Rainbow City and work for the New Age? Gladys Hefferlin cautioned her readers that such people were doomed to disappointment. Only certain individuals had been chosen by the Three to go to Rainbow City—not because they were "worthy," but because they were needed there. Rainbow City was not open to the curious. "No one can buy his way into Rainbow City," she wrote; adding,, "We ourselves, who are the North American spokesmen, cannot enter

Rainbow City at this time. Therefore we cannot promise entry to anyone else."

The Hefferlins faded into obscurity in the early 1950s, but Rainbow City was not forgotten. In 1960, UFO writer Michael Barton, known to his readers as Michael X, published a small book titled *Rainbow City and the Inner Earth People,* a curious mishmash of the holes-in-the-poles hollow-earth idea, the Hefferlin Manuscript, and the Shaver Mystery. Here we learn that the Inner Earth people are far from a homogenous group; some are Masters, some are dero, and some are ordinary humans. But since the New Age is coming, the Masters—with the help of the "Guardians," their friends from Venus—are slowly "removing" the dero and other destructive beings from the planet. "Both the astral and physical levels of the inner earth," Barton wrote, "are being cleaned out in preparation for the coming Golden Age." The Masters and the Guardians used Rainbow City as their way-station when passing in and out of the South Polar Opening.

Barton claimed to have discovered these facts in psychic conversations with a number of astral entities through a channel he called "Telethot." Using Telethot, he contacted a Master named Ramel and asked about the nature and history of the inner earth. Ramel told Barton there was someone on the astral plane who wanted to speak with him: "His name is Marshall B. Gardner."

> MG: Marshall Gardner here. I am happy to meet you, Michael. Your writings are very interesting to me. Especially your newest book dealing with Rainbow City and the Inner Earth inhabitants. I can help you considerably in these matters as you probably realize.

> [Michael] X: Yes, thank you. It is a great pleasure to meet you. My first question is, do the polar openings really exist?

> MG: The poles are but phantoms as my book revealed. I find more openings into the earth than I ever dreamed when in the flesh.... One located at the North Pole region, but not at the spot present-day exploration has covered. The opening is at a distance some 1800 miles from the Pole. Another opening is 2400 miles from the South Pole. These openings are not nearly as large as I had calculated in my book... nor are they easy to find. The inner earth people keep these entrances well concealed and camouflaged by their advanced scientific and technical abilities.

> X: Is there a Rainbow City?

> MG: There is a city at the South Pole entrance into the Cavern World. It is known as Rainbow City because the effect of the "Southern Lights" colors the city with beautiful rainbow tints.

There was another writer who kept Rainbow City alive as well—a man who proposed that the hidden war between planets, between the human race and the Snake People, continues secretly to this day. Robert Dickhoff told us that the day was not far off when it might be necessary to choose between Mars and Venus in an interplanetary Armageddon. In the end a new Messiah was to arise, but to meet him, a side trip to Mongolia is necessary.

Chapter 10

Agharti

Once, the Yellow Emperor was sleeping in broad daylight. He dreamt that he was taking a walk in the kingdom of Hua-hsü, a country that lies even further west than the westernmost continent Yen-chou, and to the north of the northernmost continent T'ai-chou, and I do not know how many thousand or ten thousand miles from China. Neither ship nor chariot will do for the journey. One can only travel there in one's mind.

—The *Book of Lieh-tzu,* Second-fourth century AD.

In 1922, Ferdinand Ossendowski (1876–1945), a 46-year-old Polish scientist who had lived most of his life in Russia, published in Warsaw *Przez Kraj Zwierzat, Ludzi i Bogow,* a chronicle of his adventures in Central Asia. When translated into English and published in America as *Beasts, Men and Gods,* it was immediate best seller, reprinted over twenty times within a year of its release. Ossendowski's story was draped heavily with an aura of the supernatural, so much so that his translator, Lewis Palen, felt prompted to advise readers that although the tale might seem "too highly colored to be real," Dr. Ossendowski was no wide-eyed dreamer—he had been thoroughly trained "for careful observation," and he was first and foremost a man of science. Palen's caveat was needless, however, for readers and reviewers alike found themselves too caught up in the doctor's unashamedly exotic prose to care whether or not it was strictly accurate.

Ossendowski's life until that year had been a turbulent one. After his graduation from the University of St. Petersburg in the 1890s, he wandered through Siberia, Mongolia, and western China for several years and fell in love with their wild emptiness. He returned to Europe and earned his doctorate in Paris in 1903, but left for Siberia almost immediately afterward, where he became more and more involved in politics. He was first a chemical expert for the Russian Army during the Russo-Japanese War of 1905, later the president of an abortive "Revolutionary Government of the Russian Far East," and finally a political prisoner, sentenced for his activities against the Tsarist government. After his release from prison, he was living in the Siberian town of Omsk, teaching chemistry and physics, when the Bolshevik revolution exploded. Ossendowski had been active in the short-lived White Russian government and was profoundly anti-Communist, so the Bolsheviks pursued him and a small group of fellow Whites through Siberia and into Mongolia. From Mongolia he crossed into China and finally made his way to Europe to write his story, an indictment of the Bolsheviks. *Beasts, Men and Gods* is a poetic work of propaganda, a highly romanticized tale of a few good men running with death at their heels through a land of superstition. It is also the story of a strange prophecy.

The King of the World

Ossendowski was as intrigued with legends and with the occult as he was with politics. As he fled through "Mysterious Mongolia... the Land of Demons," he paused frequently to speak with Buddhist monks and lamas about the traditions associated with lakes, caves, and monasteries. There was one story he said he encountered everywhere in Central Asia; he called it "The Mystery of Mysteries," the legend of a Messiah-figure known as "The King of the World."

In the Mongolian town of Narabanchi, Ossendowski was led by a lama into the small temple and shown a small room dominated by a low throne. The lama told him that one night in the winter of 1890, a group of horsemen rode into Narabanchi, entered the temple, and demanded that all the lamas gather in that room. When all had assembled, one of the horsemen seated himself on the throne and removed his cap. Everyone present

> fell to their knees as they recognized the man who had been long ago described in the sacred bulls of Dalai Lama, Tashi Lama, and Bogdo Khan. He was the man to whom the whole world belongs and who has penetrated into all the mysteries of Nature. He pronounced a short Tibetan prayer, blessed all his hearers and afterwards made predictions for the coming half century. This was thirty years ago and in the interim all his prophecies are being fulfilled.

As the King of the World spoke, candles and incense burners lighted themselves, and when he had finished, he and his men vanished into the air; "behind him remained no trace save the folds in the silken throne coverings."

After telling his tale, the lama went to pray and left Ossendowski to contemplate the throne. "It was wonderful and difficult to believe," the doctor wrote, "but I really saw there the strong and muscular figure of a man with a swarthy face of stern and fixed expression about the mouth and jaws, thrown into high relief by the brightness of his eyes. Through his transparent body in white raiment I saw the Tibetan inscriptions on the back of the throne. I closed my eyes and opened them again. No one was there but the silken throne covering seemed to be moving..."

Again and again in *Beasts, Men and Gods,* the shadowy figure of the King of the World was invoked against the background of political unrest. Russia, Mongolia, and China were at that time locked in battle over control of Central Asia, with Mongolia bullied by its larger neighbors. Ossendowski implied that the King was the true ruler of Asia who would soon rise from his subterranean empire, the land of Agharti, to lead the children of Genghis Khan to great deeds and conquests once again. Another lama Ossendowski encountered told him that sixty thousand years ago, a holy man had led a tribe of his followers deep into the earth. They settled there, beneath Central Asia, and through the use of the holy man's incredible wisdom and power, and the labors of his people, Agharti became a paradise. No evil could penetrate its borders; destruction and death were forbidden there. Its population now numbered in the millions, and all were happy and prosperous. But the King of the World's command was not limited to Agharti; he ruled "invisibly" millions of Central Asians living on the surface as well. "They will accomplish his every order," the lama told Ossendowski.

Still another lama described Agharti's capital as a stately metropolis encircled by towns of wise priests and scientists who controlled powers beyond the comprehension of the Westerner. The King's palace sat atop a great subterranean mountain and was guarded on all sides by the mansions of the Goro, an elite squadron of priests who could harness "all the visible and invisible forces of the earth." The first Goro, he who had originally brought these forces under control, was named Om; he was honored in Buddhism's best-known mantra, "Om! Mani Padme Hum." The lama who told the doctor these things described some of the other powers of the King and the Goro:

> By [the King's] order, trees, grasses and bushes can be made to grow; old and feeble men can be made young and stalwart; and the dead can be resurrected. In cars strange to us they rush through narrow cleavages inside our planet.... Some of them course among the stars, observe their events, their unknown peoples, their life and their laws.... If our mad humankind should begin a war against them, they would be able to explode the whole surface of our planet and transform it into deserts.

As Ossendowski repeated these stories, he never made it clear whether he believed in the legend of the King of the World or not. Only in the last few pages of the book does it begin to grow plain that he was presenting the legend as an allegory of that once-popular notion called politely "The Restless East" and more bluntly "The Yellow Peril." Ossendowski fled through Mongolia as that country witnessed the most violent era in its history since the days of the Khans, and he seems to have believed that war and revolution were awakening the teeming masses of the East from their slumber of a thousand years and inciting them to conquer the world once again. He tried to be subtle about it, but the message was surely there. He wrote that "as I traveled through Eastern Mongolia to Peking, I often thought:

"And what if? What if whole peoples of different colors, faiths and tribes should begin their migration toward the West?"

He didn't answer his question directly, but offered us instead the prophecy the King of the World had given the lamas of Narabanchi on that winter's night in 1890. The King told them that over the next fifty years, war and materialism would devastate the earth: "The crowns of kings, great and small, will fall.... There will be a terrible battle among all the peoples. The seas will become red.... the earth and the bottom of the sea will be strewn with bones." But he would send a people who were then unknown to "tear out the weeds of madness and vice with a strong hand." They would "found a new life on the earth purified by the death of nations." Evil would be driven out, and from the wreckage of a half century of battles—in other words, in 1940—

three great kingdoms would arise, to flourish peacefully side by side for seventy-one years. But the three kingdoms were doomed to fight each other for eighteen years, and at the climax of the bloodshed in the year 2029, the people of Agharti would rise out of their cavern world. With the King of the World at their head, they would establish a paradise on the earth's surface.

The political usefulness of such a prophecy was clear. Knowing what we do of Ossendowski's history, it is not far-fetched to perceive the "King of the World's prophecy" in the context of the book as the doctor's own curse against the Bolsheviks who had recently killed many of his friends and relatives and chased him from his beloved Siberia. It isn't surprising to see Ossendowski's vision of a new Mongolia rising to crush the Bolsheviks in turn. But the legend of the King of the World may have affected the history of Mongolia in another way.

As Ossendowski passed through the country, Mongolia was in chaos. The fragmented native peoples were fighting both the Chinese, who had for a long time controlled most of the country, and the Bolshevik Red Army, which was trying to wrest it from the Chinese. At the same time all sides were threatened by the Japanese, who had built up the most powerful military force in East Asia. But a curious figure occupied the eye of the hurricane. In October of 1920, Baron Roman Ungern von Sternberg, the commander of a detachment of White Russian cavalry, took his troops into Mongolia and led them in an attack on Urga (now Ulan Bator), the Mongolian capital, which was then held by the Chinese. The Baron had announced to the Mongolians that he was the heir to the power of the Khans, and that he had come to lead them in the conquest of all Asia, and perhaps the world. Ungern's attack on Urga was unsuccessful and his men were forced to retreat, but his words and his crazed courage inspired many Mongolians. Soon ten thousand volunteers had joined his original force of eight hundred, and with their help the Baron easily took Urga in February of 1921; the Chinese who were not slaughtered fled the city in confusion.

Ossendowski met the Baron while passing through Urga and spent several days under his protection. In the light of later events, he depicted Ungern as a doomed, harsh, unforgiving man, but one with a profoundly mystical nature—a convert to Buddhism who expected the same asceticism from his troops that he did from himself. The Baron, according to Ossendowski, knew he would not live to see his empire take root, but he was determined to fight for Mongolia until the end. Before they parted, Ungern said to the doctor:

> I shall die!... but no matter, no matter.... The cause has been launched and shall not die.... The tribes of Jenghiz Khan's successors are awakened. Nobody shall extinguish the fire in the heart of the Mongols! In Asia there will be a great state from the Pacific and Indian Oceans to the shore of the Volga.... It will be the victory of the spirit. A conqueror and leader will appear stronger and more stalwart than Jenghiz Khan... he will keep power in his hands until the happy day when, from his subterranean capital, shall emerge the King of the World.

Ungern appears to have been something of a proto-Nazi as well, both in his brutality and his racial pride. He boasted at length to Ossendowski about the knights, generals, mystics, and alchemists who had been his mighty Teutonic ancestors. The Baron tortured and executed hundreds of men during his military career, but he was particularly hard on Jews; after capturing Urga, he ordered his troops to round up any Jews they found and shoot them. Yet he protested to Ossendowski that some of his most trusted assistants were Jewish.

Another of Ossendowski's lama informants told him that soon after Ungern came to Mongolia, he sent a young prince to find Agharti and deliver a message of greeting to the King of the World. The prince returned with a letter from the Dalai Lama in Tibet, so the Baron sent him a second time. This time "he did not come back."

Not long after Ossendowski made his escape from Mongolia, Ungern decided it was time to begin the assault on the despised Communists. Although some of his officers had suspicions the Baron was losing his mind—his forces were still struggling with bands of Chinese and Bolsheviks in the country around Urga—Ungern's army rode across the border and attacked the Siberian town of Troitskosavsk on May 22, 1921. The Red Army was ready for them and pushed them back into Mongolia without much trouble. But a group of Mongolian Communists, who had just formed the Mongolian People's Government and put together a rag-tag army of their own, asked their Soviet allies to please get Ungern out of the country so they could take Urga. The Red Army obliged and chased the Baron back into Siberia again. Most of the Baron's Mongolian followers grew tired of riding back and forth and deserted, and many of his White Russian officers followed suit. Ungern eluded capture for two months, but to little purpose; Urga was taken easily by the Mongolian People's Government in the Baron's absence, and Mongolia was declared a Communist nation on July 11. Finally, Ungern's remaining men turned him over to the Soviets in disgust, for his defeats had loosened his hold on reality almost totally; he was court-martialed and executed in Siberia on September 15. Thus did the man who wished to conquer Asia in the name of the King of the World—if we are to believe Ossendowski—meet his end.

Shambhala

Ossendowski left Agharti and the King of the World behind to write a scathing biography of Lenin and a half-dozen accounts of his own travels in Africa and the Middle East, but the legend he had set in motion was nurtured by an even more colorful figure. Nikolai Konstantinovitch Roerich (1874–1947), known to his English-speaking readers as Nicholas Roerich, was a twentieth century mystic and Renaissance man. Although little remembered today, he was in the twenties and thirties a highly respected and prolific artist and designer with a softened Art Deco style; he produced many thousands of paintings and drawings of exotic landscapes, images from myth and folklore, and incidents from Russian history (like Ossendowski, he was an exiled White Russian). He had designed sets and costumes for the Ballet Russe before the revolution, and he is probably best known today for his designs for Igor Stravinsky's ballets *Petrouchka* and *Rite of Spring*. Fired by a nostalgia for a romanticized "dawn of history," he also helped the composer write the scenario for *Rite of Spring,* and Stravinsky in turn dedicated the ballet to Roerich.

He traveled extensively all over the world in search of artistic and spiritual inspiration, but his favorite quarter of the globe was Central Asia, from the Urals to the Himalayas. Between 1924 and 1929, Roerich, accompanied by his wife Elena and their sons Georges (an archaeologist) and Sviatoslav (an artist), made five Asian expeditions, and the traditions and legends of the peoples he encountered supplied him with the material for a series of books on the mysteries of Asia. One of them, *Shambhala* (1930), deals in a roundabout way with the King of the World and Agharti.

Roerich was a believer in the transcendental unity of religions—in the notion that one day the Buddhist, the Muslim, and the Christian would realize their separate dogmas were husks obscuring the kernel of truth within. All his works embraced the belief that all faiths awaited a new age in which this chaff of dogma would be stripped away, humanity would toss aside its discords, and all would come together in a paradise of universal brotherhood. His symbol for the coming paradise was Buddhism's land of Shambhala.

Nicholas Roerich, author of *Shambhala,* in a moody and mysterious portrait of the 1920s. Roerich charmed many people with his claims of hidden wisdom in the thirties, but ended his life exiled from the US, in trouble with the IRS.

Shambhala—for Buddhists the hidden land in which the teachings of the *Kalacakra* ("Wheel of Time") Tantric school are kept in their purest form— seems a paradise to the Westerner. Its people live a hundred years, have the power to cure themselves of all illnesses, read the thoughts of others, and see into the future. The palace of the King of Shambhala is fitted with skylights made of lenses, enabling him to see beings living on other planets. In his book *The Way to Shambhala* (1980), Edwin Bernbaum, who spent several years working and studying with Tibetan lamas in Nepal, writes of other wonders from Kalacakra texts: "The King also possesses a glass mirror in which he can see scenes of whatever is happening for miles around; lamas familiar with modern technology explain it as a kind of television screen that enables him to monitor the events of the outside world. Descriptions of 'stone horses with the power of wind' suggest that Shambhala has the technology to make aircraft of metal." Similar texts reveal how the people of the hidden kingdom transmute chemical substances and use natural forces, like the wind, to supply energy. In other words, the Shambhala of Tibetan Buddhism is not too different from Ossendowski's Agharti.

It is similar to Agharti also in its form. In the Kalacakra teachings, Shambhala takes the shape of an eight-petaled lotus blossom surrounded by huge snow-covered mountains. Eight regions—the "eight petals"— form the outer circle of the kingdom, and at Shambhala's center lies Kalapa, the home of the King, surrounded by a ring of even higher mountains. Each of the eight petal-shaped regions is the home of twelve princes, so the image is similar to Ossendowski's description of the palace of the King of the World surrounded by the mansions of the Goro. Similar also is the Tibetan belief in Shambhala's mission on earth. There is a prophecy that Shambhala will have thirty-two kings, each ruling one hundred years. The first king, Sucandra, ruled during the life of the Buddha Gautama in the sixth century BC. As the reign of the thirty-second king approaches, conditions on the rest of the earth will grow progressively worse; people will become brutal, power-hungry, and materialistic, and a race of barbarians will arise, led by an evil king, who will conquer—he thinks—the entire world.

But as this evil one is about to clinch his hold on the peoples of earth, the mists that have concealed Shambhala for thousands of years will lift, and all the barbarians will gather outside the kingdom. The tyrant will lead the attack, but the thirty-second King of Shambhala—Rudra Cakrin, called "The Wrathful One with the Wheel"—will ride out of his kingdom and crush the barbarians in a great battle. With the tyrant and his forces slaughtered, all the world will become Shambhala; one text tells us "the perfect age will dawn anew." Disease and poverty will end, and all will live to the age of a hundred. The teachings of the Kalacakra will spread throughout the world, and many will gain enlightenment. This age will last at least a thousand years, and the final battle which begins it is due between two and five hundred years from now. The prophecy of Rudra Cakrin's victory over the barbarians circulated freely among the Mongolians at the time Ossendowski passed among them; it is ironic that Sukhe Bator, leader of the Mongolian People's Government, composed a march for his troops in the war against the Chinese and Baron Ungern's men which ran: "Let us die in this war and be reborn as warriors of the King of Shambhala!" It is not difficult to see where Ossendowski might have learned of the King of the World's prophecy.

It was probably not in Mongolia, however, that he heard the name Agharti. Shambhala is not a subterranean country in Buddhist tradition, but a hidden valley somewhere to the north of Tibet. Scholars of Tibetan religion have attempted to identify Shambhala with a real place in Central Asia for many years without much success; Afghanistan, Turkestan (in the modern Soviet Union), India, and the Gobi Desert have all been candidates. But the most likely spot for a Shambhala—if we see it as a historical location from which the Kalacakra teachings came to Tibet—is the vast expanse of western China known today as Xinjiang. Here are several huge windswept basins between the Kunlun, Tien Shan, and Altai Mountains—the Tarim Basin, the Turfan Depression and the Dzungaria Basin—all of which supported flourishing, cosmopolitan civilizations during the first thousand years AD. Shambhala may also not signify a *place* so much as a culture—the nomadic culture of old Siberia and Mongolia. The Bon religion, which was the native belief of Tibet before Buddhism first appeared there in the seventh century AD, was dominated by shamanistic traditions, and they may have come to Tibet in ancient times from the Altaic and Mongolian peoples. Bon tradition holds that its teachings first came to Tibet eighteen thousand years ago from Olmolungring, a hidden kingdom northwest of Tibet. Olmolungring was the earthly paradise, the center of the world from which spiritual energies flowed in all directions.

Central Asia, with many of the locations discussed in Chapter 10. The search for Shambhala and Agharti has centered here.

In Buddhist tradition, Shambhala assumed many levels of meaning. While on an external level it retained from the Bon myths its identity as an earthly paradise and a source of wisdom, it also came to signify the "land" of the Buddha-nature, peace, and bliss. In the *Kalacakra Tantra*, Rigden Dragpo, one of the Kings of Shambhala, defeats in battle a barbarian king, Lalo-Desum, who symbolizes the three Lords of Materialism known as the Lala-Desum—the Lord of Form, the Lord of Speech, and the Lord of Mind—who had enslaved the human race. Rigden Dragpo's victory was the victory of the transcendent Buddha-nature over mind and matter. A leading lama of the Kalacakra school has warned us against trying to express Shambhala only in physical terms: "its appearance," he says, "varies according to one's karma. For example, one and the same river will be seen by gods as nectar, by man as water, by hungry ghosts as pus and blood, and by some animals as a place to live in. Therefore, it is difficult to say specifically what anything is."

It is also difficult to write of Eastern traditions in a manner valid for matter-enslaved Westerners. Nicholas Roerich, who so fervently desired to bring East and West together, stressed the nearness and reality of the Shambhala-to-come by implying there was a physical land of Shambhala, built out of matter, *on* or *in* the earth. His book *Shambhala* opens with Roerich quizzing a lama on a mountainside in the Himalayas about the hidden kingdom. The lama feigns ignorance at first, but when Roerich demonstrates his knowledge of the Shambhala tradition, he responds with word of the King of Shambhala, whose name is Rigden-jyepo:

> Verily, the time is coming when the Teaching of the Blessed One will once again come from the North to the South... great things are coming. Probably the ray from the tower of Rigden-jyepo has reached all countries.
>   Like a diamond glows the light on the Tower of Shambhala. He is there—Rigden-jyepo, indefatigable, ever vigilant in the cause of mankind. His eyes never close. And in his magic mirror he sees all events of earth.

But where was this earthly Shambhala? We begin to get a hint in a later chapter, when Roerich tells us of a legend of the Chud, a mysterious people who "once upon a time" lived in a fertile valley of the Altai Mountains. The Chud were content until a ruthless Tsar conquered their valley and forced them into serfdom. Their pride smarted under the Tsar's oppression, but they remained docile and industrious until the day one of the Chud discovered a white birch, a tree that had never been seen in the valley before. They had among them a prophecy: when a white birch appeared among them, they were to leave the face of the earth. They gathered their belongings and filed into a secret cavern in a low hill. They sealed the cavern's mouth with stones, and none of the Chud have been seen since. "Only sometimes," said the old man who told Roerich the tale, "can you hear the holy people singing; now their bells ring out in the subterranean temples. But there shall come in the glorious time of human purification, and in those days, the Chud shall appear again in full glory."

Later, as Roerich's party passed through Xinjiang, they crossed an area honeycombed with caverns. They heard the hollow sound of their horses' hoofs upon the hills, and "our caravan people called attention to this, saying, 'Do you hear what hollow subterranean passages we are crossing? Through these passages, people who are familiar with them can reach far-off countries.'" When the Roerichs passed the mouths of caves, the caravan people said, "Long ago people lived there; now they have gone inside; they have found a subterranean passage to the subterranean kingdom." Roerich was not specific about *which* subterranean kingdom, but he implied it was Shambhala. "Only rarely," his caravan driver continued, "do some of them appear again on earth. At our bazaar such people come with strange, very ancient money, but nobody could remember a time when such money was in usage here."

When Roerich asked the lama of the opening chapter about these tales—and whether such passages might lead to the hidden kingdom—the lama replied in circuituous fashion that yes, sometimes the people of Shambhala come out into the world, emerging to bring us gifts which aid us in our struggles on the surface. "Even Rigden-jyepo himself appears at times in a human body," the lama said, and then described a scene that sounds as if it had been lifted directly from Ossendowski's book:

> By night or at early morning before sunrise, the Ruler of the World arrives in the Temple. He enters. All the lamps at once kindle themselves. Some already recognize the Great Stranger. In deep reverence the lamas gather. They listen with the greatest attention to the prophecies of the future.
>
> A great epoch approaches. The Ruler of the World is ready to fight.... The planets are manifesting the new era. But many cataclysms will occur before the new era of prosperity.

This suspicious quotation is not Roerich's only "borrowing" of material he described as coming directly from his own conversations with the people of Central Asia. He was for many years involved with the Theosophists (I have never been able to discover whether he was a member of the Society or not; his biographers disagree), and he was familiar with H.P.B.'s, Annie Besant's, and C.W. Leadbeater's writings on "Shamballa," the city of Masters they claimed was concealed by the sands of the Gobi. Roerich wrote in *Shambhala* of stories he said he had heard in Mongolia of "how the sands of the great desert shift, and for a moment disclose treasures of the entrances of subterranean kingdoms. But none would dare to touch those treasures." Compare this quote with one from H.P.B.'s *Isis Unveiled*: "the Gobi sand moves regularly from east to west before terrific gales that blow continually. Occasionally some of the hidden treasures are uncovered, but not a native dare touch them." Roerich sometimes appeared to have gathered at least as much of his material on Central Asia from Western occultists as from Central Asians.

Roerich did, however, present himself in the West as one in contact with the Masters of Central Asia, and he gathered about him a large group of American and European disciples who were convinced he spoke to the Masters regularly. One of them was the metaphysician Claude Bragdon, who wrote in his introduction to Roerich's travel diary *Altai-Himalaya* (1929) that "one may regard Roerich as an envoy of those powers which preside over the life and evolution of humanity in the same sense that gardeners preside over a garden." And indeed Roerich styled his personal appearance as a Western occultist might imagine a Master; for his photographs he wore long, brocaded Oriental robes, shaved his head, and kept his beard immaculately forked. The political historian Arthur M. Schlesinger, Jr. described Roerich in the early thirties as a "small, bald man, with his soft voice and white beard, billing himself as the exclusive representative of the White Brotherhood of the Far East."

His most famous disciple was Henry Wallace, Franklin Roosevelt's third-term Vice President. While serving as FDR's Secretary of Agriculture, Wallace wrote many letters to Roerich beginning "Dear Guru;" these letters nearly found their way into the newspapers when Wallace was FDR's running mate in 1940, and they finally did appear—and ruined Wallace's political career—in 1948, when Wallace was running for President and conservative columnist Westbrook Pegler published them as the "Guru Letters." Wallace convinced FDR to participate in one of Roerich's more exoteric campaigns in April of 1935—the signing of the Roerich Peace Pact at the White House. Here twenty-two countries, including the United States, agreed to place a special banner (which Roerich identified as the Banner of Shambhala) on museums, libraries, monuments and other repositories of culture so that in wartime, they would not be blown up, looted, or burned. It was one of Roerich's most sensible and popular ideas, but it never went much further than the signing and was soon forgotten in that era's combustible global political climate. Wallace had also sent Roerich on another Central Asian expedition in 1934; he was supposed to search for drought-resistant grasses on the Central Asian plateaus, but according to an article in *Newsweek,* Department of Agriculture officials "freely admitted" he had also been sent "to look for signs of the Second Coming," most likely the coming of the King of Shambhala.[1]

Roerich had already seen one sign in August of 1927, after building a large white shrine in the Shara-gol Valley of Xinjiang and consecrating it to Shambhala. Soon afterward, one of their caravaneers saw something strange in the sky:

> We all saw, in a direction from north to south, something big and shiny reflecting the sun, like a huge oval moving at great speed. Crossing our camp the thing changed its direction from south to southeast. And we saw how it disappeared in the intense blue sky. We even had time to take our field glasses and saw distinctly an oval form with shiny surface, one side of which was brilliant from the sun.

Today it would be a typical UFO sighting, and one not taken too seriously—in another of his books, Roerich describes the same sighting, but he not only describes the object differently, he has it travel south*west* instead of south*east.* But discussing it later with the lama who had told him of Rigden-jyepo, Roerich was told it had been a sign from Shambhala. "The protecting force from Shambhala follows you in this Radiant form of Matter. This force is always near to you but you cannot always perceive it.... Did you notice the direction in which the sphere moved? You must follow the same direction."

---

[1]It appears, however, that Roerich's main goal on this expedition was to establish a White Russian government in Siberia; see the fascinating article "The New Deal and the Guru" by C. J. Errico and J. S. Walker in *American Heritage*, March 1989, p. 92.

It does not seem to have been, however, the direction to an earthly—or subterranean—land of Shambhala.   Like most alternative-reality writers, Roerich hinted at many more wonders than he described plainly.   Despite the suggestions he dropped here and there in his books about hidden passages beneath the Tibetan plateau and underground lakes beneath the Potala (at that time the Dalai Lama's residence in Lhasa), the thoughtful reader is hard put to conclude that Roerich ever found that hidden valley or subterranean paradise. For the purposes of his work, however, it was not really necessary to find a physical Shambhala any more than it had been necessary for Ossendowski to demonstrate the existence of Agharti.   For both writers, the symbol and the prophecy of both hidden lands had been the important things.   Ossendowski saw Agharti as the sleeping power of the East, waking to rise and crush Bolshevism.   Roerich conceived of Shambhala as the archetypal paradise the world was to become when East and West—and science and religion—united.   The Ruler of the World was in Roerich's eyes not only Rigden-jyepo, but also Maitreya, the Buddha-who-is-to-come, as well as the Messiah of the Jews and Christ in his Second Coming.   The coming race from Shambhala were the fully realized human beings of the new era.   In his book *Heart of Asia*, Roerich defined Shambhala not as a kingdom but an event—the great coming together of all the world's people:

> Above all conventionalities, above all separation, are to be seen some sparks of peaceful world unity. In the name of this peace of the world... it is a great joy to pronounce here the Sacred Word of Asia, Shambhala.
>
> You have noted that the concept of Shambhala corresponds to the aspirations of our most serious Western scientific research.... In their striving, the Eastern disciplines of Shambhala and the best minds of the West, which do not fear to look beyond the outworn methods, are uniting.
>
> How precious it is to ascertain that the East and West are united in the name of free knowledge.

Roerich, for whom the world was soon to become Shambhala, for whom the approaching battles of World War II were only harbingers of the final battle for the hidden kingdom, stressed in the end that although a physical Shambhala would be a great wonder, it wasn't essential.   It was the prophecy of a united world that was important, and the hidden kingdom was its symbol.

But symbolic countries aren't much fun to believe in, and Western alternative-reality proponents, who prefer to take their myths literally, have little patience with them.   Among the great pile of ancient-astronaut books that appeared in the wake of von Däniken's *Chariots of the Gods* were two by one of Roerich's *chelas,* Andrew Tomas: *We are Not the First* (1971) and *Shambhala, Oasis of Light* (1973), Tomas revealed in them that after the First World War, the Masters of Shambhala sent a fragment of a mysterious stone to Europe. This stone—which Tomas said is known in Tibetan legend as Chintamani, an object brought to earth many centuries ago by space travelers from the Sirius system—is kept in a tower in Shambhala, broadcasting rays that influence the destinies of nations. The fragment sent to Europe aided in the establishment of the

League of Nations, and when its mission was accomplished, the Masters asked Roerich to return it to Shambhala, which he did, evidently after his UFO sighting of 1927.

But the idea of an earthly Shambhala/Agharti and the true meaning of the King/Ruler of the World's prophecy intrigued occultists decades before Tomas wrote his books. In their hands, the subterranean empire of Agharti became welded firmly to the hidden valley of Shambhala, and both became actual—and often sinister—nations filled with wonders that were all too real.

"Tales from Tibet"

Madame Blavatsky mentioned Shambhala a few times in *The Secret Doctrine* as an "island" or oasis in the Gobi Desert, the sanctuary of Lemuria's "elect" after their home continent had disappeared into the Pacific, playing for her in Asia the same role Shasta played for H. Spencer Lewis in California. It was only one hidden sanctuary among many in H.P.B.'s writings, but her successors Annie Besant (1847–1933) and C.W. Leadbeater (1847–1932) gave it a much greater role in later Theosophy. In his book *The Masters and the Path* (1925), Leadbeater wrote of the "oasis in the Gobi Desert called Shamballa,[2] often spoken of as the Sacred Island," where the Lord of the World—whose Hindu title is Sanat Kumara—dwells with his three pupils, the Pratryeka Buddhas. They are the earth's four greatest adepts; although human in appearance, their bodies "differ widely from ours in constitution, being rather garments assumed for convenience than bodies in the ordinary sense, since they are artificial and their particles do not change as do those of the human frame. They require no nourishment, and remain unchanged through thousands of years." The Lord of the World looks like a youth of sixteen, but his face and eyes are filled with an "omniscient, inscrutable majesty, conveying such a sense of relentless power that some have found themselves unable to bear his gaze, and have veiled their faces in awe." H.P.B. was one of the few mortal initiates to be presented to Sanat Kumara in Shamballa, he wrote, and she found the force of his personality almost more than she could endure.

The Lord of the World, according to Leadbeater and Besant, was the leader of the "Lords of the Flame," the group of infinitely wise beings from Venus whom H.P.B. had called the "Serpents and Dragons of Light." They had come to humanity's aid during Lemuria's fall, bringing us the arts of civilization to start anew, and for their trouble they were later maligned as devils and evil spirits by the Christians. Sanat Kumara remained on this planet to guide its development, and with the help of his three pupils, he wields all the powers of nature, both creative and destructive. He controls the weather, the evolution of plant and animal life, earthquakes, and the rhythm of the tides. "He is the

---

[2]In this section, I shall use the Theosophical spelling "Shamballa" to differentiate the Theosophical city of Masters in the Gobi from the Shambhala of Buddhist tradition described earlier in this chapter.

force," wrote Leadbeater, "which drives the whole world-machine, the embodiment of divine will on this planet." When humanity has moved on to the planet Mercury, his pupils will succeed him as Lords of their own worlds.

Alice A. Bailey (1880–1949), a renegade Theosophist, took these teachings about Shamballa and made them even more central to her own scheme of the cosmos. Bailey was an upper-class Englishwoman who claimed she was visited throughout her life by one of H.P.B.'s Masters, whom she called "The Tibetan." Under his guidance, she produced and published a heavy shelf of occult books—perhaps the best known is *A Treatise on Cosmic Fire*. In her books, Sanat Kumara became the director of a bustling worldwide organization of spiritual beings; Shamballa is their headquarters, a city of seven gates somewhere in the Gobi. The city was built of matter which is simultaneously physical and etheric; thus the seeker after Shamballa can find it only after he or she has developed "etheric sight"—otherwise it is invisible. From the city Sanat Kumara leads his Hierarchy of Masters in focusing the spiritual energies of the earth upon humanity in preparation for the oncoming Aquarian Age, in which Christ—who is also Maitreya—will appear on earth again.

At the same time, the notion of the subterranean empire of Agharti (which did not appear by name in Theosophical writing) influenced a wider circle of alternative-reality writers after the publication of Ossendowski's book. One such book, and one very much in the Ossendowski/Roerich tradition, was *Darkness Over Tibet* (1935) by Theodore Illion, which purported to be a chronicle of the author's experiences in Central Asia. Illion wrote that he was given directions by an Initiate to an underground city in a remote Tibetan valley; he traveled there and discovered a strange settlement of Initiates and their zombie-like servants. The living quarters were just beneath the surface, but a vast complex of temples and sanctuaries lay further down, connected by tunnels miles long. At first Illion believed the Initiates were working for the "Powers of Light," but after he met the Prince, a tall man with a long white beard, he was certain that all the talk of virtue was a show and the underground city was a city of evil. His suspicions were confirmed when, trying to escape, he blundered into the kitchen and saw the zombie-like servants preparing dinner by cutting up a corpse. Although Illion filled his book with authentic-seeming details of Tibetan culture, the effect of the book is stagey—more like a work of heavily allegorical fiction than a real chronicle. Some features of his underground city are delightfully mysterious, however; when Illion first arrived at the city, he wrote that he saw on the surface the opening of an incredibly deep shaft. He tossed a few stones into the shaft and stood silently on the edge, but never heard the stones hit bottom. Later, he passed the opening again with one of the Initiates:

> "This shaft must be very deep," I observed.
> "How do you know it is a shaft?" asked Narbu.
> "I have explored it a little," I answered.
> He seemed greatly surprised.
> "It is immeasurably deep," he observed, "but no one except the Prince of Light and a few of the highest Initiates who are called Lords of Compassion know where it leads to.

Anyone who would find out where it leads to and what it is used for would have to die....
There are such secrets."
  "Who would kill him?"
  "No one. He would die automatically the following night."

Illion presented his description of this city of the "Powers of Shadow" as
the truth behind the legend of Agharti. In the introduction to the book he
wrote, "The existence of an Underground City in Tibet is occasionally hinted at
by well-informed people in the forbidden country, although the stories are often
extravagant and turn the Underground City... into a 'Mighty Underground
Empire inhabited by millions of people.'"

Such tales were not lost on Ray Palmer and the readers of the Shaver-era
Amazing Stories. In 1946 Palmer published the first in a series of highly sensational articles by Vincent Gaddis, "Tales from Tibet." Gaddis, who was later to
gain fame for his sensational UFO writings, blended the mystery/paranoia of
the Shaver Mystery with Illion's and Ossendowski's stories, and painted Tibet
in the foulest colors possible. He implied it was a nation of sorcerers and devil-
worshippers—a land that broadcast "currents of sheer evil" to the rest of the
world under the fearful leadership of the so-called "King of the World," who
lurked in the subterranean city of Agharti like the King of the Dero. In a later
article, "Tunnels of the Titans," Gaddis hinted darkly that Agharti's domain
was not limited to Central Asia, but stretched throughout the world. He quoted
H.P.B.'s description of the vast tunnel system of South America, and then mentioned a "strange rumor" he had heard: that the thirteenth Dalai Lama had not
died in 1933 as everyone had thought, but had forseen the coming of great troubles to Asia, arranged for a false successor, and fled to a hidden retreat in the
Andes. How had the Dalai Lama reached South America unknown and unseen? Gaddis could not say for certain—"the miles are long between the Andes
and the highland of Tibet"—but might not he have used a great tunnel beneath
the Pacific? He cited a magazine story to the effect that strange figures in Indian
costume, "but with Mongolian facial features" and carrying prayer wheels, had
been spotted in the mountains of Ecuador. Were they part of a hidden empire of
sinister Tibetan "holy men"?

  Several readers protested Gaddis's execration of Tibet, and among them
was a man who signed himself EDONI—"E plus D equals zerO plus N equals I."
EDONI contended that while there were "various centers" in Tibet from which
"mighty forces of evil are being poured out upon us constantly," the country
was also the home of one of "the most powerful centers of *good* in the entire
universe." This center was Shamballa, also known as Agharti. EDONI included a "true description" of the King of the World to correct Gaddis's slander-
ing portrait, and Palmer placed it in an article of its own, titled "THE KING OF
THE WORLD?" EDONI said the King had come here "ages ago from the planet
Venus to be the instructor and guide of our then just dawning humanity."
When humanity was at last ready for the blessings he had preserved for them
beneath the earth, he would "emerge and establish a new civilization of peace
and plenty."

But Palmer was forever impatient with humanity-isn't-ready-yet oc-cultists, and he didn't take the idea of the King of the World very seriously. He asked the King a question: If you can bring peace to the world, why not do it now, when we need it? "We, the people of Earth, ask: What man can judge another? Wars must end now! Judge not, Great One, lest you be judged. For we ARE ready for peace!"

The King of the World did not respond to Palmer's challenge immediately, but the letters arriving at *Amazing* asking for more information about the King and his subterranean realm did inspire several of his writers to produce fiction on the theme. Soon after "Tales from Tibet" appeared, Palmer ran a novel-length story by Heinrich Hauser titled "Agharti." It suggested that the Nazis had built enormous underground cities beneath Germany during the war and named them "Aghartis" after the land of Tibetan legend. When they realized the war had been lost, Hitler and the high officials of and scientists of the Third Reich—accompanied by a select group of storm troopers and another of beautiful women—se-creted themselves in the Aghartis, where the Nazi scientists labored relentlessly over "monstrous V-7 atomic rockets" and other super-weapons de-signed to conquer an unsuspect-ing world. Fortunately for the world, however, one of the V-7s malfunctioned, exploded, and de-stroyed the Aghartis in a mas-sive earthquake.

THE KING OF THE WORLD?

Is there an underground cave city called Agharti ruled by a Venusian who holds our future hopes?

ALL through the world today are thousands of people who claim to have knowledge of an underground city, not specifically located although generally assumed to be in Tibet, called Agharti, or Shambala. In this city, they say, is a highly developed civilization ruled by an "Elder" or a "Great One" whose title is among others "The King of the World." Some claim to have seen him, and it is also claimed that he made at least one visit to the surface. It is also claimed that when Mankind is ready for the benefits he can bring, he will emerge and establish a new civilization of peace and plenty.

To quote the words of a "witness": "He came here ages ago from the planet Venus to be the instructor and guide of our then just dawning humanity. Though he is thousands of years old, his appearance is that of an exceptionally well-developed and handsome youth of about sixteen. But there is nothing juvenile about the light of infinite love, wisdom and power that shines from his eyes. He is slightly larger than the average man, but there are no radical differences in race."

Apparently the ruler of Agharti is a man; apparently he possesses great power and science, including atomic energy machines. Apparently also he is dedicated to bring to us great benefits. Apparently he has power to end warfare on the surface at will. We, the people of Earth, ask: What man can judge another? Wars must end now! Judge not, Great One, lest you be judged. For we ARE ready for peace!

The King of the World, as pictured in the May 1946 *Amazing Stories*

Another story, "The Man from Agharti" by the husband-and-wife team of John and Dorothy de Courcy, told of the visit of a young college professor and his wife to the sub-Tibetan Agharti, where they met the wise and beneficent King of the World. The King told them that the world would soon be cleansed by an atomic war, which would burn off the dross of surface humanity and signal his own arrival as ruler of a reborn outer earth. In the story the King—

indirectly, of course—answered Palmer's earlier question as well. When Mary (the young woman of the story) asks the King why the world cannot be cleansed without mass destruction and death, he answers as would most "secret tradition" occultists: "If there was a way, it would be done that way. You will understand better later on and then you will change your point of view.... If man chooses to remain at peace, we will certainly not object and if he follows the path of blood, it is his choice to make. Either way, it will work toward his eventual betterment."

The de Courcys who wrote "The Man from Agharti" seem to have narrowly missed meeting a real man from Agharti in 1946. They wrote to Palmer that "a tall man wearing a long blue or black overcoat and a dark hat drawn down to conceal his face" had appeared at two former residences of theirs and asked the landlord for their forwarding address. The landlord in San Francisco forgot their address temporarily, and the landlord in Portland misplaced it; but both times the mysterious visitor asked the landlord to write the de Courcys if possible and tell them, "The man from Agharti seeks you. I bear a message from the King." They asked Palmer to publish their current Seattle address, and he did—but he added, "We don't think you'll hear from this bird. If the King of the World exists, and we have no proof at all that he does, it would seem that he does not skulk around in long coat and lowered hat brim." If he was so foolish not to contact *Amazing* for their address, the only message the couple were likely to receive would be, "Can you spare five dollars for a nice fellow?"

Agharta

And then in 1951 a truly—and unintentionally—comical version of the Agharti legend appeared when Robert Ernst Dickhoff, "Ph.D., D.D., Messenger of Buddha," who affected the title of "Sungma Red Lama" and described himself as "a dedicated, sworn to honesty philosopher," published *Agharta: the Subterranean World* from his small combination bookshop and "Dordjelutru Lamasery" in New York City. Although Dickhoff presented himself as the American spokesman of a hidden network of Buddhist princes and lamas of the "Aghartan philosophy," it was painfully obvious to the reflective reader that his information about subterranean realms came not from any secret brotherhood of priests, but from *Amazing Stories* and the Hefferlin Manuscript.

Dickhoff's scenario for the genesis of the human race was similar in many ways to the Hefferlins'. Two and a half million years ago, he wrote, a party of Martian "super-scientists" traveled to Earth in their "space spheres" to colonize the planet. They landed in the subtropical Antarctic continent and out of a mass of red clay created the first human beings. The Martians told our ancestors that they of Mars were the Elder Gods and that the human race had been created to serve them; the Martians quickly put the new humans to work building the seven great cities of Antarctica. But as the work progressed, the sinister inhabitants of Venus looked over at what was happening on Earth and decided they wanted the planet for themselves. Soon fleets of Venusian cruisers were landing in remote locations to drop off raiding parties that harassed and destroyed settlements of humans and Martians wherever they could find them. These Venusians were none other than the infamous Serpent People; they resembled crocodiles but walked erect, had humanoid hands and feet—but with six fingers or toes plus a thumb—and averaged fourteen feet tall. They also possessed a good deal of sophisticated and deadly weaponry, and as their raids grew more frequent and daring, the Martians and their human servants were forced to excavate huge cities under the surface for defense, connected by tunnels thousands of miles long. Two of the greatest of the subterranean cities were Shambalah, beneath what is now Tibet, and Agharta, under what is now the Tzangpo Valley of China. But the Martians continued to actively colonize the surface world as well, and as their human children learned to run a civilization on their own, the Martians helped them until they could withdraw from direct involvement in surface affairs.

The Martian Elders did not want to abandon complete control of the human race, however, so they arranged to reincarnate themselves into human bodies and became great teachers and political leaders of the two continents Atlantis and Lemuria, which were then rapidly filling with human settlers. All went well until the Venusians realized what the Martians were doing; soon they too were reincarnating themselves as humans, particularly in Atlantis. The reincarnated Venusians became the notorious Black Magicians of Theosophical lore and seized control of the Atlantean government. The Black Magicians provoked the Atlanteans to attack their former allies the Lemurians with the atomic weapons the Magicians provided them, and in the end both sides destroyed each other under the force of tons upon tons of nuclear warheads. Atlantis and Lemuria sank into their respective oceans, and in the catastrophe the earth tipped on its axis and sent the cities of Antarctica to the bottom of the world, freezing all of them permanently except for Rainbow City.

The Martians and Venusians, not to mention the human race, were almost wiped out in the conflict, and both races of aliens, now completely in human form, went "underground" in both senses of the word. The headquarters of the Martians was Shambalah, and the Venusians wrested control of Agharta from the Martians. They held Agharta for a million years, and streams of evil magicians and hypnotists—who incited petty wars and squabbles among humankind—issued from its caverns. But in 1948, an army of five hundred lamas from Shambalah, led by the reincarnated Martian Grand Lama, invaded Agharta and exterminated "the Evil Master of evil masters, who called himself 'King of the World[3]'" and all but a few of his host of sorcerers. Those few who had survived the attack and fled into the surface world were easy to recognize, Dickhoff said; they referred to Agharta by its Venusian name, "Agharti."

Although their numbers had been decimated, the evil magicians and their allies on Venus were working as diligently as ever in the early 1950s to conquer the earth. History was repeating itself; as they had in Atlantis, the Venusians, posing as scientists, had "discovered" atomic power for the human race, and were tempting governments into stockpiling heaps of ever-more-so-

[3]Remember that EDONI had revealed in *Amazing Stories* the King's Venusian origins.

phisticated nuclear weapons. The Venusians were also keeping the nations of the world in constant dissension. "You can find these serpents well represented in the U.N. Council," Dickhoff wrote, "saying many pretty things, which are in themselves time-devouring, meaningless, expensive to the taxpayer and an outright nuisance, since they are aimed to confuse the already snarled issues." All the while, the evil ones were plotting to annihilate the human race; after triggering World War III, they would fly over the earth in the confusion, "scooping up humans by the thousands from the streets of cities and towns." The unlucky captives would be taken to the Gobi Desert, where the Venusians would devour them "in a fantastic bacchanal supreme, by gorging down the flesh torn from still living humans into the facial apertures they call mouths."

But the Martian forces, rallying in Shambalah, Agharta, and Rainbow City, were not about to let the Venusians undo all their work without a fight. Dickhoff was evidently in contact with the Hefferlins or Borderland Science, for in *Agharta* he supplied a good deal of information about Rainbow City and the Ancient Three that did not appear in the generally available portions of the Hefferlin Manuscripts. He revealed, for example, the names and roles of the Three: "Raj Rutan, skilled in material things, Raj Ruzzan, skilled in cultural arts and the mental angle, and Rani Khatani [the female member of the Three] of the spiritual angle." He also passed along a report from Emery about a Venusian serpent nicknamed "Junior," who committed suicide when the army of the Ancient Three tried to capture him alive. Junior's body was saved, however, and permanently preserved for study in a huge plastic cylinder in Rainbow City. The forces of the Three also found and destroyed several huge subterranean vaults filled with thousands of Venusian serpents lying in suspended animation until "serpent-dominated men would find and free them, thus arousing them into instant evil action."

But Dickhoff was not entirely on the side of the Ancient Three either; he found the Martian "Elder Gods" almost as warlike as the Venusians, and unwilling to share their technology and mental powers with their human children. He advocated a path of peace, following the teachings of the Buddha, and he believed that the Buddha Maitreya would soon appear upon the earth to usher in the New Age, in which war would be no more (he was unclear about just where Maitreya fit in among the Martians and Venusians, but the Buddha evidently disapproved of both sides). But to demonstrate to both the Elder Gods and Serpent People that the people of Earth had come of age, Dickhoff urged humanity to perfect space travel as soon as possible and build a fleet of its own spaceships as a deterrent.

In the meantime, however, signs of the paradise to come were beginning to appear, at least to Dickhoff. Since in the New Age all seasons would be spring, he cited several newspaper articles reporting freak heat waves with flowers blooming in New Jersey in January of 1951. He mentioned the rumors of Tibetans lurking in the Andes which had appeared in *Amazing Stories,* and reported that strange lights had recently been seen beaming from the mountains of Ecuador; were they greeting a squadron of spaceships from Mars, he wondered, or from Venus? He felt something mysterious was definitely happening in Ecuador, and pointed to the Otovallo Indians of that country as an example. "They certainly look like Tibetans," he wrote, "wearing their traditional queues and living in dwellings of an ancient Chinese style." The Otovallos obviously knew what was going on, but "you cannot make an Indian talk for all the money in the world, when he decides that the answer is not meant for white men's ears." Was this mysterious activity the harbinger of the coming paradise on earth, or of an impending cataclysm? Dickhoff was not entirely sure himself. "Whatever comes of this," he concluded, "time will tell."

From "Agharttha" to "Arghati"

The notion of a subterranean empire beneath Central Asia has had a strong influence on the inner-world mythos since Ossendowski's *Beasts, Men and Gods* first appeared in the 1920s, and we shall see in the next two chapters how strong that influence was. But how much of the notion is truly Asian and how much originated in the imaginations of Western occultists? Agharti appears to be a blend of Eastern and Western myth; we might compare it to a better-known but similar Western creation—Shangri-La. James Hilton, the British author of *Lost Horizon* (1933), the novel which made "Shangri-La" part of our cultural baggage, was inspired to create his paradise after reading either a garbled report of the Shambhala tradition brought from Tibet by a European missionary or one of Roerich's books, or both. The Agharti legend, it appears, was created by a Westerner in a similar way.

That Westerner was not Ferdinand Ossendowski, however, but an eccentric French writer named Joseph-Alexandre Saint-Yves (1842–1910), who took the spurious title of "Marquis J.-A. Saint-Yves d'Alveydre." Saint-Yves was a strange mixture of occultist and political philosopher; he promoted in his books the establishment of a form of government called *synarchy,* supposedly the opposite of anarchy. He taught that the body politic should be treated like a living creature, with a ruling spiritual and intellectual elite as its brain, and the trunk and limbs—the workers, soldiers, and technicians—contentedly following the elite's orders. In his final work, *Mission de l'Inde en Europe* (Mission of India in Europe), published posthumously in 1910, Saint-Yves revealed the existence of an ideal synarchic government, the subterranean empire of "Agarttha."

Saint Yves d'Alveydre, whose stories of "Agarttha" inspired later tales of the land of Agharti.

Saint-Yves claimed to have been initiated into Agarttha's mysteries by "a high official of the Hindu church," who was actually an expatriate Brahmin who had fled India for political reasons and set himself up in Le Havre as a dealer in exotic birds and a teacher of Asian languages. He taught Saint-Yves a good deal about Indian traditions, but their association ended when Saint-Yves argued with his teacher over spiritualism. The Brahmin considered Western table-turning and spirit guides dangerous and foolish, and he demonstrated the depth of his feelings—so said Saint-Yves—by pulling out a knife. Saint-Yves found himself without a teacher, but he soon discovered that his training enabled him to receive telepathic messages from the Dalai Lama in Tibet, as well as make astral journeys himself. In *Mission de l'Inde,* he described what he had seen on his out-of-body trips to Agarrtha.

Saint-Yves's depictions of Agarttha were sometimes expansively vague. "Agarttha," he wrote, "forms the mystical zero, the undiscoverable. Zero—that is to say all or nothing, all by a harmonious union, nothing without it, all by synarchy, nothing by anarchy.... Agarttha means uncapturable by violence, inaccessible to anarchy." The best information he would give regarding its location was a hint that it was somewhere beneath the Himalayas, but he added that it would be useless for the profane to search for it.

Like Ossendowski's subterranean empire, Agarttha was populated by millions of happy souls, governed by a synarchic hierarchy of 5000 "pundits" or teachers, 365 "bagwandas," twelve "supreme gurus," and finally a "Sovereign Pontiff." The Pontiff's palace contained a great library not unlike those of H.P.B.'s and Doreal's Masters—it was filled with 556 centuries of human culture and wisdom, guarded from "all profane glances." And like Doreal's Masters, the "mages of Agarttha" had to descend into the infernal regions below them to work at bringing the earth's chaos and negative energy to an end. "Each of these sages," Saint-Yves wrote, "accomplishes his work in solitude, far from any light, under the cities, under deserts, under plains or under mountains."

He also revealed that parts of the underworld were inhabited by monsters and wild people, creatures "half-human, half-simian." The Agartthians themselves were unusual beings; Saint-Yves repeated a story he said he had heard from a man who had lived in the Malabar Islands, about a group of Agartthians who had settled there. They were over six feet tall, double-jointed with elastic bones, which made them exceedingly graceful and agile, stronger and more beautiful than surface humans. Their ears had a "double cavity" and their tongues had been surgically split, which enabled them not only to listen to two conversations simultaneously, but speak all human languages, imitate animals, or sound like two people speaking at once.

These superior beings were the true authors of synarchy, Saint-Yves wrote, and for thousands of years Agarttha had "radiated" synarchy to the rest of the world, which in modern times had chosen foolishly to ignore it, especially the people of Europe. As long as Europeans persisted in their anarchical government systems, the doors of Agarttha would be closed to them. He believed Europe was about to destroy itself through anarchy, and its only hope was for its people to open their hearts and minds to synarchy; until that day arrived, he was not able to reveal the location of Agarttha or the names of its mages. In the meantime, he complained, he was the prey of cynics, who hurled at him "sarcasm upon sarcasm, insult upon insult, calumny upon calumny…. Who is the man who has ever brought humanity a fistful of truths without being repaid by plenty of persecution?" It did not occur to Saint-Yves that most of his ideas—like his plans to make food from algae or construct a machine, the "archaeometer," that would determine the origins of religious ideas— or his well-known habit of in his later years of setting a place at table for his dead wife did not inspire confidence in the minds of most people in Agarttha's existence. Even Saint-Yves's father is supposed to have said of him, "Of all the lunatics I have known, my son is the most dangerous."

But Saint-Yves did have his followers, and in the late 1880s they set up a "Martinist" lodge in Paris, purportedly to continue the teachings of Louis Claude de Saint-Martin, an eighteenth-century French occultist. In fact the lodge promoted many of Saint-Yves's own teachings, including synarchy and the role of Agarttha in world history. The Martinist lodges multiplied in France until the coming of the First World War, influencing the ideas of several important occultists of that day. One of them was Rudolf Steiner, the founder of Anthroposophy, an offshoot of Theosophy which remains a major occult school today and which includes a philosophy of education that led to the founding of the Waldorf schools which can be found in many modern cities. Steiner incorporated much of synarchy into his book of socio-political theory, *The Threefold Commonwealth,* so Saint-Yves's idea is not entirely dead.

The Martinist lodges also flourished in the troubled political atmosphere of turn-of-the-century Russia, where they often served as meeting places for anti-Tsarist revolutionaries. Considering Ossendowski's political background, it seems likely that he was a member of one of these lodges, perhaps when he was studying in St. Petersburg, and it was probably here that he learned of Agarttha, that was to become "Agharti"—perhaps through mistranslation—in *Beasts, Men and Gods.* There is neither an "Agarttha" nor an "Agharti" in any Asian tradition that the few Asian scholars who have looked into the matter have been able to discover, and the words "Agarttha" and "Agharti," which are supposedly Sanskrit names, do not correspond to any known names in that language; in fact, they don't even transliterate properly. There was also little of the Shambhala tradition in Saint-Yves's Agarttha; it was more Hindu than Buddhist in spirit. Some of Saint-Yves's details, like the mystical library, corresponded more to Western occultism than Eastern tradition. It thus appears that Ossendowski grafted the name and subterranean location of the French occultist's mythical kingdom onto the Shambhala tradition he found in Mongolia. He did it in a way, ironically, that continued Saint-Yves's use (intentional or not) of the subterranean empire as political metaphor.

There remains, of course, another intriguing possibility—that the "Mad Baron" Ungern von Sternberg, a man obviously interested in the hidden destinies of races, had been a member of one of the Russian Martinist lodges. He might have added Agarttha to the Shambhala tradition he found was so strong among his Mongolian soldiers. Unfortunately, there is no evidence—besides what is available in Ossendowski's book—that Ungern had ever heard of Agarttha, so this possibility will have to remain only that. Ossendowski is the more likely myth-manipulator, though, for he let some highly suspect remarks slip from the tongues of his glib lamas. One of these lamas told him that after Atlantis and Lemuria sank into the sea, their people migrated into the cavern cities, including some beneath the Americas, and that the inhabitants of these American cavern cities are worshipful subjects of the King of the World. Such remarks sounds less like those of a Mongolian lama and more like those of an H. Spencer Lewis or an Edgar Larkin.

Another French occultist, René Guénon (1886–1951), brought Saint-Yves and Ossendowski together in his book *Le Roi du Monde* (The King of the World), first published in 1927. Guénon, like Saint-Yves, was convinced that the West was destroying itself through its materialism and stress on quantification while ignoring the "ancient tradition" of spirituality. He was so disgusted with the ways of the Europeans that he converted to Islam and spent the last twenty years of his life in Egypt. He lambasted modern occult groups like the Theosophists for trying to blend Eastern and Western traditions and preaching a New Age when the world was in fact rapidly reaching the end of the *Kali Yuga,* one of the great world-cycles of Hindu tradition in which the world would need to pass through a long series of cataclysms before it was purified. The true nature of the Ancient Wisdom had to be concealed during this era, and nobody who claimed to possess it in the West truly understood it. Agarttha, wrote Guénon, was the "cave" in Mount Meru—the world-mountain of Hinduism—and the symbol and prototype of all great temples and centers of initiation. The subterranean location of Agarttha was both a symbolic and a literal expression of Agarttha's status as the source and storehouse of the ancient traditions and the King of the World was the spiritual ruler who would guard the world's wisdom until the world had been purified. "The symbol of the cave and that of the heart are very close," Guénon wrote. "The fragmentary information," he continued, "that Madame Blavatsky was able to gather on the subject—without fully understanding its true significance—gave birth to her conception of the 'Great White Lodge,' which we should call not an image, but quite simply a caricature or imaginary parody, of Agarttha."

Guénon acknowledged the similarity of Saint-Yves's and Ossendowski's stories, but where a skeptical scholar might conclude that the former had been the source of the latter's ideas[4], Guénon pointed to the two stories as independent verifications of one another. How, he asked, could Ossendowski in Central Asia have read Saint-Yves, whose work was published in Paris? Ossendowski's background in both politics and occultism, as we have seen, however, made him a likely advocate of Saint-Yves's ideas.

All of the foregoing does not negate the fact that there was a subterranean-paradise tradition in Asia; there was such a tradition in China and Tibet, but it shared few details with Agarttha/Agharti. Between about 300 and 1000 AD, many reports of subterranean paradises were written in China—in fact, one

---

[4]Guénon wrote, "There were hostile and skeptical critics, of course, quick to accuse Mr. Ossendowski of plagiarizing Saint-Yves, and supporting their case by pointing out the parallel passages in the two books: there are in fact a good number which show an astonishing similarity even of detail."

work, *The Report Concerning the Cave Heavens and Lands of Happiness in Famous Mountains,* by Tu Kuang-t'ing (850-933), listed ten "cave heavens" and thirty-six "small cave heavens" supposed to exist beneath Chinese mountains, some of which had their own skies and suns. In one typical Chinese subterranean-paradise tale, a man entered a cave in a mountain near his home while collecting medicinal herbs, and decided to explore it as far as he could. After walking ten miles, he suddenly found himself in a beautiful land "with a clear blue sky, shining pinkish clouds, fragrant flowers, densely growing willows, towers the color of cinnabar, pavilions of red jade, and far-flung palaces." He was met by a group of lovely, seductive women, who brought him to a house of jasper and played him beautiful music while he drank "a ruby-red drink and a jade-colored juice." Just as he felt the urge to let himself be seduced, he remembered his family and returned to the passageway. Led by a strange light that danced before him, he walked back through the cave to the outer world; but when he reached his home village, he did not recognize anyone he saw, and when he arrived at his house, he met his own descendants of nine generations hence. They told him that one of their ancestors had disappeared into a cavern three hundred years before and had never been seen again.

Such stories have more to do with the Fairyland tradition than with Agharti, however, and probably played the same dreamy role in the lives of Chinese peasants as the stories of the Fair Folk did for their European counterparts—the land where work is not necessary, where one's desires can walk around freely, and where time is so expanded that a few happy days pass in paradise while generations of pain and tribulation go by in the outer world. Perhaps stories like these are better indicators of the true nature of "hidden lands" than tales like those of Saint-Yves or Ossendowski.

The prophetic nature of Agharti has kept it alive, however, although like all myths it changes with time. A few years ago, browsing in a bookstore, I saw a copy of *Doomsday 1999 A.D.* (1981) by Charles Berlitz, one of those gloomy the-cataclysm-is-coming books that have always been with us. In Berlitz's book was a reference to the "mysterious and mystical tradition" of the King of the World, who prophecied "hundreds of years ago" (remember, the prophecy was supposed to have been made in 1890) the battles which would tear the world apart before he and his people, the people of "Arghati," would emerge from their underground kingdom and establish a new order on the earth.

Chapter 11

The Strange World of Dr. Bernard

> Fear is sharp-sighted, and can see things under ground, and much
> more in the skies.
>   —Cervantes, *Don Quixote*

The Shaver Mystery and all the Masters-from-the-Under-world theories accompanying it, which had blazed up so brightly at the end of the Second World War, had smoldered into a pile of ashes by the middle of the fifties. The novelty of the idea of very wise or very evil beings hiding under cities or inside mountains had worn off for most people, and seemed out-of-place in that prosperous, optimistic decade. But Ray Palmer's magazines—*Search, Flying Saucers,* and a few others that appeared and disappeared—continued as forums for wild ideas. Palmer would print anything sufficiently screwball to keep his readers entertained; it made no difference whether it could be proven or not. In the pages of *Flying Saucers,* Palmer chronicled his struggles with the government conspiracy—an unholy alliance of the Air Force, the FBI, and the CIA—at work concealing the existence of the saucers from the public. A UFO had been shot down by an Air Force jet, he hinted, but the Air Force had covered it up; government scientists had made radio contact with an extraterrestrial civilization, he had heard, but they were denying it; the Army had found the wreckage of a crashed spaceship and thrown the corpse of its alien pilot into a top-secret freezer for study, he suggested, but the crash site had been cleaned up so tidily that no evidence remained for civilian researchers. *Search* was a more conventional occult magazine; it was filled with tales of psychics, ouija boarders, astrologers, abominable snowcreatures, and the secrets of the pyramids.

Articles by and about Shaver appeared in Palmer's magazines regularly; in one issue of *Search,* for example, readers learned that the dero had stolen thousands of washing machines from the surface because "they are too stupid to either use the wash machines of the ancients... or build wash machines of their own." But it seemed by the late fifties that everything that could be said for or against Shaver's ideas had been said many times over. Palmer was after a timelier, more brain-boggling cause to champion. He toyed for a while with the then-controversial "Hoxsey Cancer Cure," which like its successors Krebiozen and Laetrile was banned by the U.S. Government although it had supposedly effected hundreds of cures. Palmer also promoted for a time the prophecies of "Doc" Anderson, a burly Georgia psychic and showman who bent steel pipes around the back of his neck between predictions (Anderson announced early in 1957, for example, that nuclear war would begin in China before the year ended). But none of Palmer's sideshows caught fire until he revealed, in the December 1959 issue of *Flying Saucers,* the truth about the UFOs. They were not extraterrestrial craft at all—they came from earth!

"Donuts on the brain"

Beneath the breathless title "SAUCERS FROM EARTH! A Challenge to Secrecy!" Palmer presented what he claimed was "the results of years of research." Not only were the saucers real and visiting us daily from a mysterious earthly location, but all the major governments of the world, despite their constant denials of the existence of UFOs, knew where they were coming from. The truth about UFOs was, he said, "the world's top secret." If it was revealed to the public, the news would disrupt the "political and economic status quo," "topple governments," and incite "widespread panic." What was this terrible secret?

Palmer had some years before read Marshall B. Gardner's *Journey to the Earth's Interior,* and he had now come upon some evidence suggesting that Gardner just might have been correct. The earth, Palmer hinted in his article, was not round with a North Pole and a South Pole—maybe it was hollow and "donut-shaped," with openings where the poles should be, and the interior was populated, perhaps, with a "highly scientific and advanced race." Some of the proofs he offered were straight out of Gardner—the circular magnetic pole, the frozen mammoths drifting out of the North Polar Opening, and the birds and musk oxen migrating north for the winter—and at least fifty years out of date. But to Gardner's hoary proofs, Palmer added others utilizing more recent technology. Didn't the Van Allen radiation belt, he asked, which had recently been detected encircling the earth, take the form of a vast "donut," with its "hole" passing through the polar regions? Why had every attempt so far by the United States to launch a satellite into polar orbit failed, and why hadn't any of the crashed payloads been recovered? Was it possible these satellites had been "sucked" into one of the polar openings?

But such circumstantial evidence was a minor part of Palmer's case for a donut-shaped earth. He meant to propose that the U.S. government had known of the existence of the polar openings since 1947, and that one of America's greatest explorers had passed thousands of miles into both of them. In 1947 and 1956, he revealed, Admiral Richard E. Byrd had flown far beyond the spurious North and South Poles, respectively—but the wonderful new lands Byrd had found within the earth had been kept secrets from the American public. The truth had been carefully concealed in the roundabout way the Navy described Byrd's flights to the press. In 1956 the Navy released a bulletin that Byrd had "accomplished a flight of 2700 miles from the base at McMurdo Sound, which is 400 miles west of the South Pole, and penetrated a land extent of 2300 miles beyond the Pole." And when Byrd returned from the Antarctic, he told reporters: "The present expedition has opened up a vast new land." Where, Palmer asked, was this "vast new land" *beyond* the Pole? Obviously it wasn't in the Antarctic continent the geographers had mapped out for us—that, he said coyly, was all *north* of the South Pole, not beyond it.

But Byrd had made even more amazing discoveries, Palmer said, on his flight past the North Pole in 1947. Before he left, Byrd had told the press: "I'd like to see that land beyond the Pole. That land beyond the Pole is the center of the great unknown." Once in the Arctic, the Admiral had flown 1700 miles "beyond" the Pole before returning to his base. While aloft, he reported over his radio that he was not passing over an Arctic waste, but a lush country of tree-covered mountains and ice-free lakes. At one point he saw a "monstrous animal moving through the underbrush," an animal Palmer hinted *might* have been a mammoth.

To fully appreciate the bombshell he had dropped, Palmer advised his readers to look closely at a globe. A moment's inspection of the Arctic regions revealed that there *was* no land within several hundred miles of the North Pole, and that the timberline was well over 1700 miles to the south, far into Canada, Alaska, and Siberia. So where *was* Byrd during his flight? "What have we here?" Palmer asked. "We have the well-authenticated flight of Admiral Richard E. Byrd to a land beyond the Pole that he so much wanted to see.... Apparently, he had his wish gratified to the fullest, yet today, in 1959, nowhere is that mysterious land mentioned. Why? Was that 1947 flight fiction? Did all the newspapers lie? Did the radio from Byrd's plane lie?"

The conclusion was obvious. Byrd had discovered a "vast new land" inside the earth, and the United States government (and probably that of the Soviet Union by now) knew a good deal about that mysterious land but was keeping the information secret. Given the frequency of UFO sightings, continued Palmer, and the furtive behavior of government officials where UFOs were concerned, it was a good bet that the inner world was the saucers' true home. Palmer's argument was hung on the thinnest of logical threads, but he ended the article in one of the crescendoes of certainty that were his trademark:

> The Flying Saucer has become the most important single fact in history. The questions raised in this article must be answered. Admiral Byrd has discovered a new and mysterious land, the center of the great unknown, and the most important discovery of all time. We have it from his own lips, from a man whose integrity has always been unimpeachable, and whose mind was one of the most brilliant of modern times.
> Let those who wish to call him a liar step forward and prove their claim!
> Flying saucers come from this earth!

Unfortunately, Palmer had made a serious error. Dozens of readers wrote him immediately to tell him Admiral Byrd had been nowhere near the North Pole in 1947; both the 1947 and 1956 expeditions had gone to the *South* Pole. A few readers even went back and combed through the newspapers for that year, but none of them found any mention of Byrd flying over any Antarctic forests, any monstrous animals in the underbrush, or even any underbrush. Such obvious errors cast Palmer's "years of research" into doubt, and he knew it. In the next issue of *Flying Saucers* (February 1960), he was forced to admit he had gotten his information from *one* very strange book, and that information had not been exactly correct.

Early in 1959, Palmer had received in the mail a review copy of a new book, *Worlds Beyond the Poles,* by one F. Amadeo Giannini. This little work, which its author paid three thousand dollars—in those days a great deal of money—to have printed, is perhaps the archetypal crank book. As we see him through its pages, Giannini seems the archetypal crank; he spent his life promoting a revolutionary theory of the nature of the universe that seems only marginally comprehensible, and he saw himself, as do many would-be revolutionary theorists, as a martyr for his cause. He liked to refer to himself in the third person, as "the new Columbus."

As a young man in 1926, Giannini had been wandering through a New England forest when he had a vision. Guided by "his extrasensory perception," he suddenly realized that the earth was not round, but sort of spindle-shaped, and the North and South Poles were illusory points. The earth's surface, he perceived, did not end at the points of the spindle but continued into space and curved back over our heads. What looked like stars, planets, galaxies, and comets were actually "globular and isolated areas of a continuous and unbroken outer sky surface." This meant that these seemingly "heavenly" bodies weren't heavenly at all, but points on the vast land surface of the universe, *part* of which was the earth's surface. There was no need to develop rockets to explore space, wrote Giannini, for "space" was an illusion created by the refraction of the lenses of our eyes, telescopes, and cameras. All we needed to do to reach "Mars" or "Venus" was to climb into an airplane (or amphibious vehicle) with a very large tank of gas and fly (or drive) there. When Admiral Byrd flew *beyond* the poles he had proven Giannini correct—the earth did not "end" at the poles, but continued into "vast new lands."

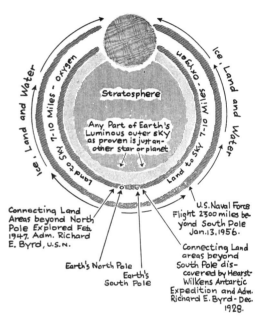

One of F. A. Giannini's diagrams of his continuous universe does not, as he admits, make the spindle-shape of his proposed earth very clear, but it does at least show the continuous land surface of the cosmos in his theory. From Giannini's *Worlds Beyond the Poles* (1959).

Giannini insisted throughout *Worlds Beyond the Poles* that Byrd's flights had demonstrated the "physical continuity of the universe" (the official name of his theory) beyond any doubt. But his lack of knowledge about Byrd's polar expeditions was appalling; Giannini seemed to have read nothing about them but a few newspaper and magazine articles, and he even got the facts from them confused. He transposed the 1947 Byrd Antarctic expedition to the North Pole for no reason—except perhaps symmetry—while retaining details from the actual

South Polar operation. He described the routes of both the 1947 and 1956 flights incorrectly, as if they had been straight lines; yet maps of Byrd's flight paths on both occasions—loose zigzag routes past the Pole and around the Antarctic coastal regions—had been published in practically every newspaper in the world.

Giannini probably plucked the phrase "beyond the Pole" from an article in the October 1947 *National Geographic,* written by Byrd and titled "Our Navy Explores Antarctica." The Admiral referred several times in the article to a "Mystery Land beyond the Pole," but he made it clear that this Mystery Land was neither the highway to outer space nor the gateway to the inner world. He used the phrase to describe the millions of square miles of Antarctica's interior surrounding the so-called "Pole of Inaccessibility," a point approximately 78° south latitude and 70° east longitude—"the most difficult spot," wrote Byrd, "left on earth for man to reach." It was the very large chunk of Antarctica that was in 1947 still unmapped and unexplored. In that year Byrd and his men did photograph, chart, and claim a large and previously unseen portion of the Antarctic for the United States, but the Admiral never found any "vast new lands" in the sky, on the earth, or under the earth, he didn't know were there to begin with.

Thus was Admiral Byrd's name linked with a discovery he was never aware he had made. After Giannini used Byrd's "discovery" to support his theory, in which the earth was far from hollow, Palmer borrowed it and turned it inside out to support his own version of the hole-in-each-pole hollow-earth theory. Palmer barely concealed his contempt for Giannini's ideas, but was not averse to using Giannini's misinterpretation of Byrd's statements for his own articles in *Flying Saucers.* Even after Palmer learned of Giannini's errors, he continued writing about the "land beyond the poles" as if nothing had happened, and his use of Byrd's flights as "evidence" passed into the heart of the hollow-earth mythos, where it has remained ever since.

In the February 1961 *Flying Saucers*, Palmer printed a letter from Giannini which suggested that Byrd had flown to the Arctic after leaving the Antarctic in February of 1947, but that U.S. Naval Intelligence had covered up the Arctic flights. Neither Palmer, he wrote, nor his reading audience "KNOW where Rear Admiral Richard Evelyn Byrd was during the *entire month of February*, 1947.... Mr. Palmer is considerably at fault in his quoted contention, 'Giannini stakes his verity on the New York Times accounts.' Giannini does no such thing." The newspapers refused to print the truth, Giannini said; however, the U. S. Office of Naval Intelligence could reveal much. "BUT, but, will they. That would require a measure of moral stamina which is almost too much to expect."

Palmer was soon ranging farther and farther afield for material suggesting the earth took the form of a donut, and it did not take him long to find the writings of Theodore Fitch. Fitch was an Iowa evangelist who believed in a Gardnerian hollow earth, and that the inner world was the true location of the Garden of Eden. In a shower of pamphlets, he described how the human race had been cast out of the earth's interior and how the inner world was populated today by "small brown men" who espoused Communism and flew UFOs powered by "free energy." Fitch reinterpreted scores of Biblical quotations to demonstrate the inner world's existence, and Palmer passed the evangelist's rendering of the Book of Job along to his own readers. Was it possible that Job 26:7 referred to the North Polar Opening when it said that God "stretcheth out the north over the empty place, and hangeth the earth upon nothing"? Other passages supposedly described the ice that gripped the Arctic verges—"Out of whose womb came the ice? and the hoary frost of heaven, who hath engendered it? The waters are hid as with a stone, and the face of the deep is frozen" (Job 38:22-30)—and the glowing clouds that lit the inner world: "Dost thou know when God disposed them, and caused the light of his cloud to shine?" (Job 37:15).

The long series of articles Palmer wrote for *Flying Saucers* throughout 1960 and 1961 supporting the idea of a hollow earth generated, as usual, plenty of mail from his readers. Many were convinced that Byrd had in fact entered the polar openings, and they congratulated Palmer for unveiling another "conspiracy of silence" on the part of the government and the scientists. Others wrote him long letters refuting each of his arguments in tiny detail, but nobody ever won a debate with Ray Palmer that way. He printed each critical letter in full, and then chided the writer for singling him out for unfair harrassment. "It SEEMS to us," he responded to one such letter, "that everybody challenges us with criteria which they FAIL to use in challenging authorities considered more authoritative. How would it be if we went to college, and collected a half-dozen degrees? Would that influence you to accept everything we said without question or challenge? What this editor has striven for his entire career is to induce people to challenge EVERYTHING." Palmer, who had never attended college—except for a short stint at a Milwaukee business college—loved nothing more than to set whoopee cushions on the chairs of the Ph.D.-laden "authorities," and a few of his readers saw his game and made rude noises at him in return. One told him he had "donuts on the brain;" another wrote, "Do you know where I think the hole is? In your head."

But there was at least one holder of a Ph.D. who followed the debate in *Flying Saucers* over the true shape of the earth in deadly earnest. He was stepping forward to warn us that if we wished to survive the nuclear holocaust which was to strike within the next decade, we had better stop talking about the inner world and start preparing to settle there. His name was Walter Siegmeister, but he was better known as Dr. Raymond Bernard, A.B., M.A., Ph.D.

The once and future super-race

Raymond W. Bernard (I will refer to him by his more-familiar pseudonym) is best-known today for his book *The Hollow Earth* (1963), which is still the most widely-read book on the subject, and the only book on the hollow-earth theory available in most libraries. But Bernard's belief in a hollow earth was only a small facet of his larger obsession—restoring the degenerate human race of the twentieth century to the beautiful and nearly immortal super-race it had been millions of years ago. He detailed his plans for the resurrection of our race, and its ultimate doom in a cloud of fallout if his words were ignored, in some forty volumes on "Biosophy," the "scientific world religion of the New Age." Among his fondest hopes were the abolition of all meat and cooked foods from the human diet, the end of the menstrual period in the female sex, and—perhaps—the elimination of the male sex.

Bernard was born Walter Siegmeister in 1901 to a family of Russian non-practicing Jews in New York City. His father was a doctor, and as an adolescent Bernard's fascination with the differences between the sexes led him to search his father's medical books. His interest went far beyond the average adolescent's; he wanted to know not only the what and how of sex, but also the why. He was, he wrote later, particularly troubled by "the mystery of menstruation… the cause and nature of this hemorrhage that afflicts girls, and from which boys are free." But the medical books did not tell him what he wanted to know, and by the time he reached his twenties he had set himself firmly upon a search for the answers to the enigmas of sexuality and childbirth. His feeling about the physical act of sex, however, seems to have been one of disgust; judging from his writings and what is known about him, it is possible that he abstained from sex throughout his life.

Walter Siegmeister (Raymond Bernard) in 1943.

Bernard's Biosophy was nothing new; it went back to the beginning of the "health-food" tradition in America. Sylvester Graham (1794–1851) preached in the 1830s that virtue was to be found in vegetarianism—particularly the consumption of whole grains—fresh-air exercise, and sexual abstinence. Graham, who is remembered by the whole-grain crackers named after him, believed that meat stimulated the base passions and took away the body's ability to resist disease. One of Graham's followers was John Harvey Kellogg (1852–1943) of cereal fame, who believed that whole-grain breakfast cereals encouraged continence.

As a young man, Bernard also became immersed in the world of the occult. He read deeply in the works of the Theosophists and Rudolf Steiner's Anthroposophists, especially those works which told the stories of Atlantis and Lemuria and described the evolution, migration, and degeneration of races. He took his bachelor's degree at Columbia University in 1924 and his master's degree and doctorate in education at New York University in 1930 and 1932, respectively. But his Ph.D. dissertation demonstrated his interest in the occult; its title was "Theory and Practice of Dr. Rudolf Steiner's Pedagogy."

I have seen two photographs of Raymond Bernard. The first was taken in 1933, soon after his graduation from NYU and about the time he moved to Florida, where he began spending his days taking long nude swims, setting up a colony for people who believed in "natural living," and publishing a health-food newsletter called *Diet and Health.* In the photo he looks much like the son of Rasputin—a dark suit, a long bushy beard, slicked-down hair, and a pair of very dark, intense, staring eyes that reach out of the picture. He was clearly a man of strong beliefs, and in the pages of *Diet and Health,* between ads for powdered kelp and "Hydrocotyle Asiatica, the Rejuvenative Herb," Bernard began issuing a warning he would cry until the end of his life. Urban, industrial society was unhealthy, he said, and its continued growth would signal the collapse of Western civilization. His Lake Istokpoga Colony was supported by G.R. Clements, another "health" writer who was actually a real-estate shyster; through Bernard, Clements offered parcels of Florida land near Lake Istokpoga to grow pineapples, avocadoes, papayas, and other semi-tropical fruits. Unfortunately, all too often the land was unsuitable for such crops, or else periodic frosts would kill the plants. Clements fooled even Bernard, telling him he could earn $5000 growing papayas—Bernard wanted the money so he could go to India and study with "the Masters"—but Bernard never got the hang of papaya growing, and instead sold repackaged animal feed as health foods, making elaborate promises about their benefits, just to survive. As a result of all this creative advertising, both Clements and Bernard were threatened with legal action and Bernard thought it prudent to leave the country.

Bernard had hired one of the "natural livers," John Wierlo, as an assistant at the Lake Istokpoga Colony, and when Wierlo decided to travel to Ecuador in 1940 to escape civilization, Bernard followed the next year. He had been searching for what he called a "New Promised Land," an isolated spot far from the cities, anyway. He claimed that he wished to gather about him those who wanted to leave material things behind, and where only pure, raw food would be eaten. Once again, however, his manner of promoting his cause was not as pure as it might have been. Wierlo, who later changed his last name to Lovewisdom, told the story after Bernard's death.

The second, more conservative, photograph I have seen of Bernard was taken when he was well into his attempt to start his New Promised Land. It appeared in a sensational article in *The American Weekly* for May 9, 1943: "Hope to Breed a Super-Race in Ecuador's Secret Jungles." The article's author, J.M. Sheppard, recounted in titillating prose his interviews with Marian Windish, a "24-year-old girl hermit who lived two years in the Ecuadorean jungle without clothes, cooked foods, weapons or medicines," and John Wierlo, a "blond giant of 24 years... 200 pounds of solid bone and muscle, clad in native garb after his two years preparation in the jungle." Sheppard also interviewed the man who meant to bring them together "to begin a Super-Race," Dr. Walter Siegmeister:

At forty years of age, Dr. Siegmeister has the skin of a child, a complexion a movie star would envy and the most unusual eyes I've ever seen—brown, extraordinarily large and of such depth and fire that they draw one's attention inexorably. Yet the manner of the man is one of meekness and solemnity.

Bernard painted for Sheppard the paradisical society he proposed to create with his two young disciples and their offspring-to-be (whom Sheppard called the "Modern Master Child"). He was inviting others to join them as well on thousands of acres of the eastern slopes of the Andes—after they passed the two years of probation. All would be absolute pacifists, killing neither other humans in anger or war nor animals for food. All would eat nothing but raw fruits, vegetables, and nuts, without salt. "All the material things for which men fight and connive are forbidden, even clothing," Bernard told Sheppard. "There will be no money, nor valuables of any sort, though perhaps the harvesting and saving of a few nuts and seeds may be considered capital. If this makes us capitalistic, so are the squirrels capitalistic."

Bernard believed that children born in such surroundings, eating only pure, uncooked food—the very conditions, he told Sheppard, under which the Buddha had been born—would grow to be a race of huge, physically perfect, spiritually enlightened beings, living a blissful, childlike existence. In his jungle Eden, no one would work for anyone else, and no one would rule; their riches would consist not of material wealth, but of "health, happiness, and understanding.... This is the super-race idea, as old as civilization, and the only solution." Bernard felt that thousands of people from all over the world, attracted by a wealth that could only be shared, not stolen, would come to Ecuador to join the colony. But he underestimated the desire of almost everyone for at least a modicum of comfort and material things. His colony idea went nowhere, and it was just as well, for Sheppard had been fabricating the entire story and, with Bernard's help, many of the accompanying photographs as well. Marian Windish, another "natural liver," was actually married to another man, and she and her husband had long been friends of Wierlo's, but Sheppard and Bernard made Wierlo, without his permission, the "father of the New Race" because he looked more the part (Wierlo wrote that he "refused to consent to the 'super-baby' creation scheme"). Sheppard also, according to Wierlo, "photographed bearded Siegmeister with long hair down, in a robe, walking on water (with supports just below the surface) and other 'miracles'." They had also, in an earlier issue of *American Weekly*, "faked some stories about meeting Tibetan Masters with prayer wheels on a nearby mountain"—the same stories picked up by Vincent Gaddis for his "Tales from Tibet" series in *Amazing Stories* and by Robert Dickhoff for his *Agharta*! Wierlo wrote: "With such perversion of facts, both Sheppard and Siegmeister were banned from use of U.S. Mails, and Sheppard banned by Ecuadorian Immigration Department."

Despite all of this fakery, Bernard seems to have been sincere in his desire to set up a real "super-race" colony, if not in the way it was marketed. He went back to the United States, this time to California, selling health foods and books with titles like *Are You Being Poisoned by the Foods You Eat?* and *Super-Health thru Organic Super-Foods* under the name of Dr. Robert Raymond, A.B., M.A., Ph.D. (since he couldn't use the mails under his real name), but not for long. Undeterred by the failure of his Ecuardorian paradise, he was soon back in the tropics. He lived in Hawaii for a while, Guatemala for a while—there selling his books and foods under the name of Dr. Uriel Adriana, A.B., M.A, Ph.D.— and Puerto Rico for a while, searching for another spot to begin his super-race. He didn't find the paradise in which he would spend the rest of his life, however, until 1955. In that year he purchased with some money his mother had left him a large tract of property near the town of Joinville on Sao Francisco do Sul Island off the coast of the state of Santa Catarina in southern Brazil, about 200 miles south of Sao Paulo.

Here he also settled on the pseudonym he would use for the rest of his life, Dr. Raymond Bernard, A.B., M.A., Ph.D. One of the first books Bernard wrote under his new name was *Escape from Destruction* (1955), which became one of the basic manifestoes of Biosophy, and one in which his search for a super-race took a new direction. Like other alternative-reality works of the 1950s—such as Robert Dickhoff's *Agharta* and the books of George Adamski and his fellow flying-saucer "contactees"—*Escape* warned us that the human race had come dangerously close to committing atomic suicide, and that our every move was now being observed by benevolent but all-powerful extraterrestrials. Even now, Bernard wrote, nuclear testing was filling the atmosphere of the Northern Hemisphere with fallout that was slowly poisoning the planet. He had learned from a Puerto Rican psychic named "Mayita," a woman "whose body functions as an interplanetary radio," that between 1965 and 1970 a global nuclear war was to begin. When the year 2000 arrived, there would be no living thing left on the surface of the earth.

But Mayita cushioned her prophecy; she told Bernard that not everyone would perish in the holocaust. Certain individuals who had purified their bodies and prepared themselves for the New Age would gather in the Southern Hemisphere, far from the showers of fallout. These pure ones would be picked up in UFOs and safely removed to Mars, where they would watch in comfort the slow, painful destruction of their unregenerate brothers and sisters on the earth. Bernard told his readers that Sao Francisco Island was to be one of these gathering places; it was located at a latitude far from the centers of nuclear conflict. Winds from the Antarctic would sweep it free of fallout long after life elsewhere had been wiped out. John Wierlo wrote that this claim was false:

> Being on the same latitude as Antofagasta, Chile (a fallout-free region protected by the High Andes to the East), he figured he could say he was in the fallout protected belt, which was an absolute lie. Likewise he claimed a breeze from the Antarctic blew the fallout away from the Joinville area. In turn the Catholic University at nearby Rio de Janeiro reported the heaviest fallout in South America to be there.... Yet Siegmeister filled U.S. Health Food stores with "Dried-Bananas-Free-From-Fallout" from South America's unprotected east coast in Brazil.

Much of *Escape from Destruction* was devoted to Bernard's retelling of the true story of the human race, which was the prelude to the sad state of the modern world. He wrote that he had first heard the story from Mayita, but the story he heard corresponded amazingly with his own ideas about a vegetarian super-race. By 1955 Bernard had come to believe that women were by far the superior sex, and men were an unfortunate mutation which was—contrary to male-dominated scientific doctrine—unnecessary for reproduction. As a result, his story of our origins sounds much like a mythology devised by a community of modern radical feminists:[1]

Throughout her life, Bernard wrote, Mayita had been visited almost daily by a tall, imposingly beautiful woman "with long golden hair that reached down to her feet, and large deep blue eyes, and skin as pink as a babe's." This woman called herself the Great Mother and told Mayita she lived on the sun, which was not, as humans believed, unendurably hot. Its temperature was actually pleasant, and when it was seen from space, the sun was dark; only when its rays struck our atmosphere did they radiate light and heat.

The Great Mother said she had given birth to all life within the solar system parthenogenetically. About 150,000 years ago she brought from her womb the first members of a race of superwomen much like herself; no males were born because there was no need for them. This long-lived race of great, wise, and beautiful women lived happily on the planet Uranus for 50,000 years and would have continued to do so had not an unfortunate accident occurred—a mutation causing the birth of "a defective... and sterile female": the first male. Despite the happiness and perfection of the society around him, young Lucifer grew up—not unexpectedly—feeling very inferior because he was unable to bear children like his sisters. To compensate, he convinced himself that his difference made him a superior being. He believed he had been born as the new ruler of the solar system, destined to replace the Great Mother. But he realized that to replace her, "he would have to create a race of his own, as She did."

Lucifer was gifted with great powers of persuasion, and he convinced several of his sisters the time had arrived to begin reproducing both male and female children through a union of the two sexes. Using electromagnetic waves—the sex act "had not yet," in Bernard's words, "degenerated into... copulation"—Lucifer impregnated them with a new race of children both female and male. These new children were noticeably smaller and sicklier than the daughters of the Great Mother, but Lucifer was beside himself with pride. The Great Mother, however, was shocked and and saddened by Lucifer's treachery, and when he showed no regret for his actions, she felt she had no choice but to exile him, his wives, and his children to the planet Saturn. There Lucifer took

---

[1] In fact, it does resemble strongly the scenario of human history advanced by Elizabeth Gould Davis in her passionately-argued book *The First Sex* (1971), which has since it appeared been popular among radical feminists. Davis contended that the male sex is indeed a mutation (she wrote that the male *y* chromosome is a "degeneration and a deformity of the female *x* chromosome"), and that "it seems very logical... that originally there was only one sex—the female," which reproduced parthenogenetically. Until about three thousand years ago, she claimed, humanity enjoyed in fact the "Golden Age" of so many mythologies—a matriarchal civilization worshipping peace and practicing strict vegetarianism. She suggested this civilization may have originated on the Antarctic continent, which before the poles shifted was called Atlantis.

the name of Satan and settled in, delighted with the prospect of a world to rule. The story of the expulsion of Lucifer and his family is thus the origin of the Christian myth of the fallen angels.

For another 50,000 years Satan ruled Saturn autocratically, displaying to the utmost the supremely masculine traits of anger, violence, and vengefulness. But his children thrived and multiplied until he decided to conquer and colonize another planet of the solar system and extend his power. The Great Mother's daughters had settled on all habitable planets save Earth, so Satan sent a great fleet of spaceships to the earth, filled with his descendants, who became our ancestors. Satan ruled them by "telepathic remote control," and as time passed they worshipped him as Saturn, Jupiter, Jehovah, God the Father, and Allah. He ordered them at last to commit that most horrendous of sins in Bernard's eyes, "to kill animals in sacrifice to him, and eat their flesh, violating the Great Mother's primal law of vegetarianism." This violation led rapidly to human sacrifice and battle: "He inspired them to wage endless wars in his honor, inciting his followers who worshipped him under one name to slaughter others who worshipped him under another."

Thus the history of the human race on the earth was the history of a continual degeneration. Even the children of Satan who first arrived on the planet, as degenerate as they were, were gods and goddesses compared to modern men and women. They were larger, healthier, and more intelligent, and because they had not yet stooped to eating meat and engaging in physical sex, they lived for hundreds of years. It was not until the race had settled in Lemuria some 25,000 years ago that we took those final steps in our descent, and the rapid decline they brought about caused the atomic war which sank Lemuria and Atlantis in a cloud of radioactivity. The survivors of that catastrophe were left struggling at a very primitive level, and only slowly developed into the present human civilization. But we were fooling ourselves, Bernard warned, if we thought we were progressing, for today we were on the brink of repeating the disaster that befell the two Lost Continents.

The greatest tragedy of all, however, was the state to which Woman had sunk. Once the queen of creation, she had been enslaved by the appetites of the tyrannical male sex. Bernard lamented that sexual intercourse, which the Great Mother had forbidden so strongly, had

> converted a long-lived, disease-free superhuman race into a short-lived, diseased human race, as recorded in the Book of Genesis. The apple that Eve ate was evidently the act of animal copulation, which was not natural for humans, though natural for animals. This act brought all the misery and suffering to humankind. Woman's painful childbirth and periodic menstrual hemorrhage are among the consequences not of an original sin but of the continuance of this mistaken practice...

But it was possible for women, even in their modern degenerate condition, to free themselves from menstruation, and to give birth painlessly and parthenogenetically; they had merely to abstain completely from animal food in any form, tobacco, alcohol, caffeine, and especially from sexual intercourse. Total chastity would help both sexes live longer as well, Bernard wrote, for he—like the mad general in the film *Dr. Strangelove*—believed the "vital fluids" produced by the gonads kept the body youthful. The sex act drained away the vital fluids and brought on rapid aging and senility; only abstinence allowed the body to absorb them. This idea, too, had been popular in the American health-food community for years; it was based on the Biblical story of Onan (Genesis 38:7-10), who "spilled his seed on the ground" and was slain by God, and Leviticus 15:16-18, which warned that "if any man's seed of copulation go out from him," he was "unclean." Sylvester Graham and John Kellogg believed that semen should remain within the body to resist illness.

At the end of her message through Mayita to Bernard, the Great Mother said she had been observing our society's headlong rush to nuclear suicide with great sorrow; when her people's observation ships had flown overhead as signs of her concern, they had been mistaken as hostile "flying saucers". Although the end of life on the earth was not far away, she was preparing a fleet of space-ships to take those who had purified themselves in accordance with her laws to Mars, where a flourishing colony of her children dwelled. Both men and women lived among them, although the two sexes were separated; all were strict vegetarians, and disease was unknown. The highest members of Martian society had so purified their bodies that they ate nothing at all; they lived entirely on the air they breathed and the perfumes of certain flowers. The earth people brought to Mars would begin as vegetarians, but all would eventually attain this state of absolute physical purity. The pilots of the Martian saucers would select those to be taken from the earth "by the degree of phosphorescent brain glow emitted by the pineal gland. This glow results from oxidation of lecithin, a golden phosphorus substance that is conserved in the body by continence, and lost by incontinence."

But the time, warned Bernard, was short. He sent out his plea in *Escape from Destruction*—all those who wished to leave the earth before its life was obliterated, and join the New Age of humanity on Mars, should begin the process of physical purification as soon as possible. "Since the worthy people are now scattered, living in cities," he wrote, "it is impossible for flying saucers to save them until they are first gathered in some distant land with broad open spaces, far from areas of the earth which are contaminated by radioactivity." He invited all his readers who were ready to begin this purification to join him on Sao Francisco Island and await the coming cataclysm and the landing of the Great Mother's spaceships.

Dr. Marlo and the men from Masars II

But Bernard, curiously, also hedged his bets in *Escape from Destruction* by suggesting that if we were not to be picked up by the extraterrestrials, we had another option open to us: moving underground. He had recently read one of Shaver's articles in Ray Palmer's *Mystic* magazine which had recounted the story of the Titans moving underground to escape poisoning on the earth's surface, and Bernard wondered whether we might not do the same thing. Perhaps we might find some of the abandoned cities of the ancients and live there after the Last World War had struck.

It appears that Bernard had known about the Shaver Mystery for many years (he had been advertising in Palmer's magazines for some time), but several events now conspired to move the home of his "super-race" from outer space to inner space. In 1956, browsing through a bookshop in Sao Paulo, he discovered a book called (in English) *From the Subterranean World to the Sky,* by the Brazilian writer and Theosophist O.C. Huguenin.[2] Huguenin's thesis, according to Bernard, was that UFOs had first been constructed by a technologically sophisticated race of Atlanteans twelve thousand years ago, just before their home sank into the ocean. They climbed into their saucers and migrated through the polar openings into the inner world, where they have lived ever since; we of the surface are descendants of the more primitive races the Atlanteans left behind. Huguenin asserted that the behavior commonly attributed to UFOs made little sense if they were extraterrestrial craft, but a great deal of sense if their origin was subterranean. If the saucers were extraterrestrial, he asked, why did the same types of craft keep hanging about year after year, watching us but never making any attempt to contact our governments? If they merely wanted to use us as subjects of an anthropological study, they could have gotten their results long ago and returned to their distant home. But since the saucers first appeared in great numbers immediately after the development of nuclear weapons and had continued appearing as if they were regularly patrolling the surface, it made sense that they came from a point close by that shared our atmosphere and water. Perhaps the UFO pilots were monitoring the radiation levels on the surface with a mind to preventing radiation entering their home: the inner world.

Huguenin shared with two other Brazilian theosophists, Professor Henrique de Souza (described by Bernard as an "archaeologist and esotericist") and Commander Paulo Strauss of the Brazilian Navy, the belief that it was to the subterraneans' advantage to fool us surface folk into assuming their craft came from other worlds. The idea of an inner world seemed so fantastic to most people that nobody bothered looking down—they watched the heavens instead. But Professor de Souza, particularly, had known the truth for some time. Members of the Brazilian Theosophical Society in the city of Sao Lourenzo frequently saw strange spacecraft landing near the Society's headquarters; men "of great stature" would leave the ship, greet de Souza, and hurry inside for conferences on matters of esoteric importance. In 1956, Commander Strauss toured Brazil, lecturing on the true home of the saucers; he disclosed, among other things, that the earth was indeed a great hollow sphere, and the mighty empire the UFO pilots called home was named Agharta. It was a technological wonderland a thousand years ahead of us.

---

[2] I have searched for years for a copy of this book, but Bernard's reference to it is the only evidence I have been able to discover that it actually existed. It is almost certain that it has never been translated into English.

In 1957 Bernard traveled to Sao Lourenzo to pay a visit to Professor de Souza. He described the meeting in one issue of his new *Biosophical Bulletin*:

> On the sofa in the back of the room sat a young girl, looking about 18 years of age. Much to my surprise she was introduced as [the Professor's] wife, though he was over 70, and was told that she is a subterranean woman, and really over 50 years of age, but retains her youth, since subterranean people live much longer than we do.
>   The professor began the conversation saying, "I just returned from a visit to the Sub-terranean World, where I am well known. I have frequently visited the city of Shamballah and once had the key to the door that leads to this city."

De Souza told Bernard there were a number of tunnel entrances to the inner world in Brazil. One of them, in the Roncador Mountains of the Matto Grosso, was the passage into which Colonel Percy Fawcett and his son Jack had disappeared on their ill-fated expedition into the Brazilian wilderness in 1927. The Professor said Fawcett and his son were still alive in a subterranean Atlantean city, but "are not permitted to leave lest they be forced to reveal its whereabouts." The Roncador tunnel entrance was guarded by "the fierce Chavantes Indians," who would calmly kill any intruder. But de Souza gave Bernard a password that would enable him to pass the Chavantes and enter the tunnel. He told Bernard that the tunnel descended through several levels of subterranean cities and farms, but it finally ended in the great hollow at the center of the earth. The various levels were inhabited by descendants of the peoples of H.P.B.'s three great lost continents, Hyperborea, Atlantis, and Lemuria. Bernard described these races in a way that linked them clearly to his story of the Great Mother.

The Hyperboreans, he wrote, who "composed the central world government in Shamballah" and were known as "the Perfect Ones," were a race of tall, beautiful superwomen who reproduced parthenogenetically. The Lemurians were a transitional race, partially degenerate but beardless, and the ancestors of the Polynesians and East Asians. The Atlanteans were slightly more degenerate, but still superior enough to surface humanity to serve as the basis for the gods and goddesses of classical times (although as Bernard moved more deeply into the UFOs-from-the-inner-world phase of his mythology, the Atlanteans came to represent in his writings all three races of subterraneans). Bernard assigned to these subterranean races a revised version of his historical scenario from *Escape from Destruction*. Humanity had begun as a race of superwomen created on Hyperborea by the Great Mother: "This was the Golden Age represented by Eden." But the birth of Lucifer and his expulsion to Lemuria signaled the beginning of our degeneration, which culminated when Atlantis and Lemuria destroyed themselves. The wisest and most virtuous of the Atlanteans and Lemurians were visited by the Great Mother and shown tunnels hidden under the earth, through which they migrated to safety in Agharta. There they had lived peacefully ever since, safe from the cataclysms of the surface:

> These people use no money. Neither do they have to labor. They live free from worry. There is no exploitation, no scarcity, no conflict, no disharmony among them. Nor is

there any crime…. The sexes are segregated, each living in complete freedom. Due to their diet, these people are naturally chaste and free from all sexual tendencies which they regard as unnatural and pathological.

In his 1960 book *Nuclear Age Saviors* Bernard described his search for the concealed entrances to Agharta that began after his meeting with Professor de Souza. He never found any of them himself, although he spent many months trying to find a guide into the Matto Grosso who could lead him to the right tunnel. He claimed to have spoken with many Brazilians who had stumbled into the subterranean world while exploring caves, however. One man told Bernard he had

> traveled through a smooth-cut, illuminated tunnel for three days, 20 hours a day, accompanied by two subterranean men he met at its entrance, until he came to an immense illuminated space filled with buildings and fruit orchards and where lived men, women and children, also various animals, including lions and tigers, who were as tame as cats and dogs. The sexes lived apart and the women all looked as if in their teens, even though some were centuries old. Also these people were all an exact copy of each other, with no variation. Women… were all virgin mothers.
> One of the children ran over to him, apparently unafraid, and when he tried to pick it up (which is forbidden among these people) an avalanche of rocks fell upon him, but did not harm him, leading him to believe that they were projected images rather than real rocks. He escaped to the outside through an exit tunnel.

Bernard admitted he could not guarantee the veracity of such stories, since most of those offering to lead him to the subterranean world, "knowing of the writer's interest in this subject," requested a large payment for their services in advance. Bernard never wrote about it directly, but the pained tone in which he retold some of the stories sounded as if he tendered payment during these years to more than one "guide," who vanished soon afterwards—and not into a tunnel. But he believed "where there is smoke there is fire," and he never gave up his search of rural Brazil for *the* tunnel entrance. Although Bernard had often been involved with tricksters and been a trickster himself, his own blind faith in his beliefs seems to have led to his own deception as often as he deceived others, and it was about to fool him again.

His faith in the existence of the subterraneans was encouraged when his correspondents and followers in the United States sent him Theodore Fitch's pamphlets and Ray Palmer's hollow-earth articles from *Flying Saucers.* One day in 1959, at about the time Palmer's first article appeared, Bernard had also received a letter from a man named Ottmar Kaub, secretary to Dr. George Marlo, the head of a St. Louis organization, UFO World Research:

> You have very kindly kept me on your mailing list for the past several years. I have been a vegetarian for twenty years and have desired to have a place to live in your community on the island of Sao Francisco…. I have been wanting to write to you for some time, but was not sure that you had an understanding of the flying saucers and the people living under the earth…

[Dr. Marlo] has been taken inside the earth via the North Pole opening on many different trips on a flying saucer. He is in constant touch with the saucer people and in conference with them.

Because of his position and the orders he is under, he does not seek or desire any publicity whatever, and this letter is not for publication or showing to anyone outside of our group, because various governments and air forces do not want certain information given publicity...

The various governments have all the information that we have, but in order to avoid panic by the lunatic fringe and perhaps from many other vital reasons of security, they wish this information to be kept among those who are not mentally affected by it...

In the exchange of letters that followed between St. Louis and Sao Francisco Island, Bernard learned that Dr. Marlo had been in touch for the past several years with two beings named Sol-Mar and Zola who lived in Masars II, a subterranean city beneath South Africa. Marlo claimed that he had made more than sixty trips in their spaceship, some to the North Pole region, where one entered the inner world through a "curve" instead of a hole, and some to Masars II itself[3]. He said the subterraneans called themselves Terras, and their home looked much like the outer world, except that it was lit by a small sun that never set. Besides Masars II, Marlo told of five other inner-world cities: Eden, Delfi, Jehu, Nigi, and Hectea. With an ideal climate, living things grew much larger; the Terras stood between twelve and fourteen feet tall, tortoises were twenty-five feet long, and birds with wingspans of thirty feet laid eggs two feet in diameter. Grapes were as large as oranges, and apples were the size of a man's head.[4]

Technologically, the Terras were a millenium ahead of us on the surface. Their saucers, like Fitch's, operated on "free energy" and made the trip from St. Louis to Masars II in a little less than an hour. Marlo, in his letters both to Bernard and to the members of UFO World Research, protested that although the big governments of the world knew the saucers came from the inside, government officials added to the popular misconception of UFOs as extraterrestrial vehicles by refusing to speak out and reveal the truth. The Terras themselves enjoyed confusing the issue by picking up naive surface people—the contactees—taking them for saucer rides, and fooling them into believing they had been to Mars or Venus and back. But these days had come to an end. Sol-Mar and Zola had chosen Marlo as their "Good Will Ambassador;" he had been shown the wonders of the inner world and entrusted with the truth about the saucers. He had been chosen partly because he was "worthy," but mostly, he admitted because he looked like Prince Neri, Sol-Mar and Zola's leader (a UFO buff who visited Marlo in St. Louis in 1960 described him as short, plump, balding, and pink-cheeked). Marlo wrote in one of his letters that Sol-Mar and Zola kept call-

---

[3] It appears that Marlo borrowed the name of his inner-world metropolis from one of the early contactee books, George Hunt Williamson's *The Saucers Speak* (1953). Williamson and some friends allegedly received messages from extraterrestrials from "Masar" or "Masars," which they learned later was Mars, on an impromptu ouija board.

[4] Marlo lifted these details directly from an inner-world novel by Willis G. Emerson, *The Smoky God* (1908); see Chapter 13.

ing him "The Boss" and this embarrassed him: "I say it should be the other way around because if it was not for them I wouldn't take any trips to the *Inner Earth.*"

Ottmar Kaub's protests to the contrary, however, it soon became clear that both he and Marlo were *very* interested in publicity and money. A group of Marlo's correspondents, intrigued with his story and hoping that they too might be offered rides to Masars II by the two Terras, investigated Marlo's background and found no evidence he possessed the Ph.D. he claimed. They did discover he was a door-to-door salesman who had become interested in UFOs and had gone into the business, hawking memberships in UFO World Research for $3.50 each. Marlo promised members they would head Sol-Mar and Zola's list for trips to the inner world, and he and Kaub wrote dozens of letters to prominent ufologists, politicians, and entertainers, inviting them to take saucer rides. Most of them, including Ray Palmer, did not take Marlo and Kaub seriously and ignored their offers. But the members of UFO World Research, who were very anxious to take saucer rides, were always disappointed. Marlo would set a place and time for the saucer to land and pick up its passengers, but on or before the scheduled day he would call and say the trip had regretfully been canceled because Sol-Mar and Zola had an urgent errand to perform in the inner world. Rumors about Marlo flew wildly within the UFO community in 1960—one of the rumors ran that President Eisenhower had made a secret trip to the California desert with Dr. Linus Pauling to meet Sol-Mar and Zola and take a short saucer ride. But Marlo's long string of empty promises brought him under merciless ridicule in the UFO press; it was not long before the Good Will Ambassador of the Inner World was laughed at and forgotten.

Bernard put great faith in Marlo's promises for a long time, however, and in his books *Nuclear Age Saviors* and *Flying Saucers from the Earth's Interior,* Bernard wrote glowingly of Marlo's sincerity and genuineness. In his letters and newsletters he claimed Marlo had promised to settle with him on Sao Francisco Island, and he would then be able to send Sol-Mar and Zola on regular trips to the United States to bring the "fit" back to Brazil.

Armed with Marlo's assurances, Bernard started a new campaign for members for his island community. Several psychics had told him that nuclear war would begin in 1965, so those who desired to purify themselves and join the elect in Agharta had to hurry. Those who came to the colony would be immediately placed on a gradual vegetarian diet, beginning with the elimination of meat and culminating in a diet entirely of fruit. An adept in yoga would train the colonists in exercises designed to speed physical purification and encourage sexual abstinence. "Naturally," Bernard wrote, "none may enter into the company of the Sages who is not resolved to live in strict chastity as they do. They do not want any "problem cases" on their hands. The mental cases better remain behind and be eliminated with the rest of the unfit. Only the fit can survive."

Bernard bristled, at least publicly, at the accusation—one which had found its way into the UFO press—that his colony was a racket designed to take money from trusting believers. He said he had spent $43,000 purchasing the property, but he claimed repeatedly that while those who could afford to do so would pay the "Aghartan Order" $150 an acre for their bit of farm and orchard land on the island, nobody who sincerely desired to join the colony would be turned away for lack of money. One's wealth was not as important as one's desire to live a chaste, fruitarian life.

He seems to have relied on Sol-Mar and Zola to help him in just this way—to provide a free U.S.-to-Brazil shuttle service for poor but sincere believers. A seventeen-year-old girl wrote Bernard early in 1960, full of hope:

> I am afraid I've subjected myself to the ridicule of everyone because I believe you.... We have seen two groups of flying saucer crafts.... We were not exactly surprised at the flying saucers, just a little overwhelmed and awe-stricken with admiration for such people who fly them. I just wish we could know and contact such people and be one of them. Since we saw the crafts, all of us seem to be somewhere else—just don't seem to give a hang about anything much. I can't stand to see those strange beautiful elusive things go drifting and dancing on the wind, yet so far, far away!.... If a person was accepted, could they take anything? Maybe—just a pet? A little yellow cat, maybe, that's awfully precious? Or a dog?
>
> Dad says... he'd like to be one of them, those people you call the Atlanteans, and have peace and security and things we've never had. We'd give up everything if only we knew that it will be waiting for us—a place and people who accept us and want us too. It would be a beautiful dream and both of us kids would study and learn.

Bernard printed her letter in one of his bulletins and assured her he was doing all he could to help her and her family. "We wrote to Dr. Marlo," he replied, "to put you all on the passenger list of his next flying saucer trip to Santa Catarina, and I am sure he will do so.... I hope it will not be long before you will all be here, and from here I hope you will go to the New World inside the earth, where all your troubles will be over and a new life of peace and happiness will await you."

Unfortunately, none of these things were to come about. Dr. Marlo—through the letters of Ottmar Kaub—kept promising the imminent arrival of Sol-Mar, Zola, and himself in Brazil, but he kept having to postpone, and postpone, and postpone. Usually agents of the U.S. Government stepped in to "forbid the flight;" several other times Marlo was called away to Washington D.C. on mysterious errands or for meetings with unnamed "high officials." After nearly a year of "delays," Bernard finally realized he had been hoaxed; he came to believe, in fact, that Marlo did not exist. "I am trying to get Kaub to confess that he fooled us all," Bernard wrote angrily at the end of 1960 to an American follower. It was a bitter blow for Bernard; since his "secret password" from Professor de Souza had gotten him nowhere, Marlo had been his closest link to the subterraneans. He continued his harangues in the *Biosophical Bulletin,* but he was not quite as confident. "Don't come here," he wrote, "expecting Dr. Raymond Bernard to bring you to the Atlanteans. He is hot on their trail, and must first meet them himself. After he does and he secures their permission, he will bring qualified refugees to them. The first step is to come to Santa Catarina, the New Holy Land. The next step is to enter the tunnels."

Bernard returned to his search for a Brazilian tunnel entrance, and he hoped to lure some of his American followers to Sao Francisco Island to help him. But his recruiting pitches bore little fruit; the only people who seem to have gathered on the island were a few poor Brazillians and German immigrants from nearby Joinville. When his American correspondents wrote him of their searches for entrances to the inner world in the caves and mountains of Arizona, New Mexico, and northern Mexico, Bernard became especially disturbed; he pleaded with them not to explore the dero-haunted caverns of North America. He felt the dero were the "outcasts and degenerates" expelled from the Lemurian "Motherland" thousands of years ago, and their presence beneath America explained the growth of juvenile delinquency in American cities. Desperate to convince his American readers to join him in Brazil, he went to work on his final book, *The Hollow Earth*.

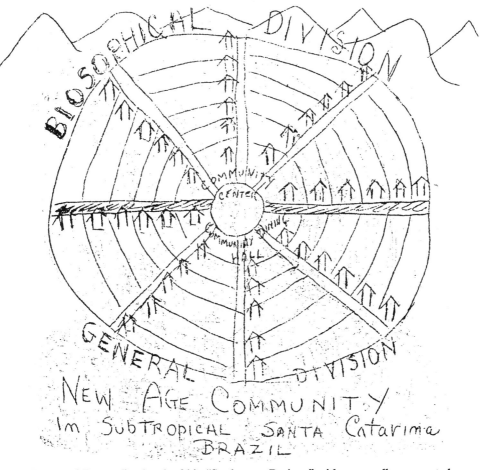

Raymond Bernard's sketch of his "Settlement Project," with a sexually segregated "Biosophical Division" and a non-segregated "General Division," from one of his mimeographed "Aghartan Order" newsletters of about 1960.

The Hollow Earth and its aftermath

The Hollow Earth is almost more interesting as an exposition of what Bernard did *not* know about the inner world than of what he did. Most of the book is a mishmash of pages-long quotes from the writers discussed so far— William Reed's list of questions, Marshall Gardner's "proofs" that neither Pole was ever reached, Ferdinand Ossendowski's description of the King of the World and his realm, and Ray Palmer's evidence for a donut-shaped earth. Although Bernard must have read Palmer's admission that Byrd had gone to the South Pole instead of the North Pole in 1947, he rested his case on Byrd's 1947 *North* Polar flight. He felt the U.S. government had covered up the Arctic flight of 1947: hadn't it been "almost completely forgotten until Giannini mentioned it in his book"? The evidence he presented was selected carefully to support his thesis; he presented dozens of quotes from nineteenth-century explorers—cribbed from Reed's book—as incontestible proof of an inner world, while ignoring or denying the feats of the twentieth-century explorers who *had* reached the poles. He believed Peary, Amundsen, the crew of the submarine Nautilus, and all the others had been fooled by faulty navigation instruments, or their real discoveries had been covered up by their governments.

It was with his argument dealing with government cover-ups that Bernard most clearly contradicted himself, and demonstrated how desperate he was to convince his readers the earth was hollow. Early in the book he claimed the U.S. government had learned of the existence of the inner world, and of the true home of the UFOs, when Admiral Byrd made his flight *beyond* the North Pole in 1947, but the truth had been immediately suppressed. Near the end of the book, he turned around and argued that the subterraneans first appeared in the outer-world atmosphere after 1945 to warn us of the dangers of nuclear weapons, but their mission failed because our governments didn't believe they, or their saucers, were real. The subterranean saucer pilots, he continued, have a good reason to mislead us into believing they come from other planets; they were fearful the governments of the outer world would "make a mad rush to send their aircraft through the polar openings to claim this territory as their own." Such an attempt at conquest would be a sorry mistake, for the superior subterraneans would be forced to use their "death rays" to disintegrate our pitiful armies and air forces; since the subterraneans were pacifists, it would pain them greatly to slaughter us.

Instead of an invasion of the inner world, which would be doomed from the beginning, Bernard suggested that a party of surface explorers who had accepted the superiority of the subterraneans journey by zeppelin through one of the polar openings to sit humbly at the subterraneans' feet and absorb their wisdom. As their zeppelin passed the ninetieth degree of latitude, the crew would watch the outer sun disappear and be replaced by the smaller, dimmer, reddish sun that shines eternally inside the earth. Strange new plants and animals would appear as the craft cruised slowly over the inner lands, and zoologists would be enthralled by the appearance of species thought long dead, like the mammoth. At last the beautiful cities of the Atlanteans would appear in the distance, and the explorers would be warmly met and shown the wonders of the subterranean civilization. They would be given a profound message to take back with them about the folly of building nuclear weapons. Armed with this message, the expedition would return to the surface to be hailed "not merely as the greatest explorers in history but as true Nuclear Age Saviors."

Perhaps Bernard sensed that the idea of an inner world was surprising enough for most people; most of his usual themes are nowhere to be seen in *The Hollow Earth*. There is very little about the atomic war to come in 1965, and no significant mention of the virtues of chastity and a fruitarian diet. His colony project limped on, however. In one of his last published statements, sent in 1964 to ufologist Timothy Green Beckley, Bernard said he had gathered a hundred men, women, and children on his island.

He also claimed to have twenty or more "explorers" in his service, hunting for entrances to the inner world in the Brazilian wilderness. One of them, referred to only as "R.K.," told Bernard he had encountered an old hunter in the mountains of Santa Catarina who led him to an enormous tunnel hidden in a cliffside. Within the tunnel R.K. found a "strange immense air vehicle" resembling a zeppelin and met its pilot, who was from the inner world. R.K. tried to take a picture of the craft, but the pilot would not allow it. He was invited to take a short ride in the vehicle, however; once R.K. was inside, the pilot drew blinds over the windows ("perhaps to guard important secrets") and began flying the ship down the tunnel at supersonic speed. After half an hour of descent, R.K. felt the craft resume a horizontal flight, and a large window opened in the floor, revealing a great city shining in the red glow of the inner sun. The subterranean pilot allowed R.K. a leisurely look, then shut the window and returned to the surface. Before leaving R.K. the pilot told him to return soon with Dr. Bernard, and the three of them would return to the city of "Shamballah, world capital of the Subterranean World of Agharta." There Bernard would be honored at a great banquet by the King of the World and his millions of subjects as "the first inhabitant of the earth's surface to establish communication between the Upper World and the Subterranean World."

Bernard called R.K.'s trip "THE GREATEST FEAT OF EXPLORATION IN HISTORY" and renewed his call for more colonists to join his triumphant entrance into Shamballah. It would be only a short time before "the Chinese Dragon starts to spit forth atomic fire," and he wanted to be the Noah of the twentieth century, rescuing the worthiest of surface humanity. He reasserted that the colony was "entirely humanitarian and non-commercial"—for "the subterranean people use no money and require no payment of those they accept in their subterranean cities."

He continued his pitchmaking until the summer of 1965, when his correspondence suddenly stopped. Letters sent to him from the United States were returned from the Joinville post office stamped "deceased," and soon word reached the American UFO community that Raymond Bernard had died of pneumonia on September 10, at the age of 64. Wierlo wrote that "those who saw... Bernard" in the year before his death "described him as 'filthy and disgrace to Americans,'" with a disregard for germs. Not all his followers accepted the news of his death, however, and all sorts of rumors arose quickly among American hollow-earthers. Soon it was generally believed among them that Bernard was still alive—he had merely disappeared while searching for another tunnel entrance. Perhaps R.K.'s report had been true, and Bernard had been flown down to Shamballah and remained there. As late as 1976, a prominent UFO newsletter printed a letter from a reader in Puerto Rico:

> I write to you at the request of Walter Siegmeister. He is alive and in excellent health. I just met with him last week.... He comes to see me often from his present home in Masars II, a colony in Agharta. I have learned many amazing things from both him and his friends from the interior of our Earth. I plan to travel to live with him there very soon...

How pleasant it would be to believe that Bernard, after all his years of searching, reached the inner world at last.

If he did, it might make up for the confused image of himself he left among students of ufology and the hollow-earth idea. I corresponded with several of those who wrote regularly to Bernard and subscribed to his newsletters during the late fifties and early sixties, and most believed he was sincere. But a few of them, as well as several UFO journalists of that time, believed he was a fake, running a real-estate racket in worthless South American land and swindling the gullible with stories of subterranean cities, and it appears they were at least partially correct. One writer, Daniel Cohen, believes Bernard may not have existed at all. Cohen, former editor of *Science Digest* magazine and author of many books debunking various alternative-reality beliefs, suggested in his book *The World of UFOs* (1978) that Raymond Bernard was really Ray Palmer. *The Hollow Earth*, Cohen wrote, "sounds like Palmer, it certainly concentrates on many of Palmer's favorite themes, and it quotes generously from the writings of Ray Palmer." Cohen seems to have been unaware of Bernard's several dozen other books—although one can hardly blame him, since most of them have never been published in any form other than mimeographed-and-stapled booklets—promoting a fruitarian diet, parthenogenetic childbirth, or the value of sexual abstinence. These themes were definitely *not* Palmer's style. Palmer himself had a low opinion of Bernard. When one of his readers asked Palmer what he knew of Bernard, he replied in a 1970 issue of *Flying Saucers*:

> He is a pen name for a person we believe to be Walter Siegmeister, who at one time sold lots on an island off the "Horn" in South America, where he claimed there was an entrance to the inner world, and where he intended to found a colony with himself as the boss. Get away from the radioactive menace of the atomic bomb, he said.
>
> While we are at it, the Bernard book... is entirely his work, and all references to me, and material from my magazines, are pilfered, without permission, and I have been quoted and misquoted, entirely out of context, and many times falsely...
>
> As Siegmeister, he owes me a large sum for unpaid advertising early in the beginning of my magazines. THAT I would be interested in getting! But his book(s) are no more reliable than his credit.... Look into the Siegmeister affair and you'll find... some pretty big real estate frauds. He sold half the Atlantic Ocean to suckers who feared for their lives from atomic radiation in the atmosphere.

At this writing, twenty-five years after his death, with large gaps in the information available on his life, it is difficult to make any hard conclusions about the life, personality, or motives of Raymond Bernard/Walter Siegmeister. But after reading many of his books, bulletins, letters, and most of what others have said and written about him, Bernard indeed seems to me to have been something of a swindler. But he was a swindler serving his own naive ideal. He doesn't appear to have interested many people in giving up meat and sex and "moving to the inner world," and he never appears to have gotten rich from his schemes; he rather seems to have been a surprisingly sincere (in his ends, if not his means), stubborn, frightened man who clutched desperately to an idea neither history nor reason supported—the survival of a supremely "pure" and childlike super-race either on the earth or in the earth or on another planet. Despite the broad trickster streak in him, his beliefs are those of one filled with the desire to escape the complexities of adult life on the "surface" world of wars and laws and economics and run back to the womb, or at least to infancy. For most of his later life the central figure of his personal mythology was the Great Mother, who ruled a community of her eternally childlike offspring. Although the descriptions of the Atlanteans within the earth were often colored by the science-fiction imagery of those around him, Bernard never strayed far from the image of an untroubled, supremely happy race of vegetarians living in purity. They had neither sex nor money nor work to tangle their lives in their enclosed Eden.

Bernard was genuinely disturbed by the secondary role of women in society, and in his strange way, one of the major labors of his life was pointing a way in which women could free themselves from the tyranny of men. He believed sex was at the root of this tyranny, and if sexual desire, which he called unhealthy, could be eliminated, the sexes would be equal. Sexual desire was caused by eating animal foods: "Imagine a race of people," he wrote in one of his bulletins, "who live as strict vegetarians and who do not consume sex-stimulating proteins, as is the case with the Atlanteans. Among these people, the sexual tendencies that obsess surface people are entirely absent." In his descriptions of the subterranean Atlanteans, he stressed repeatedly that the two sexes lived separately, independently, and entirely free. Childbirth was painless for the women, and since it was parthenogenetic, men had no responsibility in the process at all. Although Bernard never spoke to the issue directly, his "ideal" subterranean society—unless it was constantly reinfused with men from the surface—would soon have no males at all, for parthenogenetic offspring are always female.

These beliefs, not the size or location of the polar openings or the true origin of the UFOs, are the core of Raymond Bernard's writings. He was a truly archaic believer in the holiness and power of the Great Mother—the Earth Mother as Provider and Protector—and the mythic civilization she ruled. He wrote of a life in which all her children who remained pure would also eternally remain happy, secure children. Bernard himself was trapped in a complex adult world of space flight and nuclear weaponry, but he never stopped looking for her country, his true home.

Since his death he has become a symbol of the faith that sustains every believer in an inner world. While researching this chapter, I placed requests in several UFO-oriented publications asking for information about Bernard, and two of the replies I received were especially intriguing. The writer of one described an out-of-body vision of Bernard prevented from reaching the entrances to the tunnels by evil magicians from the astral plane. The other was a note on a small piece of paper, which I quote here in full:

> Walter Krafton Minkel: [*sic*]
>   The Man whom you wonder about so much is living in a remote quiet place near the little village town of Houston, Missouri. Yes, he does exist...
>   Let this satisfy your curious thoughts. Leave it at that, my friend, leave it at that.
>   Anon.

Chapter 12

The Nazis and the Hollow Earth

> Well do I remember, as a child, contemplating with wondering awe the great Kyffhäuserberg in Thuringia, for therein, I was told, slept Frederic Barbarossa and his six knights. A shepherd once penetrated into the heart of the mountain by a cave, and discovered therein a hall where sat the Emperor at a stone table, and his red beard had grown through the slab. At the tread of the shepherd, Frederic awoke from his slumber, and asked, "Do the ravens still fly over the mountains?"
>
> "Sire! they do."
>
> "Then we must sleep another hundred years."
>
> But when his beard has wound itself thrice around the table, then will the Emperor awake with his knights, and rush forth to release Germany from its bondage, and exalt it to the first place among the kingdoms of Europe.
>
> —Sabine Baring-Gould, *Curious Myths of the Middle Ages*

Near the end of the First World War, a young German pilot named Peter Bender was shot down over France and spent the rest of the war in a French POW camp. Recuperating from his near-mortal wounds, he found in one of the camp huts a pile of old American magazines, and among them were several copies of the *Flaming Sword,* the magazine of the Koreshans. Bender, who knew English well, lay in his cot fascinated by Cyrus Teed's concave earth and womblike cosmos, and when he was released and returned to Germany after the war he began searching for some proof for Teed's ideas. He didn't have to look far to satisfy himself. In the city library of Worms am Rhein, Bender found a copy of Teed's book *The Cellular Cosmogony,* and as soon as he read of Ulysses Grant Morrow's triumphant demonstration of the earth's concavity with the Rectilineator, he became a convert to Koreshanity for the rest of his life. The ideas he found in *The Cellular Cosmogony,* in fact, struck such a deep emotional chord in Bender that he convinced himself that he was the current incarnation of Koresh, and that it was his mission to spread Koreshanity to Germany, and from there to the rest of the world.

Bender had little interest, however, in the religious aspects of Koreshanity—in Teed's Anglo-Israelitism or his prophecies of a constricted new age. Bender was obsessed by one idea—an enclosed, clockwork universe—and he pursued it with single-minded vigor. He spent the twenties and thirties writing furiously, as Symmes and Gardner had, to scientists, politicians, newspapers, and universities. He simplified Teed's tangle of optical "laws" and complex planetary polarities to a more easily comprehensible mechanism, the "Phantom Universe." At the center of the concave earth, Bender suspended a large navy-blue sphere. Around it the sun—a glob of molten rock about 150 miles in diameter—and the moon and planets, which were smaller molten globs, revolved at different speeds and distances in an almost total vacuum. The dark sphere itself was flecked with even smaller globs, which appeared to us as the stars. The atmosphere, which was only some forty miles thick, bent the rays of the sun, moon, and stars so they appeared to be passing overhead, but night and day itself was caused by the positions of the Phantom Universe and the sun. If the sun was situated between us and the dark sphere it was daytime; when the sun went behind the sphere, it was night.

Bender, like Symmes and Gardner, was ignored by the geologists and astronomers, but like them he won a few converts here and there to what he called the *hohlweltlehre*—the hollow-earth doctrine. In the early 1930s, as Adolf Hitler's shadow began spreading over Germany, Bender and his wife took jobs as teachers of English and mathematics at a Frankfurt school which prepared Jewish emigrants in the languages and ways of their prospective homelands. The school's dynamic Jewish headmistress, Hedwig Michel, listened to Bender's talks and read his writings, as well as those of Cyrus Teed, until she too converted to Koreshanity. When Nazi pressure on the Jews grew unbearable and the school was forced to shut down, Bender wrote to the Koreshans in Estero—with whom he had been corresponding for years—and asked them if they would sponsor Michel as an immigrant. They replied that they would welcome her. She left Germany on the last scheduled shipload of Jewish immigrants bound for the United States, and from not long after her arrival until her death in 1982 at the age of ninety, Hedwig Michel was the driving force behind the dwindling colony of Florida Koreshans.

Yet not long after Bender helped her leave Germany, he was to write in one of his articles, "An infinite universe is a Jewish abstraction. A finite, rounded universe is a thoroughly Aryan conception." While the professors paid no attention to Bender, many members and sympathizers of the National Socialists read his writings with great interest. One of Bender's old comrades from his days as a flyer was Hermann Göring, the man who was to become commander of the Luftwaffe and *Reichsmarschal* of the Third Reich. Göring did not forget Peter Bender. It was through his influence that Bender received an opportunity to officially test his belief—a test that resulted in Peter Bender's death.

The Magdeburg Project and the Rügen Island Experiment

National Socialism had a strange love-hate relationship with occultism and revealed science. It is well known that the Nazi Party grew from the alliance of several small political-nationalist-occultist organizations that clung to the underbelly of post-World War I German culture, most notably Munich's rabidly anti-Semitic Thule Society. The Thule Society, which appears to have gained a reputation among occultists as a major force behind National Socialism far beyond what it actually deserved, was formed in Munich in 1918 in reaction to a short-lived Bavarian Socialist government led by the Jewish intellectual Kurt Eisner; its goal was the revival of Teutonic culture, symbolism, and mythology (Thule itself was the Aryan Atlantis—H.P.B.'s Hyperborea under another name). Non-occultist Hitler biographer Robert Payne wrote that Thule was "ostensibly a literary club devoted to the study of Nordic culture but in fact a secret political organization devoted to violent anti-Semitism and rule by an aristocratic elite". The Society seems to have functioned only until 1933, when the Nazis banned it. It is also well known that several of the leading Nazis, including Rudolf Hess and Heinrich Himmler, and to a lesser degree Hitler himself, were advocates of reincarnation, astrology, and the Atlantean (or Thulean) origins of the "Nordic race." Yet not long after they seized power in Germany, the Nazis began a systematic persecution of occult groups; storm troopers raided booksellers throughout the mid-thirties to confiscate and destroy occult books and magazines, break up occultist meetings, and force astrologers and spiritualists to abandon their work. Many occultists, in fact, were executed or sent to concentration camps. Himmler, the *Reichsführer SS,* is supposed to have said after he ordered the purge of the astrologers, "In the Third Reich we have to forbid astrology.... We cannot permit any astrologers to follow their calling except those who are working for us."

Several alternative-reality theories flourished alongside Nazism, however; one of the best known was the "Cosmic Ice Theory" of Hans Hörbiger (1860–1931), an Austrian inventor and mining engineer. Hörbiger proposed that the earth had, throughout its history, captured four successive moons from space. Each of the moons, including the present one, and all of the planets of the solar system, were balls of rock coated with ice hundreds of miles thick, and the stars were simply huge ice blocks reflected in the rays of the sun. Over thousands of years, Hörbiger wrote, each of the earth's moons, caught in the deadly pull of gravity, spiraled slowly closer to the earth. As each icy moon approached, it gradually froze our oceans and brought great ice ages to the earth, until the interaction of gravitational forces broke the moon to pieces, showering the earth with a deluge of ice and rock, followed by a flood of the melting oceans. The destruction of our third moon was, of course, the end of the last Ice Age and the source of the worldwide legend of the Flood (here Hörbiger anticipated Immanuel Velikovsky), and the few human survivors of the cataclysm were venerated by their descendants as the parents of modern humanity.

The Cosmic Ice Theory, with its icy catastrophes so reminiscent of the *Gotterdamerung* of Teutonic myth, was highly appealing to many of the Nazis and their sympathizers. Hitler himself was inclined to believe in Hörbiger's cosmology, and Himmler was a committed supporter. The Hörbigerians issued pamphlets and broadsides throughout the thirties that declared: "Our Nordic ancestors grew strong in ice and snow; belief in the World Ice is consequently the natural heritage of Nordic Man," and "Just as it needed a child of Austrian culture—Hitler!—to put the Jewish politicians in their place so it needed an Austrian [Hörbiger] to cleanse the world of Jewish science." It has even been suggested—although without much evidence to support it—that Hitler's invasion of Russia failed because his Hörbigerian meteorologists told him that the winter of 1941-42 would be mild, where it was actually so severe that the German Army, sent east without proper cold-weather gear, suffered more than a million casualties.

   Peter Bender's *hohlweltlehre,* however, did not enjoy the Cosmic Ice Theory's popularity among the leaders of the Reich.   One of Bender's disciples, Johannes Lang, applied to Hitler's cultural minister, Alfred Rosenberg, in 1938 for permission to give public lectures on Bender's teachings.   Rosenberg, one of the Reich's most fervent believers in Atlantis as the Aryans' homeland, turned Lang down, condemning the *hohlweltlehre* as "completely unscientific."   Nevertheless it had two sterling opportunities—with official support and the top technology available at the time—to prove itself.   In 1933, just as Hitler was coming to power, an engineer named Mengering, who was employed by the Prussian industrial city of Magdeburg, had read Bender's articles with great interest and made a proposal to city officials.   Mengering wanted to test Bender's theory, and he felt that the best way to do it would be to construct a large rocket, launch it straight up, and see whether it would strike the opposite side of the earth.   He asked the Magdeburg officials for the money to stage the test, and while they had little interest in the hollow-earth idea, they decided that a rocket launching would make a magnificent holiday spectacle for the coming June.   So they awarded Mengering 25,000 marks to have a rocket constructed that would launch a man to at least the height of one kilometer, where he would be ejected and parachute back to earth.   If the rocket kept going up until it reached New Zealand, so much the better.

   The German science writer Willy Ley, who knew many of the men involved in the project, described the enterprise as short-lived and plagued with problems.   Although Mengering hired scientists and mechanics who were later involved with construction of the infamous V-2 rockets, rocket technology in 1933 was simply not ready to launch a man even a few feet into the air.   Mechanical failures beset the test motors—several of them exploded during the construction of the rocket—and the finished rocket seemed unable to leave its launching pad.   In one trial flight, it reached a height of six feet, a screw fell out of the gas tank, and the engine stopped.   In another trial it reached the top of the launching rack, paused there, and slowly settled back to earth with the engine running.   When the day of the grand spectacle arrived, two weeks after the appointed date, the rocket was wisely ignited without a human passenger.   It hooked itself momentarily on its now-warped launching rack—the Magdeburg officials, concerned about the runaway budget on the project, had only allowed for a wooden launching rack, which had been caught in a storm during the delays—flew off horizontally, and landed gently on its side a thousand feet from the disappointed crowd.   After skidding over the ground for another thirty feet, the engine sputtered out.   That was the end of the Magdeburg project; most of the city shopkeepers who had pledged their money to the undertaking refused to pay up, and the embarrassed Mengering was only able to collect 3200 marks. The concavity of the earth remained unproven.

   More torturous—and ultimately tragic—was the story of the Rügen Island Experiment, the *hohlweltlehre*'s second opportunity to prove itself. Throughout the thirties and during the war, a number of officers in the German Navy explored several methods for locating enemy vessels that smelled strongly of the occult. A retired Austrian architect and occultist named Ludwig Straniak, for example, was whisked to the Naval Research Institute in Berlin in the early years of the war when a committee of officers visited him and discovered that he could detect the locations of German ships at sea using a technique he called *pendelforschung*. This technique was nothing other than a new variation of the old occult tradition of radiesthesia or pendulum-swinging; Herr Straniak would spread a large map of the Atlantic on a table, concentrate on a photograph of the ship he wished to locate, and swing a steel pendulum, shaped like a cube and a cubic centimeter in size, over the map. When its swing changed, Straniak announced the location of the ship. He trained several naval officers in this method, and they swung their pendulums dutifully over maps for much of the war trying to find Allied warships, but *pendelforschung* did not seem to work well at all when the ships in question were not German and when their location was not known in advance by someone at the Institute.

The same officers who investigated *pendelforschung* also discovered the *hohlweltlehre*—thanks to Bender's old-cronyship with Hermann Göring—and were quick to realize its naval implications. If the earth was indeed, as Bender said, hollow and concave, it should be possible, using advanced photographic techniques, to detect from Germany the position of the British fleet in the North Sea and the Atlantic, since the curvature of the earth wouldn't get in the way. Bender had said, as Teed had, that we were unable to see the upward curvature of the horizon because the rays of the visible spectrum were severely refracted by the atmosphere, giving us the illusion of a convex planet; but Bender also suggested, and the Naval Research Institute officers agreed, that infrared rays were hardly refracted at all. So in 1942, at great expense to the Reich at a critical point in the war, the officers pushed through, with Göring's tacit approval, a new experimental project. A crew of researchers was sent to Rügen Island in the Baltic Sea under the direction of physicist Dr. Heinz Fischer. Fischer, who resented being dragged away from his own work to test what he considered a crackbrained idea, pointed a special telescopic camera using infrared filters at approximately a 45° angle into the sky to photograph areas of the Baltic and North Seas where the British Navy might be found—if the earth was concave. Fischer and his assistants made hundreds of photographs of the sky, and each was searched carefully for the warships. Not a single ship, British or otherwise, could be found in any of the photographs, despite microscopic examination and adjustments and readjustments of the equipment. The experiment was quickly ordered shut down.

The complete failure of the project on Rügen Island infuriated the Nazi High Command; they felt that Bender and the officers at the Institute had made fools of the Reich and themselves. Even Göring must have felt angry and foolish, for when Peter Bender, his wife, and a group of some of Bender's most fervent suporters were sent soon after to one of the death camps, the *Reichsmarschal* did nothing to help them.

Although Bender became one of the Third Reich's countless victims, the *hohlweltlehre* itself did not die. Two of Bender's disciples, Karl Neupert and Johannes Lang, survived the war and began publishing booklets and little magazines espousing a concave earth almost immediately after the Reich surrendered. Neupert prepared *hohlweltlehre* tracts in German and English and mailed them all over the world, and after Neupert's death in 1949, Lang pressed on in the pages of his journal *Geokosmos*. Lang clung to the concave earth even after the arrival of space flight; in one *Geokosmos* article of the early sixties, he published photographs of the earth taken by the American Mercury astronauts to demonstrate how the atmosphere lining the shell of our planet warps light and deceives us into thinking that the earth is really convex.

And—somewhat incidentally—it was in Germany in 1953 that Godfried Bueren, a 70-year-old patent attorney and occultist, lost a battle with the German Astronomical Society when he tried to prove in court that the *sun* was hollow. Instead of a hollow earth with a little sun inside, Bueren claimed that after years of studying the sun, he had concluded it consisted of two spheres—an outer shell a million miles in diameter heated to 1,000,000° Celsius through bombardment by cosmic particles, and an interior planet 600,000 miles in diameter floating in the center of the solar shell. The planet was covered, Bueren said, with an ultra-lush form of vegetation which absorbed the sun's heat, transformed it into chemical energy, and rendered the inner planet a tropical paradise. Sunspots were merely small holes that appeared in the shell from time to time and allowed us a peek at the dark, fertile world within.

Bueren was as stubborn and self-assured as Symmes and Gardner, but he was unwise enough to put his money where his mouth was; he announced that he would pay 25,000 marks (about $6000 in those days) to anyone who could prove him wrong. The German Astronomical Society, disgusted by Bueren's "silly ideas" and the attention they were attracting in the press, took up the cudgel and had little trouble deflating his theory, even when the arguments for both sides had been presented to a jury of West German scientists Bueren himself had chosen. But he refused to pay the Society, sniffing, "People who want to cash in on the money do not even pay attention to what I have to say." The astronomers took Bueren to court, arguing that "Science cannot always say what is correct, but we have advanced so far as to be able to say what is wrong. And Herr Bueren's theory is most definitely wrong." The court ruled in favor of the Society, and Bueren was ordered to pay not only the 25,000 marks, but a year's interest and court costs as well. He left the court grumbling that the jury of scientists who had ruled against him had been "intimidated."

Fascism, racism, and occultism

During the 1970s, the Devil, who had grown vague and unfashionable in mainstream religion and culture, suddenly returned with a vengeance. He possessed small boys and teenage girls in countless paperback novels and horror movies. The massive renaissance of fundamentalist Christianity returned him to a major religious role as the necessary opponent of Jesus's plan to redeem humanity and as the necessary author of evil in a jumbled, violent world. He has also become the subject of a growing number of serious theological and historical studies. We have refused to let the Devil die; it appears that in a world in which so much evil occurs so apparently at random, we need him. In the years since the end of the Second World War the figure of Adolf Hitler has come to assume a similar role in the Western mind; our image of the Führer saluting lines of goosestepping soldiers, sending millions of "undesirables" to their deaths, and spellbinding the German masses has come to symbolize much that is supremely evil. He has become the Devil personified of the late twentieth century, and since his death our emotional selves have been reluctant to let him die.

Almost moments after the reports of Hitler's suicide on the last day of April 1945 hit the newspapers, rumors billowed around them like clouds of dust. The May 7, 1945 issue of *Time* carried, tongue somewhat in cheek, a report from the anti-Nazi "Free German Press Service" based in Stockholm; it revealed that the Führer had not died in the Berlin bunker at all. A Plauen grocer named August Bartholdy, who served as Hitler's double, had died in his place, and Hitler himself had escaped to an unknown refuge. James Byrnes, U.S. Secretary of State under Harry Truman, added fuel to the fire in his book *Speaking Frankly* (1947) when he described a conversation with Josef Stalin at the Potsdam Conference: "In speaking of our visit to Berlin, I asked the Generalissimo his views of how Hitler had died. To my surprise, he said he believed that Hitler was alive and that it was possible he was then either in Spain or Argentina. Some ten days later I asked him if he had changed his views and he said he had not." Stories about "Hitler's escape" from occupied Germany and into hiding appeared regularly in American and European newspapers during the postwar years, encouraged by the arrests of Adolf Eichmann and other Nazis who had gone into hiding. Several "Capture Hitler" funds were set up by public-spirited Americans who believed the Führer was still alive.

The idea that Hitler or other Nazi "masterminds" left Germany before V-E day and lurk somewhere on earth today, plotting a Fourth Reich, survives in books like Ira Levin's best-selling *Boys from Brazil* and its spinoffs. In a world filled with terrorism and political chaos, there is something both titillating and reassuring in the notion that it *isn't* chaos, that a vast conspiracy of evil moves over the world unseen. Such ideas are popular among occultists as well; theoreticians of the "hidden wisdom," who regularly paint sweeping battles between Good and Evil on spiritual and physical planes for their disciples, have often been drawn to the figure of Adolf Hitler. For many occultists, the Führer was an initiate of the inner circles of power, a great magician who destroyed himself by following the Left-Hand Path, the way of annihilation. Others have suggested Hitler was possessed by the demons he called up; still others believe he was a "psychic vampire," drawing his power to hypnotize crowds from their souls, draining away his listeners' spiritual energy and their will to resist him.

The myth of Hitler-the-Magician was streamlined into a strange book by the occultist Trevor Ravenscroft, *The Spear of Destiny* (1973). Ravenscroft claimed that Hitler immersed himself in the occult as a young man in Vienna, where he was an avid student of yoga, Eastern religions, and Teutonic myth. Hitler's studies led him to an obsession with the so-called "Spear of Longinus," one of the holy relics of the Hapsburg dynasty displayed in Vienna's Hofburg

Museum. The Spear, in two sections once joined by a silver sheath, is supposedly the head of the actual spear used by the Roman centurion Gaius Cassius Longinus to dispatch Christ on the cross, and Hitler was well acquainted with the Spear's reputation as a vessel of power.

The "Spear of Longinus."

Ravenscroft quotes the tradition: "There is a legend associated with this Spear that whoever claims it, and solves its secrets, holds the destiny of the world in his hands for good or evil." Hitler realized, wrote Ravenscroft, that if he could take possession of the Spear he could lead the German people to the conquest of the world, and all his plans for the next thirty years revolved around claiming the *Helige Lance,* as the Germans called it, for his own. When he returned, toughened but disillusioned, from World War I, a bookseller friend brought him into the arms of the ultra-right-wing Thule Society, and it was there that Hitler took his fatal step into darkness.

The Thule Society appeared on the surface a cranky cult of anti-Semites, but it was in reality, according to Ravenscroft, a circle of the darkest of black magicians. One of the Society's leaders, the poet and drug addict Dietrich Eckhart, initiated Hitler into the secrets of the Left-Hand Path "in a monstrous sadistic magic ritual" in which the Führer-to-be was consumed and possessed by "evil and non-human intelligences." Driven by these powers and his own twisted desire for conquest, it was only a short time before Hitler rose from nowhere to the Chancellorship of Germany and set the nation on the path to war. No sooner had he occupied Austria in 1938 than he traveled to Vienna and shut himself up, alone, with the Helige Lance. The Spear and the other Hapsburg relics were moved to Germany not long afterward. Possession of the Spear did not, however, protect Hitler from losing the war, and he ordered the relics hidden beneath a medieval fortress in Nuremburg as the Allies began rolling into Germany in 1945. The Americans who occupied Nuremburg found the hiding place, however, and returned the relics to the new Austrian government to be replaced in the Hofburg Museum, where the Spear has been displayed ever since.

Actually, there is no real evidence that Hitler had any special interest in the Spear, although he did take possession of the Hapsburg relics and move them to Nuremburg as a symbol of his "unification" of the Germanic people under the swastika. Ravenscroft's magical history of the Reich tells us more about his own passions than Hitler's. But there is more to *The Spear of Destiny* than the Spear itself. There is also the story of Dr. Karl Haushofer, a sinister figure who was both a German general in World War I and an academic; as a professor he developed and promoted "Geo-Politics," the notion that every people can conquer the world if it can only control its own home territory. This abstraction concealed Haushofer's belief that Aryan man was fated to rule the world after he had conquered Europe and Central Asia, his traditional "homeland." Rudolf Hess was Haushofer's assistant as a young man, and Geo-Politics was highly regarded by the leaders of the Third Reich. Ravenscroft revealed that Haushofer was also an initiate of the inner circle of the Thule Society, as well as of an even more secretive Japanese brotherhood, the Green Dragon Society, and he rubbed shoulders with many of the dark adepts of the East. Under his guidance, Hitler was able to establish contact with two orders of evil magicians who dwelled in cave cities beneath the Himalayas, the "Order of Schamballah" and the "Order of Agarthi." Starting in 1926, Hitler sent Nazi expeditions to Tibet every year until 1942. During the early expeditions, the Nazis met with both orders, but only one—the adepts of Agarthi—agreed to assist them in their rise to power. The adepts of Schamballah refused to help Hitler, not because he wasn't evil enough, but because he wasn't materialistic enough. Schamballah, Ravenscroft wrote, was dedicated to tempting humanity into the morass through the pursuit of wealth and material things, and was already working with "certain Lodges" in England and the United States.

Agarthi, however, specialized in setting up dictators and spreading oppression, and sent a party of Tibetan adepts back to Germany with the Nazis in the early thirties to settle in Berlin, Munich, and Nuremburg. The Nazi leaders referred to the Tibetans as "The Society of Green Men," and Himmler made their teachings the centerpiece of his shamelessly occultist *Ahnenerbe,* the SS "Department of Ancestral Heritage," set up to trace the origins and characteristics of Aryan man. The Green Men worked for the Nazis throughout the war, aiding them in battle on the psychic plane, but after the Russian victory over the Germans at Stalingrad in 1942, their influence went into eclipse. Near the end of the war, said Ravenscroft, Hitler was so angered by their failure to change the war's course that he ordered their rations reduced to those of the concentration-camp prisoners. When the Russian Army reached their quarters east of Berlin, the Green Men were found naked and laid out neatly in rows; each had committed hara-kiri (a most un-Tibetan form of suicide) rather than submit to their Soviet captors.

Ravenscroft neither could nor would offer any proof for his marvelous tales of an occult Reich. When *The Spear of Destiny* was reviewed in the German journal *Die Drei*, reviewer Christoph Lindenberg revealed the results of some research he had done in Vienna about people and places there at the time Hitler was supposed to have been lured into the occult. It showed several very large factual errors in Ravenscroft's story (for example, the bookseller Pretsche, who is supposed to have introduced Hitler to both occult literature and drugs, never appears to have existed). But that such tales exist at all in occult circles, and that they appeal to the reading public, is a tribute to the emotional aura surrounding the name Hitler. They are also, in a small way, tributes to the power of the Agharti/Shambhala myth. The writings of Ossendowski, Roerich, and Guénon have influenced European occultism since they were first published in the 1920s, and it is very possible that Agharti and Shambhala were real places for Himmler and the other occult-minded Nazis. The British folklorist Geoffrey

Ashe has suggested that the King of the World's prophecy in *Beasts, Men and Gods* was not only well-known to the Nazis, but a heady stimulant to their desire to remake the world. Ashe writes of the prophecy:

> It begins with a vague series of horrors which more or less fits the First World War. The King goes on to speak of the war's aftermath, and the action he will take through his own secret influence. "Then I shall send a people, now unknown, which shall tear out the weeds of madness and vice with a strong hand and will lead those who still remain faithful to the spirit of man in the fight against Evil. They will found a new life on the earth purified by the death of nations. In the fiftieth year only three great kingdoms will appear." The first two sentences could have been applied, by Hitler and his associates, to the rise and assumed mission of the Nazi movement. Purifying the earth "by the death of nations" could mean the extermination of the Jews and other lesser breeds... The "fiftieth year" from the prophecy was 1940. In that year Germany, Italy and Japan, "three great kingdoms," formed the Tripartite Alliance which was intended to dominate the earth. The attacks on Russia and the United States followed, both acts of apparent lunacy which might yet have been supposed to make sense if the Alliance had the King's blessing.

The notion that the Axis powers felt themselves to be the armies of the King of the World, mysterious and intriguing as it is, suffers from an overwhelming lack of proof. It first appeared in print, to my knowledge, in *The Morning of the Magicians* (1960), the French occult bestseller by Louis Pauwels and Jacques Bergier. Pauwels and Bergier gave a version of the Agharti myth which has been kicking around Europe in various forms for decades; its Theosophical origins are obvious. "Thirty or forty centuries ago" a technological civilization thrived in the midst of what is now the Gobi Desert, but an atomic war or other catastrophe devastated the culture and its survivors migrated westward, some to northern Europe, some to the Caucasus Mountains. But others—the authors quote Guénon's *Le Roi du Monde* to the effect that these others were the adepts, "the All-Knowing, the sons of Intelligences from Beyond"—traveled south to settle in the Himalayas. Some of the adepts succumbed to the temptations of the dark powers, while others remained faithful to helping humanity progress; they split into two communities dwelling in cities deep beneath the mountains—Agarthi, the city of goodness and meditation, and Schamballah, the city of "violence and power whose forces command the elements and the masses of humanity, and hasten the arrival of the human race at the 'turning point of time.'" In the authors' scenario, it was the adepts of Schamballah, not Agarthi, with whom the Reich sealed their sinister covenant, and who traveled to Germany to aid the Nazis. They write of one of the Schamballah adepts:

> In Berlin there was a Thibetan monk, nicknamed "the man with the green gloves," who had correctly foretold in the Press, on three occasions, the number of Hitlerian deputies elected to the Reichstag, and who was regularly visited by Hitler. He was said by the Initiates to "possess the keys to the Kingdom of Agarthi."

Once again, Pauwels and Bergier give no documentation at all for these tales, but that, of course, only deepens the mystery.

Robert Charroux, a French author of Theosophical inclinations whose books inspired Erich von Däniken, wrote in his *The Gods Unknown* (1969) of a European occult society, the Grand Lodge of Vril, active in the 1960s. The Lodge considered itself the external manifestation of the adepts of Agharti/Shamballa, and the successor to the mantle of the Thule Society (Charroux reveals in passing that Baron Ungern von Sternberg, before he traveled to Mongolia, had been initiated into the inner circle of Thule—an intriguing notion, but again without proof). The Lodge appeared to be another product of the Saint-Yves-Ossendowski-Guénon tradition, with an emphasis on a racist/religious New Age. Charroux, who frankly found the Lodge's beliefs distasteful and puzzling, quoted from one of their publications:

> The Master of the Three Worlds enthroned at Shamballah or K.B.L. [Charroux either doesn't know or doesn't say what K.B.L. stands for] is named Lucifer or Odin. The forces of K.B.L., the principles of which are set out in the Vedas and the Tibetan Bardo Thodol, will act as a synarchy "to unite the yellow races, as the most numerous, with the fair nordic races, as the most capable, in a joint struggle against the forces of evil....
> "The Master of the Three Worlds, whose initials are K.R.T.K.M., reigns at Shamballah over a community of Magi, the *Green Men*, who constitute the cosmic synarchy Tchun-Yung, or the Direct Middle Way." These magi are the descendants of Venusian ancestors and claim to be the successors of Zoroaster and Mahomet; their mission is to revive the "true ritual of the Black Stone."

The Lodge, according to Charroux, expects the imminent return of "the next Buddha," who will usher in the Golden Age, "the end of the Kali-Yuga, the casting out of the Joten and the cacodaemons from the governmental centres of the earth, and of the 100,000 years of evil karma inherited from the darkness of Atlantis."

Beneath the tangle of words and symbols from a jumble of European and Asian beliefs, it isn't difficult to sense the Lodge's goal—a world run by a magical fascism, in which the vast majority of humanity would be "capably" ruled by an Aryan elite. Such conceptions of the New Age are not limited to the members of the Grand Lodge of Vril, however. Several chroniclers of the occult, including Jacques Vallee in his *Messengers of Deception* (1979) and Francis King in his excellent study *Satan and Swastika* (1976), have noted how many occult "revelations" share the racial and political beliefs of the ultra-right. These similarities are due in part to the theocratic nature of millenarian "New Age" visions, both occult and religious, in which paradise will come soon, but only for the believer. There are other racist and anti-democratic elements in occultism, however, that we need trace no further than Theosophy and the groups that splintered from it.

We have had a taste of Helena Blavatsky's racial theories already, in Chapter 7; they reflected, in part, the racism of Western society at large in that day. But many of her nineteenth-century prejudices were carried on in the teachings of her twentieth-century followers. Her ideas continued as basic to mainstream occultism—the foundation upon which Rudolf Steiner, Alice Bailey, and many of the UFO-era occultists built their doctrines. The idea of an "elite" of Masters and their pupils has remained central, as has the notion of a spiritual evolution that is often determined by one's race. Both are found in the writings of Vera Stanley Alder, for example, who was a onetime Theosophist and disciple of Alice Bailey; she wrote a very popular series of occult books in Britain in the thirties and forties. One of them, *The Initiation of the World* (1939), contains a description of the spiritual situation in India before the coming of Krishna—whom Alder equates with Christ—that drips with racism:

> ... Brahma was the one eternal God, worshipped earnestly by the noble and ascetic Aryan priests and their followers. Very different was the religion of the fanatical, superstitious, astrally-focused coloured peoples. They worshipped the god Siva whom they had degenerated into a terrible tyrant, who thrived upon lust, blood and cruelty. So strong and prolific were the coloured races of India that they threatened to smother the new growing Aryan population, and supplant the reign of Brahma with that of the dreadful Siva. The white Aryans began to succumb to the fascination which the coloured race often exercises upon the whites, and to intermarry with the conquered people.
> The new white race was in grave danger.

The Brahmans, wrote Alder, recognized the danger in time and introduced the caste system, and when Krishna arrived on the earth, he gave the peoples of India a religion of many levels "to suit these castes," its simplest form, of course, being that of the "coloured peoples." Alder also included in *The Initiation of the World* a diagram of "racial types" such as a "Lemurian-type" stereotypical Black man with a vacant expression, a small cranium, and enormous lips, an "Atlantean-type" Asian with an inscrutable but faintly sinister appearance, and the "Aquarian" type of Aryan who will usher in the New Age, a large-eyed, delicately-featured blond man.

Raymond Bernard attempted to explain the existence of races by suggesting that Aryans are closest to the original "optimal" super-humans of the inner world, and the other races had deteriorated, more or less, from the Aryan:

> The inhabitants of Agharta, living under optimal biological conditions, approximate to the pure Nordic type, being blonde, fair-skinned, and blue-eyed. The blonde races are those who more recently left the Subterranean World and lived for the least time under the unfavorable conditions of solar radioactivity, soil depletion and wrong diet on the earth's surface, while the races that were exposed for the longest period of time to the harmful rays of the sun and general unfavorable effects of life on the earth's surface turned darker, and under the tropical sun, turned black.... Similarly the hair turns black and the eyes brown. All races, including negroes, were originally blonde and blue-eyed...

In other words, the darker one is, the more degenerate.

Anti-Semitism, too, appears in occult literature with surprising frequency. An example from 1979 which is both amusing and alarming is a publication, *Revelations of Awareness*, issued by a group in Olympia, Washington called Cosmic Awareness Communications. This group claimed to be the vessel and voice of "Cosmic Awareness," the Force that governs the universe and speaks through a succession of mediums in a peculiar style. Awareness always refers to itself in the third person ("this Awareness indicates...") and calls all human, super-human, and quasi-human beings "entities." The medium in 1979 through whom Awareness spoke was Paul Shockley; while in a state of trance he answered questions touching on all sorts of political, social, and occult controversies, and the answers always painted the cosmos as a stage of a great battle between the forces of Awareness and Evil.

The government of the United States, according to Cosmic Awareness, had been taken over by a cabal of "greedy, power-hungry bankers... the Rockefeller-Rothschild Beast conspiracy to destroy the economy." The Rockefellers and the Rothschilds, working with "Luciferian" extraterrestrials and the Soviets, had created a race of "organic robotoids," android-like beings who took the places of people in positions of power and did the conspirators' bidding. Awareness revealed that then-President Jimmy Carter was a robotoid, as were many top officials in the U.S. government. The robotoids were manufactured by the Russians in the mountains near Las Vegas and programmed with the entire life history of the person they were intended to replace, down to memories of childhood experiences and family nicknames. Such careful planning made them difficult to detect, although Awareness admitted that until recently, a trained eye could spot their physical limitations:

> ... they showed no Adam's apple; they did not eat in public, for they have no need for food. They used pills, and when caught in a situation whereby they were required to eat, would eat only soup or light salad...
>
> This Awareness indicates that these entities generally had a mottled skin, something like pizza crust. This Awareness indicates these entities often had a walk that was reminiscent of a penguin or duck, a kind of waddle back and forth...

Now, however, improved technology had eliminated these defects. Today's robotoids were provided with great physical and occult powers; they "have machines which allow them to listen to the thoughts of others, which allow them to teleport... [and] have the ability to create pain and nausea and sickness in others," as well as accidents and death. If this sounds familiar, Awareness also indicated "that these entities are slaves. The Bigfoot creatures are slaves, and those dwarfs and those entities beneath the ground known as Deros, or detrimental robots, these are also slaves." The Bigfoot and the dero were "tools" of the Antichrist, working in concert with the International Bankers (a term which has long been a euphemism for "powerful Jews") and the Soviets from a subterranean headquarters. So far the Cosmic Awareness scenario sounds suspiciously like a science-fiction version of the notion of a Jewish/Communist plot to take over the world that first appeared in the "Protocols of the Elders of Zion," a "Jewish" plan for financial/political conquest fabricated by Russian anti-Semites at the turn of the century. The "Protocols" enjoyed a wide circulation in Germany between the two world wars, and helped fuel the fires of Auschwitz and Buchenwald. But Awareness has more to tell us about the Jews.

According to Awareness, Jehovah, the "god of the Jews," was not a god but a proud, technically skilled extraterrestrial who biologically engineered the human race, which he tended for a time like flowers in a garden. But after a time, he let most of humanity reproduce wildly on its own while he concentrated on his favorite strain—the Hebrews. "The actions of Jehovah," Awareness indicated, "created through DNA duplication a race of Hebrews, who were basically reflections of Jehovah—these entities reflecting the rebellious attitudes of Jehovah and carrying on certain attitudes of superiority, love of power, jealousy, vengeance and a feeling of being righteous..." Jehovah's fellow extraterrestrials, the virtuous members of the "Intergalactic Federation," regarded Jehovah as a "renegade;" they sentenced him to an Earth exile until he corrected his behavior. To help Jehovah, the Confederation sent Jesus to earth to help the Hebrews rid themselves of their superior attitudes—Awareness indicated that Jesus was not a Hebrew, but an extraterrestrial—but most of the Jews would have none of Jesus's teachings and crucified him. For their foolhardy act, the Jews have been forced for the past two thousand years to work the evil out of their karmas, but they have found it difficult to relinquish their pride because they have been so successful at accumulating wealth: "This Awareness indicates that Jehovah basically is a money god. This Awareness indicates that the Hebrew or Jewish culture moved for thousands of years using the economic systems in a manner that allowed advantage to those who followed the Lord God Jehovah..." Finally, however, the Wheel of Karma brought the rise of the Nazis and the Holocaust, but even in these disasters the Jews themselves were at fault:

> ... it boils down to the fact that the persons who began setting up Hitler, and pressed the issues which led to World War II; the entities who created the environment and who allowed the persecution of the Jewish people, were, to a large extent, *of Jewish origin*, in the cult known as Zionism. This Awareness indicates this information can be quite shocking to many entities...

Awareness indicated further that Hitler was visited by an emissary from the subterranean headquarters of the Antichrist/International Bankers conspiracy who told the Führer that "he would receive great power in conquering the world by following the orders and direction of these forces from the Luciferian levels."

Such obvious racism and anti-Semitism are not found often in occult and UFO literature, but an objective reader will find elitist, anti-democratic ideas lurking beneath the surfaces of many alternative-reality "revelations," just as they lurk beneath many of the "revelations" of religious fanatics. Let us look now at how a notion that was born mostly of pure fancy and sensationalism—the idea that UFOs are craft built by escaped Nazis preparing another attempt at a worldwide Reich—became a magnet for occultists of a fascist bent.

Argentina? Antarctica? Agharta?

It all began logically enough—if not sensibly enough—during the Red-scare days following the Second World War. When flying saucers were first reported in great numbers, the question was asked: could they have been built by an earthly government? The major theory along these lines, one that was examined in some detail by the Air Technical Intelligence Command (ATIC) of the U.S. Air Force, was described by Edward J. Ruppelt in his *Report on Uniden-*

tified Flying Objects (1956):

> When World War II ended, the Germans had several radical types of aircraft and guided missles under development. The majority of these projects were in the most preliminary stages but they were the only known craft that could even approach the performance of the objects reported by UFO observers. Like the Allies, after World War II the Soviets had obtained complete sets of data on the latest German developments. This, coupled with rumors that the Soviets were frantically developing the German ideas, caused no small degree of alarm.... Wires were sent to intelligence agents in Germany requesting that they find out exactly how much progress had been made on the various German projects. The last possibility, of course, was that the Soviets had discovered some completely new aerodynamic concept that would give saucer performance.

But this theory was discarded by the ATIC within a year after its investigation had begun. "Every intelligence report dealing with the Germans' World War II aeronautical research," Ruppelt continued, "had been studied to find out if the Russians could have developed any of the late German designs into flying saucers. Aerodynamicists at ATIC and at Wright Field's Aircraft Laboratory computed the maximum performance that could be expected from the German designs.... The answer was, 'No, there was no conceivable way any aircraft could perform that would match the reported maneuvers of the UFO's.'" The engineers were convinced that no human pilot could bear the stresses dealt by the impossibly speedy zigzags of UFO flight patterns in the atmosphere. The Air Force soon abandoned the idea of human-built UFOs and began examining the theory that they were extraterrestrial craft (which they soon, as every frustrated UFO fan knows, discounted as well).

Ruppelt's book was widely read in the UFO community, and his hints of advanced "German secret weapons" were added to the rumors of a "hidden empire" of escaped Nazis by several of the more sensation-minded UFO writers during the late fifties. "Michael X" Barton, whose ideas about Rainbow City were mentioned in Chapter 9, published a small book in 1960 titled *We Want You—Is Hitler Alive?* that assembled the rumors in the most gee-whiz-laden prose to be found outside a comic book. Michael X recalled the story, widely reported during World War II, that Admiral Dönitz had made a curious announcement to the people of the Reich in 1943: "The German submarine fleet is proud of having built for the Führer in another part of the world, a Shangri-La on land, an impregnable fortress!" Where was this fortress? Barton, using such "reliable" sources as the *Police Gazette*, answered: Argentina, and most probably Patagonia, where Dönitz and his men purchased enormous tracts of desolate ranchland during the war. In the last months before Germany's surrender, reported Barton, Hitler and much of the Nazi High Command, many leading German scientists, and some $750 million were secretly brought to Argentina by U-boat. Today, he continued, the Nazis were busy preparing secret weapons almost beyond our comprehension in isolated secrecy:

> Please give your closest attention to what I am about to say. It is new and startling information. I ask you to keep this information in strictest confidence. It is for mature minds only.

LISTEN! Inside the "Sanctum Sanctorum" of the Hitler forces in Patagonia, what do you imagine you and I would find, if we were permitted to travel unmolested past the gates of the Hideout? Would we, dear friend, meet with the surprise of our lifetime? Would we come upon certain underground installations—factories—staffed by German scientists? There for what purpose?

To design, build, and test what we would call *"UFO's"!*

Barton then revealed that German engineer Viktor Schauberger had proposed and designed several saucer-shaped aircraft for the Luftwaffe in 1940, and printed photos of two scale models Schauberger supposedly flew by remote control, utilizing "electro-magnetic power." Barton then compared several photos of alleged UFOs taken in the United States during the fifties to the models—the resemblance was close but hardly exact—and concluded that many saucers considered extraterrestrial by ufologists *might* have been built by Hitler and his scientists in Patagonia. If the concealed Nazis perfected their secret technology, their UFOs might soon lead a new *blitzkrieg*:

What do you think would happen if a whole fleet of UFOs manned by earthlings from a secret place on Earth were to actually make a landing in Berlin? Or in Washington, D.C.? What if they—the pilots of the earth-built UFOs—made use of "electromagnetic" devices to cause all electrical power systems in those big cities to go completely, utterly DEAD?

Imagine it.... No electricity for lights, communications, or for anything else.... Our military couldn't even send up its Nike guided missles to intercept the UFOs, since they are fired electrically! Then a voice is heard in the air: "Your city, your nation is helpless. We are here to bring a new way of life to this world. We ask you not to fear but to follow these instructions at once...!"

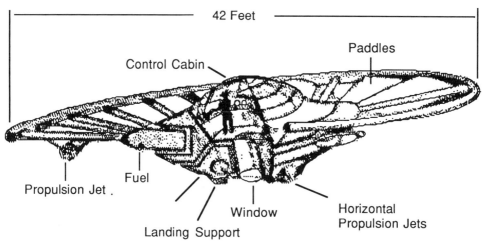

One of the "German flying saucer designs," published in the English-language version of
Der Spiegel in 1950.

About the same time Michael X painted this lurid scenario in his book, there appeared in the UFO magazines the story of Reinhold Schmidt, a sixty-year-old Nebraska grain buyer who claimed he had been taken for rides by a friendly group of saucer pilots from Saturn. Most of Schmidt's story was unremarkable as contactee stories go—he claimed the Saturnians took him on sightseeing jaunts to the North Pole and to Egypt, where he was shown a secret crypt beneath the Great Pyramid containing the cross upon which Christ had been crucified (it had been placed there for safekeeping when Christ was flown back to his home on Venus). But there was one detail many of the UFO writers found interesting: Schmidt reported that the Saturnians spoke English with a German accent, and they conversed telepathically among themselves in High German. For those who have little trouble connecting the details of contactee stories with the memories and subconscious of the contactee, the German is easily explained—Schmidt was the son of German immigrants and spoke High German with his parents as a child.[1] But there were those in the UFO community who made much of the German-speaking saucer pilots, such as the anonymous writer of a letter to Ray Palmer in the August 1960 issue of *Flying Saucers*. In the midst of the controversy surrounding Palmer's arguments in favor of a "donut-shaped" earth, the letter-writer carried Michael X's argument one step further:

> Now—the one thing in Mr. Schmidt's story that is intriguing is that the men in the ship spoke German, which Mr. Schmidt could understand. It is also interesting that they were fixing something that had gone wrong, which was the reason (ostensibly) that the ship had landed there. It would seem from this that these individuals were not CENTURIES ahead of us, but perhaps only a few years! Could they be (earth) people from "the mysterious land beyond the poles"?
>
> And, Ray, since you printed evidence that there IS such a land, I am reminded of information that was available to a few people back in 1945, and was published in a national magazine between four and eight years ago—that Adolf Hitler might not have perished at all in the Berlin bunker, but might have escaped by submarine, first to Argentina, and LATER TO ANTARCTICA!
>
> ... Add to all this the fact that Jewish people have been frantically trying to learn about the saucers.... Mr. George Adamski, at least on one occasion, perhaps more, has addressed a banquet composed of mostly Jewish people. Could it be that they are looking for the origin of the saucers BECAUSE of this possibility of a connection with Hitler?

In 1975, a new book, *UFO's—Nazi Secret Weapon?* appeared in the UFO community. Unlike the somewhat foggy political stances of previous writers linking the Nazis to the saucers, the authors of this book—Christof Friedrich and another man known simply as Mattern—made no bones about their sympa-

---

[1]Perhaps we don't even need to go that far to dismiss Schmidt's story. On one of his alleged trips with the Saturnians, they flew over Southern California and pointed out the location of a mine of quartz to Schmidt; they told him this remarkable quartz cured cancer. After the splash of publicity that surrounded his tale began to subside, Schmidt came to Southern California and issued stock in the mine, which he sold to well-to-do widows fearful of cancer. Unfortunately, he didn't own the mine, and he finally found himself indicted for fraud in 1961, convicted, and sent to prison.

thies. The back cover contained a plea for donations to "Free Rudolf Hess!" Friedrich, the pen name of one Ernst Zündel, a German who had emigrated to Canada after the end of the Second World War. Zündel was the head of Samisdat, a Toronto-based organization that published and sold through the mail such items as collections of Hitler's and Goebbels's recorded speeches on tape and Third Reich choral and marching music, advertised as "inspiring and nourishing food for the Aryan soul." Samisdat also sold books titled *The Hitler We Loved and Why, Allied War Crimes* ("Read about the mass extermination—genocide—practiced by the so-called humanitarians of France, Britain, and the United States in their insane war against the women and children of Europe"), and *The Six Million Swindle* ("exposes the profit motive... behind the manufacture and sale of wartime anti-German hate propaganda, specifically the hoax of the so-called six million holocaust of Jews who supposedly died in 'Nazi extermination camps.' Another look at the Zionist Big Lie").

After giving us a brief personality sketch of the Führer—"Hitler never thought anything impossible; he never accepted defeat"— Friedrich and Mattern described the massive arsenal of ultra-advanced secret weapons the Reich was preparing to use against the Allies near the end of the war. The German scientists and engineers had tested prototypes of surface-to-air missiles, a "sound cannon" that could kill or paralyze enemy troops using sound waves, and delta-winged jet fighters. If the German Army had only been able to keep the Allies at bay for six more months, the authors tell us, the outcome of World War II would have been very different.

The pride of the Reich's secret weapons labs was the *flügelrad,* or flying saucer, capable of speeds beyond 2000 km/hr. By the end of the war, the Germans had built and flown three prototype saucers, all based on Viktor Schauberger's designs and all using his "electromagnetic" power system. Although still in the testing stage in 1945, the flügelrads were often spotted by Allied pilots, who called them "foo fighters" or "Kraut meteors," terms long familiar to the UFO buff for unidentified flying objects seen during the war. While plans for most of Germany's secret arsenal fell into the hands of the Allies after V-E day, the flügelrad scientists and their craft escaped, with the Führer himself and a band of crack troops known as the "Last Battalion," to a sector of Antarctica called "New Schwabenland" by the Germans. Located almost due south of Africa, New Schwabenland had been claimed for the Reich by a German expedition in 1938,[2] and the escaped Nazis traveled there by way of Argentina in a fleet of U-boats stocked with oil and precious metals needed for saucer production. In the icy reaches of New Schwabenland, the Nazi scientists continued refining their weapons, and the Last Battalion began preparing the struggle for a Fourth, and permanent, Reich.

Although the public knew nothing of Hitler's escape besides a few rumors discounted by their governments, the Allied governments themselves learned

---

[2]Actually, after the Reich occupied Norway in 1940, Hitler claimed all of Antarctica, since Roald Amundsen, the man who first reached the South Pole, was a Norwegian.

quickly of the Reich's Antarctic hideaway and the Last Battalion's plans. In 1946, under the guise of a "scientific expedition," eight nations sent a cooperative military mission to Antarctica. The American mission was led by Admiral Richard E. Byrd, who commanded a fleet of thirteen fully-armed U.S. Navy ships and four thousand men. Byrd was sent by his government not to explore, wrote Friedrich and Mattern, but to wipe out the Nazis and capture their arsenal. Unfortunately for Byrd, the Allies had not counted on just how advanced the Germans had become. When the Admiral located the Nazi base early in 1947, he dropped an American flag there "to warn Hitler;" but the Führer responded to Byrd's warning with a show of force. "Within 48 hours," the authors tell us, "four of Byrd's planes had been lost, some without a trace and others without any survivors." They also surmised that Hitler turned the sound cannons on Byrd's troops, paralyzing and disorienting them until they were left wandering helplessly on the ice. "Admiral Byrd hastily abandoned all his efforts and disembarked, with all his force, for home;" he realized he had met more than his match. Naturally, all reports of Byrd's defeat were hushed up by the U.S. government. Once back in Washington, the Admiral suggested to his superiors that the Antarctic be used as an atomic test range, but as soon as his proposal reached the newspapers, a large fleet of UFOs was sighted "flying over the nearby Congressional buildings and the White House in perfect 'typically-German' formation. Many UFO researchers have been puzzled about that particular flight. Was it a demonstration of strength?" After the sighting, the authors chuckled, nothing more was said about dropping atomic bombs on Antarctica. Perhaps, they said, we should chalk up another victory for the Last Battalion.

Friedrich and Mattern thus concluded that the UFO mystery was no mystery at all—the saucers were the reconaissance craft of the hidden Nazis. Reinhold Schmidt's story excited them; didn't the pilots of the "Saturnian" craft look like Aryans and speak German? Didn't they treat Schmidt in the "friendly and correct" manner typical of German soldiers? Most conclusively, didn't their ship bear a strong resemblance to one of the Schauberger models?

One of Viktor Schauberger's 1940 magnetic-power saucer designs.

The authors then intimated that the story of the surviving Nazis might include even deeper secrets. After pausing to wonder whether the scientists of the Reich might not have had the technical assistance of "visitors of other galaxies" when developing the flügelrads, Friedrich and Mattern asked whether the Nazis might have discovered during their polar explorations "that there is indeed an 'Inner Earth'":

Nordic legends and sagas have long recounted very inspiring tales of a perfect society of blue-eyed, blond Germanic giants who dwell in the inner earth.... Could it mean that the German nation is indeed a colony, either from the German-speaking "Saturnians" with whom Reinhold Schmidt conversed or are they the outer-earth beach head of the inner-earth civilization?

Was this the reason, they asked, why the German people are "different," why they are such "superb" soldiers, why they are "leading the world in precision engineering and technology"—in other words, why the Germans are so obviously superior to other peoples? Was Adolf Hitler "planted" among the greatest race of the surface world by this extraterrestrial or subterranean super-race "to pull back Western civilization from the brink of degenerate self-destruction"?

Friedrich and Mattern left these questions unanswered, but they reminded us that even after so many decades in hiding, it was very possible the Führer was still alive beneath Antarctica. Hitler, they pointed out, was a "health-conscious" vegetarian and teetotaler, a man certain to live a long life. They also speculated that one reason Hitler chose the Antarctic as his hideaway was the marvelous preservative effect of its low temperatures—would not the cold cause all creatures, including humans, to "age much less quickly"? They ended with a warning that members of the Last Battalion might be walking and working among us today, covertly fighting Hitler's fight "to prevent the extinction of the White race." They were "soldiers, labourers, teachers, students, scientists... male and female, young and old." When the time was right, when the signal arrived from the Reich's Antarctic fortress, the Last Battalion would "spring into action."

Soon after *UFOs—Nazi Secret Weapon?* was published, Friedrich put out another title, *Secret Nazi Polar Expeditions,* which dangled more questions before the reader. During the 1938-39 German expedition to New Schwabenland, he wrote, an exploration party discovered a great crevasse in the ice. They

Samisdat's announcement of a proposed flight to Antarctica
to search for hidden Nazi bases and the inner world.

found in its depths a mighty cavern rich with minerals, part of an enormous natural tunnel system leading far into the earth which was warmed comfortably by volcanic activity in the area. Did these caverns lead to the inner world? Friedrich only piqued our curiosity by noting how convoys of U-boats were sighted off the Norwegian coast in the last days of the war, heading northward past the Arctic Circle. He also reminded us that the Reich had active bases in Greenland, Lapland, and Spitzbergen for many months into 1945:

> Obviously Nazi Germany was up to Something Big, but what? Was there a short cut from the Arctic to Antarctica? Did the Nazi expeditions discover a more direct way to Antarctica via Greenland, Spitzbergen, or the North Pole?... Only time will tell us what really is up there or down there, or should we say, *in* there?

Ernst Zündel and his comrades at Samisdat began making plans soon after to discover what was *in* there. In 1978, he sent through the mail an announcement, with a snappy "Achtung!" at its head, for a proposed "Samisdat Hollow Earth Expedition." For the curious sum of $9,999, Samisdat's readers, tired of the "official CIA-KGB alibi that all UFOs are extraterrestrial," were invited to reserve their seats in a specially-chartered airliner that was to fly from New York to Rio de Janeiro to Antarctica. The airliner would be repainted for the occasion with a huge swastika, presumably so Hitler and the Last Battalion would know the plane was filled with kindred souls and not shoot it down (Friedrich later hinted that this was precisely what happened to the 747 full of tourists that crashed on Antarctica's Mt. Erebus in November 1979). The Samisdat party would circle the South Pole and New Schwabenland, searching from the air for the Nazi UFO bases and for the entrance, if one exists, to the Inner World. In his announcement Friedrich made a plea for "cold, hard cash up front"; he estimated the cost of the expedition at "well in excess of $2,000,000," $500,000 of which would be for chartering the airliner and for the special paint job, but the knowledge revealed would be "worth every dollar." To raise cash for the expedition, Samisdat produced a special flügelrad frisbee, complete with swastika decal, sold through the mail and at science-fiction and UFO conventions. Although I attempted to follow the progress of the proposed expedition, I heard no more about it after 1980, probably because Friedrich's alter ego, Ernst Zündel, had other things on his mind. In 1981 Zündel was prohibited by Canada's postal minister from using the mails under pressure from a Canadian Holocaust activist. In the mid-eighties Samisdat returned to publish the memoirs of "Hitler's guru," an Indian woman named Savitri Devi, under the title *The Lightning & the Sun*. "Were the ancient sanskrit laws of the universe compiled in the Bhagavad Gita the secret source of Nazi strength?" asked the ad.

In 1985 Zündel was taken to court for printing false statements about the Holocaust in his book *Did Six Million Really Die?* (a potential criminal offense under Canadian law), and his trial became a Canadian *cause celebre*. During his trial his defense lawyer suggested that Zündel did not really believe that the Nazis created any UFOs and that his UFO-oriented books were written only for the publicity they brought him. Those books, his attorney suggested, sold better than his "revisionist" histories of the "so-called 'Holocaust'," and they made it easier for Zündel to appear on talk shows to preach his real message—that the Holocaust never really happened. Zündel was found guilty and sentenced to prison for fifteen months, although he served only a few days, but his appeals continue at this writing (in mid-1989).

There have been others who have seen the inner world as the home of the Nordic race, and one of the most interesting of them is Captain Tawani Wakawa Shoush, a Native American of the Modoc people. In the seventies, Shoush led an organization, based in rural Missouri, called the International Society for a Complete Earth. The Society used as its emblem the crest of the Thule Society: a sword in front of a swastika ringed with oak leaves. Shoush said he was a retired U.S. Marine Captain and a pilot whose goal was to fly a dirigible into one of the polar openings and establish contact with the Arianni, the "tall, blond, blue-eyed super-race" that rules the inner world. The Arianni, he wrote, spoke "a language very much like German," lived in "cities built of shimmering crystal," and used their saucers—again called flügelrads—to patrol the skies of the surface world and keep an eye on us. In a 1978 interview with newspaper columnist Bob Greene, Shoush claimed that his organization's use of the swastika was as a "Nordic symbol," and had nothing to do with the Nazis. "As you probably realize," he told Greene, "the swastika has been known in various cultures for thousands of years." He also said that "people will call us crackpots, will try to ridicule us and even stop us. But we are not crackpots. We are a small group, made up of physicians, engineers and pilots."

Shoush sold copies of what he claimed was a suppressed diary kept by Admiral Byrd during his *North* Pole flight of 1947. This booklet, intriguingly, contains a preface by one "Dr. William Bernard, D.D., Ph.D." The diary itself, written in comic-book prose worthy of Michael X or Guy Ballard, describes Byrd's awe building as he draws nearer to the Pole. He looks down and suddenly sees vegetation instead of ice:

> There should be no green valley below! Something is definitely wrong and abnormal here! We should be over ice and snow!... Our navigation instruments are still spinning, the gyroscope is oscillating back and forth!...
> The light here seems different. I cannot see the sun anymore. We make another left turn and we spot what seems to be a large animal of some kind below us. It appears to be an elephant! NO!!! It looks more like a mammoth! This is incredible! Yet, there it is!

Byrd and his radioman find themselves flying over "rolling green hills." The exterior temperature climbs to 74° Fahrenheit. Suddenly three flying saucers marked with swastikas appear from nowhere and surround the plane, taking the controls from Byrd's hands with a mysterious force. The saucer pilots tell the Admiral to relax, and they land the plane near a city "pulsating with rainbow hues of color." The gasping Byrd is escorted by two tall, blond, handsome men into the presence of a wise, aged man called "the Master," who informs Byrd that he has passed into the inner world of the Arianni. The Master gives him a message: surface humanity has discovered a power not meant for such a primitive people—atomic energy—and it must cease tampering with this power or suffer a new Dark Age of destruction, like the Dark Ages of history but worse. The Master does not believe the people of the surface will listen to him, but even if they do not, he holds out to Byrd the hope of eventual regeneration:

> We see at great distance a new world stirring from the ruins of your race, seeking its lost and legendary treasures, and they will be here, my son, safe in our keeping. When that time arrives, we shall come forward again to help revive your culture and your race...

Byrd, completely awed by what he sees and hears in the land of the Arianni and returns to Washington with the Master's message, but he is ordered by "top security forces" to remain silent "for the good of humanity." The final entry in the diary, dated just before Byrd's death in 1957, concludes, "I have faithfully kept this matter secret as directed all these years. It has been completely against my values of moral right." He leaves the diary behind "so the secret shall not die with me."

After reading this booklet, I wrote to Shoush and asked him whether the U.S. government had made any attempt to verify the information it contained and to reach the inner world. "Yes," he replied, "the Government sent an Expedition, it was met and destroyed; the Government has absolutely curtailed all information on this matter.... Only a private Expedition with pure motives will be allowed to pass the Magnetic Maelstrom that guards the Polar Apertures. So it is only a matter of sending Spiritually Honest Persons in this quest; they must be as little Children." At that time (1978) Shoush also said he was negotiating with Germany's Messerschmidt and Japan's Mitsubishi to build him a zeppelin for the journey. "It is only a matter of money," he wrote, "and Courage."

In 1980 I wrote Shoush again to ask how his expedition plans had progressed. He answered by sending me a photocopy of an article which had appeared in the Winter 1979-80 *Search* magazine, "Return of the 'Spear of Longinus'." The article, by a Wilhelm Bernhardt—whom we can safely assume is the "Dr. William Bernard" of the Byrd diary—reveals that the Spear of Longinus was *not* returned to the Hofburg in Vienna after the war. The Hofburg Spear is only a clever copy of the real Spear, which Hitler sent into hiding in a cave in New Schwabenland via a U-boat mission called "Mission Walkure Zwei" in 1945. In July of 1979 a group of Germans led by a Colonel Max Hartmann (whom, says Bernhardt, was an aide to Martin Bormann and was on good terms with the Führer) journeyed by ship and airplane to "Deutsche Antarctica" to reclaim the Spear.[3] After a short stop in Missouri to show their prize to Bernhardt, the article continues, the team returned triumphantly to Germany. "Colonel Hartmann and his little party," Bernhardt concluded, "successfully completed Mission Walkure Zwei! The world will hear from the

---

[3]Due to the fact that it is practically impossible to reach the Antarctic continent in the middle of winter due to the raging storms and incredibly low temperatures, no expedition *ever* leaves for Antarctica in July. Shoush said it was made in July "for reasons of secrecy," but this claim alone casts suspicion on his story.

Spear of Longinus again, for once more it has been claimed!... Whomsoever claims the spear and solves its secrets, holds the destiny of the world in his hands for good or for evil!!!" This expedition, wrote Shoush, was his Society's 1979 mission. "It was a most wonderful success!... As plans are now, a second mission will be sent in 1981." But I heard no more from the International Society for a Complete Earth.

The emblem of the Thule Society was also used by the International Society for a Complete Earth.

The notion of an inner world still appears to be a popular one among the members of the far Right. The Fall 1987 "Sons of Liberty" book catalog, published out of a conservative church in Metrarie, Louisiana, was definitely a list of political books: "How to Get the Reds out of all Mass Communications Media," "Jewish World Conspiracy," "U.N. is Spawn of Illuminati," and "Adolf Hitler's Contribution to European Peace" were a few of the titles. Yet there was one non-political book on the list, standing out in its uniqueness: Raymond Bernard's *The Hollow Earth*.

The golden rope and the bottomless pit

Lest we are tempted to consider the beliefs of those like Friedrich/Zündel and Shoush merely a lot of ultra-right-wing blustering, we should pause to consider the ideas of another admirer of Adolf Hitler who wanted to find his way into an inner world. His name is Charles Manson, and in 1969 he was the leader of a notorious "Family" of young women and men responsible for some of the bloodiest murders in American history. Manson was loudly anti-Black and anti-Semitic; he often told Family members that "Adolf Hitler had the best answer to everything." He was, like the members of the Satanist groups and motorcycle gangs with whom he associated, enamored of swastikas; he carved one into his forehead during his 1970 trial, and his female disciples immediately did likewise. All members of the Family had to be Aryan.

Manson's beliefs were, like Manson himself, confused, and they tended to change depending on whom he was talking to, but he felt strongly that a black/white race war was imminent. He told the Family that the blacks would rise up to slaughter the whites, and he called this racial Armageddon "Helter Skelter," convinced he had heard it prophecied in the Beatles song of that name. Susan Atkins, one of the Family, told authorities after her arrest that the Family's murders had been committed to incite Helter Skelter, "to instill fear in the establishment and cause paranoia. Also to show the black man how to take over the white man." Manson felt that blacks couldn't do anything properly until a white person showed them how to do it first. Helter Skelter, according to Atkins, would be "the last war on the face of the earth... all the wars that have ever been fought built one on top of the other." At the end of the struggle, the blacks would take over the world for forty years, but at last they would realize they were "unfit" to rule. Then Manson and his Family of chosen people, who had spent the forty years in hiding, would emerge to be declared the new rulers of the earth. They planned to spend those forty years in the inner world.

During his trial, Manson said:

> There's been a lot of talk about a bottomless pit. I found a hole in the desert that goes down to a river that runs north underground, and I call it a bottomless pit., because Where could a river be going north underground? You could even put a boat on it. So I covered it up and called it the Devil's Hole and we all laugh and joke about it. You could call it a family joke about the bottomless pit. How many people could you hide down in this hole?

In 1968 the Manson Family commandeered a ranch in the Mojave Desert near Death Valley and spent several months there, meditating under the influence of various drugs, engaging in a variety of sex acts, riding around the desert in stolen dune buggies, and talking to prospectors. Manson heard from one of the prospectors a jumbled version of a Hopi emergence myth similar to the Zuni myth retold in Chapter 1, and he convinced himself that the entrance to the Inner World out of which the Hopi had come at the beginning of time was hidden somewhere in Death Valley. There have long been prospectors' tales told in the area of caves large enough to hold a city beneath the valley floor, carved by an underground river called the Amargosa. Manson sent Family members on regular searches for the entrance to these caves in their dune buggies. Finally he came upon a formation in Nevada's Amargosa Valley, just over the state line, known as Devil's Hole, a hole in the floor of a cave filled with water hundreds of feet deep. Gazing into the hole, Manson suddenly realized that this was the entrance to the inner world. The water was a door placed there, he said, by the Inner-World inhabitants to keep surface intruders out. Soon Manson began having drug-induced visions of the wonders awaiting the Family in the world below; food grew on trees and fountains gushed with chocolate.

In his book *The Family* (1971), Ed Sanders told how Manson conceived a plan for initiating Helter Skelter not long after he found Devil's Hole. The murders were only part of the plan—they were to be murders that looked like the work of black militants, murders that would anger the white establishment "pigs." The whites would begin persecuting the blacks, and the persecution would anger the blacks to the point of violence; Helter Skelter would begin. Manson and the Family would be ready for their escape from their home base on the Spahn ranch near Los Angeles when it began, and he had members of two motorcycle gangs gather an arsenal of guns (in case the Family had to fight its way to Death Valley) and blaze a trail across the desert to the Hole far from the main highways, where blacks and police would be lying in wait. He put together a fleet of dune buggies for the journey to the Hole, and at the Hole itself there would be hidden a truck with a winch and a coil of thousands of feet of special gold rope, which he planned to pay for by putting his female disciples to work as topless dancers. He also planned to hire a contractor to pump the Hole dry, so when Helter Skelter arrived, the Family could flee to the dry Hole and slide down the golden rope to the inner world of chocolate fountains. There they would, according to Manson's interpretations of the Beatles and the Book of Revelations, increase to 144,000 white men, women, and children, while the rest of the white race was slaughtered or enslaved by the blacks.

It didn't happen quite that way. After the murders, the blacks did not rise up in violence, but the Los Angeles Police did come after Manson and the Family, although not for the right reasons at first. Manson and the Family fled to Death Valley, although they had never bothered to follow through with the rest of their plans. There was no truck with a winch and no coil of golden rope waiting for them, and Devil's Hole was (and is) still filled with water. The Family and the police played hide and seek until Manson was, at last, found hiding in a bathroom cabinet at the Death Valley ranch. No one ever reached the Bottomless Pit, except perhaps—through no fault of their own—the Family's two dozen known and suspected murder victims.

Chapter 13

The Inner World in Fiction

> In the first place please bear in mind that I do not expect you to
> believe this story.
>
> —Edgar Rice Burroughs, *At the Earth's Core*

The interior of the earth has never been popular as a sub-
ject or a setting for fiction. It may be that more novels have been written about
the Inner World than about bowling or raising chickens, but I doubt it; only
three dozen or so subterranean-world novels have been published, in English at
least, in the last three centuries. If someone were to stand somewhere on an
American college campus and ask any hundred students passing by to name all
the fiction they can describing adventures inside the earth, chances are that at
least eighty of them, and possibly more, would be unable to think of one title.
The other twenty would undoubtedly name the only inner-world novel
which has attained classic status, Jules Verne's *A Journey to the Center of the
Earth*, and perhaps five of the same twenty would be science-fiction fans and re-
call Edgar Rice Burroughs's *Pellucidar* series.

All the other novels about an interior world have been forgotten by everyone but historians of fantasy and science fiction and the small fraternity of
hollow-earthers, and most of them, frankly, are forgettable. Who today without faith in the divine wisdom of a hollow earth, for example, would enjoy
reading DeWitt C. Chipman's flatulent novel *Beyond the Verge*? Published at the
turn of the century (and reprinted by Ray Palmer in the early sixties), *Beyond
the Verge* described the migration of the Ten Lost Tribes of Israel through the pre-
Columbian North America and into the North Polar Opening, a journey from
the turbulent battlefields of the surface world into the paradise God revealed to
them within the earth. What self-respecting modern reader can sit through two
hundred pages of soupy melodrama broken up by long discussions of the revealed "divine laws" that held the hollow earth together?

> "God's laws are immutable [marvels the hero], and he who planned gravity, on the sur-
> face of the sphere, can place it likewise within the sphere. I can see if the crust of the earth
> is two thousand miles thick, that if a ball of iron should fall a hundred miles into the
> crust of the earth, every yard of its fall would decrease its speed, until it reached a point
> where the attraction of the inner crust equalized that of the outer, and the ball would
> come to a rest, being held in equilibrium by equal attractions, and I can now see how the
> water on the inside is held in position. Blessed be the name of the Lord!"

Luckily, not all inner-world novels are wrapped in such a gassy cloud of
divine revelation; there are a few whose authors stressed adventure and imagi-

nation in the subterranean world, and they are among the strangest fruits on the tree of fantastic fiction. In Bibliography B I have assembled an annotated list of many other inner-world novels; with this chapter, they include almost every one which has, to my knowledge, been published in English. Here, however, are close looks at eight of the most unusual, worthwhile, and/or influential of them: Willis George Emerson's *The Smoky God*, Edgar Allan Poe's *Narrative of Arthur Gordon Pym*, Ludvig Holberg's *Journey of Niels Klim*, Mary Lane's *Mizora*, William Bradshaw's *Goddess of Atvatabar*, John Uri Lloyd's *Etidorhpa*, Edward Bulwer-Lytton's *The Coming Race*, and Herbert Read's *The Green Child*. But first there should come a glance at the two works of inner-world fiction that have not been forgotten.

Verne's caverns and Burroughs's burrows

Jules Verne (1828–1905) appears to have known little and cared less about John Cleves Symmes and his Theory of Concentric Spheres when he wrote *A Journey to the Center of the Earth* in the early 1860s. Verne told the tale of Professor Otto Lidenbrock, a hard-boiled German scientist, his faint-hearted nephew Axel, their stolid Scandinavian guide Hans, and their trek into the crater of Sneffels, an extinct Icelandic volcano. Armed with ropes and "Ruhmkorf coils" (a sort of primitive electric torch) and following a trail left by the alchemist Arne Saknusemm in the sixteenth century, the three men descended hundreds of miles through volcanic passages until they reached a subterranean sea, an ocean "horribly wild—so rigid, cold, and savage." The inner sea occupied a vast cavern filled with clouds and was "lit up like day" by electric currents, and Axel's description of the sea mentioned Sir John Leslie's hollow-earth theory, not Symmes's:

> Deep shadows were cast beneath, and then suddenly, between two clouds, there would come a ray of unusual beauty, and remarkable intensity. And yet it was not like the sun, for it gave no heat.
> The effect was sad and excruciatingly melancholy. Instead of a noble firmament of blue, studded with stars, there was above me a heavy roof of granite, which seemed to crush me.
> Gazing around, I began to think of the theory of the English captain, who compared the earth to a vast hollow sphere in the interior of which the air is retained in a luminous state by means of atmospheric pressure, while two stars, Pluto and Proserpine, circled in mysterious orbits. After all, suppose the old fellow was right!

Verne was hardly arguing for a hollow earth, however—his intent was quite different. Although his party of adventurers met with wonderful sights—a forest of giant fungi, a herd of mastodons and their twelve-foot-tall "antediluvian" human shepherd, and a battle between an icthyosaur and a plesiosaur—Verne's aim in *Journey* was to acquaint his readers with some basic geology and paleontology in the guise of a rousing saga. As the party descends, his Professor Lidenbrock spends whole chapters lecturing Axel—who, despite his claims of scientific knowledge, seems to be as ignorant of basic science as

Verne's average reader—about the nature of volcanoes, underground rivers, strata formations, and prehistoric fauna and flora. Until the adventurers' climactic (and impossible) exit from the interior world, shooting out of the crater of Sicily's Mount Etna during an eruption while sitting on a raft of petrified wood, Verne stayed within the known—if speculative—scientific doctrine of his time. Lidenbrock was presented as a protegé of the nineteenth-century English scientist Humphry Davy, who proposed the earth was solid and cool throughout, except for a few pockets of volcanic activity. Most scientists of Verne's time believed, equally incorrectly, that this planet was completely molten beneath its thin crust, but this judgement was hardly unanimous. Verne's Lidenbrock could say with confidence to his skeptical nephew in the first chapter, "Neither you nor anybody else know anything about the real state of the earth's interior," for in 1864 geology was barely out of its infancy.

Edgar Rice Burroughs's *Pellucidar* books, on the other hand, are adventure stories pure and simple; Burroughs (1875–1950) had no axe to grind regarding the interior of this planet. He cared not a fig about scientific fact and was happy to toss it out the window whenever it got in the way of the action. I am not a fan of Burroughs's writing; I find the three Pellucidar books, *At the Earth's Core* (1922), *Pellucidar* (1923), and *Tanar of Pellucidar* (1930), unpleasantly macho and violent from end to end. Burroughs's male characters are usually either heavily-muscled, square-jawed heroes or heavily-muscled, slack-jawed villains, and *all* his female characters seem to be athletic sex kittens with flowing hair. They spend all three books fighting each other and a menagerie of prehistoric beasts with an armory of weapons—swords, daggers, clubs, bows and arrows, spears, pistols, rifles, cannons, and fists. Probably for these reasons the books in the Pellucidar series, like Burroughs's other books, have been loved by generations of adolescent and pre-adolescent boys.

Here is the basic plot: David Innes, the heavily-muscled, square-jawed hero, who has inherited a mining business, is approached by Abner Perry, the inventor of an "iron mole," a machine capable of digging speedily into the earth after deep veins of ore, and the two agree to test it out. But during the test, Innes and Perry discover the mole is stuck on a downward course and is heading straight toward the center of the earth. After futile attempts to turn the mole around, they begin running out of oxygen; but at the last moment the mole surfaces into the sunlight. Innes and Perry soon realize that they are not on the surface of the earth, but in Pellucidar, a beautiful but deadly land open at the poles and lit by a small sun that sits always at the center of the sky ("pellucid," which means "admitting light," appears to refer to the outer sun's light shining through the polar openings). In a country in which it is eternally noon, there is little sense of time or direction, and Innes and Perry wander away from the mole to be captured by a group of Sagoths, sub-human creatures described as "strikingly similar in aspect to the Negro of Africa." The Sagoths take them, with other Pellucidarian humans they have rounded up, as prisoners to the city of the Mahars, the ruling creatures of Pellucidar.

The Mahars are a race of flying reptiles somewhere between crocodiles and pterodactyls in appearance, but highly intelligent. They communicate among themselves, and to a limited extent with the Sagoths, by projecting their thoughts "into the fourth dimension, where they become appreciable to the sixth sense of the listener." The Mahars consider the humans of Pellucidar a race of domestic animals, and keep them both as slaves and for food. Perry discovers, after deciphering some of the Mahar books, that the race of Mahars is of one sex:

> "Once the males were all-powerful [Perry tells Innes], but ages ago the females, little by little, assumed the mastery. For other ages no noticeable change took place in the race of Mahars. It continued to progress under the intelligent and beneficent rule of the ladies. Science took vast strides. This was especially true of the sciences which we know as biology and eugenics. Finally a certain female scientist announced the fact that she had discovered a method whereby eggs might be fertilized by chemical means after they were laid—all true reptiles, you know, are hatched from eggs.
>
> "What happened? Immediately the need for males ceased to exist—the race was no longer dependent upon them. More ages elapsed until at the present time we find a race consisting exclusively of females."

When one remembers that women had received the vote in the United States in the wake of a great burst of feminist activity just before Burroughs wrote *At the Earth's Core,* his anti-feminist sentiments aren't hard to miss. But is it possible that Raymond Bernard read the Pellucidar books? This instance is only one of many in which the female sex plays an important—and often dominant—role in an inner-world novel.

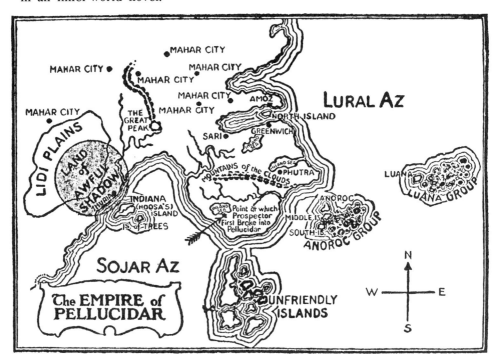

A map of Pellucidar, from Edgar Rice Burroughs's
At the Earth's Core (1922).

The rest of the series is basically one battle after another. Innes escapes, fights his way back to the mole, and returns to the surface to gather together books and technological equipment, and plenty of guns and ammo, to bring the blessings of civilization to the primitive people of Pellucidar. And after a great deal of bloodshed he becomes David I, Emperor of Pellucidar, alongside Dian the Beautiful, his athletic Pellucidarian wife with the flowing raven hair.

A fourth book set in Pellucidar, *Tarzan at the Earth's Core* (1930), is a bridge between Burroughs's Pellucidar series and his Tarzan series, with characters from both. Heavily-muscled, square-jawed Jason Gridley receives a radio message from Abner Perry in Pellucidar—David Innes has been captured by the Korsars, a race of pirates originally from the outer world who had sailed into Pellucidar through the North Polar Opening. Gridley travels to Africa and convinces Tarzan to accompany him on a zeppelin expedition into Pellucidar to free Innes. Tarzan agrees, and he falls in love with the jungles of Pellucidar while Gridley falls in love with Jana, another athletic inner-world maiden. After a few dozen battles and hair's-breadth escapes, their party is captured by the Horibs, a race of snake people—could this novel have influenced Doreal and the Hefferlins?—whose "blood ran cold in their hearts." Tarzan and Gridley escape easily from the talons of the Horibs, however, and by the end of the book have left all their enemies utterly pulverized. These are not intellectually challenging books.

The Smoky God

In the first chapter of *Tarzan at the Earth's Core,* Jason Gridley tells a skeptical Tarzan that a "very complete exposition" of the hollow-earth idea was to be found in two books, which he unfortunately doesn't name. One of them was "written about 1830," so it is a safe guess it was *Symzonia,* the best-known work to come out of Symmes's theory. Gridley says the second work is "of more recent time." While this "more recent" work might well have been Gardner's—the zeppelin trip and the eternal sun could have been taken straight from *A Journey to the Earth's Interior*—it might also have been a novel by one of Burroughs's fellow Californians that first appeared in 1908: Willis George Emerson's *The Smoky God*.

Emerson (1856–1918) was a Los Angeles banker and real estate broker who wrote westerns and romances on the side. *The Smoky God*, however, does not read like an adventure story written in an odd moment—it is the work of a believer in a hollow earth, written perhaps in a flush of enthusiasm after reading William Reed's *Phantom of the Poles*. Emerson buttressed his fictional account of a pair of accidental inner-world explorers with a mass of footnotes taken from the reports of the nineteenth-century explorers quoted by Reed. On some pages of Emerson's novel, the notes take up more space than the text.

Emerson presented the tale as true and told by himself. Several years previously, he wrote, he had become friendly with Olaf Jansen, an aged Swedish fisherman who had retired to a tidy cottage in Pasadena, not far from Emerson's home. On his deathbed, Jansen called Emerson to his side to reveal to him the story of his journey as a young man to the paradise inside the earth. He presented Emerson with a manuscript copy and maps of the travels he had kept secret for half a century:

Olaf Jansen and his father meet the giant inhabitants of the inner world, from W. G. Emerson's *The Smoky God* (1908).

In April of 1829 Jansen and his father, a believer in the Nordic gods Odin and Thor, left Stockholm for the fishing waters of the Arctic. A storm caught their boat and drove it towards the North Pole, but after a time of drifting endlessly north they realized they had passed over the icy verge of an opening to the inner world. They found themselves sailing a warm expanse of open sea lit by a dull red sun, which rose slowly until it reached the zenith, where it remained. Finally the Jansens encountered a vast ship filled with singing giants twelve to fourteen feet tall, who greeted them politely and brought them to Jehu, one of their cities. There they learned to speak the giants' language, which Jansen wrote was "much like Sanskrit." They learned also that the giants worshipped their small sun, which they called "the Smoky God" because of its hazy glow. Jansen's father was convinced they had reached the "paradise to the North" of Nordic belief, the home of the original Odin and Thor. It was also the original homeland of the human race.

After a year in Jehu, the Jansens were placed in an anti-gravity monorail and taken to Eden, the capital of the inner world, where they had an audience with the ruling High Priest, a wise but hulking fellow even larger than the other giants. He asked them questions about their journey from the surface to the inner world, and he offered them the hospitality of the country for as long as they wished to remain. For another year the Jansens toured the inner world and saw all its wonders.

Emerson's inner world was a paradise in every sense of the word, as well as humanity's birthplace. Through the voice of Olaf Jansen, the author said, "in the beginning, the world was created by the Great Architect of the Universe, so that man might dwell upon its "inside" surface, which has ever since been the habitation of the 'chosen'." He likened the earth to a house: "A man builds a house for himself and his family. The porches or verandas are all without, and are secondary. The building is really constructed for the conveniences within."

Everything, said Jansen, was larger and more beautiful in the inner world. Gold was common and used everywhere for decoration. Crops were huge and abundant; bunches of grapes were five feet long, with single grapes as large as an orange, and apples were as large as a man's head. The inner world's race of giants lived as long as eight hundred years. They loved music, and wherever Jansen and his father traveled there, they heard the giants singing.

At the end of two years inside the earth, living among this race of wise, peaceful, and beautiful giants, the Jansens decided to return to Sweden. As they left, the giants gave them a complete set of maps of the inner world and all the egg-sized gold nuggets they could carry. The current carried them through the South Polar Opening and into the Antarctic Ocean, but it was not long before another storm struck their boat. Jansen's father was swept away and drowned, the boat sank, all evidence of their visit was lost, and Jansen barely scrambled onto an iceberg and drifted with it until he was rescued by a whaling ship. Its captain, after listening to Jansen's tale, thought him mad and had him placed in irons until Jansen pretended his exposure to Antarctic cold had made him temporarily delirious. He continued to dissemble when he arrived back in Stockholm, swearing to himself to tell only his family of his experiences. Unfortunately, his mother had died during his absence and when he told the remainder of his relatives, they thought him mad as well. It was not long before one of them had Jansen committed to an insane asylum, where Jansen remained for twenty-eight years. On his release, he swore never to mention the inner world to anyone again and moved to Norway, where he became a successful fisherman with his own fleet and enough money to retire prosperously in America. It was not until death approached that he decided to write his adventures down, redraw the maps from memory, and leave them in Emerson's hands.

Jansen concluded his tale with his—and William Reed's, and presumably Emerson's—belief that the shell of the earth is only a few hundred miles thick, and that gravity is centered within the shell. Emerson, in his afterword, stated that while it was impossible for him to divine the truth behind Jansen's story, he intended "at some later date" to give Jansen's manuscript and maps to the Smithsonian Institution for further investigation.

Although *The Smoky God* has long been forgotten even by fantasy fans, it has remained popular among hollow-earth proponents. In the early 1960s, Ray Palmer reprinted it in a paperback edition with all the beautiful color illustrations of the original in the midst of his flurry of "donut-shaped earth" articles. "Dr." George Marlo, the man who started UFO World Research and claimed frequent trips to the inner world, evidently was familiar with *The Smoky God*, for his descriptions of subterranean people, cities, and animals were taken almost word for word from Chapter Four of Emerson's book. Several of the "quickie" alternative-reality paperbacks that appeared during the *Chariots of the Gods?* craze of the mid-1970s mentioned the hollow-earth theory, and in some of these Jansen's story was discussed as if it had really occurred; Jansen became a real Scandinavian fisherman instead of a fictional character created by Emerson to stimulate interest in the notion of an inner world.

But the most telling legacy of Emerson's book may be the idea of a "perfect" race of wise and beautiful Nordic giants living happily within the earth while surface folk cling precariously to the outside of the planet in varied states of "degeneration." When Christof Friedrich wrote in *UFOs—Nazi Secret Weapon?* about "Nordic legends and sagas" that "have long recounted very inspiring tales of a perfect race of blue-eyed, blond Germanic giants who dwell in the inner earth," it may well be that he was not inspired by real Nordic myths as much as by Emerson's book.

Poe and *Pym*

Edgar Allan Poe (1809–1849) is not usually associated with the idea of an inner world, and it is true that he never wrote anything clearly describing a hollow earth or its inhabitants. There is nevertheless ample evidence that he was intrigued by John Cleves Symmes's theory and that it influenced his writing. Three pieces of Poe's fiction—his short story *MS. Found in a Bottle* (1831), his longer attempt at a scientific fantasy *The Unparalleled Adventure of One Hans Pfaal* (1835), and his unfinished novel *The Narrative of Arthur Gordon Pym* (1838)—deal with the notion of some kind of openings at the North and South Poles. As Poe lay dying in Baltimore in 1849, he spent hours in a delirious state, calling loudly for "Reynolds"—the same Jeremiah Reynolds who had been Symmes's best-known disciple. In the same issue of Poe's magazine, the *Southern Literary Messenger*, which contained the first installment of *Arthur Gordon Pym*, there was an article by Poe praising Reynolds's speech promoting Antarctic exploration before the House of Representatives in 1836; he spoke glowingly of Reynolds and his ideas on other occasions as well. The two men were never more than acquaintances, but Symmes's former disciple and his causes fascinated Poe for years.

MS. Found in a Bottle, for which Poe was awarded a fifty-dollar prize by the *Baltimore Sunday Visitor* in 1833, an award that attracted the notice of the literati to its author for the first time, is a typically tortured Poe story. The nameless narrator, who has taken to the sea to satisfy his "nervous restlessness," finds himself—the only survivor of a shipwreck off the island of Java—aboard a Flying-Dutchman-style ghost ship propelled toward the Antarctic by a savage and mysterious current. Although filled with a sense of doom, he is curiously elated by the wild journey: "It is evident that we are hurrying onward to some exciting knowledge—some never-to-be-imparted secret, whose attainment is destruction. Perhaps this current leads us to the southern pole itself." This "never-to-be-imparted secret" suggests nothing so much as the dark underside of Symmes's "golden secret," Poe's twist on the elusive discovery the Captain so desired. Poe's narrator reaches the edge of that secret and apparently pays for the discovery with his life. Approaching the Pole in terrible darkness, pulled between "stupendous ramparts of ice," the ship is suddenly caught in a vast whirlpool and sucked down to oblivion. Poe appended a note to the story that several years after its completion, he found a copy of one of Mercator's sixteenth-century maps of the world "in which the ocean is represented as rushing, by four mouths into the (northern) Polar Gulf, to be absorbed into the bowels of the earth; the pole itself being represented by a black rock towering to a prodigious height." The image he saw on Mercator's map came from the the writings of those European proto-geologists who, like Athanasius Kircher, taught that the oceans were sucked into the earth at the North Pole and expelled at the South Pole. This idea survived even in *The Smoky God*, in which the ocean currents of the inner world flow naturally from the North Polar Opening to its southern counterpart.

The Unparalleled Adventures of One Hans Pfaal, Poe's half-satirical, half-serious tale of a Dutch balloonist's flight to the moon, was written partly as a reply to a similar story by one of his professors at the University of Virginia, George Tucker's *Voyage to the Moon* (1825). Tucker's voyager turned back at one point to examine the earth's polar regions: "I returned to the telescope, and now took occasion to examine the figure of the earth near the Poles, with a view of discovering whether its form favoured Captain Symmes's theory of an aperture there; and I am convinced that that ingenious gentleman is mistaken." Poe's Hans Pfaal did not agree. Looking down on the North Pole from a height of 7254 miles, Pfaal saw very definite evidence of a polar opening:

> Northwardly from that huge rim [of ice] before mentioned, and which, with slight qualification, may be called the limit of human discovery in these regions, one unbroken, or nearly unbroken, sheet of ice continues to extend. In the first few degrees of this its progress, its surface is very sensibly flattened, farther on depressed into a plane, and finally, becoming *not a little concave* [Poe's italics], it terminates, at the Pole itself, in a circular centre, sharply defined, whose apparent diameter subtended the balloon at an angle of about sixty-five seconds, and whose dusky hue, varying in intensity, was, at all times, darker than any other spot upon the visible hemisphere, and occasionally deepened into the most absolute blackness.

Having tantalized the reader, Pfaal watched this dark spot drift slowly out of sight as he proceeded moonward. What could it have been but the entrance to an unknown inner world? What Poe imagined lay within that great darkness can only be imagined, but *The Narrative of Arthur Gordon Pym* gives a hint of the direction his speculations took.

Poe appears to have used *MS. Found in a Bottle* as the jumping-off place for *Pym*. But he blended it with Reynolds's pleas for an exploratory voyage to unlock the secrets of the Antarctic, the nautical memoirs of Benjamin Morrell, Jr., which he had recently read, and a good deal of the basic plot and details of *Symzonia*. Morrell's memoirs, like the pseudonymous Seaborn's tale, suggested that ice-free waters lay beyond 82° south latitude, and Poe's story, which begins as a straightforward seafaring yarn, grows darker and more dreamlike the farther south it moves from Nantucket to the warm lands beyond the ice rim. Pym, who tells the story, stows away in a southbound ship, survives a mutiny, and is picked up by the captain of the *Jane Guy*, a whaling vessel. Pym convinces the captain to head for the uncharted waters of the Antarctic, and once beyond the ice of the 82nd parallel, the story becomes strangely similar to *Symzonia*. In both books, the ships' crews find the remains of unknown beasts on the shores of strange islands. Both Seaborn and Pym spend several pages describing the ways of the penguins they encounter. In both books there is a feeling of anticipation, of being on the edge of a great secret; Seaborn goes on to discover the inner-world continent he names Symzonia, and Pym alludes several times to discoveries he makes to the south that he never quite reaches.

Both *Symzonia* and *Pym* are filled with images of racial conflict, especially *Pym*. In *Symzonia* Seaborn remarks pointedly on the whiteness of the inner-world inhabitants' skins, and the manner in which the Symzonians punish those convicted of a crime—they exiled their criminals to an island near the southern verge and exposed to the direct rays of the sun, which darkened their skins and shortened their lives. In *Symzonia* Seaborn—suggesting how the humans of the surface world who think themselves civilized are really the sunburnt stepchildren of a more perfect race—also effectively, if unconsciously, tells one how one's virtue can be seen in the whiteness of one's skin. Poe, who was unashamedly racist and a strong defender of slavery throughout his life, took Seaborn's suggestion and twisted it into an allegory of eternal division between the black and white races.

When the *Jane Guy* has passed the icy rim and sailed into the warm and temperate waters of the unknown South—a region very similar to the lands within the southern verge found by Seaborn in *Symzonia*—she reaches a dark island, Tsalal, in a strangely dark sea. All the native creatures of Tsalal are black; even the stones of the island are black. The natives who meet the ship are "jet-black... clothed in the skins of an unknown black animal," and their teeth are black as well. The natives recoil at first from the light skins of the ship's crew, and refuse to approach "several very harmless objects, such as the schooner's sail, an egg, an open book, or a pan of flour"—in other words, anything white. They seem friendly, however, and the crew slowly come to trust them. But just before they are about to depart Tsalal for the south, the crew are ambushed and killed, except for Pym and his friend Peters, in the way Poe found most horrendous—they are buried alive beneath an avalanche triggered by the natives. Pym and Peters hide on the island for several days, and during this time discover a series of chasms on the island which take the form of ancient letters, although they remain a mystery to Pym. At last they make their escape in a canoe, taking with them a native prisoner. The canoe is pulled southward by a current much like the one in *MS. Found in a Bottle* into an ocean which slowly turns a milky white and is enwreathed in a strange white mist. Their prisoner grows more anxious the further south they travel, crying "Tekeli-li!" in terror when Pym pulls a white handkerchief from his pocket. At the last moment of the story, the black man dies of fright as the canoe approaches the rim of a great abyss:

> And now we rushed into the embraces of the cataract, where a chasm threw itself open to receive us. But there arose in our pathway a shrouded human figure, very far larger in its proportions than any dweller among men. And the hue of the skin of the figure was of the perfect whiteness of the snow.

Here the story breaks off, with Poe's concluding note mourning the sudden death of Arthur Gordon Pym in New York. What does this ominous ending signify? There have been many interpretations—one Poe scholar thinks the figure is simply the figurehead of a ship that rescues Pym and Peters and returns them home, but others believe the author intended to show his readers a world of spirits at the South Pole, or a Symzonia-like utopia within the earth, but almost all agree the story was left unfinished. In his concluding note, Poe said, "The loss of two or three final chapters (for there were but two or three) is the more deeply to be regretted, as it cannot be doubted they contained matter relative to the Pole itself, or at least to the regions in its very near proximity; and as, too, the statements of the author in relation to these regions may shortly be verified or contradicted by means of the Governmental expedition now preparing for the Southern Ocean." Anticipating great discoveries, it appears that Poe decided to remain vague; but what is the meaning of the all-black natives of Tsalal and their great fear of the whiteness to the south?

Poe's concluding note continues with an analysis of the letter-shaped chasms on Tsalal. Poe writes that he has examined the figures and arrived at their meaning—one set of shapes takes the form of the Ethiopian verb "to be shady," and the other the Arabic verb "to be white" accompanied by the Egyptian for "the region of the south" and an outstretched figure of a man pointing southward. Poe ends the note with an invitation for more investigation into the meaning of the hieroglyphics, and with a pseudo-Biblical quotation that sounds like the voice of Yahweh: *"I have graven it within the hills, and my vengeance upon the dust within the rock."*

Poe scholar Sidney Kaplan, in his introduction to a 1960 edition of *Pym*, analyzed the letter-chasms in detail and concluded that Poe meant readers to intuit them as a message written in the stones of Tsalal by the hand of God as an eternal damnation of the black race and its eternal separation from the white race. Kaplan wrote that Poe was influenced by *Symzonia* while writing *Pym*—Kaplan called Poe's work "Pymzonia" at one point—and if the two books were compared, the symbolism of the hieroglyphics would become clear. The utopian white race of Symzonia, whom Poe may have seen as God's "chosen" race dwelling in "the region of the south" (that is, within the South Polar Opening) exiled their wicked to an island on the verge. Poe turned these exiles into the evil and supremely black natives of Tsalal, living in terror of the white race that had cast them out and reacting in fear and hatred to anything white. Kaplan argued convincingly that Poe, who loved cryptograms and mystification, placed words for "black" and "white" in various languages throughout the story, as well as other fragments of his basic message. For example, "Tekeli-li," the natives' cry of terror, can be related to the Bible story of Daniel deciphering the famous "handwriting on the wall" to Belshazzar, who was about to die: "Mene, Mene, Tekel, Upharshin." "Tekel" signifies "Thou art weighed in the balances, and art found wanting," and such were definitely Poe's feelings toward the black race.

Had Poe continued with those final "two or three chapters" of Pym's story past the encounter with the great white figure at the entrance to the chasm as the Pole, he might have described a mighty race of virtuous beings as white as the Tsalal natives were black. This race might have been based on the Symzonians, but Poe's "Symzonians" would not have been like Seaborn's. They would have been transformed into something more vivid and more awesome by Poe's skill as a writer, just as he turned Seaborn's stiffly sketched voyage into a journey to a dream world. Despite Poe's racism, it would have been fascinating—if such really *were* his intentions—to read his description of the inner world, and it is a shame he chose to remain so vague about what he felt lay at the far end of the earth.

Inner-world satires

Although Poe chose not to complete his story and carry Arthur Gordon Pym to a lily-white utopia, there have been many other writers who have created utopias and dystopias within the earth to satirize the cultures and institutions of the surface. Imaginary voyages to subterranean realms began appearing in the early years of the eighteenth century. Two of the first were French—an anonymous *Narrative of a Voyage from the Arctic Pole to the Antarctic Pole through the Center of the World* (1723) and *Lamékis, or the Extraordinary Voyages of an Egyptian through the Interior World* (1737) by the Chevalier de Mouhy. The first of these anticipated both Symmes and Friedrich Klopstock by placing entrances to the inner world at the Poles; the second depicted a subterranean colony of Egyptian Masters in the Rosicrucian mold. But the best-known and best-conceived of the early inner-world novels is *The Journey of Niels Klim to the World Underground* (1741) by Ludvig Holberg. Holberg (1684–1753) was born in Norway but lived most of his life in Denmark, where his novels and many comic plays earned him a reputation as "the Moliere of the North" and the founder of modern Danish literature. *Niels Klim* is similar in many ways to its English predecessor, Jonathan Swift's *Gulliver's Travels* (1726), and both enjoy an equal popularity in their respective homelands even today. In both, a man of this world visits a series of imaginary countries in which the foibles of contemporary society are exaggerated and ridiculed.

Holberg presented the tale in the form of a manuscript written by Niels Klim and discovered by his heirs after his death. In the year 1665, the manuscript begins, Klim graduates from the University of Copenhagen and returns to his native Norway, but he is unable to find a suitable job, so he decides to occupy himself by exploring a deep cave at the top of a nearby mountain. Some friends lower him in on a rope, but the rope breaks and Klim falls, like Alice in Wonderland, through the shaft until he passes completely through the earth's crust. He is amazed to discover a small sun with its own system of planets within the great hollow of the globe, and soon finds himself in orbit around the little sun. He tosses a piece of bread from his pocket, and it quickly goes into orbit around him. Klim is proud to find himself a planet with its own satellite, but after three days in orbit—by which time he is growing rather bored—he is knocked out of his orbit by a griffin, who drags him down to the planet Nazar. Nazar is inhabited by a race of sentient trees—small trees with human heads and branches that end in hands (the more branches one is born with, the more honored is one's position in society) and feet instead of roots, which give the tree-beings a slow, waddling gait.

Klim finds himself in Potu, one of the tree-countries, in which many of the conventions of European society are reversed. Holberg disliked his contemporaries' constant pursuit of fashion and their endless religious, legal, and political squabbles; thus in Potu, there is no interest in fads or fashions, and religious disputes are illegal. In the Potuan courts, the judge—who is often female—arrives at a legal verdict only after long meditation, and once her ruling is announced, both prosecution and defense agree to its wisdom. Klim is judged by the Potuans too flighty and too enamored of folly—in other words, too human—to hold a high position in their society, so he is given, much to his disgust, the job of King's messenger. Because he is the only one on Nazar with long legs, Klim is commissioned by the King of Potu to tour the entire planet (Nazar is only 600 miles in circumference, so the walk takes him only a few months) and report his discoveries to the Potuans.

While Potu is presented as a utopian society (even the name *Potu* is *utop* spelled backwards), Klim finds the other cities and states of Nazar filled with follies and strange customs. In one city Klim passes through, Holberg—who was an early feminist—satirized the treatment of women among his contemporaries by reversing their sexism. Here men are forced to do the housework, care for the children, and keep their noses out of public affairs; aggressive women flirt with shy young men on the street, and Klim notes how a group of male prostitutes are punished as criminals while their female customers are unmolested by the authorities. In another part of Nazar, criminals are considered ill and treated with medicines while sick people are jailed. On his return to Potu, Klim's journal is published to popular acclaim, but his hoped-for promotion to a higher position never materializes. Desperate to impress the Potuans with his wisdom—and not realizing it is his obvious desperation that lowers their opinion of him—he proposes a "reform" of sex roles in Potuan society along strictly sexist European lines. To his amazement, he is judged a criminal for attempting to abridge the rights of half the population of Potu and ordered banished to "the firmament"—in other words, the inner surface of the earth's outer shell.

Klim is marched out to the wilderness, where a great bird picks him up and deposits him in a land on the firmament in which animals are wise and civilized, while humans live in a primitive state. After making his escape from a nation of cultured monkeys, Klim takes the education of the humans in hand and trains them in battle and the art, previously unknown in the inner world, of making guns and gunpowder. Eventually he becomes the humans' ruler, and after leading them successfully in war and conquering several of the animal nations, he is crowned Emperor of a good part of the firmament. But power goes to Klim's head, and his pride incites his formerly faithful subjects to revolution. Driven from his palace, Klim hides in a cave in the countryside, falls into a great hole in its floor, and finds himself where he began, in the mountains of Norway. Staggering from the mountainside, his imperial robes in rags, he meets some peasants who convince themselves he is the Wandering Jew. But Klim eventually finds one of his old friends, who had long ago given him up for dead and who cautions him to say nothing of his adventures to anyone, lest he be persecuted as a heretic. With his friend's help, Klim finds a job at last as the curate of a tiny Norwegian community's church, and he concludes his story with the admission that although his curateship offers him little satisfaction—after all, he had been Emperor of most of the inner surface of the earth—he has repented his pride and performs his few duties "with the contentedness of a philosopher."

A cross-section of the earth from William R. Bradshaw's *The Goddess of Atvatabar* (1892).

As strange as Klim's discoveries may have been, Holberg found an even more extravagant successor a century and a half later when William R. Bradshaw wrote his subterranean epic *The Goddess of Atvatabar* (1892). Bradshaw (1851–1927), a New Yorker born in County Down, Ireland, was known in his day primarily as a prolific magazine poet; *Atvatabar* was his only work of fiction. He seems to have poured all of himself into his tale, which was illustrated by eight artists and published to rave reviews. The *Daily News* of Lowell, Massachusetts called it "the most remarkable work of fiction ever produced," and the Savannah, Georgia *Morning News* said it was "sultry with the breath of love, terror, and delight." Today none but a few fantasy connoisseurs know of Bradshaw's opus, however, for his writing style can be described best as Victorian rococo, and the work of eight illustrators in one volume imparts a schizophrenic feel. Still, *Atvatabar's* large, elaborately bound first editions command top prices among fantasy book collectors.

The Goddess of Atvatabar is the story of Lexington White, a wealthy, adventurous American who uses his millions to construct a ship, the *Polar King*, and outfit an expedition bound for the North Pole. Using a newly-formulated explosive called Terrorite, White blasts a hole through the icy rim surrounding the polar regions and sails into a vast area of open water. The *Polar King* finds itself within the North Polar Opening instead of at the Pole, and White is barely able to put down a mutiny attempt by a crew fearful of descending into the "infernal regions." But all is well again when the crew realize that the inner world is much like the outer, even though the sun never sets and gravity is reduced by nine-tenths; one member of the crew who weighs 175 pounds on the surface is shocked to find his weight reduced to seventeen pounds. As White and his coterie of scientists speculate whether the inner world is inhabited, a group of bizarrely uniformed soldiers appears alongside the ship, flying with motorized wings. One of White's scientists listens to their speech and realizes it is merely English with the letters mixed up (Bradshaw provides a letter-substitution chart so the reader can translate their words; *wayleal*, for example, means "soldier"), and soon White is able to present himself to them as the leader of the first exploring party from the outer world. The soldiers offer their nation's hospitality and conduct the *Polar King* to Kioram, the main port of the land of Atvatabar.

Atvatabar lies partly beneath the eastern coast of the United States and partly beneath the North Atlantic. Its fifty million people possess a more sophisticated technology than the surface world; the Atvatabarese had been using artificial lights, railroads, and phonographs for centuries, as well as airplanes for travel and vehicles in the shape of mechanical ostriches called *bockhockids* for cavalry and police mounts. They used for power not steam or electricity, but "magnicity," a force "generated by the two powerful metals terrelium and aquelium."

The Atvatabarese have a complex and unusual set of religious beliefs as well. Their deity is Harikar, the "Universal Human Soul," and his devotees, who dwell in the sacred city of Egyplosis, worship him by forming into male-female couples, known as "twin souls," who are required to remain chaste and funnel all their passions into performing wonders in Harikar's name. In honor of White's visit, the priests and priestesses of Egyplosis perform endless, ornate ceremonials, described in ecstatic excess:

> At the waving of the fans by the adepts, plants issued from the hands of every god of gold, clothing the throne in one endless wreath of brilliant crimson blossoms.... Again the fans waved and the flowers changed to bloom all snowy-white, while the foliage became blue.
>
> The adepts disappeared at a given signal and thereupon entered another band of beautiful girl adepts, who seated themselves, each body in a crouched mass with flowing drapery, around the base of the throne. These priestesses were in a state of catalepsy. The ego, or soul, in each case had been separated from the body, which floated in a state of apparent death. They had so developed their will by thinking enormous thoughts, yearning for spiritual power, that they could suspend the functions of the body and give all their existence to the soul.... [I]t was stated their souls were floating freely in the dome above, in blessed converse, and that their reincarnation would afterward take place.

And sure enough, when the lights are doused White gasps as there appear floating in the dome as "nude spectres the fifty souls of the priestesses who crouched beneath."

Harikar's "spouse" and representative on earth was a woman selected to fill the sacred office of Goddess of Atvatabar. The present Goddess was the beautiful Lyone, with golden flesh and hair "of a pale sapphire-blue color, that fell in a waving cloud around her shoulders." When White and Lyone meet, they fall in love, and although they must keep their love secret, they lead for a time an idyllic existence as they tour the wonders of Atvatabar. She shows him the gardens of Tanje, where grow creatures half-animal and half-plant which provide several of the book's most bizarre illustrations. In a strange satire of Darwinian evolution, Lyone shows White the Gasternowl, an orchid evolving into a cat; the Yarphappy, an ape-flower; and the Jugdul, a plant with "strange faces" in its roots and a flower "surmounted by a weird, small head" with a long nose. "We do not know as yet what kind of animal life will evolve from the plant," Lyone says of the Jugdul, "but the botanists and physiologists of Atvatabar are agreed that at least two new species of animal will be developed." She also takes White to the temple of the grand sorcerer Charka beneath Egyplosis, where a few thousand twin souls, dancing ecstatically while wired to a terrelium-aquelium dynamo, produce showers of precious gems out of the air.

But it is not long before Aldemegry Bhoolmakar, the King of Atvatabar, learns of Lyone's forbidden romance. He orders White out of the country and executes the Goddess for her sacrilege, but her followers, led by the infuriated White, rebel against the King. Armed with its Terrorite guns, the *Polar King*, with White in command, forces the entire Atvatabarese Navy to surrender. Charka brings Lyone's body back to his temple, and he hooks her to his magical dynamo; as White watches, she is returned to life by the ecstasy of ten thousand twin souls, and the reunited couple are crowned the new King and Queen of Atvatabar.

At the end of the story, Lexington White prepares to leave the inner world with Lyone to announce his discoveries to the surface world. But he leaves the reader with the promise of a sequel, for "many continents remain yet unknown to me, to explore which shall be my ambition." He has heard rumors of distant parts of the inner world where mountains "rise so high that there is no weight on their summits, and where torrents of water roll upward... of rocks of gold suspended in the air," and "of tribes dwelling on floating islands in the empyrean." But the sequel never appeared, and Bradshaw's inner-world fairytale sits alone like a huge gilded allegorical sculpture in a suburban tract house—grotesque and overwhelming, but fascinating.

Brave new races

Holberg's and Bradshaw's books are quaint and amusing, and very much products of their times. But two other inner-world novels written over a century ago, and outwardly very much like *Niels Klim* and *Goddess of Atvatabar*, have a strangely contemporary ring, particularly in the way they deal with the issues of women's roles, political power, and technology. The first is Edward Bulwer-Lytton's *The Coming Race* (1871), a story of an ultra-evolved subterranean society by an author who had a profound effect on the development of historical and occult fiction. Bulwer (1803–1873), best known today as the author of the historical extravaganza *The Last Days of Pompeii* (1834),[1] is no longer read much—his style is almost as convoluted and melodramatic as Bradshaw's—but in his day he was one of the most popular authors in the world. He was an aristocrat who consorted freely with the highest of Victorian society, as well as its most notorious occultists, such as Eliphas Levi. His occult novels *Zanoni* and *A Strange Story* influenced Mme. Blavatsky and Henry Olcott, and several of his notions, particularly that of a brotherhood of Masters dwelling unseen among us, affected the development of Theosophy.

The Coming Race, published anonymously shortly before Bulwer's death, was a utopian novel and a satire of several levels. The anonymous narrator is a young American who accompanies a mining engineer into a deep chamber of a mine where strange lights and sounds have been seen and heard. But as they begin the descent into the deepest part of the mine, the engineer falls to his death, and when the narrator reaches his body, he is frightened by the appearance of a huge, dinosaur-like reptile and runs until he finds himself on a great road, brightly lit by lamps, leading to a small but majestic town. He comes to a monumental building carved into the stone of the cavern, and out of the building steps a tall, stunning figure. He is wearing wings, folded to his knees, and a tiara of gems, and he carries a bright metal staff:

Edward Bulwer-Lytton, author of
The Coming Race (1871).

> But the face! It was that which inspired my awe and my terror. It was the face of a man, but yet of a type of man distinct from our known extant races.... Its colour was peculiar, more like that of the red man than any other variety of our species, and yet different from it—a richer and softer hue, with large black eyes, deep and brilliant, and brows arched as a semicircle. The face was beardless; but a nameless something in the aspect, tranquil though the expression, and beauteous though the features, roused that instinct of danger which the sight of a tiger or serpent arouses. I felt that this manlike image was endowed with forces inimical to man.

The narrator cowers in terror, but when the strange man touches him with his hand and his staff, all fear vanishes. He follows the man to his home, where he is put into a trance. While in this state the subterranean man, whose name is Aph-Lin, and his daughter Zee learn English from him. When he awakes after several weeks, he is shocked to find the subterraneans conversing with him calmly, but his shock turns to awe as he learns more about their society.

---

[1]He is also widely known for the famous opening line, "It was a dark and stormy night..."

The subterraneans are of a race called the Ana, who migrated into the honeycomb of caverns within the earth after a flood in the outer world thousands of years before the Biblical flood. The Ana evolved much faster than the humans who remained on the surface, and possessed a thriving technology—for example, all the Ana had the ability to fly with wings they wore. Their history, however, demonstrated that at one time they fought wars and wrangled over political issues much as surface humans still did. But that period had ended thousands of years before when the scientists of the Ana discovered *vril*, a mysterious force drawn from the atmosphere which soon became so pervasive in the lives of the Ana that they came to refer to themselves as the *Vril-ya*. All members of the Vril-ya carry a vril-staff, like the wand held by Aph-Lin, and operate it with a specially-evolved thumb and palm. Vril can do almost anything, and the modern reader encountering Bulwer's description of the force is immediately reminded of the promises held out by proponents of nuclear power in the beginning of its development:

> It can destroy like the flash of lightning; yet, differently applied, it can replenish or invigorate life, heal, and preserve.... By this agency they rend way through the most solid substances, and open valleys for culture through the rocks of their subterranean wilderness. From it they extract the light which supplies their lamps, finding it steadier, softer, and healthier than the other inflammable materials they had formerly used.

But the real impact of vril lay in its accessibility; all members of the Vril-ya held equal control of it, and such power in the hands of every individual requires *détente* of the most extreme kind:

> The fire lodged in the hollow of a rod directed by the hand of a child could shatter the strongest fortress.... If army met army, and both had command of the agency, it could be but to the annihilation of each.... There were no professional lawyers; and indeed their laws were but amicable conventions, for there was no power to enforce laws against an offender who carried in his staff the power to destroy his judges.

It is intriguing to consider what the result might be if every man, woman, and child in America were given a portable atomic bomb; in the case of the Ana, it turned them into a supremely cool and democratic race of Vril-ya with no crime, poverty, or violence. All shared equally in work and wealth, and government was almost superfluous. If one of the Vril-ya was unhappy with his community, he banded together with other venturesome Vril-ya, moved to another unoccupied cavern, and settled there.

The satire in *The Coming Race* is aimed at a number of targets, all controversies that are still with us. Bulwer, a political conservative and aristocrat by inclination as well as title (he was made Lord Lytton by Queen Victoria), found the democratic pretensions and rabid patriotism of many of the Americans he had met irritating, and he made the protagonist of his story American to place in his mouth patriotic blusterings that would have done Marshall B. Gardner proud. When Bulwer's narrator first arrives in the land of the Vril-ya, Aph-Lin asks him about his own people, so he describes the outer world as he sees it: "I touched slightly, though indulgently, on the antiquated and decaying institutions of Europe, in order to expatiate on the present grandeur and prospective pre-eminence of that glorious American republic, in which Europe enviously seeks its model and tremblingly forsees its doom." He concludes his description with a prediction of America's future, of a day when "the flag of freedom should float over an entire continent, and two hundred millions of intelligent citizens, accustomed from infancy to the daily use of revolvers, should apply to a cowering universe the doctrine of the Patriot Monroe."

The Vril-ya themselves are a satire on both feminism and socialism. At the time Bulwer wrote *The Coming Race*, the Franco-Prussian War had just ended and the intellectual circles of Europe buzzed with discussions of the equality of humanity, the dignity of the laborer, and the rights of women, all of which struck him as naive. Bulwer believed women were passive and nuturant, designed by God and Nature to be wives and mothers. He made the Gy-ei, the women of the Vril-ya, caricatures of nineteenth-century feminists—they are larger and stronger than the male Vril-ya, aggressive, outspoken, superior scholars (in abstract, but not mechanical subjects), and the initiators of romantic relationships. Aph-Lin's daughter Zee is seven feet tall, one of the strongest fliers of the Vril-ya, and a professor—despite her youth—in the College of Sages. But once a Gy had selected her husband and married, she showed her true colors; she hung up her wings, supported her husband in all his interests and projects, and dedicated herself to raising her family. Bulwer suggested that once the feminists had "sown their wild oats," they would settle down to the "true role" of their sex.

Shortly after completing *The Coming Race*, Bulwer wrote that its real theme was the impracticality of utopias. With the culture of the Vril-ya, he created a straw utopia to knock down. The narrator, awed at first by the Vril-ya, eventually realizes that their lives are static and just plain dull. No important art, literature, or music has been composed among them for centuries, for the conflict which gives birth to great art has been eliminated. There is peace and beauty among the Vril-ya, he admits, but no excitement:

> ... if you would take a thousand of the best and most philosophical of human beings you could find in London, Paris, Berlin, New York, or even Boston, and place them as citizens in this beatified community, my belief is, that in less than a year they would either die of *ennui*, or attempt some revolution by which they would militate against the good of the community, and be burnt into cinders [by vril].

The narrator barely escapes being burnt to a cinder himself. When Aph-Lin eventually judges him a danger to the community, Zee—who has fallen in love with him, even though he is terrified by her dimensions and her forwardness and spurns her—comes to his rescue. Taking him in her arms, she flies him back to the mine from whence he descended and sorrowfully leaves him there. He rejoins human society without revealing his experiences to anyone, but—in what should be by now a familiar device—as his death approaches, he has "thought it my duty to my fellow-men to place on record these forewarnings of the Coming Race," whom he fears will one day conquer the outer world, vrilstaffs in hand. He prays "devoutly... that ages may yet elapse before there emerge into sunlight our inevitable destroyers."

The Coming Race has a message for us of the late twentieth century that Bulwer could not have anticipated—the notion of a "vril," a limitless, ubiquitous energy source that is placed in the hands of all with neither cost nor restriction. The vril-staff has become almost an organ of the body for the Vril-ya; the entire society is designed around its use. Vril is the ultimate fantasy of an energy-starved world, and the nightmare of every utility corporation and power cartel. The story of the Vril-ya is the story of how the use and distribution of energy and technology can transform society almost beyond recognition.

Vril is also Bulwer's greatest legacy to occultists, who have interpreted the meaning of his force in several ways. H.P.B. believed vril was a real force in the control of the Masters. "The name vril may be a fiction," she wrote in *The Secret Doctrine*, but "the force itself is doubted as little in India as the existence itself of their Rishis, since it is mentioned in all the secret works." A number of European and American occult schools, following her lead, identified vril as the energy of life, a force anyone could gather and store in his or her body. An anonymous work, *Vril, or Vital Magnetism*, published in Chicago in 1911, traced the word *vril* to the Atlantean root *vri*; it descended through Sanskrit to Latin, from which Bulwer borrowed it for his novel. This little book also claimed that water contains a certain amount of vril, which is best extracted by drinking in small sips instead of gulps; it recommended we drink through straws, enabling the tongue and mouth to experience the vril as "a peculiar feeling or sense of gratification which is unknown to those who *pour* the water down their throats."

In the 1920s an enterprising businessman named Robert T. Nelson sold small cylinders of a substance he called "vrilium" to be worn as pendants or lapel pins; Nelson told buyers the vrilium emanated a powerful radiation both into the atmosphere and the body of the wearer, eliminating disease germs and invigorating the internal organs. Business was so good that in 1944, after Nelson's death, his son Robert Jr. started the Vrilium Products Co. in Chicago and sold the cylinders, or "Magic Spikes," at $150 apiece to thousands of eager buyers. The Mayor of Chicago wore one to the 1948 Democratic National Convention and told reporters it had healed a bone abscess. But in 1950, the younger Nelson was hauled into federal court by the Food and Drug Administration for making "false and misleading" claims about vrilium. When several of the Magic Spikes were opened and their contents were analyzed by an independent laboratory, they were not found to contain any substance comparable to Bulwer's vril, but instead a few pinches of barium chloride, commonly used as a rat poison.

Every critic who comments on Bulwer's novel has noted the sexual symbolism behind vril ("virility") and the phallic symbolism of the vril-staff. It is easy to read his anti-feminist satire—with vigorous Amazons toting power-charged wands—as a Freudian nightmare. Some occultists, like the right-wing Grand Lodge of Vril mentioned in the previous chapter, have incorporated the sexuality of vril into their own dreams of a macho/mystical New Order. But another sexualized New Race novel, Mary Lane's *Mizora: a Prophecy* (1880–81), moved in the opposite direction. *Mizora* is the story of one woman's adventures in a feminist utopia inside a hollow earth—a world from which men have been intentionally excluded.

Vera Zarovitch, a daughter of the Russian nobility with a revolutionary spirit (it was difficult for me, while reading *Mizora*, not to picture her as a young Mme. Blavatsky), is sent to Siberia as a political prisoner, but her husband and father send her guards a bribe and enable her to escape to a whaling ship bound for the Arctic Ocean. She is to be transferred to a ship bound for France, but fate has other plans for her. The ship is wrecked, the captain is killed; the crew abandon her in an Eskimo village. She is strong and energetic and spends the winter among the Eskimos, hunting with them for food, but when she reaches the shore of an ice-free sea at 85° latitude, she builds a boat and attempts to sail northward, hoping to meet another ship. But her boat is caught in a current that carries her through a cloud of mist and into the inner world. Her descent into the polar opening, while reminiscent of Poe, is softer and more like a fall into unconsciousness than into certain death:

> ... [A]n arc of crimson fire... lit up the gloomy waters with a weird, unearthly glare. It faded quickly, and appeared to settle upon the water again in a circular wall of amber mist, round which the current was hurrying with rapidly increasing speed. I saw, with alarm, that the circles were narrowing. A whirlpool was my instant conjecture, and I laid myself down in the boat, again expecting every moment to be swept into a seething abyss of waters. The spray dashed into my face as the boat plunged forward with frightful swiftness. A semi-stupor, born of exhaustion and terror, seized me in its merciful embrace.

When Zarovitch awakes, her boat is drifting at the mouth of a gentle river in a warm, beautiful country, "an enchanted country such as I had read about in the fairy books of my childhood." Another boat, filled with beautiful blonde women, pulls alongside hers and they motion to her to follow them to a spot where the marble steps of a great building meet the shore. She is greeted there by another group of women, again all beautiful blondes, and given splendid new garments and rich food. After several months of learning to speak their language, Zarovitch discovers she has entered Mizora, a utopian country populated entirely by millions of youthful-looking blondes; she sees no men, no brunettes, and no people of other races.

The Preceptress of the National College of Mizora appoints her daughter Wauna as Vera's guide, and Wauna shows her the wonders of the country. The Mizorans have possessed for centuries a high technology, heating their homes by separating hydrogen and oxygen from water, creating "pure" chemical foods which enable them to live to a great age without aging, and living almost entirely free from the diseases of the outer world. They have been vegetarians for so long that most animal species have become extinct among them. There are no social classes in Mizora, and as among the Vril-ya, all share the labor and the wealth.

But Zarovitch is troubled by the absence of men. "Why is such a paradise for man," she asks herself, "devoid of him?" She asks Wauna where the men are and Wauna replies that she has never heard of "such beings." She asks Wauna where her other parent is, and Wauna is puzzled by the question—how could she have two mothers? Finally, speaking with the Preceptress, Vera learns something of Mizora's history.

Three thousand years ago, both sexes had lived in Mizora, a nation not unlike the United States of 1880. A cunning general had been elected president and sought to have himself elected for life and turn Mizora into a monarchy. But revolution broke out, and in the anarchy that followed, the women gathered together and formed a new government. Announcing that a government run entirely by men had led them into chaos, the women denied men suffrage for a century and set up a new matriarchal republic. One of the new government's female scientists discovered the "Secret of Life"—a method of fertilizing the ovum artificially. With this discovery came the beginnings of what was in the nineteenth century called eugenics and today would be called genetic engineering, and the women of Mizora met and decided that since men were now useless—and troublesome—no more would be allowed to be born. In the centuries that followed, genetic research eliminated more and more "undesirable" characteristics, and Mizora became a nation of uniformly blonde, uniformly beautiful, uniformly healthy women. The blondeness was not unintentional; the most unsettling conversation in *Mizora* occurs when the Preceptress shows Zarovitch the hidden gallery of portraits of men of the country's distant past:

> I had observed that dark hair and eyes were as indiscriminately mingled in these portraits as I had been accustomed to find them in the living people of my own and other countries. I drew the Preceptress' attention to it.
>
> "We believe that the highest excellence of moral and mental character is alone attainable by a fair race. The elements of evil belong to the dark race."
>
> "And were the people of this country once of mixed complexions?"
>
> "As you see in the portraits? Yes," was the reply.
>
> "And what became of the dark complexions?"
>
> "We eliminated them."
>
> I was too astonished to speak...

It is unknown how accurately this passage reflected the author's racial views. But it is significant that later in the book, when Vera returns with Wauna to the outer world and Wauna grows ill among the Eskimos, Zarovitch is unable to get any help for her from them for, as she writes, "Like all low natures, the Esquimaux are intensely selfish." Wauna dies in an Eskimo hut, and Vera travels alone to the United States, where she presents the public with her story.

I have not been able to learn much about Mary Bradley Lane, the author of *Mizora*. She wrote the story in four installments for a Cincinnati newspaper, the *Commercial*, in 1880 and 1881. The story was rescued from obscurity after the publication of Edward Bellamy's *Looking Backward* (1888), the most popular utopian novel of the nineteenth century. Dozens of utopian stories appeared in *Looking Backward*'s wake, and one of them was Lane's, published in book form in New York in 1890. The writer of the book edition's preface tells us little— only that *Mizora* attracted a great deal of attention in Cincinnati when first published, that the author "kept herself in concealment so closely that even her husband did not know she was the writer who was making the stir in our limited literary world," and that when the possibility of publication in book form was mentioned to her, Lane was "a shade indifferent on the subject." A strange story for such a passionately feminist work!

It is also eerily contemporary in several ways. There have been numerous newspaper and magazine articles in recent years about the results of human bioengineering being influenced by a culture's racism or sexism; for example, if couples are allowed to select the sex of their children, will not many more males than females be born in traditional cultures like those of India or China? In the late 1970s, a great stir was created by an article in a London newspaper about a group of lesbian separatists who planned to give birth to cloned children. Feminist literature of the 1970s and 80s has frequently speculated on the differences between a culture run by men and one run by women.

Mizora also bears an amazing similarity to the writings of Raymond Bernard. So much of Bernard's dream cosmos is there that I cannot help but wonder whether Bernard ever read Lane's book—for there we have a race of "superior" inner-world women reproducing parthenogenetically, a pervasive concern with vegetarianism and "pure" food, and a society in which women lived in complete freedom from sexual entanglements. The parallels between Bernard and Lane are remarkable, as are the parallels between the Mizorans and the Mahars of Pellucidar, although Edgar Rice Burroughs took a profoundly anti-feminist attitude in his writings. It is, however, very possible that neither Burroughs or Bernard had heard of Lane—nor of each other. If such is the case, is there something about the notion of an inner-world which lends itself to the concept of a female-dominated culture? Even in fiction the archetype of the Earth Mother makes an appearance; the territories of the interior are her territories, whether she is the Provider (as in *Etidorhpa,* below), the Devourer (as in the *Pellucidar* series), or a little of both, as in *Mizora* and *The Coming Race.*

Etidorhpa

Of all the inner-world novels I have read, none is more remarkable, or more filled with sheer weirdness, than John Uri Lloyd's *Etidorhpa* (1895), written by an author who walked the thin line between science and occultism with great success. Lloyd (1849–1936) was a pharmaceutical chemist, president of Lloyd Brothers Pharmacists, Inc., and for a time president of the American Pharmaceutical Society. He made a number of important discoveries in pharmacy by extracting drugs from plants, and he performed numerous experiments with herbs and plant-derived substances used for medical purposes, including cocaine and hallucinogenic fungi. Lloyd also, like Cyrus Teed in his pre-Koresh days, became a doctor of Eclectic Medicine and was Professor of Chemistry for many years at the Eclectic Medical Institute in Cincinnati. He was a scholar of alchemy, spiritualism, and the occult throughout his life, and his theme in *Etidorhpa* was the unity of science and "the supernatural." Lloyd believed in the existence of powers beyond the grasp of the science of his time, and in the existence of the human soul. But he felt there was nothing that truly transcended nature in angels, ghosts, the soul, and "mysterious" powers; these things were simply as-yet-undiscovered natural beings and phenomena.

Etidorhpa is a cleverly crafted story within a story. The protagonist of the outer story, Llewellyn Drury, is sitting alone in his study in Cincinnati one evening when a strange being appears from nowhere—an "old man" of indeterminate age. He looks like an Old Testament prophet in a frock coat, and he identifies himself only as "I-Am-The-Man-Who-Did-It." He has chosen Drury to listen to a manuscript he has written of his adventures, and then have the manuscript published. Drury reluctantly agrees (I-Am-The-Man pulls out a wicked-looking knife and threatens "to separate his soul from his body" if he does not) and the mysterious visitor begins to read:

In the early years of the nineteenth century, I-Am-The-Man was an upstate New Yorker obsessed with learning the secrets of alchemy. Receiving an invitation to join a secret alchemical brotherhood, he enthusiastically becomes a member, but after he learns a few of its secrets he comes to feel that such knowledge should be shared with the rest of humanity. Breaking the oath of secrecy he swore when initiated, he assembles a manuscript of the brotherhood's doctrines, publishes it, and immediately finds himself persecuted by fellow members. His books are destroyed in a fire, I-Am-The-Man is thrown into jail on a minor charge, and on his release he is kidnapped by the brotherhood and whisked away into the night in a coach that also contains a dead body. He is brought before a jury of his brothers who are hooded and masked; they tell him that he has been chosen to perform a secret task as penance for his error. Using secret formulae known only to them, the brothers transform the corpse's features into those of I-Am-The-Man, and transform I-Am-The-Man's features into those of a man of eighty; the corpse is thrown into a nearby river to be found by the authorities, and the masked brothers turn I-Am-The-Man over to a young-looking man. This seemingly young man is actually a centuries-old adept of the brotherhood—in other words, a Master—who tells him he has been assigned to explore the unknown realms of the inner world for the benefit of the brotherhood and humanity.

Lloyd's story thus far is based on "the Morgan episode" of 1826 which, although forgotten today, was extremely important in pre-Civil War American history. At that time, the Masons were held by many Americans to be plotting in their secret meetings to take over the government and worse. William Morgan, a former brewer, was accepted by the Masons of Batavia, New York, and attained the level of Royal Arch Mason, but had a falling out with his lodge and decided to publish the Masonic secrets in a book called *Illustrations of Masonry*. As soon as the book was published, however, Morgan vanished and the shop where the book had been printed was burned. Over a year later the decomposing body of a man who could have been Morgan was discovered on the shore of Lake Ontario and buried. As news of the discovery spread through the area, a hastily-called jury ordered the body exhumed and declared that it was indeed Morgan's, and it was reburied in Batavia, although another jury assembled later decided that the body was actually that of a local farmer who had drowned. The news of the first jury's decision set off a wave of anti-Masonic activity across the country in which many lodges disbanded and many political candidates ran for office, and won, on a strict anti-Masonic platform. Whether the body was indeed Morgan's was never determined, and no one could ever prove that the Masons had been responsible, but sentiment still ran so high fifty years later that enough donations were collected to erect in Batavia in 1882 a monument to Morgan forty-seven feet high with the inscription "Murdered by the Masons."

I-Am-The-Man's fate, however, is to be taken by the adept to the mouth of a cavern in the wilds of Kentucky, where he is met by a bizarre, highly-evolved amphibious being in the shape of a man without eyes, sex organs, or hair, and with slippery skin "the color of light blue putty" who is to serve as I-Am-The-Man's guide. The adept leaves him in the company of this strange guide, and the two descend through dark caverns for many days (although the guide can "see" the way perfectly) until they reach the "zone of inner earth light."

Their weight decreases steadily as they descend, and soon they are able to leap into the air and float forward for great distances, covering a dozen miles in a few minutes. I-Am-The-Man discovers that the deeper he travels, the less frequently he needs to breathe and eat and the less often his heart beats. Finally he ceases to breathe and eat altogether and his heart stops beating, yet he feels more alive than he ever has; the guide explains that with little gravity and a nutrient-rich atmosphere, the inner world is much kinder to the human body than the outer. A man living in the inner world can live for centuries and hardly age a day, for there is no strain on his body at all.

The guide restrains I-Am-The-Man from fleeing, in an illustration from J. U. Lloyd's *Etidorhpa* (1895).

Some parts of the inner-world journey that follows are similar to Verne's *Journey to the Center of the Earth*—a forest of huge fungi, a vast subterranean sea, and the guide's interminable lectures on wonders as yet unknown to outer-world science. The inner-world sea in *Etidorhpa* is, unlike Verne's, as smooth as polished glass, and the boat the guide places upon the sea, driven by an utterly silent force, travels nine hundred miles an hour. On the other side of the sea, the guide brings I-Am-The-Man to an immense, exotic mushroom; its spores contain a strange green liquid, which he orders I-Am-The-Man to drink. He drinks the liquid, and for the next four chapters I-Am-The-Man—and the reader—experience a bizarre vision: a cavern, through which he must pass, filled with the suffering souls of drunkards. It is a gallery of beings reminiscent of the sinners of Dante crossed with the spooks from the old Max Fleischer Betty Boop cartoons:

> ... [T]o my right I beheld a single leg, fully twelve feet in height, surmounted by a puny human form, which on this leg, hopped ludicrously away. I saw close behind this huge limb a great ear attached to a small head and body; then a nose so large that the figure to which it was attached was forced to hold the face upward, in order to prevent the misshaped organ from rubbing on the stony floor.

The guide spends several pages warning us how alcohol deforms the soul of the alcoholic, and I-Am-The-Man is forced to undergo ever-more-difficult tests in which he is tempted to drink. He finds himself, parched and tongue swollen, in a desert where he must sit for centuries while fiends offer him alcohol. He is visited by the beautiful love-spirit Etidorhpa (Aphrodite spelled backwards) who promises she will be his forever if he will drink—and then rejoices when he refuses.

Suddenly the vision dissolves and I-Am-The-Man finds himself standing next to his guide once again, who tells him that all the tests were given him under the influence of the drink he took at the guide's bidding, the juice of a hallucinogenic fungus. (In a footnote, Lloyd hints that he had experienced the effects of numerous hallucinogens himself before writing these very puritanical chapters).

Finally the guide brings I-Am-The-Man to the brink of a cliff on the inner edge of the earth's shell and tosses him into the emptiness; they float for hundreds of miles through space to the "Sphere of Rest," a concentric inner sphere at the point where the shell of energy holding the earth together resides and where gravity is nullified. Lloyd's view of the shape of the earth, although based roughly on Symmes's, included a framework of exotic physics which would have startled even the self-assured Captain. Matter, says the guide, is "retarded motion," and the matter forming the earth's material shell is able to hold its shape only because it rests on this sphere of pure energy, as dust might collect on a soap bubble. This "energy bubble," which is the seat of the earth's gravitational pull, lies seven hundred miles beneath the surface, and is truly the planet's soul:

> Take from your earth its vital spirit, the energy that subjects matter, and your so-called adamantine rocks would disintegrate, and sift as dust into the interstices of space. Your so-called rigid globe, a shell of space dust, would dissolve, collapse, and as the spray of a burst bubble, its ponderous side would vanish in the depths of force.

On the shore of the ocean of light filling the shell, the eyeless guide pauses on the lip of the inner sphere to hand I-Am-The-Man over to an angelic being, who conducts him into the inner surface, the Unknown Country, the land of Etidorhpa, for initiation into deeper secrets. Here I-Am-The-Man's manuscript

ends. The now-fascinated Llewellyn Drury demands to know what happened
to him in the Unknown Country, but in the style typical of the Master (for that
is what he has become), I-Am-The-Man refuses to say; he is "not permitted" to
reveal more "at this time." After entrusting the manuscript to Drury's care, he
slowly fades into the air and vanishes.

How much of Lloyd's inner world reflected his own beliefs is hard to
say. What is certain is his desire to demonstrate the inadequacies of materialistic science and the need to build a bridge joining science and religious belief.
Etidorhpa is a debate between the rational materialist (represented by Drury and
the younger, unenlightened I-Am-The-Man) and the intuitive person of spirit
(represented by the eyeless guide and the older, enlightened I-Am-The-Man). It
was a debate which likely raged in Lloyd's own mind, but he wanted science
to respect spirit, so it is the forces of intuition which are triumphant. Drury
stops I-Am-The-Man in several places during the reading of the manuscript to
snort in disbelief, and I-Am-The-Man always patiently but sarcastically demol-
ishes Drury's objections. Some of their dialogue is quite funny, if a bit simplistic
and unconvincing to the empirically-minded reader. Drury, for example, inter-
rupts at one point to express his complete disbelief in I-Am-The-Man's inner-
world adventures, and I-Am-The-Man asks him politely, "Why do you doubt?"

"Because I have never seen such phenomena, I have never witnessed such occurrences. I
must see a thing to believe it."
"And so you believe only what you see?" he queried.
"Yes."
"Now answer promptly... Did you ever see Greenland?"
"No."
"Iceland?"
"No."
"A geyser?"
"No."
"A whale?"
"No."
"England?"
"No."
"France?"
"No."
"Then you do not believe that these conditions, countries, and animals have an exis-
tence?"
"Of course they have."
"Why?"
"Others have seen them."
"Ah," he said; "then you wish to modify your assertion—you only believe what oth-
ers have seen?"
"Excepting one person," I retorted.
Then he continued, seemingly not having noticed my personal allusion:
"Have you ever seen your heart?"
"No."
"Your stomach?"
"No."
"Have you seen the stomach of any of your friends?"

"No."
"The back of your head?"
I became irritated, and made no reply...

Etidorhpa was highly praised and successful when first published privately by Lloyd in 1895, and it was soon after picked up by a major publisher and reprinted a dozen times in the following decade. It was reprinted in paperback several times in the 1970s and 80s, but it has never caught on with modern fantasy readers, probably because of its strong didactic streak. Its illustrations by J. Augustus Knapp, however, are minor masterpieces of fantasy art, its basic story *breathes* Mystery, and the eyeless guide is one of the first true *subterranean* characters—rather than a transplanted surface being—in literature. Lloyd's warnings against the evils of drink—although still relevant—seem hopelessly Victorian today, but I-Am-The-Man's drug visions do not. Lloyd's explanation of the earth as a shell of particles balanced on a bubble of energy makes little sense to modern readers, but his desire to spiritualize science still appeals to many people of all ranges of belief. *Etidorhpa* is a unique work, and I hope it is never forgotten completely.

The Green Child

After the North and South Poles were officially recognized as discovered in the first decades of this century, the number and the passion of inner-world novels declined rapidly. It became clear to all but a few that the Symmesian earth, the model for most inner-world storytellers, could never be more than a country of the imagination. The subterranean novels that continued to appear tended to be of the macho adventure/romance variety with nothing in mind but a good story in an exotic locale. Such, for example, was *The Secret People* (1935) by John Beynon (a pseudonym for science-fiction author John Wyndham), a novel set in the future year of 1964 which told of the discovery of a lost race of pygmies beneath the Sahara Desert. It had a dashing aviator hero, a good-looking heroine, and lots of action. Occasional science-fiction titles have appeared with an inner-world setting, often using as their basis the notion of a race moving underground after a catastrophe makes the surface uninhabitable. In Sidney Fowler Wright's fascinating *The World Below* (1929) we have a human race of the far future which has left the surface and evolved into two separate species—a race of Amphibians who live beneath the sea and communicate telepathically and a huge subterranean race, the Dwellers, who rule the continents but come to the surface to gather food, and then only rarely. Robert Silverberg's *At Winter's End* (1988) tells how, millions of years in the future, a race of sentient monkeys, left behind after the human race has left the planet, has dwelled in cavern worlds during the solar system's trip through a shower of huge meteors lasting thousands of years.

But of the few inner-world novels of our century, the most affecting and most memorable was written not as an adventure or science fiction, but as a modern folktale. Herbert Read's *The Green Child* (1935) is based on the twelfth-century legend of the Green Children told in Chapter 2, but expanded into the story of the realization of a man's life:

Olivero, whose story *The Green Child* tells, leaves his village in the English countryside in 1830 as a young man in search of excitement. In a few years he travels from London to Warsaw to Cadiz in Spain, where he is jailed for possession of a book by the "revolutionary" Voltaire, to Buenos Aires. There he is mistaken for a leftist political refugee and made the assistant to a general planning a revolution in the South American state of Roncador, roughly equivalent to Paraguay. The revolution is successful, and when the general retires from the office of President a few years later, Olivero, to his own surprise, is made his successor. Olivero rules Roncador wisely and well for the next twenty-five years, and it becomes in his hands almost a utopian state. When it seems to Olivero to be running itself, he grows weary of his unchallenging office. He arranges a phony assassination so his trusted assistant can succeed him and Olivero returns to England in disguise.

When Olivero arrives once more in the village where he was born, he passes a house in which a man is forcing a pale, emaciated woman who is tied to a chair to drink the blood of a freshly slaughtered lamb. Olivero bursts in through the window, confronts the man, and recognizes the woman as the survivor of the two Green Children who had been found wandering in the countryside the year of his departure:

> [Her] skin was not white, but a faint green shade, the colour of a duck's egg. It was, moreover, an unusually transparent tegument, and through its pallor the branches of her veins and arteries spread, not blue and scarlet, but vivid green and golden. The nails were pale blue, very like a blackbird's eggshell. The faint emanation of odour from her flesh was sweet and a little heavy, like the scent of violets.

Kneeshaw, the man who had tied her to the chair, tells Olivero he had married "Sally," the Green Child, fifteen years before, on the death of the old woman who had adopted her and her doomed brother. Kneeshaw, a simple, loutish fellow, had been fascinated and aroused by Sally's strangeness, but he soon grew frustrated with his exotic wife. She would not sleep or eat like a normal human; she ate only nuts, mushrooms, and raw fish, and would wander away during the night. She was emotionally cold and would not show Kneeshaw any affection, no matter how much he did for her. As she grew more distant, Kneeshaw grew angry and finally locked her in the attic and tried to force her to sleep and eat like a normal person. But she began wasting away, and Kneeshaw convinced himself that drinking fresh blood might restore her health.

Olivero, sensing Kneeshaw's rage and frustration, tries to protect Sally, but Kneeshaw attacks him and the two fight until Kneeshaw falls into the stream near the house and drowns. Olivero and Sally leave the village and walk out into the countryside to the place where she first appeared with her brother thirty years before. They wade into the stream bed hand in hand and sink down through the sand in a great bubble of air, descending until they reach a country of caverns far below the surface. Here Sally returns to her people and Olivero's new life begins.

They walk down to an immense cavern city, strange and beautiful, with a luminous atmosphere; "an everlasting light," Read calls it, "a summer evening fixed at the moment birds suddenly cease to sing." Sally steps into a warm, salty public bath in the cavern floor and falls asleep; when she wakes, her native language and knowledge of her people have been restored to her, and she remembers her real name, Siloën. She brings Olivero before the five judges who guide the subterranean society and asks that he be admitted. The judges give their consent, and set both Olivero and Siloën on the life-cycle of the Green People, an allegory of the passage of human life from stage to stage.

The lives of the Green People are exceedingly simple. Their language is entirely spoken, not written; their long life-spans are a slow promenade from the pleasures of youth to the profundities of age. As youths they band together to play games, dance, bathe, and make love to whomever they choose. When these pleasures wear thin, they become workers and craftspeople, gathering the earth-nuts and mushrooms on which they live, weaving, or polishing the beautiful gongs and crystals which are their only form of art. In middle age they spend years wrapped in philosophical debate, and in old age they become hermits, meditating on the perfection of the mineral world and preparing for death.

Read succeeds where other authors have failed in creating the alienness of a people who live and die inside the earth, who have never seen the sun or the stars. Without night, day, or seasons, they cannot comprehend cycles of time or unlimited space. When Olivero joins a group of debaters, he tries to describe the outer world for them, but they treat him as one who has had a wild dream: "It was not possible, they held, to conceive of space that was not bound in every direction by solids." Unlike people of the outer world, who conceive of freedom and perfection in terms of flight and ascent into heaven, the Green People, encased by the eternal stone of their caverns, aspire to become a part of the mineral world:

> ...[A]bove all the human breath was the symptom of an original curse which could only be eradicated after death. Death itself was no horror to them, but nothing exceeded their dread of corruption and decay: that, to them, was a return to the soft and gaseous.... Their sole desire was to become solid—as solid and perdurable as the rocks about them. They therefore practiced the rites of petrifaction. When the hated breath at last left the human body, that body was carried to the special caves, and there laid in troughs filled with the petrous water that dripped from roof and walls. There it remained until the body was white and hard, until the eyes were glazed under their vitreous lids, and the hair of the head became like crisp snail shells, the beard a few jagged icicles.... When the body was finally petrified it was removed from its watery trough and carried like a recumbent statue to the halls of the dead—caves in which the alabaster bodies were stacked, one above the other in dense rows, to wait for their final beatitude, crystallisation. When the body, no longer recognizably human, but rather a pillar of salt, took on the mathematical precision and perfect structure of crystal, then it was judged to have attained its final immortality.

Slowly the caverns were filling with these solid wedges. No man knew how far they extended into the infinite mass of the earth; all they knew was that the space they lived in was limited and that a time would come when the dwindling race would inhabit the last grotto, when the last of the race would plunge into the trough, and so fulfill the purpose of life, which is to attain everlasting perfection. For this people held that there was nothing else more acceptable to God, than to offer their body wholly to the earth, and to unite it most inwardly with that earth. That was their whole desire: to be one with the physical harmony of the earth.

When we read *The Green Child,* it is easy to see why the inner-world people of other subterranean romances and satires do not convince us they might be real. Read's description might be an anthropologist's report, for it carries a halo of truth about it. For all their fascination, Bulwer's Vril-ya, Emerson's giants, and Burroughs's Pellucidarians are only outer-world humans set inside the world to excite us, amuse us, or teach us something; only Lloyd's eyeless guide comes close, but is treated as more of an anomaly than a member of a true subterranean race. Read's Green People, however, belong in the inner world. Read, with a sure poet's touch, created a society completely dominated by and worshipful of the great womb in which it dwells. And Olivero finds that he belongs there as well; after he becomes a hermit and finally, joyfully, stiffens and dies, he is carried to the petrification trough and laid there in the arms of Siloën, who has died at the same time. Together they become a huge and perfect crystal.

The Green Child was Read's only novel, although he had a distinguished and prolific career as a poet and critic of the arts. It is a little gem which has been undeservedly ignored; perhaps one day, like a masterpiece painting forgotten in a family attic, it will be rediscovered and admired again.

Chapter 14

Why an Inner World?

> One day, maybe, I shall reach the country where nobody lacks for anything, but up to now no one has given me definite news of that country.
>
> —Voltaire, *Micromegas*

John Cleves Symmes's dream is not quite dead. It may appear to most of us that scientists and explorers have mapped the polar regions so thoroughly that there is no room left to conceal either of Symmes's Holes, but there are those who still believe that the U.S. government has chosen to keep them a secret. Geologists have made it plain that even if the openings existed the earth could not be hollow. If the planet was not a solid body, they say, it would be impossible for earthquake waves to pass through it. Locating the epicenters of earthquakes, which is done every day with great accuracy following physical laws that suppose a solid earth, would not be possible either. Yet there are those who echo the eyeless guide of *Etidorhpa*, who brazenly told I-Am-The-Man that although certain laws of physics might apply in the outer world, they do not necessarily apply in the inner world. Such a viewpoint is hard to defend today, when astronomers have demostrated so clearly that the same laws of physics that keep the earth in orbit around the sun operate in galaxies millions of light years away. Physical laws or not, however, there are still some who have not stopped looking for entrances to an inner world.

A secretive Australian organization, the Hollow Earth Society, surfaced for a short time in the late 1970s. It had been in existence, according to its letterhead, since 1818 when Symmes issued Circular No. 1 and announced that the world was hollow. Their stationery also bore the motto "At last the truth will be known," but it appeared they were still searching for physical evidence. They advised prospective members that they were only interested in recruiting those with hard information to contribute. Mr. K. H. Snell, the Society's Secretary General, told such people that the Society, which had been privately endowed, had instructed him "to offer substantial cash rewards for genuine information in a currency of your choice."

Search magazine continued publishing after Ray Palmer's death under the supervision of his widow Marjorie, reprinting some Shaver material, serving as a clearing house for Trilateral-Commission conspiracy theories, and featuring UFO and hollow-earth material stressing the U.S. government's desire to keep such matters quiet. In the early 1980s it published an ad that sounded promising: "Over 40 suspected INNER-EARTH entrances located, in the US alone!" I sent my two dollars to Bruce Walton in Provo, Utah and received a booklet of reported inner-world ruins, cities, and tunnels, but they were simply citations from the Letters column of the Shaver-era *Amazing Stories*, from the *National*

Enquirer, and from other publications of equal veracity. I wrote Walton and asked him whether he had explored any of the tunnels or verified any of the reports; he replied, very sincerely, that he had not, but he hoped to, someday. He later published an excellent hollow-earth bibliography and several other collections of articles of inner-world material, including *Mount Shasta, Home of the Ancients* (1985), a fascinating anthology of material on Mt. Shasta. Walton also established SIPAPU (Society for the Investigation of Paraspeleology, Abyssian Phenomena, and the Underworld) about the same time, and invited readers to share their experiences with him. But suddenly in 1986, at the age of 26, Walton abandoned his work, and let it be known that he "no longer wish[ed] to be contacted" regarding inner-world phenomena and ceased selling his collections.

In 1981 an author writing under the name of Floria Benton published a small book titled *Hollow Earth Mysteries and the Polar Shift* in which the idea of a massive cover-up of the earth's true nature was developed in some detail, although not very coherently. In various sections of the book, Benton suggested that the earth was secretly ruled by a superior race from the inner world, that "space beings" were regularly mating with earth women to breed a "new race," that the poles were due to shift within a few years with catastrophic results, and that we were bringing this disaster upon ourselves more quickly through nuclear testing. But all these facts had been concealed:

> Obviously, if we can prove the earth is hollow, the existence of a cover-up follows as a matter of course. A jet age and space age society such as ours could not be completely ignorant of the existence of two large openings at the poles. The fact that such a cover-up would be instituted tends to show that a catastrophe is expected. If our civilization were expected to endure another 1000 or 10,000 years, there would be no point in even attempting to cover up knowledge of the hollow earth.

The inner-world powers who secretly control our government, Benton suggested, wanted the upcoming catastrophe concealed so that the unfit members of surface humanity would be wiped out and they could come into power. Benton believed that although the U.S. government had known of the polar openings' existence since Admiral Byrd's 1947 *North* Polar flight, most scientific and government literature had systematically excluded any mention of the true shape of the earth or the polar shift. Benton's proofs were the works of Raymond Bernard, Marshall B. Gardner, Mme. Blavatsky, Erich von Däniken, and similar writers.

I also sent some money to the Science Research Publishing House of St. Petersburg, Florida for a copy of *The Incredible Cities of Inner Earth* (1979) by David H. Lewis. Lewis, who had previously published several works with a New Age slant, among them *Secrets of the Pyramids* and *Universal Oneness*, repeated with all solemnity the story of Admiral Byrd's 1947 *North* Polar expedition, mammoths and all. He then announced that a private expedition had finally reached the outskirts of a super-technological inner-world civilization a hundred miles beneath the surface in April 1979. Lewis's party had, he said, already found "ancient records" in a crypt under the Great Pyramid that revealed seven entrances to the inner world; they chose, for convenience, the United States entrance, a cavern between Poughkeepsie, New York and the Connecticut border. The expedition descended 115 miles and found one of the inner-world civilzation's ventilation units, with big exhaust fans and banks of computer controls. They returned to Poughkeepsie, evidently without taking any photographs or removing any rivets or knobs from the inner-world ventilators to prove their "discoveries." Lewis refused to give the exact location of the cavern entrance, claiming a need for absolute secrecy; "This shaft opening I speak of," he writes, "must remain free of any incumbent claims by the come-lately explorers, the curious, the rock samplers..." Apparently we are supposed to take Lewis's word for it.

A Mormon writer named Rodney Cluff revealed in 1981 that not only was the earth hollow, with openings at the poles, but that the sun shining upon the inner world is the location of the Paradise spoken of in the Book of Mormon. He noted how Joseph Smith, founder of the Mormon church, wrote, "The spirits of the just are exalted to a greater and more glorious work; hence they are blessed in their departure to the world of spirits. ENVELOPED IN FLAMING FIRE, THEY ARE NOT FAR FROM US [Cluff's emphasis], and know and understand our thoughts, feelings, and motions, and are often pained therewith." Cluff thus stated: "From this we may conclude that since paradise is a place of flaming fire and is located in the heart of the earth, then the sun discovered by polar explorers in the center of Our Hollow Earth must be the physical location of PARADISE in the spirit world of this earth." He also contended that there was a virtuous race within the earth that was trying to establish contact with the people of the outer world. "But suppose," he continued, "that the people inside Our Hollow Earth knew something which if they were able to communicate it... would endanger the hold the International Illuminist Conspiracy [whom he elsewhere identified with the Communists] has upon the world?... Ever since Admiral Byrd discovered the land beyond the polar openings, the nations controlled by the Conspiracy have been operating an offensive against the Israelite Nation inside the earth." This "Israelite Nation" is none other than the Ten Lost Tribes of Israel, who were "carried into captivity in 721 B.C. by the Assyrians but later escaped into the north country which is the hollow interior of our earth."

Cluff also told in his foreword the story of John Gagne, a fellow Mormon living in Alaska who had been researching the inner world for years. Gagne told Cluff he had met a woman who knew Admiral Byrd, and Byrd had visited with her after his 1947 *Arctic* flight and "confided information which he said he was afraid to tell the world for fear he would be condemned as insane." Byrd told her he had flown to a land beyond the North Pole filled with lush vegetation and people "large in stature," who rode monorails and flew craft "which since have become known as FLYING SAUCERS." Gagne said that when he met another woman who was a friend of the Byrd family and attempted through her to gain permission to examine the Admiral's manuscripts, "she was told that they do not let ANYONE look at Byrd's writings. They had them under lock and key." Gagne also told Cluff that soon after he came to Alaska, he met an agent of the "United States Foreign Secret Service" who "offered to take John to the Hollow Earth via float plane. But he wanted 3 million dollars to take him! Needless to say John couldn't come up with the money."

Reasons for an Inner World

Unfortunately for its advocates, all of these words and this activity add up to very little physical evidence of an inner world. Why, then, has the notion of a world inside the world continued to excite at least a few romantic souls for the past three centuries? Despite the complete lack of proof for its physical existence, the inner world holds within it several profound reasons to persevere as part of our mythical and mental landscapes:

1. **As a new world to discover**. We don't like to believe that there are no more geographical frontiers and no more unknown lands to explore and conquer. There remain, of course, both outer space and the ocean floor, but without pressure suits and breathing apparatus, both are inaccessible and inhospitable environments, and settling in either environment would require billions of dollars' worth of specialized equipment and support personnel. Neither are countries of the heart for the lone visionary. An inner world, on the other hand, would be an extension of the outer—a huge new land to survey with hiking boots, bedroll, and knapsack. In *The Hollow Globe*, William Lyon said it best, lamenting the closing of the American frontier: "What is to be done," he asked, "with that restless, uneasy mass that have always been going ahead, seeking out new territory, and preparing the way for the more quiet, stay-at-home class who only follow in the wake of the Pioneers? The required territory must be found of necessity." The inner world would be that new frontier.

Symmes, William Reed, and Marshall Gardner, like Lyon, saw it as new territory to conquer for the United States. Each of these men dreamed of himself as the new Christopher Columbus, a daring pioneer laughed at by the reactionary "wise men," but able at last to gain official support—and the last laugh—when he actually found the new world of his vision. It is easy to picture Symmes, as he limped along the lecture circuit, always holding in the corner of his mind a dream of a great stone monument in Washington, D.C. engraved "DEDICATED TO J. C. SYMMES, DISCOVERER OF THE INNER WORLD, NOW CALLED SYMZONIA." Gardner probably imagined a dozen new pages in the world atlas, all of them maps of "Gardner Land." The readers of their biographies can only feel relieved, however, that neither Symmes nor Gardner were successful in assembling and leading expeditions bound for the North Polar Opening. It is easy to imagine the sickly Symmes collapsing of exhaustion on an ice sheet and requiring his fellow explorers to carry him, or to picture Gardner sitting, arms folded, in the cabin of a zeppelin, ordering his crew to fly in endless circles around the North Pole.

2. **As the longed-for Paradise**. The English cleric Thomas Burnet, who in 1722 published a work called *The Sacred Theory of the Earth*, described

our planet in the days before the Flood as a paradise. It was a perfect sphere "without any inequality of seasons... there was no Sea then, no Mountains, nor Rocks, nor broken Caves; 'twas all one continued and regular mass, simple and compleat, as the first Works of Nature used to be." But when the people of the paradisiacal earth fell into sin, God sent great earthquakes to mar the planet's perfection. The surface, like the shell of a great egg, cracked in a thousand places, and the waters of the Great Abyss beneath the earth flooded all around the pieces, like the white and yolk around the bits of broken shell. "The Parts that stood above the Waters," wrote Burnet, "are the Mountains and Precipices that we see and admire today."

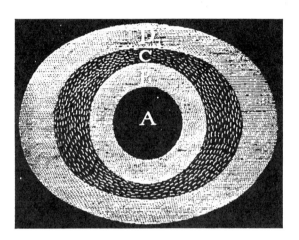

Earth in is original perfection in the shape of an egg, from Thomas Burnet's *The Sacred Theory of the Earth* (1722).

For Burnet, a paradise on earth had departed; yet reading the scores of descriptions of the inner world left by almost every one of its proponents since Edmund Halley, one is struck by how often they sound like reports of an earthly paradise. In them the inner world often sounds like the Golden Age of Greek myth, in which the landscape blossoms in an eternal springtime, the weather is always pleasantly warm, food is abundant, life is long, all know the simple truths of life, and peace and happiness are to be found everywhere. All the poor seeker from the outer world has to do is find the door.

For Cyrus Teed, finding paradise was easy—he was visited with ecstasy at the moment he realized he had been *inside* all along. Symmes, Reed, Lyon, Gardner and their followers knew where the doors to paradise were; there was one gaping wide at either end of the planet. But actually reaching them was a different matter, for the poles were in their day as inaccessible as Mars. For the later seekers, like Shaver, the Hefferlins, and Bernard, who lived in a time when the poles were reached regularly, the door was disguised and heavily guarded. Either their own government concealed it or the inner-world folk did; a few very special outer-world people were allowed inside, but most were not.

3. **As a sanctum for hidden secrets.** From the 1930s on, the inner world was most often deemed the home of the Masters, the dero, and others who kept their secrets hidden from the sticky mass of humanity. The Masters were tight-fisted with their secrets; they admitted only those who could prove themselves worthy of initiation into the Ancient Wisdom. Those who wrote of the Masters told of wonders stacked upon wonders in those subterranean

lodges—metaphysical and technological secrets held in trust until surface humanity was "ready" to accept them, and there was always the implication that most of humanity never would be "ready." Maurice Doreal told how the Atlanteans inside Mt. Shasta kept a marvelous library of "everything mankind ever did," and tended gardens of beautiful plants that existed nowhere else. Guy Ballard's Ascended Masters carelessly piled mountains of gold bars, precious gems, and wonderful machinery in their chambers beneath the Grand Tetons. H.P.B.'s "Book of Dzyan," which if properly read laid open the entire history and destiny of the universe, existed only in the Mahatmas' sanctuaries under the Himalayas.

Even Richard Shaver's subterranean spook-house was a paradise of technological secrets. The caverns abandoned by the Titans were filled with devices that could accomplish literally anything, from seeing through solid rock to improving one's sex life, from curing any disease known to reading others' minds. Shaver felt the real tragedy of the caverns was not so much the free reign of the degenerate dero as their craftiness at convincing surface humanity that they and the marvelous machines they fiddled with didn't exist. "If our scientists," Shaver once wrote, "were ALLOWED to have but one of these machines (which exist in great profusion and in fine repair) for study... our whole technical development would be accelerated beyond imagination." But the dero cleverly used the telaug rays to convince surface folk there were no caverns and to persecute anyone (like Shaver) who tried to tell us otherwise. Shaver believed the Titans' machinery, if brought to the surface, could make the earth a paradise. But the dero had to be defeated first, and the tero were too few in number to do the job themselves. The governments of the surface paid Shaver no attention, and the scientists—the ones who had the most to gain—laughed at him and ignored him. Shaver never found a "door" to the caves, either.

4. **As a Utopia.** Many of the inner-world paradises proposed in the past century have served as proving grounds for their authors' social, political, sexual, or racial ideals. Cyrus Teed brought his followers to the spot he felt was the center of the concave earth to convince everyone else about the true form of the earth and about his new doctrine. Raymond Bernard emulated the perfect inner-world society he dreamed about—a society based on sexual equality, vegetarianism, and parthenogenetic birth—on Sao Francisco Island to convince the Atlanteans of his virtue as he searched for the door to the interior. The utopian ideal has shaped much of inner-world fiction, including Willis George Emerson's society of Nordic giants, Herbert Read's race of simple, egalitarian Green People, Mary Lane's female-separatist Mizorans, and the undescribed but obviously enlightened perfect beings of John Uri Lloyd's Unknown Country. Even Bulwer's flawed Vril-ya held secrets and virtues never seen in the outer world—most notably an absolute feeling of cooperation and peace inspired by the almighty force of vril.

Those who have depicted the inner world as a land of mighty Aryans dream of a utopia free of the racial and political changes that have transformed the world in the past few decades. Europe, Great Britain, Australia, and the

United States have been taking on an increasingly Third-World character as the years pass, and those with a white-supremacist viewpoint must have found such rapid change, after so many centuries of white Western dominance in world affairs, truly terrifying. The prospect of a world in which whites rule undisputedly, where other races have been intentionally excluded, and the old ways of Nordic virility never change, must be a great comfort.

A Return to the Earth Mother

These elements of inner-world mythology have continued to wrap themselves around the archaic myth of the Earth Mother, even though at times, displayed in the flashy garb of technology, the underlying myth is difficult to see. All the talk of gaining the paradise within the earth reduces, when all is said and done, to the longing to return to the total protection of the womb. Most of the inner-world societies, despite their warmth, abundance, and wonders, are static; like the world of the Vril-ya, all one's needs are met and the only things one lacks are challenges—opportunities to take chances, experiment with new ideas, and to succeed or fail on one's own. They are the very kinds of challenges the first humans in the Native American emergence myths faced when they left the security of the Earth Mother's wombs. Reading H.P.B., Doreal, Guy Ballard, and the others who have written of the Masters, it is easy to infer that the Masters, despite their goodness and their care for their disciples, were autocratic parent figures. Since they knew exactly how humanity was to progress and what each individual's role in that development was to be, there was no room for their disciples to exercise free will. Life under Ballard's Masters, "perfect beings who never make a mistake," could never be anything but a permanent childhood of stifling security.

In many descriptions of the paradise within the earth, the writers express a strong desire to return there, as if the inner world had been humanity's first home. Often the humans of the outer world are treated as unfortunates who had been "cast out" of the interior in the distant past. This notion is stated most explicitly—but not exclusively—in inner-world fiction. "Adam Seaborn" speculated in *Symzonia* that surface humanity had descended from the criminals exiled from that inner utopia to an island on the verge, where the sun turned them darker and—by implication—less "pure." Willis George Emerson's interior world in *The Smoky God,* with its enormous fruits and vegetables, its warm, constant temperature, and dim, hazy sun is subtly but definitely womb-like. He implied that outer humanity were the shrunken descendants of giants who had been expelled from the inner world for some offense, or perhaps left the inner world, lured by a rising and setting sun and changing seasons, and could not find their way back in when they desired to return. Exposed to the harsh climate and inferior food of the outer world, their descendants grew smaller and lived shorter lives. I-Am-The-Man's guide called the outer world "bleak" and "turbulent... the roof of earth on which man exists, as a creeping parasite does on a rind of fruit, exposed to the fury of ever-present earth storms." Humanity did not belong on the surface. John Uri Lloyd's inner world is even more womblike than most; its atmosphere is filled with nutrients, so it is unnecessary to make the effort to eat. All outer-world stress is removed and one's body "floats." I-Am-The-Man's mysterious guide, a cave creature at home in a dark, warm, wet environment, might even be seen as an "adult embryo"—hairless, pale, and not totally developed. When I-Am-The-Man enters the interior, he squeezes himself into a tight, pitch-black, damp tunnel, in which he is completely at his guide's mercy.

Raymond Bernard's paradise was an unending world of childhood, ruled by the Great Mother, in which food and shelter were supplied without labor, and complications like sex and money were not only unnecessary, but forbidden. Cyrus Teed's constricting globe was designed to draw all the "chosen" together into enforced ecstasy. William Reed's dim, warm inner world and Marshall Gardner's lush subtropical paradise, both bursting with life, both sending clouds of pollen into the outer atmosphere, both serving as safe winter homes and breeding grounds for migrating animals from the outer world, have surprisingly womblike qualities for two writers who had so little interest in things mystical.

Do these similarities alert the scholar of alternative realities to an unhealthy desire on the part of inner-world proponents to escape back into the womb and avoid the responsibilities of the outer-world of sunlit consciousness and accountability? Not necessarily. They demonstrate only how the image of the all-protective, all-nuturing Earth Mother, shoved underground (as it were) by a patriarchal, urban, achieving culture, insists upon appearing wherever feeling and intuition are allowed to dominate. It appears to be the time, in fact, for the Earth Mother to return to the stage of human culture. The growth of feminism has brought with it the return of Goddess-worship alongside the monotheism of Christianity, Judaism, and Islam. The worldwide threats that industry and population growth pose to our planet's ecosystem, and the environmental movement that has grown up in response to these threats, have prompted a new look at the earth as a great being.

Eighty-foot Princess Vanue of the Titans of Nor from Shaver and Palmer's "I Remember Lemuria!" is easily recognizable as an aspect of the Earth Mother as Provider.

The cyberneticist J. E. Lovelock has proposed a theory he calls *Gaia*, in which the earth's biosphere can be perceived as a living creature. He writes that "if Gaia does exist, then we may find ourselves and all other living things to be parts and partners of a vast being who in her entirety has the power to maintain our planet as a fit and comfortable habitat for life." Lovelock demonstrates in his book how the biochemistry of the atmosphere, the oceans, and the land has somehow been able to regulate itself at just the right level for the continuance of life; whether truly conscious or not, he writes, the earth cares for us. The name Gaia was proposed to Lovelock by the British author William Golding "after the Greek Earth goddess also known as Ge." Gaia and Ge are only two of the many names the Earth Mother has had around the world.

The archetypes of birth, of the almighty Mother who holds us to her breast and feeds us, of being cast out into the cold "outer" world, of returning to her in illness and death, will be with humanity as long as there are children and mothers. It has long been said that the role of men is to *do*—to accomplish—and the role of women is to *be*—to nurture, and although women are *doing* more around the world with each passing year, the archetype behind the saying will remain with humanity as long as women are the ones who give birth. The paradises and utopias of the inner world—and in fact almost all paradises and utopias throughout history—are expressions of this desire to be accepted and nutured, not to be judged by one's accomplishments, but simply to *be*.

Just as the land of the dead had to be located somewhere nearby but inaccessible in archaic times, humanity continues to need hidden countries of the earth to stretch out mentally—landscapes that *might* lie a short journey away, places with more urgency than the purely imaginary countries of fantasy fiction. They are countries in which we can be (or might have been in some previous age) our own kings and queens and heroes, in which we can experiment with new ideas and not worry about them failing. Atlantis is one such country; Shangri-La is another. They give humanity a focus for its desires, an answer to unanswered questions, a magic dustpan into which all the stray "secrets of the universe" can be swept. The inner world is a realm of wonders that is dreamily inaccessible, but always beneath our prosaic noses, and no matter how geologically or biologically "impossible" its existence might be, the slightest possibility that the experts might be either wrong or deliberately concealing its existence will keep it alive among at least a few believers.

As much as I love the notion of an inner world, I am not one of these believers; I have never seen any evidence I consider even marginally persuasive for an inner world, and despite their occasional human failings, I see no reasons to doubt the biologists and geophysicists. Yet in a corner of my mind, I still want Agharti, Symzonia, and Masars II to lay concealed a few hundred miles down, and I'll be very happy to be proved wrong.

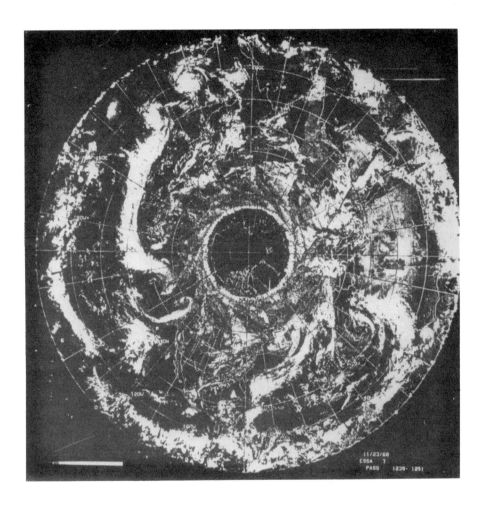

It looks like a photo of a hole at the North Pole, doesn't it?
In a 1970 issue of *Flying Saucers*, Ray Palmer touted this photo,
a mosaic of hundreds of pictures taken by an ESSA weather satellite in
1968, as proof of a hollow earth.
The US National Oceanic and Atmospheric Administration (NOAA)
disagrees, saying that in late November, when the photos were taken,
the North Polar region was dark 24 hours a day.
Other photos taken by the satellite of the South Pole at the
same time were white with ice and clouds, but inner-world
supporters claim clouds simply covered the
South Polar Opening when the photos were taken.

Bibliography A:

Source Materials by Chapter

Note: "S.P." means a source is self-published; "n.d." means a source has no listed publication date.

Chapter 1: The Earth Our Mother

Adams, Frank Dawson. *The Birth and Development of the Geological Sciences.* Williams & Wilkins, 1938; repr. Dover, 1954.

Autobiography of St. Teresa of Avila. Doubleday Image, 1960.

Bettelheim, Bruno. *The Uses of Enchantment: the Meaning and Importance of Fairy Tales.* Knopf, 1977.

Bierhorst, John, ed. *In the Trail of the Wind: American Indian Poems and Ritual Orations.* Farrar, Straus and Giroux, 1971.

Brandon, S.G.F. *The Judgment of the Dead: the Idea of Life After Death in the Major Religions.* Scribner, 1967.

Campbell, Joseph. *The Masks of God: Primitive Mythology.* Penguin Books, 1976.

Cushing, Francis H., "Outlines of Zuni Creation Myths," in the *Annual Report of the Bureau of American Ethnology*, 1896; 379–384.

Eliade, Mircea. *The Forge and the Crucible: the Origins and Structures of Alchemy.* Harper Torchbooks, 1971.

— *History of Religious Ideas*, vol. 1. Univ. of Chicago Press, 1978.

— *Myths, Dreams, and Mysteries.* Harper Torchbooks, 1967.

— *Patterns in Comparative Religion.* Sheed & Ward, 1958.

— *Shamanism: Archaic Techniques of Ecstasy.* Princeton Univ. Press, 1964.

Frazer, J.G. *The Worship of Nature.* Macmillan, 1926.

Hillman, James. *The Dream and the Underworld.* Harper, 1979.

Hughes, Robert. *Heaven and Hell in Western Art.* Stein and Day, 1968.

Joyce, James. *Portrait of the Artist as a Young Man.* Viking, repr. 1964.

Martin, Calvin. "The War Between Indians and Animals," in *Natural History*, June-July 1978, 92–97.

Mew, James. *Traditional Aspects of Hell (Ancient and Modern).* S. Sonneschein, 1903.

Mooney, James. "The Ghost-Dance Religion, and the Sioux Outbreak of 1890," in the *Annual Report of the Bureau of American Ethnology*, XIV, 2, 1896.

Neumann, Erich. *The Great Mother: an Analysis of the Archetype.* Princeton University Press, 1963.

Opler, Morris. "Myths and Legends of the Lipan Apache Indians," in *Memoirs of the American Folk-Lore Society*, XXXVI, 1940.

— "Myths and Tales of the Jicarilla Apache Indians," in *Memoirs of the American Folk-Lore Society*, XXXI, 1938.

Pennick, Nigel. *The Subterranean Kingdom*. Turnstone Press, 1981.

Ruby, Robert H. and John A. Brown. *Indians of the Pacific Northwest*. Univ. of Oklahoma Press, 1981.

Russell, Jeffrey. *Witchcraft in the Middle Ages*. Cornell Univ. Press, 1972.

Teit, James. "Traditions of the Thompson River Indians," in *Memoirs of the American Folk-Lore Society*, VI, 1898.

Verrier, Elwin. *Myths of Middle India*. Oxford Univ. Press, 1949.

Wright, Dudley. *The Book of Vampires*. London, 1914, rev ed. 1924; repr. Causeway, 1973.

Wright, Thomas. *St. Patrick's Purgatory: an Essay on the Legends of Purgatory, Hell, and Paradise, current during the Middle Ages*. John Russell Smith, 1844.

Chapter 2: The Earth's Other Children

Bergier, Jacques. *Extraterrestrial Visitations from Prehistoric Times to the Present*. Henry Regnery, 1973.

Briggs, Katharine. *British Folktales*. Pantheon, 1977.

— *An Encyclopedia of Fairies*. Pantheon, 1976.

Fontenrose, Joseph. *Python: a Study of Delphic Myth and Its Origins*. Univ. of California Press, 1981.

Green, Roger Lancelyn, ed. *A Book of Dragons*. Hamish Hamilton, 1970.

Hand, Wayland D. "California Miners' Folklore: Below Ground," in *California Folklore Quarterly*, v. 1, no. 2, April 1942.

Hartmann, Franz. *Paracelsus: Life and Prophecies*. Steiner, 1973.

Howey, M. Oldfield. *The Encircled Serpent*. Arthur Richmond, 1955.

Hunt, Robert. *Popular Romances of the West of England*. Chatto & Windus, 1881; repr. 1930.

Keightley, Thomas. *The Fairy Mythology*. G. Bell, 1880.

Le Poer Trench, Brinsley. *Secret of the Ages: UFO's from Inside the Earth*. Souvenir, 1974; repr. Pinnacle, 1977.

MacInnes, D. and A. Nutt. "Koisha Kayn, or Kian's Leg," in "Folk and Hero Tales from Argyllshire," *Publications of the Folk-Lore Society*, XXV, 1889.

Montfaucon de Villars, Abbé. *Comte de Gabalis*. Health Research, 1963.

Munch, Peter A. *Norse Mythology*. American-Scandinavian Foundation, 1926.

Shah, Sirdar Ikbal Ali. *Black and White Magic: Its Theory and Practice*. Octagon, 1952.

Spence, Lewis. *British Fairy Origins*. Watts & Co., 1946.

— *The Minor Traditions of British Mythology*. Benjamin Blom, 1972.

Vogel, J. Ph. *Indian Serpent-Lore*. Arthur Probsthain, 1926.

Willoughby-Meade, G. *Chinese Ghouls and Goblins*. Constable & Co., 1928.

Chapter 3: The Inaccessible Center

Cohen, Morris R. and Israel E. Drabkin. *Source Book in Greek Science*. Harvard Univ. Press, 1958.

Collier, Katharine Brownell. *Cosmogonies of Our Fathers*. Columbia Univ. Press, 1934; repr. Octagon, 1968.

De Camp, L. Sprague and Willy Ley. *Lands Beyond*. Rinehart, 1952.

Godwin, Joscelyn. *Athanasius Kircher: a Renaissance Man and the Quest for Lost Knowledge*. Thames and Hudson, 1979.

Goldsmith, Julian. "Mysterious Inner Earth," in *Intellect*, July 1977, 14–15.

Hilts, Philip J. "New Technology Helps Unlock Earth's Inner Secrets," Portland *Oregonian*, November 17, 1988, E1-3.

Kangro, Hans. "Kircher, Athanasius," in *Dictionary of Scientific Biography*, Scribner's, 1973, VII, 374-78.

Kenton, Edna. *The Book of Earths*. Morrow, 1928.

Ley, Willy. "The Hollow Earth," in *Galaxy*, March 1956, 71–81.

Mason, Shirley L. *Source Book in Geology, 1400 to 1900*. Harvard Univ. Press, 1970.

Orr, Mary A. *Dante and the Early Astronomers*. Wingate, 1913; new ed. 1956.

Thorndike, Lynn. "The Underground World of Kircher and Becher," in *A History of Magic and Experimental Science*, Columbia Univ. Press, 1958, VII, 567-89.

Zirkle, Conway. "The Theory of Concentric Spheres: Edmund Halley, Cotton Mather, & John Cleves Symmes," in *Isis*, vol. 34, July 1947.

Chapter 4: Symmes's Hole

Almy, Robert F. "J.N. Reynolds: a Brief Biography with Particular Reference to Poe and Symmes," in *Colophon*, 2, 1937, 227-245.

"An Arctic Theory Gone Mad," New York *Times*, Monday, May 12, 1884.

Clark, P. "The Symmes Theory of the Earth," in *Atlantic Monthly*, XXXI, 471-80, April 1873.

Darwin, Erasmus. *The Botanic Garden, a Poem, in Two Parts*. Jones & Company, 1825.

Gardner, Martin. *Fads and Fallacies in the Name of Science.* Dover, 1957.

Heiser, Alta Harvey. *Hamilton in the Making.* Mississippi Valley Press (Oxford, OH), 1941.

History of Butler County [PA]. Waterman, Watkins & Co., 1883.

Howe, Henry. *Howe's Historical Collection of Ohio.* State of Ohio (Columbus, OH), 1900.

Klopstock, Friedrich. *The Messiah, attempted from the German of Mr. Klopstock.* J. Caslon
    (London), 1769.

Miller, William M. "The Theory of Concentric Spheres," in *Isis,* vol. 33, 1941.

Mitterling, Philip I. *America in the Antarctic to 1840.* Univ. of Illinois Press, 1959.

Peck, John W. "Symmes' Theory," in *Ohio Archeological Historical Publications,* vol. 18, 1909.

"[Review of] *Symmes's Theory of Concentric Spheres,*" in *American Quarterly Review,* March 1827,
    235-253.

Seaborn, Adam (pseud.) *Symzonia, a Voyage of Discovery.* J. Seymour, 1820; repr. Arno Press,
    1974.

Sparks, Jared, attr. to. "[Review of] *Symzonia, a Voyage of Discovery,*" in *North American Review,*
    vol. xiii, New Series IV, July 1821, 134-43.

Stanton, William. *The Great United States Exploring Expedition of 1838-1842.* Univ. of
    California Press, 1975.

"Symmes and His Theory," in *Harper's Monthly,* Sept. 1882, 740-744.

Wallace, Irving. *The Square Pegs.* Knopf, 1957.

Chapter 5: Inward the Course of Empire Takes Its Way

Culmer, Frederick, Sr. *The Inner World: a New Theory.* S.P., Salt Lake City, UT, 1886.

Gardner, Marshall B. *A Journey to the Earth's Interior, or, Have the Poles Really Been Discovered.*
    S.P., Aurora, IL, 1913; rev. ed. 1920.

Lyon, William F. *The Hollow Globe; or the World's Agitator and Reconciler.* Religio-
    Philosophical Publishing House, 1871.

Reed, William. *The Phantom of the Poles.* Walter S. Rockey Co., 1906.

Vitaliano, Dorothy B. *Legends of the Earth: Their Geologic Origins.* Indiana Univ. Press, 1973.

Chapter 6: The Man Who Lived Inside the Earth

Carmer, Carl. *Dark Trees to the Wind: a Cycle of York State Years.* William Sloane Associates,
    1949.

Damkohler, Elwin E. *Estero, Fla., 1882: Memoirs of the First Settler.* Island Press, 1967.

Federal Writers Project. *Florida: a Guide to the Southernmost State.* Oxford Univ. Press, 1939.

Michel, Hedwig. *A Gift to the People.* Guiding Star Press, n.d.

Rainard, Robert Lynn. *In the Name of Humanity: the Koreshan Unity.* Unpublished Master's thesis, University of South Florida, 1974.

Sheeman, Willis G. *The Last Days and the New Age.* S.P. by Elizabeth Bartosch (Miami, FL), 1969.

"Sure He is the Prophet Cyrus," New York *Times,* Sunday, August 10, 1884, 1.

Teed, Cyrus R. *The Cellular Cosmogony, or, the Earth a Concave Sphere.* Guiding Star Publishing House, 1898, 1905; repr. Porcupine Press, 1975.

— "The Destiny of the Africo-American," in *The Flaming Sword,* VI, 22, December 2, 1893, 1-2.

Chapter 7: The Hidden Masters' Hiding Places

Besant, Annie. *The Ancient Wisdom.* Theosophical Publishing Society, 1897; repr. 1914.

Blavatsky, Helena P. *Isis Unveiled.* S.P. (New York), 1877; repr. Theosophy Co., 1931.

— *The Secret Doctrine.* Theosophical Publishing Co., 1888; repr. Theosophical Univ. Press, 1977.

Braden, Charles S. *These Also Believe: a Study of Modern American Cults and Minority Religious Movements.* Macmillan, 1949; repr. 1960.

Butler, E. M. *The Myth of the Magus.* Cambridge Univ. Press, 1948; repr. 1979.

"California Bell Legends: a Survey," *California Folklore Quarterly,* 4, 1, January 1945.

Cervé, Wishar S. (pseud. of Harvey Spencer Lewis). *Lemuria, the Lost Continent of the Pacific.* AMORC, 1931; repr. 1935.

Chaney, Earlyne. *Secrets from Mount Shasta.* S.P. (Anaheim, CA), 1953.

Clark, Ella E. *Indian Legends of the Pacific Northwest.* Univ. of California Press, 1953.

Däniken, Erich von. *The Gold of the Gods.* Souvenir, 1973; repr. Bantam, 1974.

De Camp, L. Sprague. *Lost Continents: The Atlantis Theme in History, Science, and Literature.* Gnome, 1954; repr. Dover, 1970.

Dohrman, H.T. *California Cult: the Story of "Mankind United."* Beacon, 1958.

Eichorn, Arthur F. *The Mt. Shasta Story.* Mount Shasta Herald, 1957.

Ellwood, Robert S., Jr. *Religious and Spiritual Groups in Modern America.* Prentice-Hall, 1973.

King, Godfré Ray (pseud. of Guy Ballard). *The Magic Presence.* Saint Germain Press, 1935.

— *Unveiled Mysteries.* Saint Germain Press, 1934; repr. 1939.

Lanser, Edward. "A People of Mystery," Los Angeles *Times* Sunday Magazine, May 22, 1932, 4, 16.

Larkin, Edgar L. "The Atlantides," San Francisco *Examiner,* December 31, 1913.

— *Within the Mind Maze.* Standard Printing Co., 1911.

Leadbeater, C. W. *The Masters and the Path.* Theosophical Publishing House, 1925; rev. ed. 1927; repr. 1973.

Meade, Marion. *Madame Blavatsky: the Woman Behind the Myth.* Putnam, 1980.

"Mighty I AM," in *Time*, February 28, 1938, 32-33.

"Mysteries of the Mountain," *Siskiyou Playlander* (Mount Shasta, CA), 10, 1, Spring 1979.

Oliver, Frederick S. *A Dweller on Two Planets, or, the Dividing of the Way, by Phylos the Thibetan.* Steiner Books, 1974.

Prophet, Elizabeth Clare. *The Great White Brotherhood in the Culture, History, and Religion of America.* The Summit Lighthouse, 1976.

Solovyoff, V. S. *A Modern Priestess of Isis.* Longmans, Green and Co., 1895.

Spence, Lewis. *The Problem of Lemuria, the Sunken Continent of the Pacific.* Rider & Co., 1932.

Twitchell, Cleve and Aileen Simmers. "Mt. Shasta's Mystic Quality," Medford [OR] *Mail Tribune*, March 3, 1963, II, 1.

Waite, Arthur E. *The Brotherhood of the Rosy Cross.* University Books, 1962.

Yates, Frances A. *The Rosicrucian Enlightenment.* Routledge and Kegan Paul, 1972; repr. Shambhala, 1978.

Chapter 8: The Shaver Mystery

Ashley, Michael, ed. *The History of the Science Fiction Magazine, Vol 3: 1946-1955.* Contemporary Books, 1976.

Baring-Gould, William S. "Little Superman, What Now?" in *Harper's Magazine*, September 1946, 283–288.

Beckley, Timothy Green. *The Shaver Mystery and the Inner Earth.* Saucerian Publications, 1967.

"Encounter in the Caves," in *Amazing Stories*, June 1946, 178.

Fields, Ralph B. "Inside Mount Lassen," in *Amazing Stories*, December 1946, 155–157.

Geier, Chester S. "The Shaver Mystery Club," in *Amazing Stories*, February 1947, 176–177.

The Hidden World. Vols. 1–16, Palmer Publications, 1961–64.

Hoffnagle, John H., Jr. *Letter File of Private Letters on the Shaver Hypothesis.* S.P. (Hampton, VA), 1950.

Martinelli, Emma. "An Investigator Reports," in *Amazing Stories*, October 1946, 173–177.

Palmer, Ray. *The Secret World.* Amherst Press, 1975.

"Report from the Forgotten Past," in *Amazing Stories*, September 1945, 166–173.

Shaver, Richard. *I Remember Lemuria and The Return of Sathanas.* Venture Books, 1948.

— "Proofs," in *Amazing Stories*, June 1947, 136–146.

— "The Shaver Mystery," in *Mystic*, January 1956, 9–15.

Shaver, Richard and Bob McKenna. "Cult of the Witch Queen," in *Amazing Stories*, July 1946, 8–38, 109–145.

Wentworth, Jim. *Giants in the Earth: Ray Palmer, Oahspe and the Shaver Mystery*. Palmer Publications, 1973.

Chapter 9: The Secret War with the Snake People

"Atom Attack Forecast 'This Year'," Denver *Post*, February 15, 1953, 1, 22.

Degan, W. Blake. "How About This, Hefferlin?" in *Amazing Stories*, November 1946, 178.

Doreal, Maurice. "He's Been in Caves Too!" in *Amazing Stories*, October 1946, 177–178.

— *The Inner Earth*. Brotherhood of the White Temple (Sedalia, CO), n.d.

— *Mysteries of Mt. Shasta*. Brotherhood of the White Temple, 1949.

— *Mysteries of the Gobi*. Brotherhood of the White Temple, n.d.

— *Personal Experiences among the Masters and Great Adepts in Tibet*. Brotherhood of the White Temple, n.d.

— *Polar Paradise*. Brotherhood of the White Temple, 1949.

— *Shamballa, or the Great White Lodge*. Brotherhood of the White Temple, n.d.

— *The Ten Lost Tribes of Israel*. Brotherhood of the White Temple, n.d.

Hefferlin, W. C. "Burn Water for Fuel," "Circle-Winged Plane," "The 'GHYT' Motor," and "Power!" in *Amazing Stories*, September 1946, 142, 144, 150, 157.

— "Static was Licked Twenty Years Ago," in *Amazing Stories*, October 1946, 166–168.

Hefferlin, W. C. and Gladys Hefferlin. *The Hefferlin Manuscript, Parts I and II*. Borderland Sciences Research Foundation, c. 1948.

Marranzino, Pasquale. "Bizarre Occult Haven is Beehive of Activity," *Rocky Mountain News,* August 31, 1946, 15.

Reckler, Joanne. "Mystic Mail Order Religion Survives in Hidden Valley," *Rocky Mountain News,* March 26, 1967, 20.

Williams, Franklin R. "On Static," in *Amazing Stories*, December 1946, 169–170.

X, Michael (pseud. of Michael Barton). *Rainbow City and the Inner Earth People*. Futura Press, 1960; repr. Saucerian Books, 1969.

Chapter 10: Agharti

Bailey, Alice A. *The Externalisation of the Hierarchy*. Lucis, 1957.

Bernbaum, Edwin. *The Way to Shambhala*. Doubleday Anchor, 1980.

Cooke, Millen. "A Champion for Tibet," in *Amazing Stories*, May 1946, 148–150.

De Courcy, John and Dorothy de Courcy. "The Man from Agharti," in *Amazing Stories*, July 1948, 8–59.

— "Open Letter," in *Amazing Stories*, December 1946, 173.

Dickhoff, Robert Ernst. *Agharta*. Bruce Humphries, Inc., 1951; repr. Fieldcrest Publishing, 1965.

Edoni. "Re: Tales from Tibet," in *Amazing Stories*, May 1946, 169–170.

Gaddis, Vincent H. "Notes on Subterranean Shafts," in *Amazing Stories*, June 1947, 148–151.

— "Tales from Tibet," in *Amazing Stories*, February 1946, 170–172.

— "The Truth About Tibet," in *Amazing Stories*, July 1946, 168–170.

— "Tunnels of the Titans," in *Amazing Stories*, August 1947, 162–167.

Guénon, René. *The Lord of the World*. Gallimard, 1927; trans. Coombe Springs Press, 1983.

— *The Reign of Quantity & The Signs of the Times*. Gallimard, 1945; trans. Penguin, 1972.

Hauser, Heinrich. "Agharti," in *Amazing Stories*, June 1946, 6–63, 128–168.

Hopkirk, Peter. *Trespassers on the Roof of the World: the Race for Lhasa*. Oxford Univ. Press, 1983.

Illion, Theodore. *Darkness Over Tibet*. Rider & Co., 1935.

Ossendowski, Ferdinand. *Beasts, Men and Gods*. Dutton, 1922.

Paelian, Garabed. *Nicholas Roerich*. Aquarian Educational Group, 1974.

Palmer, Ray. "The King of the World?" in *Amazing Stories*, May 1946, 179.

Roerich, Nicholas. *Altai-Himalaya*. Jarrolds, 1930.

— *Shambhala*. Stokes, 1930; repr. Nicholas Roerich Museum, 1978.

Saint-Yves d'Alveydre, Joseph-Alexandre. *Mission de l'Inde en Europe*. Librairie Dorbon Aîné (Paris), 1910.

Tomas, Andrew. *Shambhala: Oasis of Light*. Sphere Books, 1977.

— *We Are Not the First*. Souvenir, 1971; repr. Bantam, 1973.

Webb, James. *The Occult Establishment*. Open Court Publishing, 1976.

Chapter 11: The Strange World of Dr. Bernard

Barker, Gray. "Your Editor Receives Invitation for Ride in Saucer," in *Saucerian Bulletin*, January 15, 1960, 9–14.

Bernard, Raymond (pseud. of Walter Siegmeister). "Biosophy, World Religion of the Atlanteans," in *Aghartan Bulletin*, no. 403, 1–4.

— *Creation of the Superman*. S.P., n.d.; repr. Health Research, 1970.

— *Escape to the Inner Earth*. S.P., 1960; repr. Saucerian Press, 1974.

— *Flying Saucers from the Earth's Interior*. S.P., n.d.

— *The Hollow Earth*. Fieldcrest, 1963; repr. University Books, 1969 and Health Research, 1977.

— *Letters to Gray Barker from Dr. Raymond Bernard*, Saucerian Books, n.d.

— *Nuclear Age Saviors*. Health Research, 1960.

— *The Physiological Enigma of Woman*. Health Research, n.d.

— "Subterranean Researches in an Effort to Contact the Atlanteans Who Live in Subterranean Cities Under Santa Catarina, Brazil," in *Biosophical Bulletin*, no. 436, 1–3.

— "A Trip by Saucer to the Center of the Earth," in Beckley, Timothy Green, ed., *The Subterranean World*. Saucerian Books, 1971.

Bryant, Delmar H. "The Hollow Earth Hoax," in *Flying Saucers*, April 1965, 20–33.

Byrd, Richard E. "Our Navy Explores Antarctica," in *National Geographic*, October 1947, 429–522.

Cohen, Daniel. *The World of UFOs*. Lippincott, 1978.

Davis, Elizabeth Gould. *The First Sex*. Putnam, 1971; repr. Penguin, 1975.

Fitch, Theodore. "Our Paradise Inside the Earth," in Beckley, Timothy Green, ed., *The Subterranean World*. Saucerian Books, 1971.

Giannini, F. Amadeo. *Worlds Beyond the Poles: Physical Continuity of the Universe*. Vantage Press, 1959.

Kaub, Ottmar. Letters to Ray Palmer. *Flying Saucers*, June 1960, 47–48.

Lovewisdom, John (John Wierlo). *The History of Naturalistic Colonization*. S.P., n.d.

Money, John. *The Destroying Angel: Sex, Fitness & Food in the Legacy of Degeneracy Theory, Graham Crackers, Kellogg's Cornflakes & American Health History*. Prometheus Books, 1985.

Palmer, Ray. "'Byrd <u>Did</u> Make North Pole Flight in Feb., 1947!' —Giannini." in *Flying Saucers*, February, 1961, 4–11.

— "Editorial," in *Flying Saucers*, February 1960, 4, 29–34.

— "Saucers from Earth! A Challenge to Secrecy!" in *Flying Saucers*, December 1959, 8–21.

— "What the Bible Says About the Polar Mystery Area," in *Flying Saucers*, August 1960, 13–20.

— "Why do Polar Rockets Get Lost?" and "Earth's 'Center of Gravity'—Up or Down?" in *Flying Saucers*, November 1960, 8–11 and 16–21.

Sheppard, J. M. "Hope to Breed a Super-Race in Ecuador's Secret Jungles," in *American Weekly*, May 9, 1943.

Sullivan, Walter. "Antarctic Task Force Gains Military Data," New York *Times*, March 2, 1947.

Turley, Charles T. "Dr. Bernard is Alive and Well!" in *Gray Barker's Newsletter*, February 1976, 9.

Chapter 12: The Nazis and the Hollow Earth

Alder, Vera Stanley. *The Initiation of the World.* Weiser, 1972.

Angebert, Jean-Michel (pseud. of Michel Bertrand and Jean Angelini). *The Occult and the Third Reich.* McGraw-Hill, 1974.

Ashe, Geoffrey. *The Ancient Wisdom.* Macmillan London, 1977.

Atkins, Susan with Bob Slosser. *Child of Satan, Child of God.* Bantam, 1978.

Benton, Floria and Michael Alexander. *Serpents of Fire: German Secret Weapons and the Hitler/Hollow Earth Connection.* New Age Books, 1983.

Brennan, J. H. *The Occult Reich.* New American Library, 1974.

Charroux, Robert. *Legacy of the Gods.* Robert Laffont, 1965; trans. Berkley Medallion, 1974.

— *The Gods Unknown.* Robert Laffont, 1969; trans. Berkley Medallion, 1972.

A Flight to the Land Beyond the North Pole, or, Is This the Missing Secret Diary of Admiral Richard Evelyn Byrd? International Society for a Complete Earth (Houston, MO), n.d.

Friedrich, Christof (pseud. of Ernst Zündel). *Secret Nazi Polar Expeditions.* Samisdat, 1978.

Greene, Bob. "Expedition to Hollow Earth," San Francisco *Chronicle,* November 8, 1978, 12.

King, Francis. *Satan and Swastika: the Occult and the Nazi Party.* Mayflower Books, 1976.

"Legally Hot," in *Time,* February 23, 1953, 76.

Lenski, Robert. *The Holocaust on Trial.* To be published 1989.

Ley, Willy. *Rockets, Missles, and Space Travel.* Viking, 1961.

McKale, Donald M. *Hitler: the Survival Myth.* Stein and Day, 1981.

Mattern (pseud.) and Friedrich, Christof (pseud. of Ernst Zündel). *UFO's: Nazi Secret Weapon?* Samisdat, 1976.

Moore, William L., ed. *Project V-7: Hitler's Flying Discs. An Illustrated Compendium of Research and Source Materials.* S.P. (Burbank, CA), 1984.

Pauwels, Louis and Jacques Bergier. *The Morning of the Magicians.* Gallimard, 1960; trans. Stein and Day, 1964.

Pennick, Nigel. *Hitler's Secret Sciences.* Neville Spearman, 1981.

Ravenscroft, Trevor. *The Spear of Destiny.* Putnam, 1973.

Revelations of Awareness, 79–25. Cosmic Awareness Communications (Olympia, WA), 1979.

Roemer, John. "The Controversy of the Occult Reich," in *Gnosis,* 9, Fall 1988, 40–47.

Ruppelt, Edward J. *The Report on Unidentified Flying Objects.* Doubleday, 1956.

Sanders, Ed. *The Family.* Dutton, 1971; repr. Avon, 1972.

Suster, Gerald. *Hitler: the Occult Messiah*. St. Martin's, 1981.

Vallee, Jacques. *Messengers of Deception*. And/Or, 1979.

Wynants, Eric. "Notes on the Nazis: UFOs, the Holy Lance, the Vril and Thule Society, and Antarctica," in *Critique*, No. 7, 8, 1982, 41–55.

X, Michael (pseud. of Michael Barton). *We Want You! Is Hitler Alive?* Futura Press, 1960; repr. Saucerian Books, 1969.

Chapter 13: The Inner World in Fiction

Ash, Brian, ed. *The Visual Encyclopedia of Science Fiction*. Harmony Books, 1977.

Bailey, James O. *Pilgrims Through Space and Time: Trends and Patterns in Scientific and Utopian Fiction*. Argus, 1947; repr. Greenwood, 1972.

Beynon, John (pseud. of John Wyndham). *The Secret People*. George Newnes, Ltd., 1935.

Bradshaw, William R. *The Goddess of Atvatabar*. J. F. Douthitt, 1892; repr. Arno Press, 1975.

Bulwer Lytton, Edward. *The Coming Race*. Routledge and Sons, n.d.

Burroughs, Edgar Rice. *At the Earth's Core, Pellucidar, Tanar of Pellucidar: Three Science Fiction Novels*. Dover, 1963.

Chipman, DeWitt C. "Beyond the Verge," repr. in *The Hidden World*, vols. 6 (Summer 1962) , 993–1134 and 7 (Fall 1962), 1154–1213.

Emerson, Willis George. *The Smoky God, or, A Voyage to the Inner World*. Forbes & Co., 1908; repr. Fieldcrest, 1964 and Palmer Publications, 1965.

Ferguson, C. W. *Fifty Million Brothers*. Farrar, 1937.

Holberg, Ludvig. *Journey of Niels Klim to the World Underground*. Univ. of Nebraska Press, 1960.

Lane, Mary E. Bradley. *Mizora: A Prophecy*. G. W. Dillingham, 1890; repr. Gregg Press, 1975.

Lloyd, John Uri. *Etidorhpa, or, The End of Earth*. 11th ed., Dodd, Mead & Co., 1901; repr. Sun Books, 1974.

Poe, Edgar Allan. *The Narrative of Arthur Gordon Pym of Nantucket*. Introduction by Sidney Kaplan. Hill and Wang, 1960.

Read, Herbert. *The Green Child*. New Directions, n.d.

Verne, Jules. *A Journey to the Centre of the Earth*. Scribner's, 1926.

Vril or Vital Magnetism, being Volume Six of the Arcane Teaching. A. C. McClurg & Co., 1911; repr. Health Research, 1970.

Wolff, Robert Lee. *Strange Stories: Explorations in Victorian Fiction—the Occult and the Neurotic*. Gambit, 1971.

Wright, S. Fowler. *The World Below*. Shasta Publishers, 1949.

Chapter 14: Why an Inner World?

Benton, Floria. *Hollow Earth Mysteries and the Polar Shift*. Future Press, 1981.

Burnet, Thomas. *Sacred Theory of the Earth*. J. Hooke (London), 1722.

Cluff, Rodney M. *World Top Secret: Our Earth is Hollow!* S.P. (Laveen, AZ), 1981.

Lewis, David H. *The Incredible Cities of Inner Earth*. Science Research Publishing House, 1979.

Lovelock, J. E. *Gaia: a New Look at Life on Earth*. Oxford Univ. Press, 1979; rev. ed. 1987.

Walton, Bruce, ed. *Mount Shasta: Home of the Ancients*. Health Research, 1985.

Additional Works of Interest

Here is a general list of books not mentioned in the sources above which have made a contribution to the hollow-earth mythos. Fiction titles are identified with an (F). I have read most of these books; for the ones I have not, I am indebted to the second edition of *The Hollow Earth Bibliography* of Tillman Martin, Bruce Walton, Frank Brownley, and Gilbert K. Johnston, S.P. by Bruce Walton (Provo, UT), 1982.

One of the best sources of Hollow-Earth material at this writing is **Health Research**, Box 70, Mokelumne Hill, CA 95245. They have reprinted many of the most important works on the subject in inexpensive editions. **Amherst Press**, PO Box 296, Amherst, WI 54406, the press started by Ray Palmer, is still in business and sells several essential hollow-earth titles. These two sources are the *only* ones I know of for much of this literature!

Books:

Beale, Charles W. *The Secret of the Earth.* F. Tennyson Neely, 1899. (F)

Bennet, Robert A. *Thyra: A Romance of the Polar Pit.* Holt, 1901. (F)

Bergier, Jacques. *Secret Doors of the Earth.* Editions Albin Michel, 1974; trans. Henry Regnery Co., 1975.

Blaylock, James P. *The Digging Leviathan.* Ace Science Fiction, 1984. (F)

Carter, Lin. *Journey to the Underground World.* DAW Books, 1979. (F)

— *Zanthodon.* DAW Books, 1980. (F)

Charroux, Robert. *The Mysteries of the Andes.* Robert Laffont, 1974; trans. Avon, 1977.

Crabb, Riley H. *The Reality of the Cavern World.* Borderland Sciences Research Foundation, n.d.

Godwin, John. *Occult America.* Doubleday, 1972.

Haining, Peter. *Ancient Mysteries.* Hutchinson of Australia, 1977.

Harben, Will N. *The Land of the Changing Sun.* Merriam, 1894; repr. Gregg, 1975. (F)

Hartmann, Franz. *Among the Gnomes.* Occult Publishing Co., 1896; repr. Health Research, n.d. (F)

Hitching, Francis. *The Mysterious World: an Atlas of the Unexplained.* Holt, Rinehart and Winston, 1978.

Lesser, Wendy. *The Life Below the Ground: a Study of the Subterranean in Literature and History.* Faber and Faber, 1987.

Lockwood, Ingersoll. *Baron Trump's Marvellous Underground Journey.* Lee and Shepard, 1893; repr. Health Research, 1972. (F)

Marcoux, Charles A. *I Search for the Portals.* S.P. (Phoenix, AZ), 1981.

Michell, John. *Eccentric Lives and Peculiar Notions.* Thames and Hudson, 1984.

Moore, Patrick. *Can You Speak Venusian?* David & Charles, 1972.

Most, Howard H. *Shasta, Mountain of Mysteries.* Crescent Pubs., 1978. (F)

Norman, Eric (pseud. of Warren Smith). *This Hollow Earth.* Lancer Books, 1972.

— *The Under-People.* Award Books, 1969.

Norman, Ruth, and Thomas Miller. *Martian Underground Cities Discovered by Cosmic Visionary.* Unarius Educational Foundation (El Cajon, CA), 1977.

O'Neill, Joseph. *Land Under England.* Victor Gollancz Ltd., 1935; repr. New English Library, 1978. (F)

Paltock, Robert. *The Life and Adventures of Peter Wilkins.* Orig. published 1751; repr. Reeves & Turner, 1884. (F)

Roberts, Anthony and Geoff Gilbertson. *The Dark Gods.* Rider/Hutchinson, 1980.

Rockwood, Roy. *Five Thousand Miles Underground, or, The Mystery of the Centre of the Earth.* Cupples & Leon Co., 1908. (F)

Rosenberger, Joseph. *Death Merchant: The Shambhala Strike* (Death Merchant #30). Pinnacle Books, 1978. (F)

Rottensteiner, Franz. *The Science Fiction Book: an Illustrated History.* Seabury/Continuum, 1975.

Shodall, Reuben Sam. *The Enlightened Ones Beyond the Icebergs.* Exposition Press, 1966.

Sladek, John. *The New Apocrypha: A Guide to Strange Sciences and Occult Beliefs.* Stein and Day, 1974.

Smith, Cordwainer. *The Underpeople.* Sphere Books, 1975. (F)

Smith, Warren. *The Hidden Secrets of the Hollow Earth.* Zebra Books, 1976.

Stout, Rex. *Under the Andes.* Penzler Books, 1984 (orig. published in *All-Story Magazine,* February 1914). (F)

Tardé, Gabriel de. *Underground Man.* Duckworth & Co., 1905. (F)

Taylor, William A. *Intermere.* 20th Century Publ., 1901; repr. Health Research, 1969. (F)

Thomas, Eugene E. *Brotherhood of Mt. Shasta.* DeVorss, 1946; repr. Health Research, 1974. (F)

Walton, Bruce, ed. *The Inner Earth Series* (6 vols.). S.P. by Bruce Walton (Provo, UT), 1980–82.

Warren, William F. *Paradise Found: The Cradle of the Human Race at the North Pole.* Houghton Mifflin, 1886.

Wilkins, Harold T. *Mysteries of Ancient South America.* Citadel, 1956; repr. 1974.

Wilson, Don. *Our Mysterious Spaceship Moon.* Dell, 1975.

Periodicals:

There have been few periodicals which have dealt seriously with the topic of subterranean worlds. Most have been small, one-or-two-person mimeographed or photocopied newsletters, and none have lasted long. Although copies of the following publications will be exceedingly difficult to find, I include them in the name of completeness. To my knowledge, all except the last two are no longer being published.

The Hollow Hassle was published quarterly by Mary Levesque from 1972–74, and then again by her (as Mary Martin) from approximately 1981–84 from Colorado Springs, CO. It contained a wide range of speculative articles on the hollow-earth theory and related topics.

New Worlds was published by Ivan Boyes of Donn Mills, Ontario, Canada in the late 1970s; it dealt with the inner world, particularly with its relationship to the Nazis, as well as articles on UFOs and conspiracy theories.

Newsletter for the Hollow Earth Society was published by Kenneth H. Snell for the Hollow Earth Society of Sydney, Australia, approx. 1979–80. No further details available.

Pyramid Guide was a bi-monthly newsletter published in Santa Barbara, CA by Bill Cox in the late 1970s which included several inner-world articles.

Shavertron was a quarterly newsletter published by Richard Toronto of Vallejo, CA dealing with the Shaver Mystery and related topics between approximately 1980 and 1984.

The Source was published quarterly in the early 1980s by Christine Hayes of Cortez, CO; it contained information channeled to her from "the Intraterrestrials," or beings from various levels of the inner world.

Critique may still be publishing, approximately quarterly, at this writing. It bills itself as "a journal of conspiracies and metaphysics," and much of what it includes—like revisionist histories of the Nazis, Zionists, mind control in America, and the JFK assassination —will not be for everyone. It has included several fascinating articles on the hollow-earth theory, and back issues should be available. The last address I have for it is: Critique, Box 11451, Santa Rosa, CA 95406.

Search, begun by Ray Palmer, is still publishing quarterly at this writing. These days it contains much less Shaver/hollow-earth material than it did in Palmer's day, but it runs some fascinating inner-world stuff from time to time. Write Palmer Publications, PO Box 296, Amherst, WI 54406.

Index

YOU WILL ALSO WANT TO READ:

☐ **88025 PRINCIPIA DISCORDIA, or How I Found the Goddess and What I Did to Her When I Found Her,** *by Malaclypse the Younger.* Is it a joke disguised as a religion, or a religion disguised as a joke? This is the official bible of the Discordian religion which worships Eris, Goddess of Chaos. A classic of guerrilla ontology. Includes an introduction by Robert Anton Wilson. *1980, 5½ x 8½, 100 pp, illustrated, soft cover.* **$6.95.**

☐ **94027 LOOMPANICS' GOLDEN RECORDS, Articles and Features from The Best Book Catalog in the World,** *Edited by Michael Hoy.* This collection contains more than 40 of the best and most imaginative pieces Loompanics has ever published, including work by Bob Black, Jim Hogshire, Michael Newton, James B. DeKorne, and many others. The collection also features artwork by some of America's most talented artists, such as Mark Zingarelli, Nick Bougus, and Ace Backwords. *1993, 8½ x 11, 200 pp, illustrated, soft cover.* **$14.95.**

☐ **94187 ANARCHIC HARMONY, The Spirituality of Social Disobedience,** *by William J Murray, with an Introduction by Robert Anton Wilson.* "What I found by turning my back on our society-generated mythology was so profound that I had to share it — presumptuous or not — because it *indicts the social structures of mankind* and *demands social disobedience,* or living according to our inner, *heroic nature* and *not* according to the intimidation and demands of society's ideology." *1992, 5½ x 8½, 144 pp, soft cover.* **$11.95.**

☐ **94222 UNCONDITIONAL FREEDOM, Social Revolution through Individual Empowerment,** *by William J Murray, with an Introduction by Ben G. Price.* In *Anarchic Harmony,* Murray shattered the myths of the New Age and the old, showing us how to find our inner Dynamic and use it as our only barometer of right and wrong. Now he teaches us how to manipulate reality to gain unlimited freedom. "We're going to knock down the walls and rip up the floorboards that keep us imprisoned in the hellish box of 'normal life' and consensus reality," says the author. That's something worth reading, don't you think." *1993, 5½ x 8½, 260 pp, soft cover.* **$15.95.**

nd much, much more! We offer the very finest in controversial and unusual books — please turn to our catalog ad on the next page.

LOOMPANICS UNLIMITED
PO BOX 1197
PORT TOWNSEND, WA 98368
(206) 385-2230

SW94

Please send me the titles I have checked above. I have enclosed $_____ which includes
$4.00 for the shipping and handling of 1 to 3 books, $6.00 for 4 or more. *Washington residents please include 7.9% sales tax.*

Name _____

Address _____

City/State/Zip_____

Now accepting Visa and MasterCard.